Object-Oriented Software Engineering with Eiffel

Addison-Wesley Eiffel in Practice Series

Bertrand Meyer, Consulting Editor

The Addison-Wesley Eiffel in Practice Series specifically addresses the practical issues of programming with the Eiffel language and its relationship to object-oriented technology. The series provides serious programmers with pragmatic books that are technically sophisticated. Each book will cover wholly a specific aspect of Eiffel programming and will contain useful source code and/or applications that allow programmers to experiment with the concepts covered in the material. In addition to the corporate marketplace, the series will be of particular interest to academic institutions throughout the world.

Object-Oriented Software Engineering with Eiffel

Jean-Marc Jézéquel

ADDISON-WESLEY PUBLISHING COMPANY, INC.

Reading, Massachusetts · Menlo Park, California · New York · Don Mills, Ontario
Wokingham, England · Amsterdam · Bonn · Sydney · Singapore · Tokyo
Madrid · San Juan · Seoul · Milan · Mexico City · Taipei

Many of the designations used by manufacturers and sellers to distinguish their products are claimed as trademarks. Where those designations appear in this book and Addison-Wesley was aware of a trademark claim, the designations have been printed in initial caps or all caps.

The authors and publishers have taken care in the preparation of this book, but make no expressed or implied warranty of any kind and assume no responsibility for errors or omissions. No liability is assumed for incidental or consequential damages in connection with or arising out of the use of the information or programs contained herein.

The publisher offers discounts on this book when ordered in quantity for special sales.

For more information, please contact:

    Corporate & Professional Publishing Group
    Addison-Wesley Publishing Company
    One Jacob Way
    Reading, Massachusetts 01867

Library of Congress Cataloging-in-Publication Data

Jézéquel, Jean-Marc, 1964–
    Object-oriented software engineering with Eiffel / Jean-Marc Jézéquel.
      p. cm. -- (Addison-Wesley Eiffel in practice series)
    Includes bibliographical references and index.
    ISBN 0-201-63381-7 (alk. paper)
    1. Object-oriented programming (Computer science) 2. Eiffel (Computer program language) 3. Software engineering. I. Title. II. Series.
QA76.64.J49   1996
005.13'3—dc20   95-26015
                                                                          CIP

Copyright © 1996 by Addison-Wesley Publishing Company, Inc.

All rights reserved. No part of this publication may be reproduced, stored in a retrieval system, or transmitted, in any form, or by any means, electronic, mechanical, photocopying, recording, or otherwise, without the prior consent of the publisher.

Printed in the United States of America. Published simultaneously in Canada.

Text design by Wilson Graphics & Design (Kenneth J. Wilson)
Composition by Windfall Software using ZzTeX (Paul Anagnostopoulos, Joe Snowden)
Text printed on recycled and acid-free paper

ISBN 0-201-63381-7
1 2 3 4 5 6 7 8 9-CRW-99989796
First printing, March 1996

To Chantal, Gwenaëlle, Nolwenn, and Erwan.
To my parents, who helped me buy my first computer in 1980.

Contents

Preface xvii

Acknowledgments xviii

Chapter 1 **The Software Engineering Context** 1

    1.1 Introduction 1

        1.1.1 What's the Big Deal About Programming a Computer? 1

        1.1.2 Programming in the Small 2

        1.1.3 Programming in the Large 3

    1.2 The Object-Oriented Approach 6

        1.2.1 Origin 6

        1.2.2 Definitions in the Context of Software Engineering 6

        1.2.3 Object-Oriented Analysis and Design 8

    1.3 Eiffel: An Object-Oriented Language for Software Engineering 9

        1.3.1 A Software Engineering Tool 9

        1.3.2 Importance of a Language 10

        1.3.3 An Eiffel Overview 11

        1.3.4 Status of the Eiffel Language 12

PART I **Language Elements** 13

Chapter 2 **Basic Language Elements of Eiffel** 15

    2.1 The Eiffel Notion of Systems 15

        2.1.1 System and Program 15

        2.1.2 "Hello, world!" 16

2.2 Class = Module = Type 17
    2.2.1 Foundation Principles 17
    2.2.2 The Class As a Module 17
    2.2.3 The Class As a Type 18
    2.2.4 Components of a Class Declaration 19
2.3 Definition of Entity Declaration 23
    2.3.1 Entity Declaration 23
    2.3.2 Entity Expansion Status 23
    2.3.3 Constant Entities 24
    2.3.4 Default Initialization Rule for Entities 26
2.4 Statements 26
    2.4.1 Assignment 26
    2.4.2 Testing for Equality 28
    2.4.3 Sequence 29
    2.4.4 Conditional 29
    2.4.5 Multibranch Choice 30
    2.4.6 Iterative Control: The Loop 31
    2.4.7 Designing Correct Loops with Loop Assertions 33
    2.4.8 The Check Statement 37
    2.4.9 The Debug Statement 38
2.5 Routines: Procedures and Functions 39
    2.5.1 Routine Declaration 39
    2.5.2 Arguments to a Routine 41
    2.5.3 Preconditions, Postconditions, and Invariants 41
    2.5.4 Calling a Routine 45
    2.5.5 Internal Routine Body 45
    2.5.6 Once Routines 46
    2.5.7 Prefix and Infix Function Declaration 47
    2.5.8 Recursion 49
2.6 Example: Sorting Data with Eiffel 50

Chapter 3 **Object-Oriented Elements** 55

    3.1 Working with Modules 55

        3.1.1 Creating Objects 56

        3.1.2 Calling Other Object Features 58

        3.1.3 Attribute Protection and Information Hiding 59

        3.1.4 Restricted Export and Subjectivity 61

        3.1.5 Using Eiffel Strings 63

        3.1.6 Building a Linked List Class 65

    3.2 Genericity 67

        3.2.1 Generic Classes 67

        3.2.2 Generic Class Derivation 68

        3.2.3 A Standard Eiffel Generic Class: The ARRAY 68

    3.3 Inheritance 71

        3.3.1 The Dual Nature of Inheritance in Eiffel 71

        3.3.2 Module Extension 71

        3.3.3 Subtyping 72

        3.3.4 Inheritance and Expanded Types 74

        3.3.5 Implicit Inheritance Structure 74

    3.4 Feature Adaptation 76

        3.4.1 Renaming 77

        3.4.2 Redefining 77

        3.4.3 Changing the Export Status 80

        3.4.4 Other Feature Adaptations 81

    3.5 Polymorphism and Dynamic Binding 81

        3.5.1 Polymorphic Entities 81

        3.5.2 Dynamic Binding 83

        3.5.3 Type Conformance and Expanded Types 83

    3.6 Deferred Classes 84

        3.6.1 Deferred Routines 84

3.6.2 Deferred Classes 85
3.6.3 Inheritance and Deferred Classes 86
3.6.4 Deferred Classes: A Structuring Tool 88

3.7 Genericity and Inheritance 89
3.7.1 Heterogeneous Containers 89
3.7.2 Constrained Genericity 91

3.8 Case Study: The KWIC System 93
3.8.1 Presentation of the KWIC System 93
3.8.2 The KWIC Object-Oriented Software 94
3.8.3 The Class KWIC_ENTRY 95
3.8.4 The Class KWIC 97
3.8.5 The Class WORDS 99
3.8.6 The Class DRIVER 99

Chapter 4 The Eiffel Environments 103

4.1 System Assembly and Configuration 103
4.1.1 Assembling Classes 103
4.1.2 Generating an Application 104
4.1.3 Specifying Clusters 105
4.1.4 Excluding and Including Files 105
4.1.5 Dealing with Class Name Clashes 106

4.2 Assertion Monitoring 107
4.2.1 Rationale 107
4.2.2 Enabling Assertion Checking with LACE 107
4.2.3 Enabling Assertion Checking with Run-Time Control Language 109

4.3 Overview of the Eiffel Standard Library 109
4.3.1 Purposes of the Eiffel Standard Library 109
4.3.2 Required Standard Classes 110
4.3.3 Using I/O Classes: An Example 112

4.4 Interfacing with Other Languages 114
4.4.1 Declaring External Routines 114

  4.4.2 Calling External Routines 116

  4.4.3 The Address Operator 117

  4.4.4 Linking with External Software 117

4.5 Garbage Collection 118

  4.5.1 Definition 118

  4.5.2 Interest for Software Correctness 118

  4.5.3 The Cost of Garbage Collection 119

  4.5.4 Controlling the Garbage Collector 120

  4.5.5 Finalization 120

Chapter 5 Advanced Language Elements 123

5.1 Exception Handling 123

  5.1.1 Causes of an Exception 124

  5.1.2 Default Handling of Exceptions 124

  5.1.3 Trying to Repair Failures 126

  5.1.4 User-Defined Exceptions 127

5.2 Repeated Inheritance 128

  5.2.1 Definition 128

  5.2.2 Conditions for Sharing 128

  5.2.3 Replication and Selection 129

  5.2.4 Keeping the Original Version of a Redefined Feature 130

5.3 Assignment Attempt 132

5.4 Other Issues of Typing 133

  5.4.1 Changing Export Rules 133

  5.4.2 Covariance Policy 134

  5.4.3 System-Level Validity 136

5.5 Parallelism 137

  5.5.1 Parallelism and Object-Oriented Languages 137

  5.5.2 The Eiffel // Approach 138

  5.5.3 The Parallel Eiffel Approach 140

  5.5.4 The Parallelism Encapsulation Approach 142

PART II Building Software Systems with Eiffel 147

Chapter 6 From Analysis to Implementation 149

6.1 Object-Oriented Methodology 149

    6.1.1 The Object-Oriented Software Engineering Process 149

    6.1.2 An Overview of Object-Oriented Methodology 150

    6.1.3 An Overview of OMT 153

    6.1.4 Eiffel and Object-Oriented Analysis and Design 154

6.2 Case Study: An SMDS Server 154

    6.2.1 An Overview of SMDS 154

    6.2.2 Problem Requirements 156

6.3 SMDS: Object-Oriented Analysis 157

    6.3.1 The SMDS Server Problem Domain 157

    6.3.2 Object Modeling 160

    6.3.3 Dynamic Modeling 161

    6.3.4 Functional Modeling 164

6.4 Eiffel and Object-Oriented Design 166

    6.4.1 Introduction to Design Patterns and Idioms 166

    6.4.2 Design by Contract 167

    6.4.3 Encapsulation and Information Hiding 168

    6.4.4 Modularity and Coupling 170

    6.4.5 Inheritance Structure 171

    6.4.6 Routines 173

6.5 SMDS: Object-Oriented Design 175

    6.5.1 System Design 175

    6.5.2 Object Design 179

6.6 Implementation 184

    6.6.1 Introduction 184

    6.6.2 Style Guide 184

    6.6.3 Version Management 187

    6.6.4 Documentation and Indexing 188

    6.6.5 Implementation Strategy of the SMDS Server 191

Chapter 7 **From Implementation to Delivery** 193

    7.1 Verification and Validation 193

        7.1.1 Introduction 193

        7.1.2 The Testing Process 194

        7.1.3 Testing Techniques 195

        7.1.4 Specificities of Object-Oriented Testing 199

    7.2 Unit Testing of Eiffel Classes 202

        7.2.1 Class-Level Testing 202

        7.2.2 Test Development 203

        7.2.3 Test Execution and Evaluation 204

        7.2.4 Life-Cycle and Nonregression Testing 205

    7.3 Integration Testing 205

        7.3.1 Integration Strategies 205

        7.3.2 Incremental Integration 206

        7.3.3 Assembling the SMDS Server 208

    7.4 SMDS Server Acceptance Testing 210

        7.4.1 Qualitative Tests 210

    7.5 The OMT/Eiffel Approach 214

        7.5.1 Effort Breakdown 214

        7.5.2 Coding Statistics 214

        7.5.3 Reuse 215

Chapter 8 **Building Libraries: The Case of Data Structure Libraries** 217

    8.1 Library Design 218

        8.1.1 Introduction 218

        8.1.2 Domain Analysis 219

        8.1.3 Design Patterns and Frameworks 221

        8.1.4 Producing Class Libraries 223

        8.1.5 Conclusion 223

    8.2 The EiffelBase Library 224

        8.2.1 Overview 224

8.2.2 Design Patterns 227

8.2.3 Containers: The Access Hierarchy 229

8.2.4 Containers: The Storage Hierarchy 232

8.2.5 Containers: The Traversal Hierarchy 233

8.3 The **Tower***Eiffel* Booch Components 234

8.3.1 Overview 235

8.3.2 Design Patterns 237

8.3.3 Architecture of the Library 240

8.3.4 Outline of Some **Tower***Eiffel* Booch Components 243

8.4 The SiG Library 247

8.4.1 Overview 247

8.4.2 Design Patterns 248

8.4.3 Other Abstractions Related to Containers 251

Chapter 9 Building a Parallel Linear Algebra Library with Eiffel 255

9.1 Introduction 255

9.2 Encapsulating Distribution 257

9.2.1 Polymorphic Aggregates 257

9.2.2 One Abstraction, Several Implementations 258

9.2.3 Matrices and Vectors in Paladin 259

9.3 Replicated and Distributed Matrices 263

9.3.1 Sequential Implementation of a Matrix 263

9.3.2 Distribution of Matrices in Paladin 265

9.3.3 Implementation of Distributed Matrices 267

9.4 Dealing with Multiple Representations 270

9.4.1 Interoperability 270

9.4.2 Dynamic Redistribution 271

9.4.3 Matrix-Type Conversion 273

9.4.4 Polymorphic Matrices 275

9.5 Making Parallel Libraries Efficient 275

9.5.1 Optimization Techniques 275

9.5.2 Preserving User Friendliness 278

   9.5.3 Implementation Efficiency 280
   9.5.4 Reuse of External Optimized Libraries 283
 9.6 Conclusion 284

PART III Appendixes 287

A Glossary 288

B Lexical and Syntactic Elements 292
 B.1 Manifest Constants 292
 B.2 Reserved Words 294
 B.3 Syntax Diagrams 295

C Eiffel Contact List 307
 C.1 Eiffel Vendors 307
   C.1.1 Interactive Software Engineering, Inc. 307
   C.1.2 Tower Technology Corporation 308
   C.1.3 SiG Computer GmbH 309
   C.1.4 Eon Software 309
 C.2 Eiffel Forums 310
   C.2.1 NICE 310
   C.2.2 *Eiffel Outlook* 310
   C.2.3 Eiffel World 310
   C.2.4 *Journal of Object-Oriented Programming* 311
   C.2.5 USENET 311
   C.2.6 Frequently Asked Questions (with Answers) 311
   C.2.7 Mailing Lists 311
   C.2.8 World Wide Web 312
 C.3 Getting More Information About This Book 312

 Bibliography 315

 Index 327

Preface

This is a book on software engineering the Eiffel way.

Born in Dijon (France), Gustave Eiffel (1832–1923) first worked as an engineer for a railroad construction company before starting an office dedicated to the study of metallic construction. Using light steel modular structures instead of the usual design with cast iron, Eiffel built tall infrastructures featuring very good aerodynamic resistance. He built several viaducts, most notably at Bordeaux (1858) and Gabarit (1884). He also created the framework of the Bon Marché department store (1876) in Paris. He oversaw several projects in Austria, Switzerland, Hungary (Pest Railway Station, 1876), and Portugal (the Maria-Pia Bridge near Porto, 1877).

His most famous structures were the framework of Bartholdi's Liberty Statue in New York and the 300-meter Eiffel Tower, built for the 1889 universal exposition in Paris. These two world-famous landmarks were also technological marvels for that time. They paved the way for the new domain of industrial architecture. After 1890, Eiffel resigned from his business to concentrate on aerodynamic studies from the top of the Eiffel Tower. Today, more than one century after their construction, most of Eiffel's buildings are still standing and open for business.

In the software engineering domain, Eiffel is also the name of an object-oriented language that emphasizes the design and construction of high-quality software by assembling reusable software components, called *classes*, that serve as templates to make objects. Beyond classes (on which modularity is based), Eiffel offers multiple inheritance, polymorphism, static typing and dynamic binding, genericity, garbage collection, a disciplined exception mechanism, and systematic use of assertions to improve software correctness in the context of *programming by contract*.

Software engineering encompasses many more features than those offered by a computer language. Computer languages are just tools that software engineers can use (or misuse) within a larger context. The Eiffel language is a tool that has been specially designed in the context of software engineering. This book describes the tool, and provides clues on how to use it.

Chapter 1 is an introduction to the object-oriented approach within the context of software engineering. The main body of the book is then divided into two parts.

The first part of this book presents the language itself. Chapter 2 presents the basic (procedural) elements of the language: what an Eiffel program is, what the instruction set is, and how to declare and use entities (variables) and routines. Chapter 3 introduces the concepts underlying the object-oriented approach: modularity, inheritance, and dynamic binding, and illustrates them in a small case study from the management information system domain. Eiffel programs do not exist in a void, so Chapter 4 brings in environment matters: system configuration, interfacing with external software, and garbage collection. Chapter 5 closes the Eiffel presentation with more advanced issues involving exception handling, repeated inheritance, typing problems, and parallelism.

The second part of this book addresses some Eiffel software development issues. In Chapter 6, we outline how an object-oriented software engineering process may make the best use of Eiffel, concentrating on specific guidelines to facilitate the translation of object-oriented analysis and design to a maintainable Eiffel implementation. This process is illustrated by a rather large case study from the telecommunications domain. As a logical continuation of this study, Chapter 7 addresses verification and validation (V&V) issues of Eiffel software systems built in a software engineering context. Building reusable libraries is discussed in Chapter 8, which presents three competing Eiffel data structure libraries. Finally, Chapter 9 shows how Eiffel can be used as an enabling technology to master a very complex problem: the building of a parallel linear algebra library that allows an applications programmer to use distributed computing systems in a transparent way.

If you get lost at some point in terms of the Eiffel-related vocabulary, there is a short glossary given in Appendix A. An Eiffel syntax summary is presented in Appendix B, and a list of contacts closes this book (Appendix C).

Acknowledgments

This book would not exist in its present form without Bertrand Meyer (Interactive Software Engineering, Inc. [ISE]), the designer of the Eiffel language. Rock Howard (Tower Technology Corp.) and Michael Schweitzer (SiG Computer Gmbh) also helped me by providing some input on their Eiffel products (compilers and libraries).

I would also like to thank the countless people involved in enlightening discussions on the **comp.lang.eiffel** Internet newsgroup, and particularly Richard Bielak, Roger Browne, Hank Etlinger, Jacob Gore, James McKim, Jean-Jacques Moreau, Erwan Moysan, and Michel Train, who read early versions of this book and gave me a lot of feedback as well as many pertinent suggestions.

My colleagues at Irisa deserve credit for relieving me of a share of my everyday workload, thus allowing me to complete this book in a reasonable amount of time. I have a special debt toward F. Guidec, who did most of the Paladin library design, and F. Guerber, who was the main contributor on the switched multimegabits data service (SMDS) project.

Finally I would like to thank my editorial contact, Katie Duffy, for her constant support in making this book take shape.

Dr. Jean-Marc Jézéquel
Irisa/C.N.R.S.
University of Rennes

The Software Engineering Context

In This Chapter
- 1.1 Introduction
- 1.2 The Object-Oriented Approach
- 1.3 Eiffel: An Object-Oriented Language for Software Engineering

In this chapter we introduce the context of software engineering. Software construction and maintenance can benefit from an object-oriented approach. The Eiffel language, which has been designed specifically along this line, is introduced.

1.1 Introduction

1.1.1 What's the Big Deal About Programming a Computer?

Programming is easy. Nearly everybody can give the proper instructions to cook a dish or to record a movie on a VCR (though a good programming interface might be helpful). Only a handful of training hours is required for most people to learn how to write spreadsheet or BASIC programs. Even young children have little problem driving the Logo turtle back and forth on the screen.

There are few concepts, however, as widely admitted as the "software crisis." This expression was coined in the late 1960s when it appeared that most first releases of software products were notoriously buggy or delivered late or hard to maintain. Today, the maintenance of a large software system is usually more costly than the total development phase, with a fair share due to bug corrections. The overall maintenance costs can even reach three or four times the initial cost for long-life products.

What does this crisis mean? Are software engineers grossly overpaid and should they be fired in favor of teenage programmers? This approach has been tried, but it works only in Hollywood movies. As most software engineers know, the problem is actually twofold. At the micro level (also called programming in the small), we face the problem of designing and implementing correct algorithms. This activity is much like theorem proving because its complexity is of a mathematical nature. Still, it may be mastered by a single person who understands everything from top to bottom. At the macro level (also called programming in the large), we face the structural complexity of systems made of hundreds of thousands or millions of lines of code and developed by large teams of programmers. This complexity management problem is not at all specific to software systems but is amplified by the well-known software "softness."

1.1.2 Programming in the Small

The strange thing about computer science is that it has been invented *ex nihilo* to demonstrate an impossibility result in mathematics. Alan Turing built his famous mathematical model known as the *Turing machine* to prove that some properties can be undecidable (e.g., stopping the machine). An immediate and painful consequence is that computer programs cannot be proved correct in general, because *every (general-purpose) programming language is formally equivalent to a Turing machine*. This may seem a remote problem arising only in very complicated cases. Consider, however, the following program, presented in [114]:

```
input a positive number n
while n is not equal to 1 do
    if n is even then n := n/2
    else n := 3*n+1
end
print "Terminated"
```

If you are not familiar with computer science foundations, you should try to craft a proof to get some insight into its mathematical aspects.

Can you formally prove that this program terminates for all positive input values?

Since the emergence of structured programming [37] in the late 1960s, the recommended way of dealing with this kind of problem has been to build software in such a way that it can be formally proved [42]. In spite of all the effort expended since then, proving techniques cannot be applied practically to real programs, because the complexity of the proof may be much greater than the program itself (and who is going to check the proof anyway?).

What is left is a general method of software production [114] that associates partly formal correctness arguments (called *assertions*) with the programs as they are being built. This method enables the construction of robust software modules, which can then be reused safely.

The problem of software correctness takes on a new dimension when parallelism is considered. The complexity introduced by parallelism and its associated asynchronism is orthogonal to sequential complexity. Even when you restrict your programming language to the power of a finite state automaton (FSA), once you put two FSAs to work in parallel and connect them through unbounded first in, first out (FIFO) channels, you may obtain the power of a Turing machine. Thus, even for very simple examples (two FSAs with no more than three states each in [77]), you may get infinitely complex behaviors. Here again, reusing carefully designed parallel software components appears to be a promising avenue toward mastering the inherent complexity of parallel systems.

Such a programming language has a fairly low power indeed: You can't even count items *with an FSA.*

1.1.3 Programming in the Large

The size of software projects has increased by several orders of magnitudes since the 1960s such that they are out of the grasp of a single programmer. Software development is now a cooperative process. This problem is usually tackled along two different lines. On the one hand, the tools used to develop software (programming languages and environments) are continuously improving to support this scale of complexity. On the other hand, a great deal of effort is devoted to improving the *process* by which software is developed. The best results are obtained when the tools and the process fit together well.

Some effort has been devoted to adapting the notion of *total quality management* to the software industry. For instance, the ISO 9000-3 standard is an adaptation to the software world of the ISO 9001 general standard on quality assurance in industry. Other examples of this trend are variants on the ISO 9001 standard in the militaries of several countries, or the levels (Table 1.1) defined by the Software Engineering Institute (SEI) in its capability maturity model (CMM), a process-based quality management model for assessing the level of an organization's software development [69].

In this context the software development process is considered from an engineering point of view. It is generally divided into several subtasks, called *phases*. Each phase addresses different problems on the road leading from a set of requirements to a working software system. The output from each phase

Table 1.1 The SEI/CMM levels

1. **Initial** The software process is characterized as *ad hoc*, and occasionally even chaotic. Few processes are defined, and success depends on individual effort.

2. **Repeatable** Basic project management processes are established to track cost, schedule, and functionality. The necessary process discipline is in place to repeat earlier successes on projects with similar applications.

3. **Defined** The software process for both management and engineering activities is documented, standardized, and integrated into a standard software process for the organization. All projects use an approved, tailored version of the organization's standard software process for developing and maintaining software.

4. **Managed** Detailed measures of the software process and product quality are collected. Both the software process and products are quantitatively understood and controlled.

5. **Optimized** Continuous process improvement is enabled by quantitative feedback from the process and from piloting innovative ideas and technologies.

is the basis for the next. Although there is some dispute about their names and their boundaries, there is a broad agreement on the nature of these phases. In Europe, one popular approach is the V model, as illustrated in Figure 1.1 (there are several variants of the V model, such as the waterfall model [120] most popular in the United States or the spiral model [18]). The boxes represent the successive stages of a software development project, from the initial requirements down to the executable code (through analysis, design, and implementation), and then up to an operational system (through testing, integration, and delivery). The dashed lines connecting the right-hand side boxes to the left-hand side boxes suggest a match between the requirements of the descending stages and the results of ascending stages. This V model is itself the first phase in the life cycle of most large software systems, which are usually subject to several years of maintenance (both corrective and evolutive).

The study of this kind of process led to a new branch of computer science: software development methodology. This branch is the study of methods for designing and implementing software in a rational way. As with any other scientific domain, the increased complexity of a large system has been dealt with in a modular way, which breaks down problems into a manageable size.

A major breakthrough was made with the introduction of structured design [113, 119], which follows the spirit of structured programming and top-down functional design [144]. The structured-design family of methods provides a rational, systematic, and teachable process to go efficiently from a well-defined functional specification to a working implementation. However,

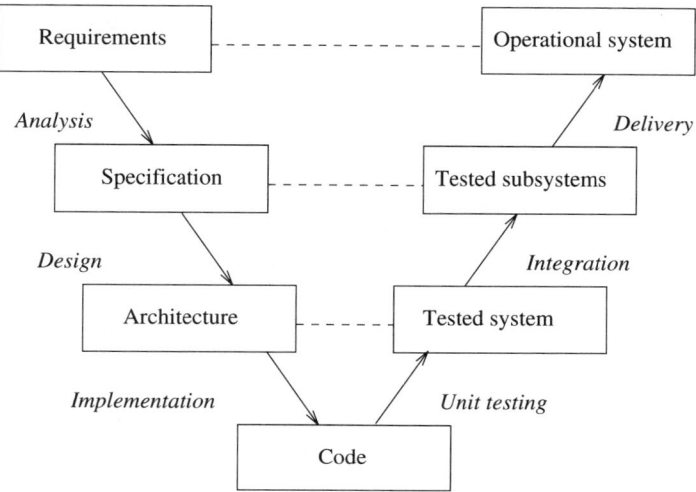

Figure 1.1 Phases of software development in the V model

for large real systems, software specifications are usually imprecise, ambiguous, unclear, and much more subject to change than other artifacts, because of the widely held belief in software "softness." When you build a house, you have to make up your mind about the disposition of the walls *before* putting on the roof. Is it possible for software systems to be relieved of that kind of constraint?

Jackson [73] showed that the main flaw of structured-design techniques is that they neglect this softness aspect of software construction. Because each module is produced to meet a precise subrequirement, no provision is made for future evolutions, nor for dealing with potential analysis or design flaws. On the premise that *entities are more stable than functions*, Jackson's system development (JSD) method recommends that the programmer start the specification of a system with the elaboration of a "real-world" model representing the stable part of the system. This model is made of *entities* performing or suffering *actions*, the temporal pattern of which is precisely defined. Functionality specifications are added to this model at a later stage. This approach makes JSD a clear winner in terms of maintenance savings, but JSD suffers from a lack of structure and too much fuzziness.

This is not to speak of reusing software components, which lies completely out of the scope of these approaches.

Another popular approach, also based on modeling, consists of building entity relationship models of the problem domain [32]. The family of methods that relies on this approach strongly emphasizes data and their organization. It is then very well suited to a relational database type of application, but may not fit so well with other problem domains.

Once the idea of analyzing a system through modeling has been accepted, there is little surprise that the object-oriented approach is brought in, because its roots lie in Simula-67, a language for simulation designed in the late 1960s, and simulation basically relies on modeling.

1.2 The Object-Oriented Approach

1.2.1 Origin

The object-oriented paradigm evolved from a set of concepts already present in computer science in the early 1970s:

- *Classes* of objects used to simulate real-world applications. In Simula-67 [38], execution of a computer program is organized as a combined execution of a collection of objects. Objects sharing common behaviors are said to constitute a class.

- Protected resources in operating systems. Hoare [66] proposed the idea of using an enclosed area as a software unit and introduced the concept of a *monitor*, which is concerned with process synchronization and contention for resources among processes.

- Units of knowledge, called *frames*, are used for knowledge representation. Minsky [104] proposed the notion of frames to capture the idea that a behavior goes with the entity whose behavior is being described. Thus, a frame can also be represented as an object.

- Data abstraction in programming languages such as CLU [48], which refers to a programming style in which instances of *abstract data types* (ADTs) are manipulated by operations that are exclusively encapsulated within a protected region.

1.2.2 Definitions in the Context of Software Engineering

Even more concretely, an object takes up space in a computer's memory, and has an associated address like a record in Ada, Pascal, or C. The arrangement of bits in an object's memory space determines that object's state.

Whereas the approaches described in Section 1.2.1 led to several paradigms in various computer science fields, the notions of *object, class, function*, and *inheritance* take a particular meaning in the context of software engineering.

Objects A computer science theoretician would define an *object* as the transitive closure of a function. More concretely, an object is an encapsulation of some state together with a defined set of operations on that state.

An object embodies an abstraction characterized by an entity in the real world. Hence, it exists in time, it may have a changeable state, and it can be created and destroyed. An object has an identity (which is a distinguishing characteristic of an object) that denotes a separate existence from other objects. The object's behavior characterizes how an object acts and reacts in terms of changes in its state. In fact, each object could be viewed as a computer endowed with a memory and a central processing unit (CPU) that can provide a set of services.

Classes A *class* is a template description that specifies properties and behaviors for a set of similar objects. From the point of view of a strongly typed language, a class is a construct for implementing a user-defined type.

Every object is an instance of only one class. A class may have no instances (usually termed an *abstract* or *deferred* class). Every class has a name and a body that defines the set of attributes and operations possessed by its instances. It is important to distinguish between an object and its class. In this book the term *class* is used to identify a category of objects and is a compile-time notion, whereas the term *object* is used to mean an instance of a class and exists at run time only.

The term object is sometimes used to refer to both class and instance, especially with languages like Smalltalk where a class is itself an object.

Features Features of an object are either *attributes* or *routines*. They are part of the definition of classes. Attributes are named properties of an object and hold abstract states of each object. Routines characterize the behavior of an object, which is expressible in terms of the operations meaningful to that object. The routines are the only means for modifying the attributes of an object, hence the encapsulation properties of an object.

Attributes also may be viewed as parameterless functions.

An object may invoke routines or read the attributes that are part of another object's *interface*. Consider, for example, a radio set. Its interface is made of:

- Buttons allowing you to select between AM and FM,
- A frequency selector,
- A display showing the current radio station.

Usually, you don't need to know how the radio set is built to use it. The same should hold for software objects.

Inheritance The *inheritance* mechanism can be used to represent a relationship between classes. Every inheritance relationship has parents called the *superclasses* and children called the *subclasses*. Inheritance allows the definition and implementation of a new class by combination and specialization of existing ones. It is a mechanism for sharing commonalities (in terms of attributes and routines) between these classes, thus allowing classification, subtyping, and reuse.

1.2.3 Object-Oriented Analysis and Design

Object-oriented analysis and design (OOAD) methods subsume the best ideas found in previous methods. They still fit quite well in the V model, even if the software development process in most of these methods does not proceed linearly but swings back and forth between phases (seamless development). Numerous OOAD methods have been documented in the literature. A 1992 survey article by Monarchi and Puhr [105] mentions more than 20 OOAD techniques. Let's try to highlight their common rationale.

More details on OOAD will be given in the second part of this book, in Section 6.1.

The first step toward an object-oriented analysis is concerned with devising a precise, relevant, concise, understandable, and correct model of the real world. The purpose of object-oriented analysis is to model the problem domain so that it can be understood and serve as a stable basis in preparing the design step.

> Object-oriented analysis is a method of analysis that examines requirements from the perspective of the classes and objects found in the vocabulary of the domain. (G. Booch)

The *design* phase starts with the output of the analysis phase and gradually shifts its emphasis from the application domain to the computation domain: The implementation strategy is defined, and trade-offs are made accordingly. Auxiliary classes may be introduced at this stage to deal with complex relationships or implementation-related matters. The output of the object-oriented design phase is a blueprint for its implementation in an object-oriented language, which is basically an extension of the design process.

See B. W. Boehm and W. Humphrey's works (17, 69) for more thoughts on this topic.

Again the boundary between design and implementation is not rigid. This seamlessness of the object-oriented approach may upset the old-time programmers who favor the well-established structured methods that feature strong frontiers between phases. A reality check might be necessary here: How often does a final product match its initial requirements? What is the situation 5 or 10 years later? Use of the same conceptual framework (based on objects) during the whole software life cycle (from analysis to implementation, testing, delivery, and maintenance) yields considerable benefits in terms of flexibility and traceability. These properties translate to better quality software systems (fewer defects and delays) that are much easier to maintain because a requirement shift can usually be traced easily down to the (object-oriented) code (see, for example, [129]).

1.3 Eiffel: An Object-Oriented Language for Software Engineering

1.3.1 A Software Engineering Tool

> A good programming language is one that helps programmers write good programs. No programming language will prevent its users from writing bad programs. (Kees Koster)

As a software engineering tool, a computer language must address both issues of

- Fostering a rigorous approach based on formal assertions when programming in the small and
- Providing support for managing the structural complexity of programming in the large.

The Eiffel language has been designed specifically to meet these requirements. It is based on the principles of object-oriented design, and achieves a careful balance between the use of sophisticated concepts and overall simplicity, consistent minimalism, and pragmatism. It brings object-oriented design and programming closer together. It emphasizes the design and construction of large, high-quality software by assembling reusable software components made of classes.

Beyond classes (on which modularity is based), Eiffel offers multiple inheritance, polymorphism, static typing and dynamic binding, genericity, and a disciplined exception mechanism, and it fosters a systematic use of assertions to improve software correctness in the context of *design by contract*.

Eiffel provides a consistent framework that fosters the design and implementation of software components that feature the following quality factors:

- **Correctness** is the ability of components to perform their tasks exactly, as defined by the requirements and specifications. Assertions available in Eiffel are elements of formal specifications that characterize the semantics of classes and their features independently of their implementation. They provide a reference against which correctness can be checked.
- **Reusability** allows software components to be used as building blocks for future software developments. Components created by others are used rather than creating new ones from scratch. The savings are not so much expected in the initial development phase (a good cut-and-paste editor

could be as efficient) as in the testing, integration, and, above all, maintenance phases of the software life cycle. Inheritance plays a major role in increasing software reusability by allowing components to be customized.

- **Extensibility** permits new functionalities to be added easily with little modification to existing software systems. With this property, software systems can be extended easily to meet new requirements. This incremental development also relies on the inheritance mechanism. It is a fundamental part of object-oriented thinking.

- **Compatibility** is the ease with which software components may be combined and assembled to build useful programs. The Eiffel approach to building software can rely on the mere notion of assembling software components. All components are orthogonal: The concept of "main program" (or entry point) does not require special syntax, therefore a class that contains the "main program" for one system may be an ordinary class in some other system.

- **Robustness** is the ability of software components to function even in abnormal conditions. This ability boils down to avoiding catastrophic behavior when things go awry. Eiffel disciplined exception mechanisms play an important role in improving robustness.

- **Testability** is the ease of preparing validation suites for software components. In Eiffel, testability relies on the underlying paradigm of programming by contract.

- **Efficiency** is the good use of resources (e.g., processor or memory) to make good trade-offs among various strategies. The clean semantics of Eiffel enables sophisticated compiler optimizations that help produce efficient components.

- **Portability** is the ability to port software components across various software and hardware environments. It is often at odds with the notion of efficiency, but sometimes (as described in the case study of Chapter 9) they can be reconciled.

- **Friendliness** is the ease of learning how to use software components. Good, up-to-date documentation as provided by Eiffel assertions and bound comments is of great help here.

1.3.2 Importance of a Language

Language shapes the way we think, and determines what we can think about.
(B. Stroustrup)

Some people still think that the technical differences between programming languages are irrelevant: A good design can accommodate any language. Clearly they are both right and wrong. Granted, a loop looks more or less the same whatever the language; and any design could be implemented with any language (remember, all languages are equivalent to a Turing machine). Few people still take seriously the old argument that method is everything, tools are nothing. If this was the case, we might as well still be writing everything in assembly language. Languages are important as tools to best support the modeling paradigm. Where there are mismatches between the modeling paradigm and the tools, manual translations must be written by programmers. This is a costly and error-prone business [81].

Object-oriented languages are close to the design concepts used to deal with ever-evolving software systems. In the context of software engineering, Eiffel is one of the most consistent and well-designed object-oriented languages on the market. It is definitively not a "universal" language (e.g., for small, one-shot programs, simpler languages may be more appropriate) nor the "ultimate" language (there will be life after Eiffel). It provides the right paradigms to address the construction of large, long-lived object-oriented software systems while staying quite easy to master, though, so Eiffel is probably an important stage in the history of language evolution.

1.3.3 An Eiffel Overview

Eiffel is a pure object-oriented language: Objects are the only things that can be manipulated at run time. It is not a superset or extension of any other language, although it retains the main lexical and syntactical conventions found in the ALGOL family of languages. Eiffel strongly fosters object-oriented programming and allows the programmer to avoid dangerous pitfalls from previous-generation languages. Still, Eiffel is an open language that does interface easily with other languages such as C or FORTRAN.

Software texts in Eiffel are made of autonomous software units called *classes*. An executable software product (a *system*) is obtained by assembling a combination of one or more classes, one of which is called the *root* of the system.

A *class* defines a type, and is also the modularization unit. It describes a number of potential run-time objects, called its *instances*. A class is characterized by its features. A *feature* is either an attribute (present in each instance of the class) or a *routine* (describing a computation applicable to each instance of the class). A routine is either a function if it returns a result, or a procedure otherwise. A routine may have formal arguments; if so, calls to the routines

12 THE SOFTWARE ENGINEERING CONTEXT

must include the corresponding actual arguments (which are expressions having a type conforming to the formal argument).

Value semantics are also available to deal with simple objects like integers and characters.

An *entity* is a name in a class text. It is either an attribute of a class, a local variable or a formal argument of a routine, or the predefined entity *result* holding a function result. An entity stands for a value at run time. This value is normally a reference to an actual object, or may be *void*.

Eiffel assertions are used for writing correct and robust software, debugging it, and documenting it automatically. Assertions include routine preconditions (which must be satisfied when the routine is called), routine postconditions (guaranteed to be true at the end of the routine), and class invariants (global consistency conditions applying to every instance of a class). Disciplined exception handling is used to recover gracefully from abnormal cases.

Eiffel classes may be generic, i.e., they may have a formal generic parameter such as T in LIST[T]. The class may use any type (class) as a generic parameter, thus making a flexible container structure such as LIST[INTEGER] or LIST[ANY_USEFUL_CLASS] easily available.

Eiffel classes may be structured in an inheritance hierarchy. Multiple inheritance is available with a set of mechanisms to manage it (renaming, selection, redefinition, undefinition, and repeated inheritance). Strict static typing is used for improving safety in a software system and dynamic binding is used for flexibility.

Entities may reference any object with a type that conforms to their declared type (hence their polymorphic nature). Dynamic binding of features to entities then ensures that the feature most directly adapted to the actual target object is selected.

1.3.4 Status of the Eiffel Language

Eiffel was created by Bertrand Meyer and developed by his company, Interactive Software Engineering Inc. (ISE) of Goleta, CA.

NICE directions are given in Appendix C.

The definition of the Eiffel language [101] is in the public domain. This definition is controlled by the Nonprofit International Consortium for Eiffel (NICE). Thus, anyone or any company can create a compiler or interpreter having to do with Eiffel. NICE reserves the right to validate that any such tool conforms to the current definition of the Eiffel language before it can be distributed with the Eiffel trademark (e.g., advertised as an "Eiffel" compiler).

There are at least four Eiffel compilers (see Appendix C). These compilers should be compatible to a large extent now that NICE has published *The Eiffel Standard Library Vintage 95* (described in Section 4.3). Note that various versions of these compilers are available for free (see Appendix C).

Part I

Language Elements

2

Basic Language Elements of Eiffel

In This Chapter

- 2.1 The Eiffel Notion of Systems
- 2.2 Class = Module = Type
- 2.3 Definition of Entity Declaration
- 2.4 Statements
- 2.5 Routines: Procedures and Functions
- 2.6 Example: Sorting Data with Eiffel

The basic constructions of the Eiffel language are the system, the class and its components, the imperative instruction set, and the assertions.

2.1 The Eiffel Notion of Systems

2.1.1 System and Program

Eiffel is a language that focuses on *software components*, not on *programs*. The *class* is the top construct of the Eiffel grammar. The notion of a "program" found in most computer languages is downplayed in Eiffel.

Building programs with Eiffel consists of *assembling* off-the-shelf and ad hoc software components, or classes. For that you have to tell the compiler (or another Eiffel environment tool, such as an interpreter) where the relevant classes are, that a particular class among them is the "root" of the Eiffel program, and that this program entry point—like the *main()* function in C—is a particular creation routine of the root class.

The exact way of doing this assembly depends on your Eiffel environment. It could be through command-line arguments. Most probably it is through a configuration file, called an Assembly of Classes in Eiffel (ACE). An ACE file

ACE files are described in depth in Section 4.1.1.

BASIC LANGUAGE ELEMENTS OF EIFFEL

```
     -- A simple "Hello, world" example

     class HELLO
     creation
5        make
     feature
        make is
              -- class entry point
           do
10            print("Hello, world!%N")
           end
     end -- HELLO
```

Example 2.1

%N is the new line character, equivalent to the \n found in C.

is remotely related to the well-known *makefile* found in UNIX or C environments, the main difference is that you don't have to deal with dependency rules nor imperative instructions. An ACE file only contains information on the root class of a system, the executable(s) name, the compilation options, and where to find the other classes needed by the system. In Eiffel, it is the job of the compiler to determine dependencies and to decide everything about the compilation and linking process.

2.1.2 "Hello, world!"

A creation procedure corresponds to the class constructor in the C++ terminology.

''Hello, world'' is the unavoidable example of one of the smallest Eiffel programs. The class listed in Example 2.1 describes objects that are only able to print "Hello, world" when they are created. The feature *make* is declared to be a creation procedure; i.e., *make* is called to create a HELLO object.

Once the Eiffel system with HELLO as its root class and *make* as its entry point has been compiled to an executable program called **hello,** it can be run as any other program.

The execution model of Eiffel is very simple: When a program is run, a single instance of the root class (here HELLO) is created (the root object), and the specified creation procedure is called. A creation procedure can be designed to create other objects (which may themselves create other objects) and do real work with them. In our simple example, the creation procedure prints the expected "Hello, world" message and exits. The program then finishes.

2.2 Class = Module = Type

2.2.1 Foundation Principles

> There is a magic number: seven plus or minus two. This refers to the number of concepts that we humans can keep in mind at any one time. (H. A. Miller)

The fewer the number of concepts in a programming language, the easier it is to learn it and to understand programs written with it. In Smalltalk, for example, everything is an object; this brings conceptual simplicity and frees space in the programmer's mind to let him or her concentrate on useful things.

The Eiffel way of liberating our minds is through the unification of the notions of module and type in the language construct called *class*. Then an object is just an instance of a class, just as you are an instance of the *homo sapiens sapiens* species. Simplification often occurs at the cost of some limitations or more complexity somewhere else. In Smalltalk, "everything is an object" leads to a complex structure of metaclasses [56, 24]. Some consequences of the Eiffel unification are discussed in Section 5.4.

Both notions of type and module existed for years, but Eiffel was the first computer language in which they were fully unified. Still, like a Janus statue, a class has two faces. Let's explore them separately.

2.2.2 The Class As a Module

Modularity helps engineers (and others) manage the complexity of systems. The principle of modularity is the key to supporting modifiability, reusability, extensibility, and understandability. A module is characterized by a well-defined interface and by information hiding. An interface should be small and simple in order for modules to be as loosely coupled as possible.

Modularity rapidly made its way into computer science through the notion of a subroutine (procedure). The next step was to consider coarser grain modularity. At the program unit level, a set of data and procedures is encapsulated in a programming module, which can be compiled separately. This idea is already present in C, where a module is just a file.

The next step was to make the notion of module part of the language. This is achieved in Modula-2 [145] (hence the name) and Ada83 [70]. In Modula-2, modules are split into specification (interface) and implementation parts. Each of these module components is compiled separately. Data types and procedures may be specified in the interface of the module without revealing their representation details. These are provided in the implementation part of the module. Any other module can only have access to the interface of the module.

Information hiding is implemented in C with the "static" declaration occurring for a variable or a function: It makes this variable or function private to the file.

In Ada a module is called a "package." It is essentially the same notion as that of Modula-2's, including a separate interface specification.

The Eiffel notion of class evolved from these notions of modules. You cannot define various types, however. Instead, you can define just one, which is identified to the class itself. As a consequence, the interface of an Eiffel class, although not described separately from the implementation part, still exists conceptually. An Eiffel class may even have several interfaces. This property is called *subjectivity*: The way you see a class depends on who you are (this is explained in depth in Section 3.1.4).

Producing interface specifications of Eiffel classes is usually done by a tool present in most Eiffel environments. Usually called *short*, this tool eliminates the need to maintain the consistency between the interface specification and the module implementation, and still retains the benefits of having an interface specification without implementation details.

2.2.3 The Class As a Type

The notion of a user-definable *data type* was already present in the ALGOL family of languages [108], and has not evolved much since then. Formally, a type characterizes:

- A domain of values and
- A set of operations applicable to objects of the named type.

In a typed language, objects of a given type may take only those values that are appropriate to the type, and the only operations that may be applied to an object are those that are defined for its type. A typing error results when one of these conditions is violated.

Depending on the moment when this typing error is detected, we can classify languages into three categories:

- Untyped (or loosely) typed language. A typing error may remain undetected until after run time. The usual error message is *"Bus Error. Core Dump"* (your mileage may vary).
- Dynamically typed language. The typing error is detected at run time, and in Smalltalk it can result in the well-known *"Message not understood"* error message (meaning an operation has been invoked on an object that didn't define it).
- Statically typed language. A program is rejected by the compiler as soon as it encounters a typing error. Eiffel is such a language. When a typing

error is detected, the usual (compile-time) error message is *"Operation xxx not defined on object yyy."*

Each approach has pros and cons. To be brief, untyped languages are useful for low-level system programming or as target languages for a compiler, but 20 years of extensive software developments with C have demonstrated the limitations of this kind of language.

Dynamic typing has made its way into software prototyping and interactive systems, and more generally into environments where the product is short lived or requires very rapid turnaround. In such a context, where the software must be as soft as possible, static type checking tools are thought to be too cumbersome, whereas dynamically typed languages give the programmer the freedom needed to get things working very quickly, and to make changes at a rapid pace.

Finally, static type checking is a must if the product is supposed to have a long and active life (e.g., requires continuous upgrading, or serves as the source of many spin-off products), or if software correctness is a prime concern—if only to save money in detecting defaults earlier in the software life cycle.

The Eiffel notion of class is actually based on the notion of an abstract data type (ADT), a type in which the allowed operations have associated formal properties defining their semantics [90, 62]. The Eiffel language constructs corresponding to these formal property specifications are the *assertions*, taken from the ADT theory. Assertions are described in more detail in Section 2.5.3, but it was necessary to introduce them here, because they belong to the Eiffel notion of type. They play a major role in constraining subtyping through inheritance, so assertions should belong to every object-oriented language notion of type (as has been proved in [92]).

2.2.4 Components of a Class Declaration

Notation for Describing Eiffel Syntax

There are several ways to formally present the syntax of a programming language. The Backus-Naur form (BNF) is the most concise, but not the most readable. Thus, we present Eiffel's form with syntax diagrams that are essentially graphical representations of the BNF. Syntax diagrams are read from left to right. The lines may loop back on themselves, indicating that a construct may be repeated. A circle or ellipse denotes a literal string that appears exactly as stated. A rectangle surrounds a construct that is defined in another syntax diagram (this construct is called *nonterminal*). A full set of Eiffel syntax diagrams is provided for reference in Appendix B.3.

ClassDeclaration

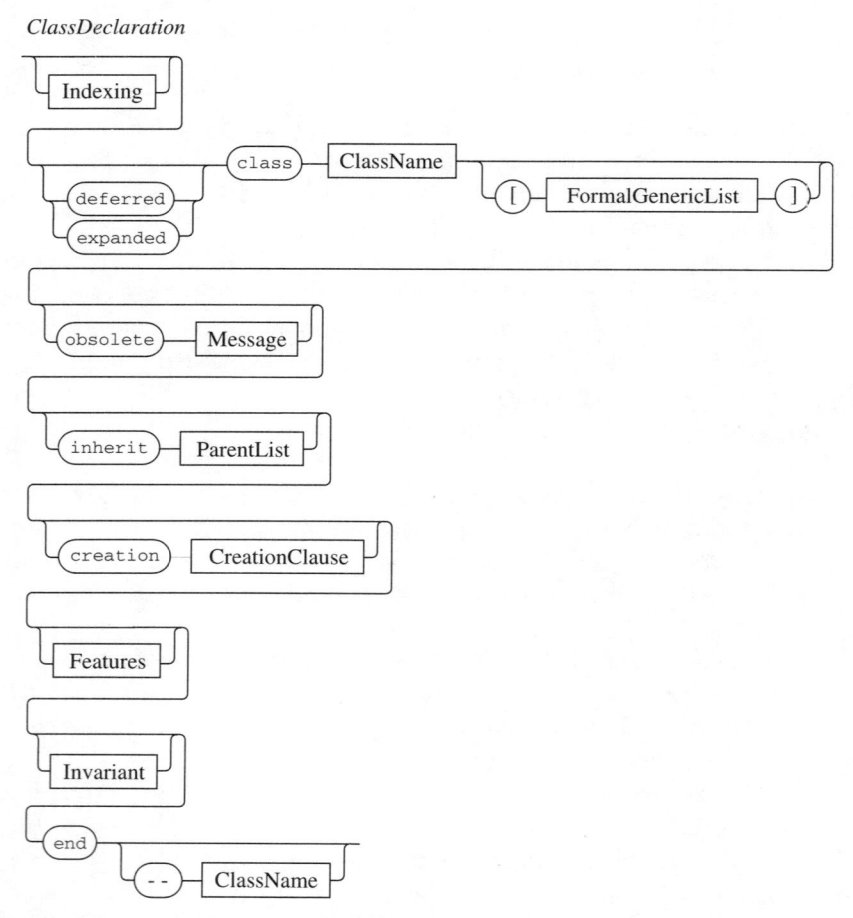

Syntax Diagram 1 The class declaration

Syntax Diagram 1 describes the syntactical components of a class declaration. It is made of the following parts:

Indexing clause, for documentation and indexing purposes. The usage of the indexing clause is described in Section 6.6.4. Until then, you may consider this clause as a structured comment.

Class header, which allows regular, deferred, or expanded classes. Deferred classes are presented in Section 3.6. Expanded classes are discussed along with the notion of entities in Section 2.3.

Class name, which is also the module name and the type name.

Generic clause, made of a list of formal generic parameters between brackets. This clause makes it possible to build classes with parameters (see Section 3.2).

Obsolete clause, which if present denotes that this class is to be eliminated from the library in future releases. More details are given in Section 6.6.4.

Inherit clause, which allows you to specify how this class inherits from other ones (see Section 3.3).

Creation clause, which specifies which routines may be called on creation of an instance of this class (see Section 3.1.1).

Feature clauses, which describes the class features (attributes and routines) grouped by exportation sets (see Section 3.1).

Invariant, which specifies the class invariants (see section 2.5.3).

The minimal class declaration in Eiffel is made of the keywords **class** and **end** separated by the class name; all other clauses are optional. The class BOOK in Example 2.2 reflects the Eiffel syntax more concretely. This class, which encapsulates a book description (basically a title, a list of authors, and an inventory number) is used in the case study of Section 3.8.

The Eiffel notion of class encompasses both notions of ADT implementation and module, that is, a program unit. In this chapter, we concentrate on the latter aspect of a class to present what is often called the imperative part of Eiffel, just considering one program unit (i.e., an isolated class), without *generic*, *obsolete*, or *inherit* clauses.

Lexical Components

On the lexical level, despite some unusual features (multiline strings, expected comments, use of the % symbol as an escape character, see Appendix B) Eiffel conforms for the most part to the way things are done in other software engineering-oriented languages. Eiffel is case independent and follows the usual conventions for the syntax of identifiers. As in Ada, comments are introduced with a double dash (--) and end at the end of the line.

However, notation conventions exist. See Section 6.6.2.

```
        class BOOK
        creation
            make
        feature
5           title : STRING
            authors : STRING
            inventory : INTEGER
            make (new_title, new_authors:STRING; new_inventory:INTEGER) is
                -- make a new book record
10              require
                    title_non_void: new_title /= Void
                    authors_non_void: new_authors /= Void
                do
                    title := new_title
15                  authors := new_authors
                    inventory := new_inventory
                end -- make
            print_description is
                do
20                  print(title); print(", by ")
                    print(authors); print(" (")
                    print(inventory); print(")%N")
                end -- print_description
        end -- BOOK
```

Example 2.2

Manifest Constants and Basic Types

A manifest constant is a literal value present in the text of the class. It has a type, deduced from the lexical structure, e.g., BOOLEAN, CHARACTER, INTEGER, REAL, BIT sequence, STRING, and ARRAY.

The usual conventions also apply here: **True** and **False** are the only BOOLEAN constants, an ASCII character enclosed in single quotes (e.g., 'a') denotes a CHARACTER constant, 42 is an INTEGER constant, and a sequence of character values enclosed in double quotes (e.g., "Hello, world") is a STRING constant. Full details on the syntax for all manifest constants are given in Appendix B.1.

A type is nothing but a class, so manifest constants are just constant instances of their classes (sometimes called *basic types*). Conversely, these classes are nothing special further than being able to have literal instances (which implies that they must be known by the compiler, which may then make several optimizations with them, but this is another story). Along with a set of other Eiffel classes, these basic types must also be the same (or at least compatible) regardless of the Eiffel compiler; this is why they are sometimes called kernel library classes.

2.3 Definition of Entity Declaration

2.3.1 Entity Declaration

At run time, only objects exist. An *entity* is a language-level notion that allows the programmer to designate objects. The notion of entity encompasses the usual notions of variable, formal parameter, and result value found in most languages. Eiffel is a strongly typed language, so every entity used in an Eiffel program must be declared, or associated to a type. As in Pascal or Ada, an ALGOL-like syntax is used to declare entities (see Syntax Diagram 2).

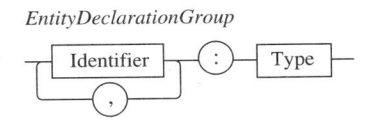

EntityDeclarationGroup

Identifier : Type

Syntax Diagram 2   Entity declarations

In Example 2.3 an entity *title* is declared to be of type STRING, and the entity *n* is declared to be of type INTEGER.

    title : STRING
    n : INTEGER

Example 2.3

2.3.2 Entity Expansion Status

An entity may either *refer* to an object, or directly *hold* it, depending on whether its type is a reference class (e.g., INTEGER_REF) or an expanded class (e.g., INTEGER), as illustrated in Figure 2.1. For both cases in this example, print(e) would display 547.

Whereas the natural semantics for entities are based on the notion of reference to an object, sometimes the expanded semantics may make more sense. This is the case when dealing with such basic notions of integers or real numbers, or when real-world modeling suggests it (a person has one head, not a reference to a potentially shared head). The choice of value vs. reference objects is simply a design decision based on the model one is trying to build.

Eiffel expanded entities correspond to C++ value *objects* or to Smalltalk immediate *objects*.

24 BASIC LANGUAGE ELEMENTS OF EIFFEL

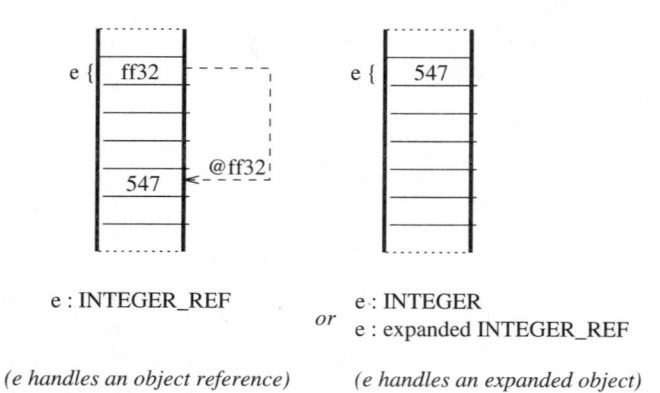

                    e : INTEGER_REF   e : INTEGER
                                        or
                                             e : expanded INTEGER_REF

                  (e handles an object reference) *(e handles an expanded object)*

On the contrary, C basic types such as int still exist in C++ as a separate notion, unrelated to the class notion. This is why C++ is sometimes referred to as a hybrid language, whereas Eiffel and Smalltalk are referred to as pure OO language.

Figure 2.1 Reference vs. expanded objects

An object may indeed have several entities referring to it, whereas an expanded object is just the run-time value of an entity. Basic data types such as BOOLEAN, INTEGER, REAL, DOUBLE, and CHARACTER are just the expanded forms of BOOLEAN_REF, ..., CHARACTER_REF and are nothing special with respect to the type system. The only thing that makes this set of classes (along with the classes STRING and ARRAY) somehow special is the possibility of declaring *manifest* constants of these types in a program text.

2.3.3 Constant Entities

Thus it does not need to be physically stored with the instance.

A *constant entity* is tied to a given object. Its value does not change at run time and is the same for all instances of a class. The syntax of a constant entity declaration is presented in Syntax Diagram 3.

The constant entity may be tied to a manifest constant as described in Appendix B.1. Example 2.4 presents a set of constant entity declarations. BIT16 and BIT8 are conceptually different classes (as for any n in BITn).

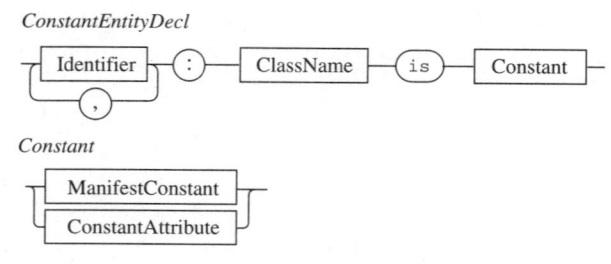

ConstantEntityDecl

Identifier : ClassName is Constant

Constant

ManifestConstant
ConstantAttribute

Syntax Diagram 3 Constant entity declaration

```
        i : INTEGER is 3
        a_negative_number : INTEGER is -864322
        a_huge_number : INTEGER is 3789641370
        PI : DOUBLE is 3.14159265453
5       message : STRING is "This is a message string"
        mask : BIT16 is 0101000011110101B
        BCD13 : BIT8 is 00010011B
```

Example 2.4

Unique Constants

Sometimes the actual value of an integer constant is not really important to the programmer: The only important thing is that each constant in a set has a unique value. To let the compiler choose a code for an integer constant, one may declare it as **unique** (Syntax Diagram 4).

This is related to enumerated types in Pascal or Ada or enum in C.

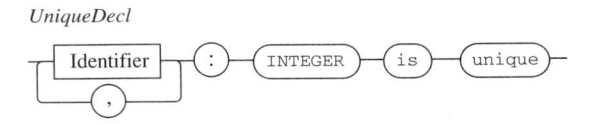

Syntax Diagram 4   Unique constant declaration

In Example 2.5, the value of a **unique** constant such as **Red** is a positive integer. If two unique constants are introduced in the same class, their values are guaranteed to be different. Furthermore, if they are declared to be in the same clause (as **Red**, **Green,** and **Blue** in our example), these constants will have consecutive values.

Unique constants may seem more primitive than the usual enumerated types found in procedural languages. However, in these languages the main use for the enumerated types is to help implement variant records or to allow clever set operations. Both concepts are superseded by object-oriented techniques: inheritance and the use of sets of anything (instead of sets of enumerated data). Still, unique constants are useful when dealing with error codes, or finite state machine state encoding.

```
        Red, Green, Blue : INTEGER is unique
        Yellow : INTEGER is unique
```

Example 2.5

Another Constant Declaration Method

The last way to declare constants is through the use of *once* functions (described in Section 2.5.6). *Once* functions allow for computed constants, and also for constants with types that cannot be expressed with the manifest constants.

2.3.4 Default Initialization Rule for Entities

The value of an entity is always defined in Eiffel. The initial value of an entity depends on its type, according to the rule described in Table 2.1 (the value *Void* denotes an empty reference).

Table 2.1 Default initialization rule for entities

Entity type	Initial value
BOOLEAN	**false**
CHARACTER	'%U' (NUL)
INTEGER	0
REAL	0.0
DOUBLE	0.0
Reference to class A	**Void**
Expanded class A	All attributes of A initialized to their default values

2.4 Statements

There are relatively few instructions in Eiffel. In this respect, it is almost minimal. All classic constructs usually found in an imperative language still exist in Eiffel, but in one instance only (e.g., there is no chance to choose among various loop constructs).

Eiffel instructions include the object creation, the assignment, the feature call, the sequence, the conditional, the multibranch choice, and the loop. Also available are the debug instruction (to include optional debugging code) and the check instruction to check an assertion at any point in the code.

For now, consider that type conformance is type equality. Its exact definition is given in Section 3.3.3.

2.4.1 Assignment

The assignment instruction allows a new value to be given to a variable provided the value type conforms to the variable one (Syntax Diagram 5).

Assignment

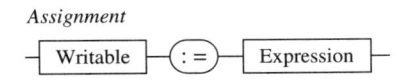

─┤ Writable ├─(:=)─┤ Expression ├─

Syntax Diagram 5 Assignment syntax

This assignment syntax is typical of the ALGOL family of languages. Consider the following assignment:

This assignment syntax is the same as in Pascal, Ada, or Modula-2.

```
target := source
```

The exact effect of this instruction depends on whether the target and the source are expanded objects or references.

- If the target is an expanded type, then the source object is copied into the target (Figures 2.2 and 2.3; on this set of figures, the rectangles represent the source and target contents). However, if the source is *Void* the assignment will fail. When something *fails* in an Eiffel program, an exception is triggered (see Section 5.1).

BEFORE   *AFTER*

source   source

target   target

```
target := source
```

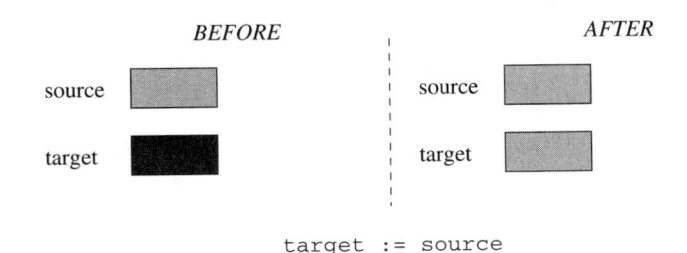

Figure 2.2 Assigning an expanded object to an expanded entity

BEFORE   *AFTER*

source   source

target   target

```
target := source
```

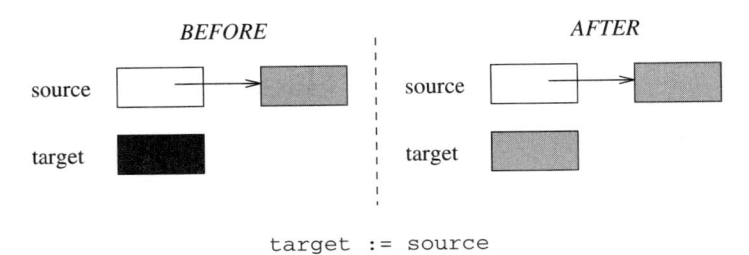

Figure 2.3 Assigning a reference object to an expanded entity

BEFORE | AFTER

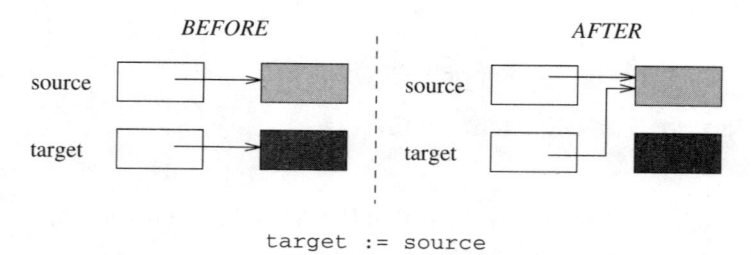

Figure 2.4 Assigning a reference object to a reference entity

Two entities are said to be aliased if their values are references to the same object.

- If the target is a reference, and

    If the source is a reference, this reference is copied to the target, and thus both target and source refer to the source object after the assignment (this is sometimes called *aliasing*). See Figure 2.4 for an example.

    If the source is an expanded object, it is cloned to a twin object, and the target then refers to this twin as illustrated in Figure 2.5.

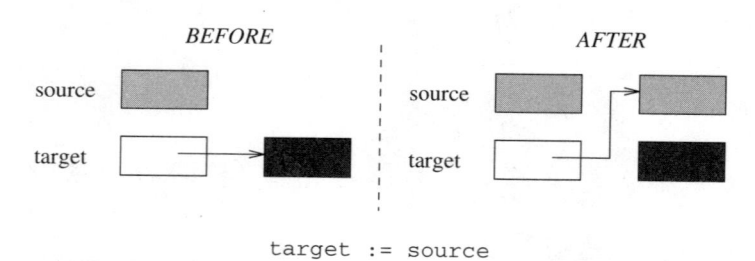

Figure 2.5 Assigning an expanded object to a reference entity

You never need to worry about memory management issues with Eiffel unless you really insist on doing so.

In both cases where the source is a reference object, it may become unreachable (lost) after the assignment instruction. In Eiffel, it is the task of the *garbage collector* to recycle this kind of unreachable memory. Section 4.5 gives more detail on how it works.

A variant of the *Assignment* instruction is called the *Assignment Attempt* (denoted **?=**). It is described in Section 5.3 in the discussion on type conformance.

2.4.2 Testing for Equality

Related to assignment is the test for *equality*, which exists in three flavors in Eiffel:

- $a = b$ tests whether a and b refer to the same object (reference equality). If both are expanded entities, it tests for the equality of their values.

- *equal(a,b)* tests whether a and b are identical objects, that is, all their fields a_i and b_i are such that $a_i = b_i$. For expanded entities, *equal(a,b)* has the same meaning as $a = b$.

- *deep_equal(a,b)* tests whether a and b have equal values if they are expanded entities or refer to isomorphic object structures; that is, all their fields a_i and b_i are *deep_equal*(a_i, b_i).

2.4.3 Sequence

The sequence is the control structure denoting that a set of instructions (called a compound instruction) must be executed sequentially, in their textual order. As illustrated in Syntax Diagram 6, the semicolon (;) is optional, and an empty sequence is a valid instruction.

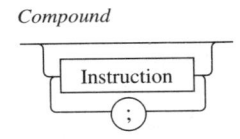

Syntax Diagram 6 The compound instruction

2.4.4 Conditional

Conditional control structures allow the selection of one of a number of alternative sequences of statements, depending on the value of some condition (see Example 2.6). The syntax of an **if** statement is presented in Syntax Diagram 7. This statement works as follows. The first condition is evaluated:

*This Eiffel conditional statement is very similar to Ada's, except that **elseif** is used instead of **elsif**.*

- If *True* then the first compound is executed and the flow of control passes to the instruction following the *end* clause.

```
if last_read_value = 0 then
   print ("zero%N")
elseif last_read_value > 0 then
   print ("positive%N")
else
   print ("negative%N")
end
```

Example 2.6

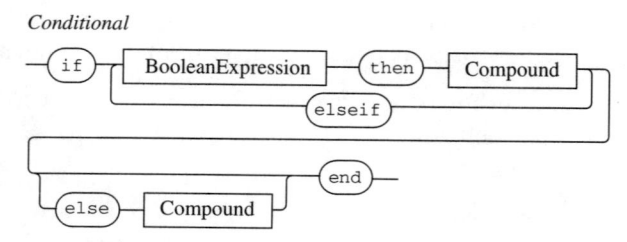

Conditional

```
──(if)──┬──[BooleanExpression]──(then)──[Compound]──┬──
        │                                            │
        └──────────(elseif)──────────────────────────┘
                                    ┌──(end)──
──┬─────────────────────────────────┤
  └──(else)──[Compound]──────────────┘
```

Syntax Diagram 7   The conditional

- If *False* then the next condition is evaluated, and so on until the last condition.
- If all the conditions have been evaluated to *False*, then the compound following the *else* clause is executed (if it exists).

2.4.5 Multibranch Choice

*This selection is in the spirit of Pascal case or C switch constructs, and has exactly the same semantics as the Ada case statement: Ada's ⇒ becomes Eiffel's **then**, and **when others** becomes **else**.*

Like the *if* statement, the multibranch choice statement selects one from many alternative sequences of statements (its syntax is described in Syntax Diagram 8).

The selection, however, is based on the value of the expression following the *inspect* clause (*inspect* expression). This value must be of the same type as the possible constant values listed in the clauses, where only INTEGER and CHARACTER constants (or intervals) are allowed.

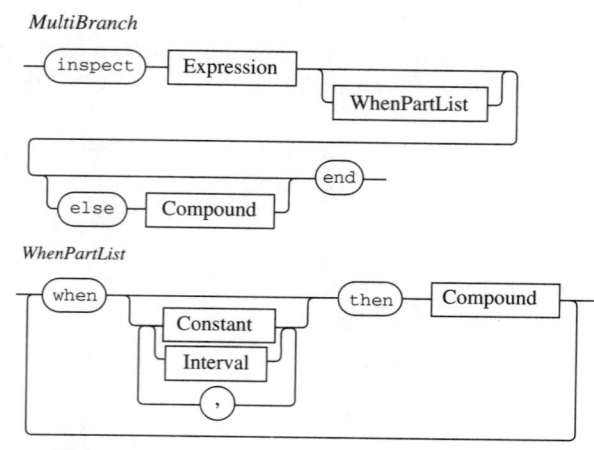

MultiBranch

```
──(inspect)──[Expression]──┬──────────────────┬──
                           └──[WhenPartList]──┘
                                    ┌──(end)──
──┬─────────────────────────────────┤
  └──(else)──[Compound]──────────────┘
```

WhenPartList

```
──(when)──┬──[Constant]──┬──(then)──[Compound]──
          ├──[Interval]──┤
          └──────,───────┘
```

Syntax Diagram 8   The multibranch choice

IntegerInterval

―[IntegerConstant]―(..)―[IntegerConstant]―

CharacterInterval

―[CharacterConstant]―(..)―[CharacterConstant]―

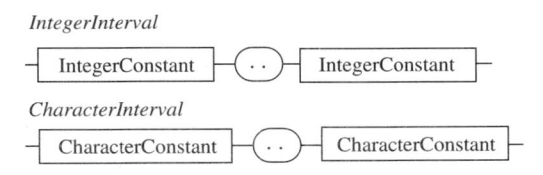

Syntax Diagram 9   INTEGER and CHARACTER interval syntax

These alternatives must be exhaustive and mutually exclusive. An *else* clause (as in the *if* statement) is available as a last alternative to cover all values not given in previous *when* clauses. Several alternatives may be declared for the same *when* clause, either by enumeration (alternatives are separated with a comma) or by range of values (the bounds of which are given and separated with two periods "..''; see Syntax Diagram 9) or any combination of both.

The effect of this statement is that the compound associated with the clause matching the *inspect* expression is executed and the control is then passed to the instruction following the *end* clause.

The multibranch choice may be the only redundant Eiffel statement. The *if* statement can always be used instead. The multibranch choice was not present in earlier versions of the language, because in procedural languages such as C or Ada, the multibranch choice statement is mainly used to select pieces of code related to variants of a data type (union in C, variant records in Pascal or Ada). This usage hampers modifiability (see, for example, [99]) because each time a component is added to or removed from the variant record, every multibranch choice dealing with the associated data structure must be changed. Object-oriented languages provide a much better solution to this problem through the use of inheritance (to replace variant records) and dynamic binding (to automatically select the relevant piece of code, see Section 3.5.2).

The multibranch choice was included in Eiffel to alleviate the syntax of dealing with input data (as in Example 2.7) while allowing the compiler to produce more efficient code.

As a general guideline, the *inspect* statement should be used mainly to discriminate among input data. Using it in another context could be an indication that the style is not really object oriented.

2.4.6 Iterative Control: The Loop

Iterative computation is a programming technique based on the repetitive application of the same process. It is a fundamental concept of computer science

```
    inspect lastchar
      when 'a'..'z' then
        print ("lowercase letter")
5     when 'A'..'Z' then
        print ("uppercase letter")
      when '0'..'9' then
        print ("digit")
      when '+','-','*','/', then
10      print ("operator")
      else
        print ("other character")
    end
```

Example 2.7

that has been used in computer languages from the beginning (in the form of a *goto* to a *label*).

An iteration is made of three main parts (Syntax Diagram 10):

1. The initialization part, to establish the initial state of the loop. In Eiffel, it is the compound following the keyword **from**.

2. The termination condition, or the Boolean expression specifying when the loop is considered finished. In Eiffel, the termination condition follows the keyword **until**.

3. The body of the loop; i.e., both the processing to be performed at each iteration and the progression code to advance toward the verification of the termination condition. In Eiffel, the body of the loop is the compound following the keyword **loop** and terminated with the keyword **end**.

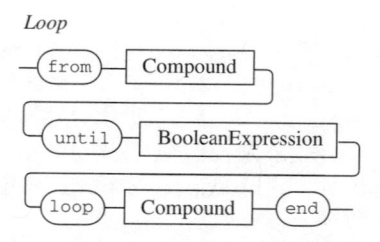

Loop

```
─(from)─[ Compound ]
─(until)─[ BooleanExpression ]
─(loop)─[ Compound ]─(end)─
```

Syntax Diagram 10 The basic syntax of the Eiffel loop construct

In Example 2.8, we compute the quotient of a number n by a *divisor* (this operation is also known as an integer division). Provided n and *divisor* are positive integers, the result of this function must satisfy:

$$Result \times divisor \leq n < (Result + 1) \times divisor \qquad (2.1)$$

```
    from remainder := n
    until remainder < divisor
    loop
        remainder := remainder - divisor
        Result := Result + 1
    end --loop
```

Example 2.8

The idea of this loop is to count how many times the *divisor* can be subtracted from n. The variable *remainder* is initialized to n, whereas *Result* is set to 0 through the default initialization rules presented earlier in Table 2.1. If the termination condition (*remainder* < *divisor*) does not hold, then the loop body is executed (*remainder* becomes *remainder* minus *divisor* and *Result* becomes *Result* + *1*). This loop body execution is repeated until the *remainder* eventually becomes smaller than the *divisor*.

The loop is a powerful construct. Imagine building programs without loops: You just lack expressive power. The drawback of the loop construct is that it is too powerful; once you have the (unbounded) loop in a language, you get the power of the Turing machine. That is, there are programs that you cannot prove correct (see the example in the introduction).

The same thing holds for recursion, which has the same expressive power as the loop.

The computer science answer to this problem is to design each loop *in such a way that it can be proved correct*. Eiffel helps you to follow this procedure, by means of the notion of loop variants and invariants.

2.4.7 Designing Correct Loops with Loop Assertions

The Notion of a Loop Invariant

A loop invariant characterizes what the loop is trying to achieve, without describing how [46]. It is a Boolean expression that must be true on initialization of the loop variables, maintained with each iteration of the loop, and held to be true at the termination of the loop. For example, a loop invariant in Example 2.8 might be $n = Result \times divisor + remainder$. In Eiffel, the loop invariant is an *assertion* that may be specified after the keyword **invariant**. The assertion itself is either a comment or a run-time checkable Boolean expression that may be tagged with an identifier. The assertion syntax is presented in Syntax Diagram 11.

Assertions checked at run time have their uses for debugging and testing, but the real value of writing down such assertions is as an aid to human thinking and reasoning about programs. It should bring you to the stage where

Assertion

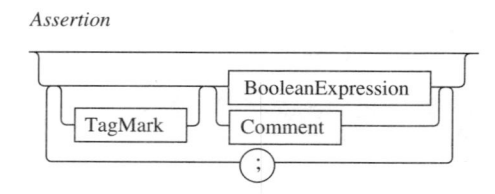

Syntax Diagram 11 Assertion syntax

you can see how in principle the software might be proved to calculate what it claims. A loop invariant describes properties that remain true on loop boundaries (initial, final, and intermediate states), so it may be given a role very much like the inductive hypothesis employed in a mathematical induction. It thus can play an important role in deriving the loop body. A loop invariant also can be used to reason about the correctness of a loop. At the end of the loop of Example 2.8 we have both:

$$\text{invariant: } n = Result \times divisor + remainder$$

and

$$\text{termination condition: } remainder < divisor,$$

which trivially implies inequality (2.1). Thus, if we reach the end of the loop, then the result will be the one we wanted. This property is called *partial correctness*. Let us see how to prove total correctness.

The Notion of a Loop Variant

Total correctness is just partial correctness *and* the proof that the loop terminates (i.e., the termination condition eventually will hold). The idea of a loop variant is to characterize how each iteration can bring the loop closer to its termination.

A loop variant is a nonnegative integer expression that is decreased by at least one at each iteration. By definition, it cannot go below zero, thus the number of iterations of a loop with a variant is bounded and then the loop eventually terminates. A suitable variant for Example 2.8 is *remainder*. It is a strictly decreasing function that takes nonnegative values only.

A loop variant has been found, so we have proved that the loop eventually terminates. This proof completes the partial correctness to give the total correctness of the loop. In other words, the loop terminates and computes the right result. In Eiffel, the loop variant may be specified after the keyword

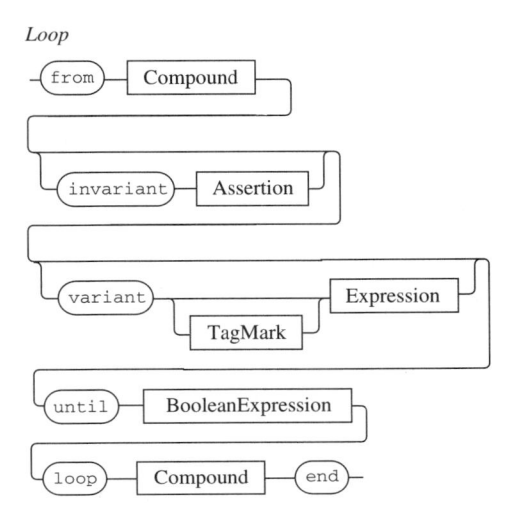

Syntax Diagram 12 The full syntax of the Eiffel loop construct

variant, as a tagged integer expression. See the full syntax of the Eiffel loop construct in Syntax Diagram 12.

So, with loop variant and invariant, Example 2.8 becomes the loop of Example 2.9.

```
from remainder := n
invariant reversible: n = Result*divisor+remainder
variant decreasing_remainder: remainder
until remainder < divisor
loop
    remainder := remainder − divisor
    Result := Result + 1
end -- loop
```

Example 2.9

Sometimes, you cannot express the loop invariant with the Eiffel assertion expressive power. Still, write it in a comment. It provides your readers with the intent of what you are trying to achieve with the loop. Consider for example the problem of computing the factorial of a number n (Example 2.10). The loop invariant ($Result = i!$) describes what the iteration has computed so far, but can only be expressed as a comment.

Designing Bug-Free Loops

Eiffel fosters the systematic design of bug-free loops (but cannot force you to do so). Here is the method:

```
        from i := 1; Result := 1
        invariant Result_is_factorial_i: -- Result = i!
        variant increasing_i: n−i
        until i = n
5       loop
            i := i + 1
            Result := Result * i
        end
```

Example 2.10

1. Design the loop invariant. It should provide a concise and preferably formal description of the properties of the loop.

2. Find the termination condition.

3. Find the variant (how the loop can advance toward its termination).

4. Write the body of the loop:

   - First deduce from the variant the progression instruction and
   - Then write the code corresponding to the restoration of the invariant.

5. Write the initialization part to set up the loop invariant.

For simple cases, steps 1 and 3 can be omitted. Still, it is a good practice to stick to the order described (termination, loop body, initialization). Example 2.10 is such a simple case, because it involves a bounded loop (i.e., the number of iterations is always n, and thus it is bounded). There is no difficulty in proving that the loop terminates.

Let us exercise our systematic design method for bug-free loops with a more complex example: a binary search. Let it be an array of integers sorted in increasing order. The feature *item(i)* gives the value of the integer stored at position i. The first position in the array is *lower*, and the last is *upper*. A *sorted* array means: $\forall i \in [lower, upper -1] \quad item(i) \leq item(i + 1)$.

// is the integer division

The problem is to find whether an integer x belongs to the array. The algorithm chosen is the binary search. Its principle is to compare x with the median element m of the array, that is, **item ((lower + upper) // 2)**.

- If they are equal, we have found x (hence we set *Result* to *True*).
- If x is smaller than m, then we have to look for it in the lower part of the array (with the same method).

- If x is greater than m, then we have to look for it in the upper part of the array (with the same method).

To apply the five-step method to solve this problem in a systematic and repeatable way:

1. First, find the loop invariant. Let l and u be the lower and upper indexes delimiting the section of the array where we look for x at a given iteration. If x belongs to the array, then x lies in between *item(l)* and *item(u)*, which by contraposition gives

$$(x < item(l) \text{ or } x > item(u)) \Rightarrow Result = False)$$

   as the loop invariant.

2. The termination condition is either that x does not belong to the array ($l > u$) or that x has been found ($Result = True$).

3. The variant is $u - l$: The range where x is supposed to be shrinks more and more.

4. The body of the loop is:

    - Make the loop progress. Let $m = (l + u)//2$. If $x < item(m)$ then $u := m - 1$ else if $x > item(m)$ then $l := m + 1$.
    - Reestablish the invariant. If $x = item(m)$, $Result := True$.

5. Set up the invariant in the initialization. $l := lower$ and $u := upper$.

The code presented in Example 2.11 directly follows from this loop design.

Finally, don't worry about the performance penalties of evaluating such assertions. As with other Eiffel assertions, their evaluation can be disabled with a kind of switch at compile or at run time.

2.4.8 The Check Statement

The *check* statement allows you to check that a set of assertions is verified at a given point in a program. Its syntax is described in Syntax Diagram 13.

In addition to reassuring yourself that certain properties are satisfied, the check statement is another convenient way to make the assumptions on which you are relying explicit for your readers.

Actual code is generated for the *check* statement only if you activate the relevant switch at compile time. As with other constructs involving assertions,

38 BASIC LANGUAGE ELEMENTS OF EIFFEL

```
            from
                l := lower; u := upper
            invariant
                in_bounds: (x<item(l) or x>item(u)) implies Result = False
 5          variant
                range_must_shrink: u − l
            until l>u or Result
            loop
                m := (l + u) // 2
10              if x < item(m) then
                    -- x cannot be in the upper part
                    u := m−1
                elseif x > item(m) then
                    -- x cannot be in the lower part
15                  l := m+1
                else -- x = item(m)
                    Result := True
                end -- if
            end -- loop
```

Example 2.11

Syntax Diagram 13   The syntax of the *check* statement

an *exception* is generated on violation of an assertion. What happens then is described in Section 5.1.

2.4.9 The Debug Statement

In C (or C++) the debug statement is often realized through the preprocessor:
`#ifdef DEBUG`
` ...`
`#endif.`

The *debug* statement enables the conditional execution of a compound statement, depending on a compilation option. The **debug** keyword may be followed by a list of manifest strings called *debug keys* (Syntax Diagram 14).

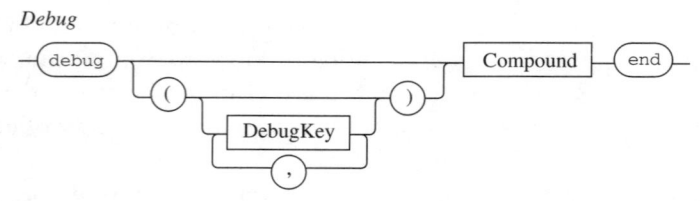

Syntax Diagram 14   The syntax of the *debug* statement

```
    debug ("TRACE","LEVEL3")
       print ("Entering the interesting part %N")
    end
```
Example 2.12

The debug code is executed if one of the debug keys has been selected (all keys also can be enabled at once). Depending on your Eiffel environment, this selection may be done either at compile time or at run time. See Section 4.2 for more details. In this example, the message will be printed only if either TRACE or LEVEL3 debug keys are activated (Example 2.12).

2.5 Routines: Procedures and Functions

As seen in Section 2.2.4, the features of a class are either attributes describing data fields or routines describing computations that are applicable to instances of that class. Routines may access or update attributes of their class. A routine returning a result is called a *function*; otherwise, it is called a *procedure*. However, Eiffel fosters a style of design that clearly separates commands, implemented as procedures, from queries implemented as *pure* functions—that is, functions without side effects (see Section 6.4.6).

Eiffel routines are called methods in Smalltalk or member functions in C++.

2.5.1 Routine Declaration

A routine declaration consists of an interface specification and its body (see Syntax Diagram 15). The interface specification reflects the abstract data type view of a routine, or signature and preconditions and postconditions. The body may be either:

external: The implementation of this routine falls out of the scope of the Eiffel compiler. More details on interfacing Eiffel with foreign software are given in Section 4.4.1.

deferred: No implementation is given for this routine. Deferred routines are presented in Section 3.6.

internal: The description of the computations the routine performs.

40 BASIC LANGUAGE ELEMENTS OF EIFFEL

FeatureDeclaration

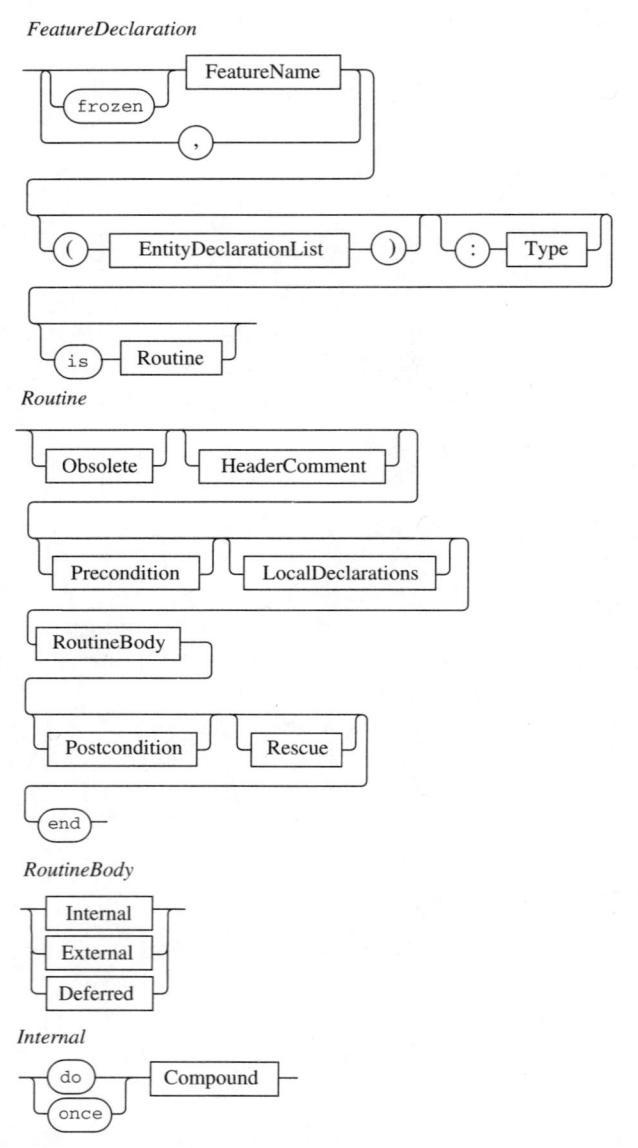

Routine

RoutineBody

Internal

Syntax Diagram 15 Feature declaration

FormalArguments

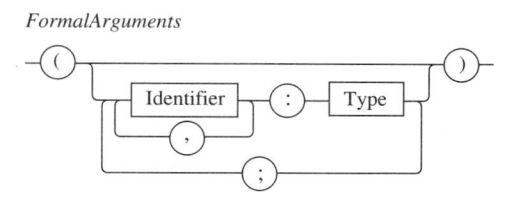

Syntax Diagram 16 Formal arguments syntax

The routine may have synonyms, i.e., various feature names may be attached to the same feature body. This is actually equivalent to multiple independent definitions with the same interface and body.

The keyword **frozen** means that the associated feature name cannot be redefined in subclasses (see Section 3.4.2).

Eiffel uses the convention opposite to C++. By default Eiffel routines may be redefined in subclasses (frozen prevents this), whereas a C++ routine may be redefined only if declared virtual in the base class.

2.5.2 Arguments to a Routine

An argument allows the routine caller to pass it information for a given execution. Within the routine, an argument is represented with a purely local name associated with a type and bears the name *formal argument* (Syntax Diagram 16).

Consider the binary search presented earlier in Section 2.4.6. It makes sense to encapsulate it within a function returning a Boolean result. Let's call this function *contains*. The corresponding declaration is then:

```
contains (x : INTEGER) : BOOLEAN is ...
```

The formal argument x is then used in the body of the routine as an entity denoting the element to look for (see Example 2.11). The *signature* of this routine is made of its name (*contains*), the type of input parameters (here INTEGER), and the type of output result (here BOOLEAN).

2.5.3 Preconditions, Postconditions, and Invariants

Like other assertions, preconditions, postconditions, and class invariants express the specification of software components and are essential for documenting and testing them. A detailed introduction to the formal aspects of these assertions can be found in [46]. As a specification tool, Eiffel preconditions and postconditions try to fulfill the goal of specifying the *what* rather than the *how*. Thus even when assertions are not easily specifiable with Boolean expressions (for example, when quantifiers would be needed), you should still try to describe them through comments.

The syntax of assertions is described in Syntax Diagram 11.

Precondition

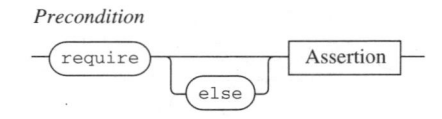

```
──( require )──┬──────────────┬──[ Assertion ]──
               └──( else )────┘
```

Syntax Diagram 17 Precondition syntax

Preconditions

A precondition is introduced with the keyword **require** (see Syntax Diagram 17) and states the conditions under which the routine may be called. The routine caller must guarantee this condition when calling the routine, or else the routine work cannot be done. More formally, a precondition is a predicate that characterizes the set of initial states for which a problem can be solved. It specifies the subset of all possible states that the routine should be able to handle correctly.

*The keyword **else** is used in conjunction with the mechanism of redefinition described in Section 3.4.2.*

For example, a precondition should be used to specify that a quotient may be computed for nonnegative integers and positive divisors only (see Example 2.13).

```
quotient(n,divisor:INTEGER):INTEGER is
    -- Integer division of n by divisor
    require
        non_negative_n: n >= 0
        positive_divisor: divisor > 0
```

Example 2.13

Postconditions

A postcondition is introduced with the keyword **ensure** and appears just before the end of the routine (see Syntax Diagram 18). The postcondition states the property that the routine must guarantee at completion of any correct call. It provides a formal specification of what the routine should accomplish. It thus can assist in the construction of the routine, and be used as a constructive proof of its correctness.

*The keyword **then** is used in conjunction with the mechanism of redefinition described in Section 3.4.2.*

In the case of the quotient function, the function specification (as described in inequality [2.1]) readily translates itself to the function postcondi-

Postcondition

```
──( ensure )──┬──────────────┬──[ Assertion ]──
              └──( then )────┘
```

Syntax Diagram 18 Postcondition syntax

```
        quotient(n,divisor:INTEGER):INTEGER is
               -- Integer division of n by divisor
            require
                non_negative_n: n >= 0
5               positive_divisor: divisor > 0
            ensure
                Result*divisor <= n and n < (Result+1)*divisor
            end -- quotient
```
Example 2.14

tion. Putting all parts together, the specification of the quotient function is as presented in Example 2.14.

An *"old" expression* is a special notation (see Syntax Diagram 19) available in postconditions only. The value of an old expression is the value the expression had before entering the routine. It appears in the routine postcondition, so it allows for the specification of the effect of the computation with respect to the previous state. Consider for example the specification of a routine to swap two elements of an array (Example 2.15). Its postcondition states that the value at index *i* is now the value that was at index *j* on entering the routine, and conversely.

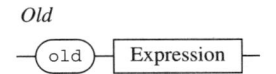

Old

─(old)─┤ Expression ├─

Syntax Diagram 19 Old expression

Invariants

Class invariants do not syntactically belong to a given routine. They actually characterize properties that the enclosing module must respect at any time.

```
        swap (i, j: INTEGER) is
               -- swap item(i) and item(j)
            require
                valid_i: i>=lower and i<=upper
5               valid_j: j>=lower and j<=upper
            ensure
                item(i) = old item(j) and item(j) = old item(i)
            end -- swap
```
Example 2.15

This relationship has a consequence for routines, because the class invariant must be true both on entering a routine (thus strengthening its precondition) and on exiting it (thus strengthening its postcondition).

Assertions and Programming by Contract

Assertions fulfill a crucial role in supporting a clear separation of responsibilities in a modular system. They foster the formalization of the contract binding a routine caller (the client) and the routine implementation (the contractor or supplier).

> Provided the client calls the contractor routine in a state in which the class invariant and the precondition of the routine are respected, the contractor promises that when the routine returns, the work specified in the postcondition will be done, and the class invariant will be respected.

If either party fails to meet the contract terms, the whole program should be considered invalid. In other words, there is a bug somewhere. The section on exception handling (Section 5.1) explains what happens next, and how Eiffel programming environments help to identify both the faulty party and the fault itself. The contract can actually be broken in two different ways:

- If the precondition was violated, then the client broke the contract. Its code should have been written to avoid this. The contractor should not try to comply with its part of the contract, but should signal the fault by raising an exception.
- If the precondition was satisfied but the postcondition was violated, the implementation of the routine did not fulfill its promises, which is commonly referred to as an *implementation bug*.

The design by contract approach provides a methodological guideline to build robust, yet modular and simple systems without resorting to defensive programming. It has a sound theoretical basis in relation to partial functions (see [99]). It is not surprising then that the notion of contractual programming is a cornerstone in the design of reusable software components in Eiffel. This approach could be emulated partially in C or C++ with the **assert.h** package. The Eiffel assertion mechanism is, however, much more powerful because it is fully integrated to the type system and the inheritance mechanism, and thus provides the necessary semantics for subtyping and subclassing. This mechanism is described in full detail in Section 3.4.2.

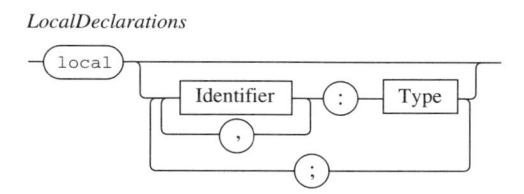

2.5.4 Calling a Routine

The only syntactical difference between a function and a procedure is that the function yields a result. Calling a function without argument presents no syntactic difference with the reading of an attribute: The caller does not need to know whether a given function is implemented with an attribute. The transmission of values between the caller and the callee consists of assigning the actual arguments provided by the caller to the formal arguments of the routine. For example, calling $q := quotient(10, 3)$ is equivalent to setting $n := 10$ and $divisor := 3$ within the function $quotient$, executing the rest of the routine, and assigning its result to q.

The semantics of this assignment are described in Section 2.4.1.

2.5.5 Internal Routine Body

A routine body may have a local declaration clause that allows the declaration of entities available within the routine body only. The name of these local entities may not override the feature names of the enclosing module.

The syntax of a local declaration clause is presented in Syntax Diagram 20; an example is presented in Example 2.16.

A local declaration clause is equivalent to the variable and constant declarations that are local to a procedure or function in C, Pascal, or Ada.

> **local**
> i, j : INTEGER
>   is_empty : BOOLEAN
>   total : REAL

Example 2.16

Functions have an additional local entity (denoted with the reserved word **Result**) that holds the result returned by the function. All the local entities (including **Result** for a function) are always initialized according to the default initialization rules for their type (see Section 2.3.4). Local entities are destroyed when the routine finishes:

- Expanded objects just vanish (are popped from the stack) and

```
            quotient(n,divisor:INTEGER):INTEGER is
                -- Integer division of n by divisor
                require
                    non_negative_n: n >= 0
5                   positive_divisor: divisor > 0
                local
                    remainder : INTEGER
                do
                    from remainder := n
10                  invariant reversible: n = Result*divisor+remainder
                    variant decreasing_remainder: remainder
                    until remainder < divisor
                    loop
                        remainder := remainder - divisor
15                      Result := Result + 1
                    end -- loop
                ensure
                    Result*divisor <= n and n < (Result+1)*divisor
                end -- quotient
```

Example 2.17

- Reference objects become unreachable (if they are not attached to nonlocal entities) and thus become fair game for the garbage collector.

Note that you never need to worry about memory management issues with Eiffel unless you really insist on doing so (see Section 4.5).

The executable part of a routine normally is introduced with the keyword **do**. It consists of a compound statement followed by an optional rescue clause, which allows it to deal with the exceptions that might have been raised in the compound (see Section 5.1). Example 2.17 presents the full definition of the *quotient* function.

2.5.6 Once Routines

Once routines are special routines. They have the same syntax, except for the keyword **once** used instead of **do** to introduce the compound statement. The first time the routine is called, it works exactly like a regular routine. Subsequent calls, however, have no effect. If the **once** routine is a function, the value it returns is the same as the value returned by the first call. This mechanism enables:

- The initialization of a data structure without an explicit initialization requirement,

functionDeclPrefix

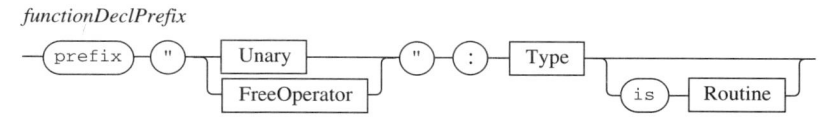

```
prefix "  Unary      " :  Type         is  Routine
             FreeOperator
```

Syntax Diagram 21 Prefix operator declaration

- The sharing of values that are computed at run time, and
- The sharing of variables among all instances of a class.

2.5.7 Prefix and Infix Function Declaration

To enable the usual practice of writing Boolean and numerical expressions (such as −2*x), two alternative forms of function declarations are provided:

- The prefix form for unary operators (functions without argument), the syntax of which is described in Syntax Diagram 21. Predefined unary operators include not, +, -.

- The infix form for binary operators (functions with exactly one argument), the syntax of which is described in Syntax Diagram 22. Predefined binary operators are listed in Syntax Diagram 23.

Free operators are sequences of nonblank characters beginning with either @, #, |, or & .

In the Eiffel standard library class BOOLEAN, we can find the declaration of the prefix function *not* giving the negation of a Boolean value (Example 2.18). We also can find in this class the usual infix operators to manipulate Boolean values (Example 2.19). The operator **and then** is called *semistrict* because it evaluates its second argument only if the first one is *True*. In the same way, the operator **or else** evaluates its second argument only if the first one is *False*. These notations allow for the usual way of describing a Boolean expression; e.g., not (a or b) implies c or else d.

This is equivalent to the notion of class variable found in Smalltalk or C++.

These operators have the same semantics as the && and || found in C and C++.

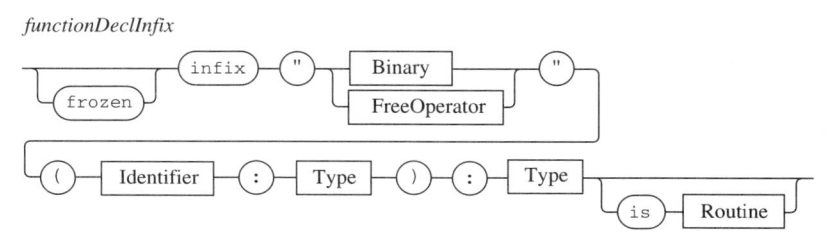

functionDeclInfix

```
        frozen   infix "  Binary       "
                          FreeOperator
        ( Identifier : Type ) : Type    is  Routine
```

Syntax Diagram 22 Infix operator declaration

48 BASIC LANGUAGE ELEMENTS OF EIFFEL

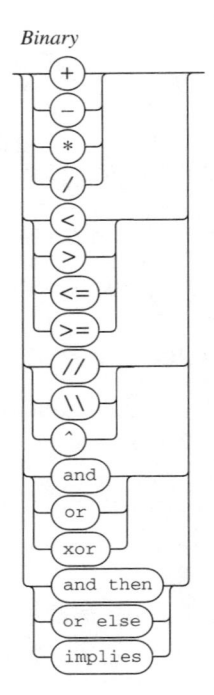

Syntax Diagram 23 Binary operator list

    prefix `"not"` : BOOLEAN
      -- *Negation.*

Example 2.18

    infix `"and"` (other: BOOLEAN): BOOLEAN
      -- *Boolean conjunction with 'other'*
    infix `"and then"` (other: BOOLEAN): BOOLEAN
      -- *Boolean semistrict conjunction with 'other'*
5   **infix** `"implies"` (other: BOOLEAN): BOOLEAN
      -- *Boolean implication of 'other'*
    infix `"or"` (other: BOOLEAN): BOOLEAN
      -- *Boolean disjunction with 'other'*
    infix `"or else"` (other: BOOLEAN): BOOLEAN
10   -- *Boolean semistrict disjunction with 'other'*
    infix `"xor"` (other: BOOLEAN): BOOLEAN
      -- *Boolean exclusive or with 'other'*

Example 2.19

Prefix and infix declarations (for arithmetic and comparison operators) are also available in Eiffel standard library classes such as INTEGER, REAL, and DOUBLE. Calling such prefix and infix functions involves writing expressions with the usual ALGOL-like syntax found in Pascal or Ada:

```
a := - b^2 * (c + d)
if a <= e // 2 then ...
```

2.5.8 Recursion

Recursion is a powerful programming technique that fosters elegant solutions for several problems. The concept of recursivity is the same in Eiffel as it is in Ada, Pascal, or C. The explicit preconditions and postconditions associated with a recursive routine, however, make it easier to produce correct implementations. A routine is said to be recursive if its body makes reference to itself, either directly or indirectly through other routines that call it.

Recursion is analogous to mathematical induction. The solution of a problem P_m is formulated supposing that each problem $p_{n-1}, p_{n-2}, \ldots, p_1$ is solved.

Consider the factorial function again. Another mathematical definition for it is:

$$\forall n \in [1..\infty[\; n! = n * (n-1)!; \; 0! = 1$$

The corresponding algorithm is given in Example 2.20.

A more interesting example is the recursive version of the binary search presented in Example 2.11. The loop invariant of this example readily transforms itself into the recursive routine postcondition: $(low > up) \Rightarrow Result = False$. The recursivity progresses by reducing the "search space": the func-

```
    rfacto(n : INTEGER): INTEGER is
            -- the factorial of n, recursive algorithm
        require non_negative: n >= 0
        do
5           if n = 0 then
                Result := 1
            else
                Result := n * rfacto(n−1)
            end; -- if
10      ensure
            positive_result: Result > 0
            factorial_computed : -- Result = n !
        end; -- rfacto
```

Example 2.20

```
    belongs_range(low, high: INTEGER; x : T) : BOOLEAN is
        -- whether x belongs to the range [low .. high]
        -- Recursive binary search algorithm in O(log(n)).
      require data_is_sorted: is_sorted
5     local
          m : INTEGER
      do
          if low > high then -- stopping condition for the recursion
              Result := false -- x not found
10        else
              m := (low + high) // 2
              if x < item(m) then
                  -- x cannot be in the upper part
                  Result := belongs_range (low,m−1,x)
15            elseif x > item(m) then
                  -- x cannot be in the lower part
                  Result := belongs_range (m+1,high,x)
              else -- x = item(m)
                  Result := True
20            end -- if
          end -- if
      ensure
          empty_implies_false: (low > high) implies not Result
      end -- belongs_range
```

Example 2.21

tion *belongs_range* calls itself recursively on a range that is smaller than the current one. The recursivity stops when an empty range is found (see Example 2.21).

2.6 Example: Sorting Data with Eiffel

In this section we try to illustrate the Eiffel constructions presented so far in a more substantial example.

Consider a data structure (typically an array) that is indexed on the interval [lower,upper]. Let us first implement a function that indicates whether a subrange of this array is sorted in increasing order. In the context of *programming by contract*, the first thing that we have to design is the contract of this function—that is, its preconditions and postconditions. We do not know what to do if the parameters of this function are not correct, so we should not try to do anything. Instead, we *must* specify that we expect correct parameters: e.g., the subrange must be included in the index domain of the array

```
      is_sorted_range (low, high: INTEGER) : BOOLEAN is
              -- are the objects in low .. high in (nonstrict) increasing order?
          require
              low_large_enough: low >= lower
5             high_small_enough: high <= upper
          local
              i: INTEGER
          do
              from i := low; Result := True
10            invariant left_subrange_is_sorted: -- [low .. i] is sorted
              variant high − i + 1
              until (not Result) or i >= high
              loop
                  Result := item(i) <= item(i+1)
15                i := i + 1
              end -- loop
          end -- is_sorted_range
```

Example 2.22

[lower,upper]. This specification gives the preconditions of lines 4–5 in Example 2.22. Like most preconditions, these are almost trivial, but nonetheless extremely useful to specify the routine behavior and also simplify debugging, because a precondition violation will give a precise error message. There is no explicit postcondition here.

The core of this function is a simple loop to check that the ith item is smaller than the next item. The invariant is thus that the subrange [low .. i] is sorted, and the termination condition is either that we find an unordered element (such that $item_i > item_{i+1}$), or that we reach the end of the subrange ($i \geq high$). An empty or a single element range is always considered as sorted. Since this is clearly a bounded loop, the variant is only helpful to double-check that we did not forget the incrementing of i within the loop. The full text of this function can then look like Example 2.22.

Conversely, consider the problem of sorting this data structure with the *quicksort* algorithm invented by C. A. R. Hoare. It is remotely based on the *bubble sort* algorithm, the principle of which is to consider pairs of neighbor items, and to move the smaller before the larger. This process is repeated until all elements are ordered. The problem with bubble sort is that the number of comparisons it requires is proportional to the square of the number of items being sorted (this algorithm complexity is thus denoted $O(n^2)$).

The *quicksort* algorithm, also called *partition sort,* is a major improvement to this method. It is based on the idea that exchanges should preferably be performed over large distances to be most effective. The idea is to consider the first item (called the *pivot*) and scan the array from the left until an item *i* such

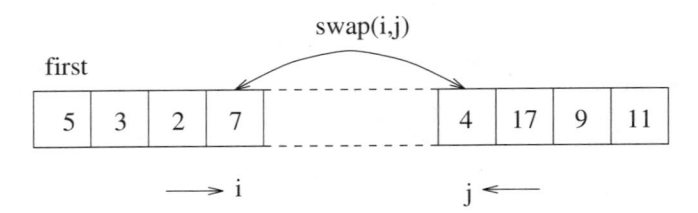

Figure 2.6 The *quicksort* "scan and swap" process

that *item(i)* > *item(first)* is found, and from the right until an item *j* such that *item(j)* <= *item(first)* is also found. Then the two items are exchanged, and this "scan and swap" process is continued until the two scans meet somewhere in the middle of the array (see Figure 2.6). The first item is then exchanged with *item(j)*, and we now get an array partitioned into a left part with items smaller than the pivot item, and a right part with items greater than it. The same process then may be applied (recursively) to both partitions, until every partition consists of a single item only (and thus is sorted). The advantage of this algorithm is that it tends to have an algorithmic complexity in $O(n.log(n))$, which brings considerable performance improvement over $O(n^2)$ when sorting large data structures.

The Eiffel implementation of this algorithm closely follows this scheme. First, let us design the precise contract of the procedure *quicksort_range(first, last)* taking as input the range to be sorted. There are two possible policies: either require correct parameters (a nonempty subrange included in [lower,upper]) and ensure *is_sorted_range(first, last)* at the end of the routine, or accept any parameters and do (and ensure) nothing in case of incorrect parameters. As displayed in Example 2.23, we have chosen the former option.

According to the *quicksort* algorithm, the body of the *quicksort_range* procedure is divided roughly into three parts: the partitioning loop (lines 12–29), the swapping of the first element with the pivot (line 30, calling the routine *swap* defined in Example 2.15), and the recursive call for both partitions if they are wider than 1 (lines 31–32). This body is surrounded with debug instructions (lines 8–11 and 33–36) that are activated with the "Recursion" key to allow the printing of the sequence of recursive calls to the procedure.

To design the partitioning loop, we start with the invariant definition that follows from the method described:

$$\forall k \in [first .. i-1] \ item(k) \leq item(first)$$

$$\forall k \in [j+1 .. last] \ item(k) > item(first)$$

2.6 EXAMPLE: SORTING DATA WITH EIFFEL

```
quick_sort_range(first, last: INTEGER) is
        -- sort elements first .. last into increasing order
        -- (quick sort algorithm)
    require range_not_empty: first <= last
    local
        i,j: INTEGER
    do
        debug ("Recursion")
            print("Entering quick_sort_range(")
            print(first); print(','); print(last); print(")%N")
        end -- debug
        from i := first + 1; j := last
        invariant
            left_lower: max_value_in(first, i−1) <= item(first)
            right_higher: (j < last)
            implies (min_value_in(j+1, last) > item(first))
        variant ends_converging: j − i + 2
        until i > j
        loop
            if item(i) <= item(first) then
                i := i + 1          -- advances i rightwards
            elseif item(j) > item(first) then
                j := j − 1          -- advances j leftwards
            else                    -- i & j have been found
                swap(i,j)           -- swap item(i) and item(j)
                i := i + 1          -- next i & j
                j := j − 1
            end -- if
        end -- loop
        swap(first, j)              -- places back the pivot
        if first < j − 1 then quick_sort_range(first, j − 1) end
        if j + 1 < last then quick_sort_range(j + 1, last) end
        debug ("Recursion")
            print("Exiting quick_sort_range(")
            print(first); print(','); print(last); print(")%N")
        end -- debug
    ensure sorted: is_sorted_range(first, last)
    end -- quick_sort_range
```

Example 2.23

```
        min_value_in(low, high: INTEGER) : T is
            -- the lowest element in the array for the range low .. high
        require
            low_large_enough: low >= lower
5           high_small_enough: high <= upper
            range_not_empty: low <= high
        local
            i : INTEGER
        do
10          from i := low; Result := item(i)
            invariant min_so_far: -- for all j in [low .. i], Result <= item(j)
            variant increasing_i: high - i
            until i = high
            loop
15              if item(i) < Result then
                    Result := item(i)
                end -- if
                i := i + 1
            end -- loop
20      end -- min_value_in
```

Example 2.24

The definition of the function max_value_in is left to the reader.

Eiffel does not feature quantifiers, so these assertions may only be expressed with comments. However, the loop is complex enough to justify some effort to allow the invariant to be actually checked at run time. We thus can design a function to compute these assertions, and use it in the invariant clause of the loop. Instead of building an ad hoc function, we may use (or reuse) more general-purpose functions, giving the minimum and the maximum items of a subrange of an array (see Example 2.24). These functions allow for the definition of the invariant as it appears in lines 13–15 of Example 2.23.

The loop variant is that either i or j must move at each step of the iteration, and the termination condition is that they cross themselves. The body of the loop is a mere translation of the core of the method described, and the initializations of i and j follow.

3
Object-Oriented Elements

In This Chapter

- 3.1 Working with Modules
- 3.2 Genericity
- 3.3 Inheritance
- 3.4 Feature Adaptation
- 3.5 Polymorphism and Dynamic Binding
- 3.6 Deferred Classes
- 3.7 Genericity and Inheritance
- 3.8 Case Study: The KWIC System

Until now we have worked within a single class, which was viewed as a module. We now describe how to use the services provided by other classes (using the example of the class STRING) and, conversely, how to make services available to other classes (for that we design a simple LISTINT class). We later introduce how these services may be made generic *and we show how to use a generic class ARRAY[T] and how to build a generic class LIST[T]. The inheritance relationship and some of the consequences it has on subtyping, polymorphism, and dynamic binding are described. This chapter ends with a medium-sized case study of a classic software engineering problem: the keyword-in-context (KWIC) system.*

3.1 Working with Modules

The *client* of a module is an object that uses the services provided by the module. The Eiffel notion of module boils down to the class. It is simply a box put

```
                    ┌─────────────────────────────────┐
                    │     RANDOM_GENERATOR            │
                    │                                 │
                    │  last_random_real │ 0.517365901 │
                    │                                 │
                    │      ( reset )    ( next )      │
                    └─────────────────────────────────┘
```

Figure 3.1 A random number generator

The interface presented by a class may depend on who is looking at it. This is called subjectivity. See the selective export clause in Section 3.1.4.

around a number of features (attributes and routines). This box has an interface (the client's view of the module), which is like a control panel with a light-emitting diode displaying the value of exported attributes and functions, and buttons allowing the user to call exported procedures. For example, the random number generator in Figure 3.1 has a function named *last_random_ real* returning (i.e., displaying) the last random real value computed by the random generator, and two procedures (namely, *reset* and *next*) to reset respectively the random generator and make it compute the next random real value. The full text of this class is given later in Example 3.8.

3.1.1 Creating Objects

Creation of an expanded object is not prohibited— it just resets the object to its default initial value.

Objects are created as instances of classes. Let *e* be an entity with the declared type SOMECLASS:

- If SOMECLASS is an expanded type (e.g., INTEGER), *e* directly holds the value of the object, and is initialized according to the default initialization rules presented in Section 2.3.4. Thus, no creation is needed.

- If SOMECLASS is a reference type (e.g., RANDOM_GENERATOR), a creation instruction is needed to dynamically allocate a new object attached to *e*.

In the simplest form, if SOMECLASS has no creation clause, a new instance of SOMECLASS is allocated, initialized (that is, its fields are given their default values), and attached to *e* by the means of a *creation* instruction made of two exclamation marks (!!) preceding the entity name (c.f. Example 3.1).

If SOMECLASS has one or more creation features, one of them must be called when the object is created. For example, the creation routine for the class RANDOM_GENERATOR is the routine *reset*, which takes as its argument a new seed value for the generator (see Example 3.8 later in this chapter). Example 3.2 illustrates how such an object can be created and attached to an entity. The effect of this instruction is the same as in Example 3.1; in addition, the *reset*

```
local
    e : SOMECLASS
do
    !!e        -- An object of type SOMECLASS is created,
               -- initialized and attached to e
end
```
Example 3.1

```
local
    e : RANDOM_GENERATOR
do
    !!e.reset(123)
               -- An object of type RANDOM_GENERATOR is created,
               -- initialized, attached to e, and then the
               -- creation procedure reset is called on e
end
```
Example 3.2

routine is immediately called on the fresh object (thus allowing it to establish the class invariant).

The third form of the creation instruction allows you to create an object instance of a subclass of SOMECLASS instead of a direct instance of SOMECLASS (see Example 3.3). More details on subclassing appear in Section 3.3.

```
local
    e : SOMECLASS
do
    !SUBCLASS!e.make(...)
               -- An object of type SUBCLASS is created,
               -- initialized, attached to e, and then the
               -- creation procedure make is called on e
end
```
Example 3.3

The last way to get a new object is to clone an existing one. The function *clone* is available in all classes to create a new object that is a field-by-field copy of the original object and has the same type (see Example 3.4).

Clone, *like print, is a feature defined in the class* GENERAL, *which is an implicit common ancestor to all classes.*

```
f := clone(e)              -- now we have equal(e,f)
g := deep_clone(e)         -- now we have deep_equal(e,g)
```
Example 3.4

If *e* is *Void*, then *f* is also set to *Void*. There also exists a variant of *clone*, called *deep_clone*, which duplicates the entire structure referenced by the original object (that is, deep clones all its fields).

3.1.2 Calling Other Object Features

In the spirit of accessing fields of a Pascal record or a C structure, the dot notation is used to call a feature *foo* of an object *obj* (see Example 3.5).

```
obj.foo                -- calls the feature foo on the object obj
```
Example 3.5

In C++, you would write obj.foo for a value object and obj->foo, equivalent to (*obj).foo, for reference objects.

This syntax is valid for any kind of feature call, so in Example 3.5 the feature *foo* might also be an attribute. Whether the object is expanded or not has no more influence on the calling syntax.

An attribute or the result of a function call are entities themselves, so the feature calls may be cascaded as in Example 3.6. If some of the features are in fact functions, they may have parameters. The formal syntax of such a call chain is presented in Syntax Diagram 24.

```
obj.foo.bar.etc        -- calls foo on obj, and then
                       -- bar on the result of foo, and then
                       -- etc on the result of bar
```
Example 3.6

The current object is called this in C++ or self in Smalltalk.

The form of the feature call itself is the same as the unqualified call defined in Section 2.5.4. Actually an unqualified call implicitly refers to the current object (denoted **Current** in Eiffel) and is thus equivalent to `Current.foo` (as far as assertion checking is concerned).

To illustrate this feature call mechanism, Example 3.7 shows a fragment of code designed to compute the mean value of a number of consecutive pseudorandom values generated by a RANDOM_GENERATOR object.

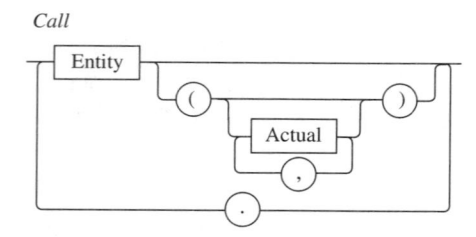

Syntax Diagram 24 Call chain syntax

```
            test_a_random_generator is
                local
                    gen : RANDOM_GENERATOR
                    i : INTEGER
5                   mean : REAL
                do
                    !!gen.reset(1234)
                    from i := 1
                    until i > 1000
10                  loop
                        gen.next
                        mean := mean + gen.last_random_real(0,100)
                        i := i + 1
                    end -- loop
15                  mean := mean / 1000
                    print("Mean = "); print(mean); io.new_line
                end -- test_a_random_generator
```

Example 3.7

Note the distinction between the command (gen.next) asking the generator to produce the next random number, and the query gen.last_random_real(0,100), which is a pure function call. That is, if we would call this function again with the same input parameters (and without calling gen.next in between), we would get the same result. This strict distinction between commands and queries is a recommended design style in Eiffel [99] (see Section 6.4.6).

3.1.3 Attribute Protection and Information Hiding

By default all features of a class are visible (exported) to every other class. Visible only means that another object can "see" the values of attributes and functions, and "push" the buttons corresponding to the procedures. Thus, an object may not modify an attribute of another object directly: the assignment obj.attribute := value is (syntactically) illegal.

A group of features appearing after a **feature** keyword can be made *private* to the class if the **feature** keyword is followed by the export clause: {NONE}. The default case in which no class is specified after a **feature** keyword is equivalent to exporting to ANY; thus, the features are made public. Conversely, exporting to the pseudoclass NONE allows a set of features to be totally hidden: They can no longer be called directly from outside of the class. In Example 3.8, the features *seed, aa, bb, invmaxint* and *uniform* are private to the class RANDOM_GENERATOR; they cannot be directly called by any client class.

A client of the class RANDOM_GENERATOR is not aware of the way it is implemented. Thus, no assumptions can be made about it: the client only sees

In C++ terms, one would say that every routine is "public," whereas attributes are read only. In Smalltalk terms, Eiffel has for each attribute an associated implicit method giving its value.

```
indexing
    description: "pseudorandom real number generator"
class RANDOM_GENERATOR
creation
    reset
feature
    reset (new_seed:INTEGER) is
            -- Reset this random number generator with a new seed
        require positive: new_seed >= 0
        do
            seed := new_seed
        end -- reset
    next is
            -- advance the generator
        do
            seed := aa + seed * bb
            if seed < 0 then
                seed := - seed
            end -- if
        end -- next
    last_random_real(lower,upper:REAL): REAL is
            -- Return an evenly distributed random number over the
            -- interval [lower, upper[.
        require non_empty_interval: lower<upper
        do
            Result := lower + uniform * (upper-lower)
        ensure
            in_bounds: Result >= lower and Result < upper
        end -- last_random_real
feature {NONE}
    seed : INTEGER
    aa : INTEGER is 987654321
    bb : INTEGER is 31415821
    invmaxint : REAL is
            -- inverse of the largest positive integer.
        once
            Result := 1.0 / (2^(31) - 1)
        end -- invmaxint
    uniform : REAL is
            -- Return an evenly distributed random number over [0.0, 1.0[
        do
            Result := seed * invmaxint
        ensure
            normed: Result >= 0.0 and Result < 1.0
        end -- uniform
invariant
    non_negative_seed : seed >= 0
end -- class RANDOM_GENERATOR
```

Example 3.8

the interface displayed in Figure 3.1. If in the future we need to change the RANDOM_GENERATOR implementation (which is probable considering the weakness of its spectral properties, i.e., the mathematical measurement of how random the number sequence is), it could be done without modifying a single character of the client's code. The client's code then is said to be *decoupled* from the actual RANDOM_GENERATOR implementation. This property is called *information hiding*. It is the main benefit of the Eiffel class-based modularity.

3.1.4 Restricted Export and Subjectivity

As a middle term between fully private and fully public features, Eiffel allows you to restrict the visibility of a set of features to a nominative list of classes (and their descendants). This list may be given between brackets after a **feature** keyword. In Example 3.9, the feature f is made visible to objects of CLASS1 and CLASS2 only.

```
feature {CLASS1, CLASS2}
    f is do...end
```
Example 3.9

This property is sometimes called *subjectivity* because the view clients get on this kind of class depends on which client is looking [14]. Consider for example a COFFEE_MACHINE class. Its interface to normal clients is illustrated in Figure 3.2.

Now consider a class MANAGER dealing with the supervision of coffee machines. It may need to access other features of the class COFFEE_MACHINE, such as the amount of cash deposited within the machine, or whether the machine requires maintenance. The class COFFEE_MACHINE then could be defined as shown in Example 3.10. The MANAGER's view of this class is displayed in Figure 3.3.

COFFEE_MACHINE

inserted_money	$ 0.25	insert_money
price	$ 0.75	deliver_coffee
is_out_of_service	○	cancel

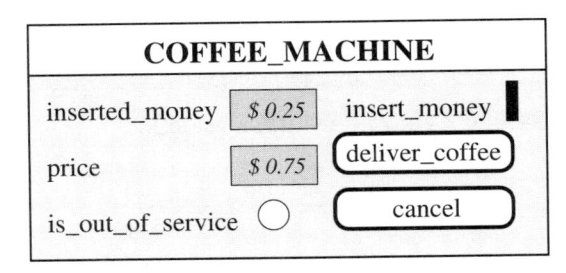

Figure 3.2 The normal client's view of a COFFEE_MACHINE

OBJECT-ORIENTED ELEMENTS

```
     class interface COFFEE_MACHINE
     feature
         is_out_of_service : BOOLEAN
         price : INTEGER -- price of a cup of coffee
5        inserted_money : INTEGER -- amount of money currently inserted
         insert_money (amount : INTEGER) is
                 -- insert money in the machine. Money is in cents.
             ensure
                 money_added: inserted_money = old(inserted_money) + amount
10       deliver_coffee is
                 -- pilot the hardware to deliver a cup of coffee
             require
                 in_service: not is_out_of_service
                 paid: inserted_money >= price
15           ensure
                 cash_added: cash = old(cash) + old(inserted_money)
                 reset_money: inserted_money = 0
         cancel is
                 -- eject the money already introduced
20           ensure
                 reset_money: inserted_money = 0
     feature {MANAGER}
         cash : INTEGER -- amount of cash stored in the machine
         needs_maintenance : BOOLEAN is
25               -- condition upon which some maintenance is needed
     end -- COFFEE_MACHINE
```

Example 3.10

COFFEE_MACHINE		
inserted_money	$ 0.25	insert_money
price	$ 0.75	deliver_coffee
is_out_of_service	○	cancel
needs_maintenance ○		cash $11.50

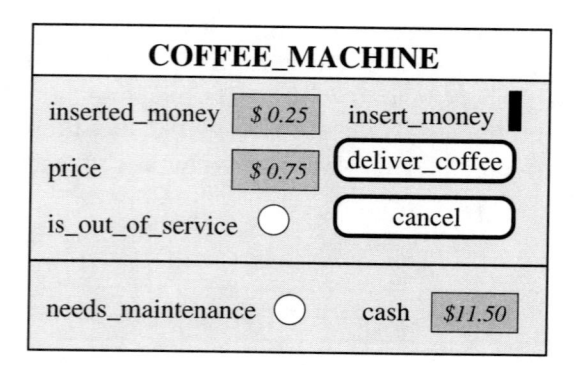

Figure 3.3 The manager's view of a COFFEE_MACHINE

```
class STRING
creation
    make
feature
    make (n: INTEGER)
        -- Allocate space for at least 'n' characters.
        require
            non_negative_size: n >= 0
        ensure
            empty_string: count = 0
```
Example 3.11

3.1.5 Using Eiffel Strings

A module that should be available with any Eiffel implementation is the class STRING. A module may be used in black-box mode by its clients (e.g., without them knowing anything about the way strings are implemented). In the next section we "enter into the box" to show how Eiffel may be used to design such modules.

This section also serves as an Eiffel string primer.

Eiffel strings (made of finite sequences of characters) are instances of the kernel library class STRING (outlined in Example 3.11). A STRING object is thus a regular Eiffel object. It may be created with the creation procedure *make*, as in Example 3.12.

```
local
    s : STRING
do
    !!s.make(80)
```
Example 3.12

Alternatively, a STRING object may get its initial value from a manifest string (Example 3.13). In that case no creation is needed, because the manifest string already exists.

```
local
    s : STRING
do
    s := "Hello, world!"
```
Example 3.13

The entity *s* attached at run time to an object declared to be of type STRING has no reason to be the sequence of characters itself. Most probably a STRING object contains information such as the actual string length and a reference to

```
            has (c: CHARACTER) : BOOLEAN
                -- Does string include c?
                ensure
                    not_found_in_empty: Result implies not empty
5           index_of (c: CHARACTER; start: INTEGER) : INTEGER
                -- Position of first occurrence of c at or after start; 0 if none
                require
                    start_large_enough: start >= 1
                    start_small_enough: start <= count
10              ensure
                    non_negative_result: Result >= 0
                    at_this_position: Result > 0 implies item (Result) = c
                -- none_before: For every i in start..Result, item (i) /= c
                -- zero_iff_absent:
15              -- (Result = 0) = For every i in 1..count, item (i) /= c
            infix "@",
            item (i: INTEGER) : CHARACTER
                -- Character at position i
                require
20                  good_key: valid_index (i)
            substring_index (other: STRING; start: INTEGER) : INTEGER
                -- Position of first occurrence of other at or after start; 0 if none
```

Example 3.14

the actual content. The content of the string can be accessed through a set of features. The specification of this feature set is presented in Example 3.14.

Strings can be compared for equality or precedence (lexicographical order) as illustrated in Example 3.15.

Other comparison operators (such as <=, >, >=, *min*, and *max*) are also available. Beware that if *s1* and *s2* are declared as STRING, (s1 = s2) is just testing the two entities *s1* and *s2* against *reference* equality; that is, it is testing whether or not *s1* is an alias for *s2*.

```
            is_equal (other: STRING) : BOOLEAN
                    -- Is 'Current' made of the same character sequence as 'other'?
                require
                    other_not_void: other /= void
5           infix "<" (other: STRING) : BOOLEAN
                    -- Is 'Current' lexicographically less than 'other'?
                require
                    other_not_void: other /= void
                ensure
10                  asymmetric: Result implies not (other < Current)
```

Example 3.15

There are three possible assignment-like operations:

1. `s1 := s2` is a reference assignment such that *s1* will be attached to the same object as *s2*. This is a classic case of aliasing, which is useful when both entities need to have access to a common underlying sequence of characters (e.g., for message or error strings). Any aliased entity can change the string's characters. The content of the string is shared by all the entities referring to it.
2. `s1 := clone(s2)` attaches to *s1* a new string object that, although consisting of identical characters, is not related to the string attached to *s2*. This is useful when you want to have a *private* copy of the string; i.e., one that is not subject to change by outside code.
3. `s1.copy(s2)` replaces the string object attached to *s1* with a copy of *s2*. It has the same effect as the previous case, except that it allows the reuse of an existing string's object. This is valid if and only if *s2* is not *Void*.

The class STRING also has a set of features designed to obtain the string status (Example 3.16). Also available are features to:

- Change the string contents (*resize, clear, fill_blank,* etc.),
- Append and prepend string representations of objects (Boolean, character, integer, real, double, string) to the current string,
- Convert the string to yield an object value (a Boolean, an integer, etc.) or to lowercase or uppercase, and
- Get a copy of a substring.

```
        empty : BOOLEAN
                -- Is string the empty string?
        count : INTEGER
                -- Actual number of characters making up the string.
        valid_index (i: INTEGER): BOOLEAN
                -- Is 'i' within the bounds of the string?
```

Example 3.16

3.1.6 Building a Linked List Class

A class may be seen as a black box. Let us "enter into the box" so we can see how to build it. Consider the notion of a list of integers as it is well known to, for example, LISP users. Basically, such a list has three features:

- The *head,* which is the first element of the list (it was known as the *car* in LISP),
- The *tail* of the list, which is also a list of integers (known as the *cdr* in LISP), and
- A function *append*, which allows the user to prepend a new head to a list.

We add a fourth one, the feature *has,* which checks whether a given integer belongs to the list. Completing this class LISTINT with more sophisticated features is left as an exercise to the reader. This list of integers is a recursive data type, because the definition of the type involves the type itself. We do not use the keyword **expanded** in the class header (see Example 3.17), so the class LISTINT is a reference type and this recursive definition does not pose a problem.

```
     indexing
         description: "Simple lisp-like linked list of integers"
     class LISTINT
     creation
5        make
     feature
         head: INTEGER
         tail: LISTINT
         make (new_head: INTEGER; new_tail: LISTINT) is
10               -- make a new list prepending 'new_head' to 'new_tail'
             do
                 head := new_head
                 tail := new_tail
             end -- make
15       append (new_head: INTEGER): LISTINT is
                 -- return a new list with 'new_head' prepended to Current
             do
                 !!Result.make(new_head,Current)
             end -- append
20       has (v : INTEGER): BOOLEAN is
                 -- does the list contain a value equal to v ?
             do
                 Result := head.is_equal(v)
                     or else (tail /= Void and then tail.has(v))
25           end -- has
     end -- LISTINT
```

Example 3.17

```
        initlist : LISTINT is
            do
                !!Result.make(2,Void)
                Result := Result.append(3)
5               Result := Result.append(5)
                Result := Result.append(7)
            end -- initlist
```
Example 3.18

```
        printlist(l : LISTINT) is
            local
                m : LISTINT
            do
5               from m := l
                until m = Void
                loop
                    print(m.head); print('%N')
                    m := m.tail
10              end -- loop
            end -- printlist
```
Example 3.19

To illustrate the use of this class LISTINT, Example 3.18 presents a routine to put the values [7,5,3,2] in such a list, and Example 3.19 prints all of the list elements.

Although this list implementation will do the job, it is deficient in several aspects. It is unnecessarily tied to the INTEGER type and its interface merely reflects its implementation. This problem illustrates the fact that building reusable components is not done for free once you adopt the object-oriented paradigm. Reusability must be a design goal, and enough resources should be allocated for it. Much better designs for list-like classes are presented in Chapter 8. Still, this simple example will serve us at several places in the following sections.

3.2 Genericity

3.2.1 Generic Classes

Building software around implementation of abstract data types (ADTs) such as the class LISTINT is the key to obtaining modular and loosely coupled systems. This technique does not in itself allow the factorization of common behavior for related ADTs (e.g., LISTINT and LISTCHARACTER). Genericity, which

ClassDeclaration

Syntax Diagram 25 Generic class declaration syntax

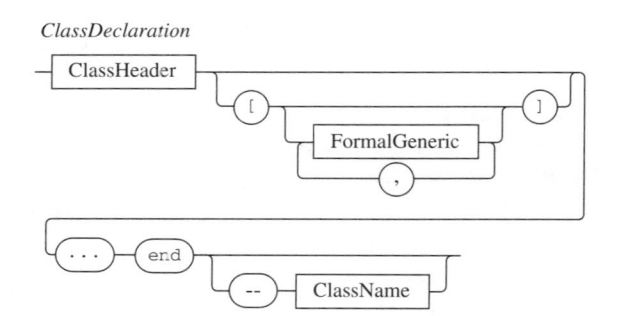

This corresponds to the notion of a class template in C++, except that the Eiffel genericity may be explicitly constrained by a type (see Section 3.7.2).

is available in Eiffel, Ada, or CLU, addresses this problem. Genericity is the ability to define modules with parameters, called *generic classes* in Eiffel. A generic class has formal generic parameters representing arbitrary types. The syntax of the generic class declaration is given in Syntax Diagram 25.

Genericity is very useful for classes that store objects (container classes). For example, we can define a generic version of the class LISTINT appearing in Example 3.17 in the previous section: This generic class LISTE[T] now describes a list containing objects of a certain type. This type is the formal generic argument that provides parameters to the class. It is denoted T in the class text of Example 3.20.

We use a French spelling for LISTE to avoid clashing with the class LIST existing in various Eiffel environments.

A generic class is not directly usable (instantiable), because it is only a class (and a type) pattern.

3.2.2 Generic Class Derivation

To derive a directly usable class from a generic one, you must provide an actual type (i.e., an actual generic parameter) for each formal generic type parameter of the generic class (Example 3.21).

The class LISTE[INTEGER] has exactly the same interface as the class LISTINT from Example 3.17. From a client point of view, they are totally interchangeable.

Genericity is only meaningful in a typed language. In Eiffel, you cannot put anything more than an integer in a LISTE[INTEGER]. In a language such as Smalltalk, there is no way to restrict the types of elements that a list contains, and then genericity would serve no purpose.

3.2.3 A Standard Eiffel Generic Class: The ARRAY

Eiffel arrays are finite sequences of generic objects, accessible through integer indices in a contiguous interval. They are instances of the generic kernel

3.2 GENERICITY

```
    indexing
        description: "Simple lisp-like generic linked list"
    class LISTE[T]

5   creation
        make
    feature
        head: T
        tail: LISTE[T]
10      make (new_head: T; new_tail: LISTE[T]) is
            -- make a new list with 'new_head' prepended to 'new_tail'
            do
                head := new_head
                tail := new_tail
15          end -- make
        append (new_head: T): LISTE[T] is
            -- return a new list with 'new_head' prepended to Current
            do
                !!Result.make(new_head,Current)
20          end -- append
        has (v : T): BOOLEAN is
            -- does the list contain an object equal to v ?
            do
                Result := head.is_equal(v)
25              or else (tail /= Void and then tail.has(v))
            end -- has
    end -- LIST [T]
```

Example 3.20

library class ARRAY[T]. Thus they are regular Eiffel objects. An extract of the interface of the class ARRAY[T] is presented in Example 3.22.

An Eiffel ARRAY is dynamic, and can be resized if necessary. This ARRAY class has much in common with the STRING class, which could have been designed as an ARRAY[CHARACTER] augmented with a set of string handling features. As for the class STRING, an entity a attached at run time to an object declared of type ARRAY is not the actual sequence of objects but an object that is likely to contain (among others) a reference to the actual contents. Thus, the earlier remarks on assignment-like operations for strings also hold for arrays.

```
    list_of_integers : LISTE[INTEGER]
    list_of_characters : LISTE[CHARACTER]
    list_of_list_of_integers : LISTE[LISTE[INTEGER]]
```

Example 3.21

```
class interface ARRAY [T]
creation
    make
feature -- Initialization
    make (minindex, maxindex: INTEGER)
    -- Make array empty if minindex > maxindex.
    -- Reallocate if necessary; set all values to default.
        ensure
            no_count: (minindex > maxindex) implies (count = 0)
            count_constraint: (minindex <= maxindex) implies
                                    (count = maxindex − minindex + 1)
feature -- Access
    frozen infix "@", frozen item (i: INTEGER) : T
    -- Entry at index i, if in index interval
        require
            good_key: valid_index (i)
feature -- Measurement
    count : INTEGER              -- Number of available indices
    lower : INTEGER              -- Minimum index
    upper : INTEGER              -- Maximum index
feature -- Status report
    valid_index (i: INTEGER) : BOOLEAN
    -- Is i within the bounds of the array?
feature -- Element change
    force (v: like item; i: INTEGER)
    -- Assign item v to i'th entry. Always applicable: resize the
    -- array if i falls out of currently defined bounds; preserve existing items.
        ensure
            inserted: item (i) = v
            higher_count: count >= old count
    frozen put (v: like item; i: INTEGER)
    -- Replace i'th entry, if in index interval, by v.
        require
            good_key: valid_index (i)
        ensure
            inserted: item (i) = v
feature -- Resizing
    resize (minindex, maxindex: INTEGER)
    -- Rearrange array so that it can accommodate indices down to
    -- minindex and up to maxindex. Do not lose previously entered items.
        require
            good_indices: minindex <= maxindex
feature -- Conversion
    to_c : POINTER
            -- Address of actual sequence of values,
            -- for passing to external (non-Eiffel) routines.
invariant
    consistent_size: count = upper − lower + 1
    non_negative_count: count >= 0
end -- ARRAY [T]
```

Example 3.22

3.3 Inheritance

3.3.1 The Dual Nature of Inheritance in Eiffel

Inheritance is a relationship between classes that fosters the definition and implementation of a new class by combination and specialization of existing ones. The new class is then called a subclass (or derived class) of its superclasses (or ancestor classes). The syntax of the inheritance clause is shown in Syntax Diagram 26.

Inheritance is characteristic of object-oriented languages. Without it, a language may only be called *object based* (e.g., Ada83 or Modula-2). Adding inheritance to such languages makes them object oriented (e.g., Ada95, Modula-3).

Inheritance has a dual nature. It provides programming by extension (as opposed to programming by reinvention [85]): A child class extends its parent class by providing more functionality. This is the module view of the class. Inheritance also can be used to represent an is-a-kind-of (or is-a) relationship, thus allowing for *classification*. This gives the type view of the class. The Eiffel type system is based on inheritance; that is, assignment compatibility is defined according to the inheritance relationship.

These two different natures of inheritance are not orthogonal. Most of the time, when you want a class B to be a kind of class A, you also like it to inherit at least a part of the code defined in A. The Eiffel's inheritance allows you to smoothly go from one extreme (the typing side, or interface inheritance, where no code is reused) to the other (the module side, or implementation inheritance, where no part of the interface is reused), or to stay at any intermediate step.

3.3.2 Module Extension

In contrast to genericity, which allows the reuse of closed modules, inheritance allows reusable parts to be customized and combined to build new classes. Inheritance makes a module always open for modification through subclassing.

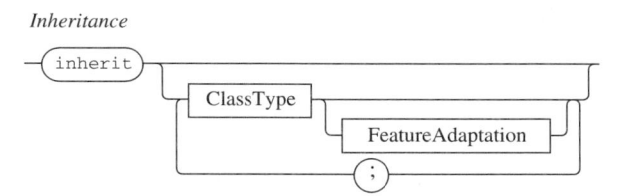

Syntax Diagram 26 Inheritance clause syntax

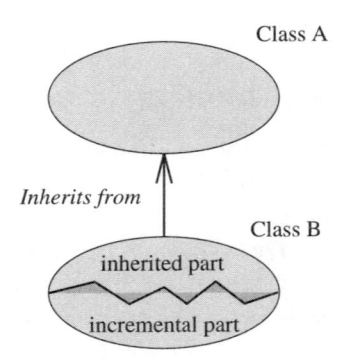

Figure 3.4 Inheritance as a module extension mechanism

Eiffel gives you full control of this customization through the mechanism of *feature adaption,* which is described in Section 3.4.

As a module extension mechanism, inheritance allows the programmer to reuse a class that is almost what is wanted, and to tailor the class in a way that does not introduce uncontrolled side effects into the other (part of the) software system using the class. It enables an incremental, nondisruptive form of programming. If a class B inherits from A, then B has two parts, an *inherited* part and an *incremental* part (see Figure 3.4).

The inherited part provides B with the same services featured by A (unless they are customized; see Section 3.4), whereas the incremental part is the new code, written specifically for B.

Consider for example the class RANDOM_GENERATOR (Example 3.8). If you need random integer (or Boolean) values, you could derive from this class a new class (e.g., MULTI_RANDOM_GENERATOR) having the same features as RANDOM_GENERATOR plus a *last_random_integer* and a *last_random_bit* feature (see Example 3.23).

3.3.3 Subtyping

Inheritance provides a natural classification for kinds of software objects. It is the software engineering counterpart of Linnaeus' classification in the natural sciences, or Bourbaki's systematic efforts to classify mathematical objects. Classification allows us to express and to take advantage of the commonality of objects.

Consider for instance the relationship between a COFFEE_MACHINE and an ESPRESSO_MACHINE. The latter is a specialization of the former: We say that the ESPRESSO_MACHINE is a kind of COFFEE_MACHINE.

```
indexing
    description: "random number generator for REAL, INTEGER and BOOLEAN"
class MULTI_RANDOM_GENERATOR
inherit
    RANDOM_GENERATOR
creation
    reset
feature
    last_random_integer(lower,upper:INTEGER) : INTEGER is
            -- Return an evenly distributed random number over the
            -- interval [lower, upper[.
        require non_empty_interval: lower<upper
        do
            Result := last_random_real(lower*1.0,upper*1.0).to_integer
        ensure
            in_bounds: Result >= lower and Result < upper
        end; -- last_random_integer
    last_random_bit : BOOLEAN is
            -- Return a single random bit.
        do
            Result := uniform < 0.5
        ensure
            evenly_distributed: -- Probability of 'Result = True' is 50%.
        end -- last_random_bit
end -- MULTI_RANDOM_GENERATOR
```

Example 3.23

When a software system is analyzed and designed using an object-oriented approach, the classifications identified during the analysis are preserved and enriched during design, and then may be directly implemented in code. This seamlessness provides better continuity between the requirements and the code: A small change in the requirements is likely to produce a small change in the code. Conversely, when a system having already reached the detailed implementation or maintenance phase needs to be modified, it is possible to reflect the changes back to the higher levels of design, specification, and analysis.

In Eiffel, subtyping is defined after subclassing. In the simplest case, if B inherits from A, then B defines a subtype of A. That is, every entity *b* of type B could be used at any place where an object of type A is expected (substitutability principle). In this case, B is also said to *conform* to A.

Generic classes are special, because they define class (and thus type) templates instead of real classes and types. We have then the following (recursive) rule to define type conformance among generic classes: A generic class B[U] conforms to A[T] only if B conforms to A and U to T. The rule is recursive, because U and T might be generic classes themselves. This conformance rule is easily extended when multiple generic parameters are used.

However, classifications are subjective matters that never quite achieve perfection. Think of the well-known example of ostriches and flying: An ostrich is a bird, a bird is a flying animal, but ostriches don't fly.

> Classification is humanity's attempt to bring a semblance of order to the description of an otherwise rather chaotic world. (B. Meyer)

The need to deal with imperfect inheritance structures (where subclasses are not true subtypes) seems universal and poses several problems, which are explored in Section 5.4.3.

3.3.4 Inheritance and Expanded Types

The values of entities declared to be of an expanded type are objects rather than references to objects. This is the only consequence of the expansion status of a class, which means that an expanded class may inherit freely from nonexpanded ones, and conversely. Whether or not the child class is expanded is never decided by parent classes (the expansion status is not inherited) but in the child itself, according to the presence or absence of the keyword **expanded** in its header. Example 3.24 presents the definition of the INTEGER class, which inherits from INTEGER_REF and adds an expanded status.

```
expanded class INTEGER
inherit
   INTEGER_REF
end -- INTEGER
```

Example 3.24

Conversely, Example 3.25 is a possible definition of the MY_INTEGER class, which inherits from INTEGER, and thus wipes out its expanded status.

3.3.5 Implicit Inheritance Structure

The inheritance structure of an Eiffel system forms a lattice (oriented with the inheritance relation) with a maximal element (the class GENERAL) and a minimal one (the pseudoclass NONE); see Figure 3.5. That is, all classes descend from GENERAL, and NONE is a descendant of every class.

Any developer-written class (e.g., A, B, C, D in Figure 3.5) without an explicit inheritance clause is considered to inherit directly from the class ANY

```
class MY_INTEGER
inherit INTEGER
feature
    new_feature is
        do
            -- something
        end
end
```

Example 3.25

(as if it included an inheritance clause of the form: inherit ANY). Then by transitivity every class (but GENERAL) inherits from ANY, and thus every type conforms to ANY (hence the name). ANY inherits from GENERAL and may be customized for individual projects or teams, thus providing for project-wide universal properties.

All the features of ANY are directly available to all Eiffel classes. The features *print*, *clone*, *deep_clone*, *equal*, *deep_equal*, *default_rescue*, *Void*, and *io*,

If you remark that a class may inherit from ANY more than once, don't worry—this is not a problem in Eiffel. It is explained in Section 5.2.

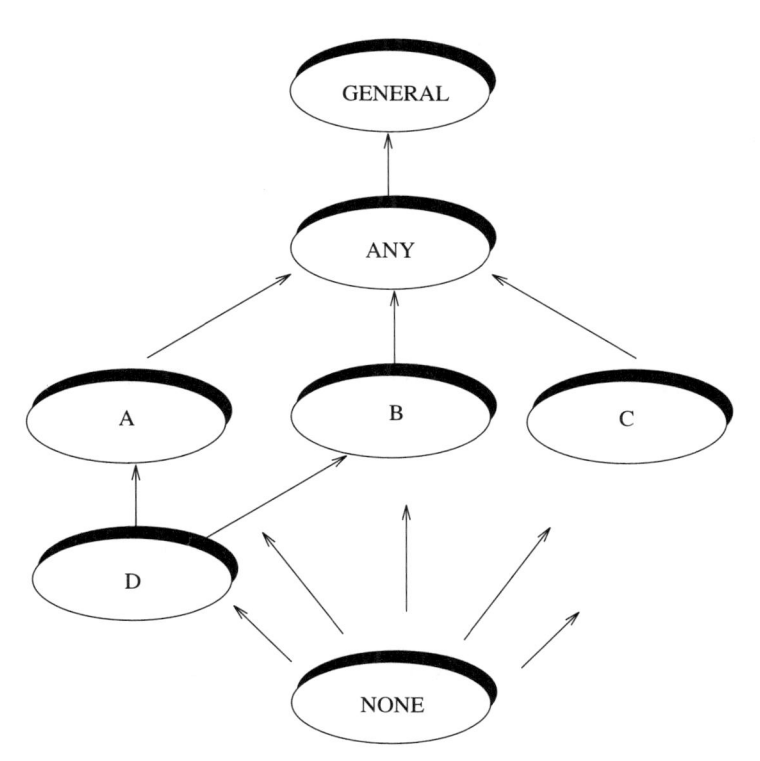

Figure 3.5 Standard Eiffel inheritance lattice

used in several previous examples of Eiffel fragments are some of the universal features that actually belong to the class GENERAL. They are not language keywords, but rather features inherited by all classes through the implicit inheritance link with ANY.

At the other end of the inheritance lattice, the pseudoclass NONE is considered to inherit from all classes. The inheritance relation is acyclic, so no class may then inherit from NONE (which is why a feature exported to NONE is private). The other use of NONE is as the type of the feature *Void* (defined in the class GENERAL). *Void* is then a value type-conformant to every class, and is used as the default initialization value for all entities of reference types. The classes GENERAL, ANY, and NONE belong to the Eiffel Library Standard described in Section 4.3.

3.4 Feature Adaptation

The reuse of Eiffel classes through inheritance may be customized on a by-feature basis. A useful analogy for this mechanism is the problem of plugging an electrical razor cord into a foreign wall outlet. The solution usually is to use a plug adaptor to convert the size and form of the connectors (and sometimes the voltage or the frequency, or both) of your cord to fit the foreign wall outlet (see Figure 3.6). What is done with this adaptor is functionally equivalent to changing the foreign wall outlet interface. As a client, you then may use the adaptor interface instead of the original one.

In Eiffel, for each individual feature inherited from a parent class, you may either inherit the feature as it is in the parent class (same name, specification [including signature, preconditions and postconditions], body, and export status [this is the default behavior]), or change any of these components

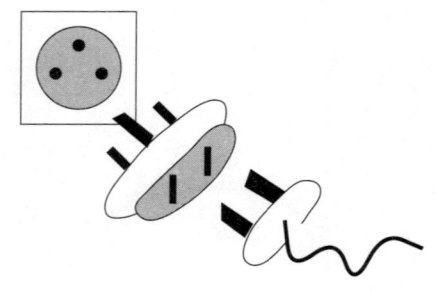

Figure 3.6 Using a plug adaptor

3.4 FEATURE ADAPTATION

FeatureAdaptation

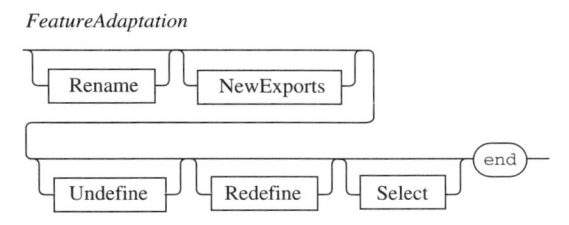

Syntax Diagram 27 Feature adaptation

with the mechanisms described in the following sections. The syntax of the feature adaptation is described in Syntax Diagram 27.

3.4.1 Renaming

Renaming gives a new name to an inherited feature. The syntax of the *rename* subclause of the *inheritance* clause is described in Syntax Diagram 28. This subclause is useful to present a more convenient interface to clients (for example, if the class VECTOR inherits from ARRAY, the feature *count* might be renamed *dimension*). Explicit renaming is also the mechanism used to solve name conflicts in multiple inheritance. Consider for instance a class VISUAL_RANDOM_BAG inheriting from the class RANDOM_BAG, which has a feature *draw*, and from the class PICTURE which also has a feature *draw*. We thus have a name conflict for the feature *draw* for objects of type VISUAL_RANDOM_BAG. In contrast to some artificial intelligence-based languages that use sophisticated heuristics to solve such name clashes, Eiffel requires you to do it explicitly through the renaming of one of the conflicting versions, as in Example 3.26.

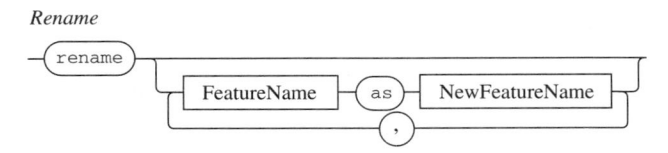

Rename

Syntax Diagram 28 Rename clause syntax

3.4.2 Redefining

Redefining the feature changes its specification or body, or both (Syntax Diagram 29). If you want to redefine a feature, you must declare it in the *redefine* subclause of the *inheritance* clause.

For example, the process by which the coffee is produced is different depending on whether you have a COFFEE_MACHINE or an ESPRESSO_MACHINE. If the

```
class VISUAL_RANDOM_BAG
inherit
    RANDOM_BAG
        rename
            draw as random_draw
        end
    PICTURE
creation
    ...
end -- VISUAL_RANDOM_BAG
```

Example 3.26

class Espresso_machine inherits from the class Coffee_machine, the *deliver_coffee* routine must be redefined, as shown in Example 3.27. This change is, however, constrained to respect the semantics of the original feature. The signature must be covariantly compatible with the original, the precondition can only be weakened, and the postcondition must be strengthened.

Covariant Signature Redefinition

The implications of the type system of the covariance rule for redefinitions are discussed in Section 5.4.2.

Syntactically the covariant signature redefinition constraint translates to the following rule. If the original version of a feature *f* takes an argument of type A and/or returns a type A (if the feature is an attribute or a function), then the redefined version may only take an argument of type B (or returns a type B), such that B is a descendant of A or A itself. The inheritance varies for both in the same direction, hence the name *covariance*.

Weakening Preconditions

If the precondition is to be changed, the new precondition follows the syntax:

```
require else new_cond
```

The precondition of the redefined routine is actually the *new_cond* or else the precondition of the original routine.

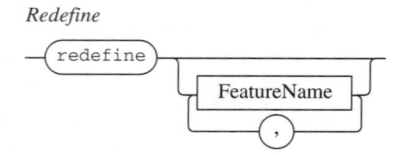

Redefine

Syntax Diagram 29   Redefine clause syntax

```
class ESPRESSO_MACHINE
inherit
    COFFEE_MACHINE
        redefine
            deliver_coffee, needs_maintenance
        end
feature
    deliver_coffee is
            -- pilot the hardware to deliver a cup of espresso
        do
            -- new method to produce the espresso
        end
    needs_maintenance : BOOLEAN is
            -- condition upon which some maintenance is needed
        do
            -- new criteria to evaluate if maintenance is needed
        end
end -- ESPRESSO_MACHINE
```

Example 3.27

Strengthening Postconditions

In the same spirit, the postcondition clause of a redefined routine must follow the syntax:

```
ensure then new_cond
```

The postcondition of the redefined feature is actually the *new_cond* and then the postcondition of the original routine. These constraints on feature redefinition provide the necessary semantics to ensure the safety of the Eiffel inheritance mechanism according to most recent works in this domain [92].

These constraints leave open the possibility of redefining a function without parameters to become an attribute (but not conversely).

Anchored Declarations

Covariance redefinition is used frequently in the Eiffel world, so a mechanism called *anchored declaration* has been designed to save a considerable amount of tedious redeclarations when dealing with signature redefinitions.

An anchored declaration has the syntax shown in Syntax Diagram 30. The *Anchor* is either **Current** or an attribute. The meaning of the declaration x : like anchor is that whenever the anchor is redeclared in a descendant class, x follows automatically. Consider for example the feature *is_equal*, as defined in the root of the Eiffel class hierarchy, the kernel library class GENERAL. This

```
                Anchored
              ┌──────┬────────┐
              │ like │ Anchor │
              └──────┴────────┘
```

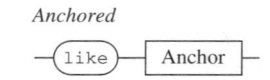

Syntax Diagram 30 The anchored declaration

```
    is_equal (other: like Current): BOOLEAN is
        -- Is 'other' attached to an object considered equal to 'Current'?
      require
        other_not_void: other /= Void
5     ensure
        symmetric: Result implies other.is_equal (Current)
      end
```

Example 3.28

anchored definition (see Example 3.28) allows an automatic redeclaration of the signature of the feature *is_equal* in any class Foo to

```
    is_equal (other: FOO): BOOLEAN
```

This *is_equal* feature may be redefined to fit special equality semantics, whereas the feature *equal* (see Section 2.4.1) may not. For example, the sets $A = \{1, 2, 3\}$ and $B = \{1, 3, 2\}$ are mathematically equal, but not Eiffel $equal(A, B)$. The feature *is_equal* may be redefined in a class SET in such a way that $A.is\_equal(B)$.

3.4.3 Changing the Export Status

The export status of an inherited feature may be changed in several ways with the *export* subclause of the *inheritance* clause (see Syntax Diagram 31). With this mechanism, you may either:

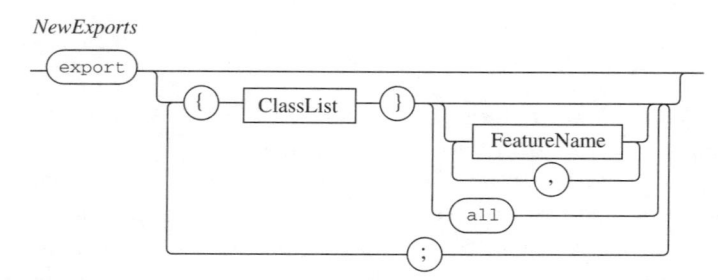

NewExports diagram: export { ClassList } FeatureName / all ;

Syntax Diagram 31 The "new export" syntax

```
    class LEASED_COFFEE_MACHINE
    inherit
        COFFEE_MACHINE
            export
5               {MANAGER,LEASEHOLDER} cash
            end
    end -- LEASED_COFFEE_MACHINE
```
Example 3.29

- Extend the export status of a set of features, or make them available to more client classes than in the parent class ("ANY" means visible by all classes), or

- Reduce it, hiding a set of features to some clients (or even to all clients if NONE is used). This option may be useful if these features are inherited for implementation purposes only.

The implications on the Eiffel type system of this is discussed in Section 5.4.1.

Consider for example a class LEASED_COFFEE_MACHINE representing coffee machines leased to special clients (instances of a class called LEASEHOLDER), who pay a rental fee, but in exchange get the money deposited in the LEASED_COFFEE_MACHINE. It is then possible for a LEASEHOLDER to access the feature *cash* with the declaration shown in Example 3.29. Any feature not specified in the new *export* clause keeps the exact export status it had in the superclass. The special keyword **all** counts for all features of the superclass.

3.4.4 Other Feature Adaptations

You may also:

- Undefine a feature (*undefine* clause), which is mainly useful for choosing one of a set of competing implementations for a feature name in some cases of multiple inheritance (see Section 3.6.3), and

- Select a feature (*select* clause) as the target for dynamic binding when there are ambiguities in some cases of repeated inheritance (see Section 5.2.3).

3.5 Polymorphism and Dynamic Binding

3.5.1 Polymorphic Entities

Polymorphism is defined in Webster's dictionary as "the quality or state of being able to assume different forms" [97]. Polymorphic referencing is the way

Expanded types are dealt with in Section 3.5.3. inheritance polymorphism appears in Eiffel. The association of a reference with an object is constrained by the type conformance rule (see Section 3.3.3): An entity x declared as being of a nonexpanded type T can be used to refer to an object of type S, provided the class S is a descendant of the class T. The entity x is then said to be of *static* type T, and capable of assuming the *dynamic* type S. More generally, an entity declared as being of static type T can be used to refer to any object with a dynamic type that *conforms to* type T.

```
e : T         -- T being a nonexpanded type
```
Example 3.30

Consider the declaration in Example 3.30. This declaration specifies that the entity *e* may only be *Void* or attached to objects conforming to T, that is, instances of T itself or subclasses of T. During its lifetime, a nonexpanded entity may refer to various objects, not necessarily having the same type (provided they conform to the entity static type), hence its polymorphic aspect. In contrast, an expanded type entity is not polymorphic, because it is really an object and not a reference to an object. In other words, objects are not polymorphic, only references are.

The *dynamic type* of an entity is the type of the object it refers to at a given point in its lifetime. A nonexpanded entity may acquire a new dynamic type in either of the following ways:

- Through a creation instruction with the third form of object creation described in Section 3.1.1. For example, if the class S is a descendant of the class T, the creation instruction of Example 3.31 creates an object of type S, attaches it to *e*, and initializes it with the creation procedure *make*, or

```
!S!e.make      -- S being a subclass of T
```
Example 3.31

- Through any assignment instruction, including actual to formal mapping of routine parameters and assignment attempt (see Section 5.3). In Example 3.32, *d* is a reference to an object of type S and *r* is a routine with a formal argument *e* of type T.

In both cases, the static type of the entity *e* is T, and its dynamic type is S.

```
e := d  -- e is now attached to an object of type S
r(d)    -- inside r, the formal argument e is attached
        -- to an object of type S
```
Example 3.32

3.5.2 Dynamic Binding

Consider a system in which instances of the classes COFFEE_MACHINE (Example 3.10) and ESPRESSO_MACHINE (Example 3.27) coexist. Let m be an entity declared of type COFFEE_MACHINE that may assume the dynamic type ESPRESSO_MACHINE at some step of the program execution. Assume that m is asked to deliver more coffee (`m.deliver_coffee`). The problem is that we cannot always know at compile time which "*deliver_coffee*" feature must be called on m—is it the one defined in COFFEE_MACHINE or in ESPRESSO_MACHINE?

The rule known as *dynamic binding* states that the dynamic type of an entity determines which version of the operation is applied. Dynamic binding allows the choice of the actual version of a feature to be delayed until run time. Whenever more than one version of a feature might be applicable, it ensures that the one most directly adapted to the target object is selected. The static constraint on the entity's type ensures that there is at least one such version.

Dynamic binding of routines to entities is the default rule in Eiffel. It is a run-time mechanism (basically a table lookup) that is *a priori* more costly than a simple procedure call. In modern Eiffel compilers, the appropriate routine is always found in constant time, whatever the complexity of the inheritance hierarchy. This time overhead tends to be small (or even negligible) for real applications. Furthermore, there are two cases in which the dynamic-binding mechanism may be bypassed in favor of a static binding:

In C++ only virtual methods are subject to dynamic binding.

- If a feature is declared to be **frozen**, it may not be redefined in subclasses. Dynamic binding is thus unnecessary.
- When compiling an Eiffel system (that is, a set of classes needed to produce an executable program), the compiler may become aware that a feature is never redefined in used subclasses, or may statically know the dynamic type of an entity (e.g., through data flow analysis). In both cases the compiler can replace the dynamic binding of the relevant features with a mere procedure call (or even its in-line expansion).

More details about compiler technology and the performance of an Eiffel program are given in Section 9.5.3 (Implementation Efficiency). Dynamic binding bypassing remains a compiler optimization that is transparent to the Eiffel programmer.

3.5.3 Type Conformance and Expanded Types

As discussed in the previous section, entities that denote expanded types are not polymorphic, because they are only *values*. If x is an entity of an expanded type A, only expanded or regular instances of class A may be assigned to

```
        i : INTEGER_REF        -- reference to an integer value
        j : INTEGER            -- an integer value
        k : MY_INTEGER         -- reference to an integer
                               -- (MY_INTEGER inherits from INTEGER)
```
Example 3.33

x. Consider the set of declarations in Example 3.33 (with the definitions of INTEGER and MY_INTEGER from Examples 3.24 and 3.25).

The assignment `i := j` is legal, and involves a copy of the value of *j* in *i*. On the other hand, the assignment `j := k` would not be legal, because although MY_INTEGER is a subclass of INTEGER, *k* does not conform to INTEGER, because INTEGER is of an expanded type.

An interesting consequence of this limitation is that operations involving expanded types such as INTEGER or REAL may be implemented as efficiently as in procedural languages, because they are never subject to dynamic binding.

3.6 Deferred Classes

3.6.1 Deferred Routines

A *deferred class* is a class with at least one *deferred feature* (that is, a feature with an implementation that is left unspecified). The syntax to declare a deferred feature is presented in Syntax Diagram 32. The feature *infix* "<" presented in Example 3.34 is an example of such a deferred feature, where the implementation part is replaced by the keyword *deferred*.

A deferred feature is equivalent to a pure virtual function in C++.

This deferred feature has a specification (a name, a signature, preconditions, and postconditions) but no implementation. By opposition, a nondeferred feature is called an effective feature (it has a specification *and* an im-

```
        infix "<" (other : like Current) : BOOLEAN is
            -- Is 'Current' less than 'other'?
        require
            other_not_void : other /= void
        deferred
        ensure
            asymmetric : Result implies not (other < Current)
        end
```
Example 3.34

deferredFeature

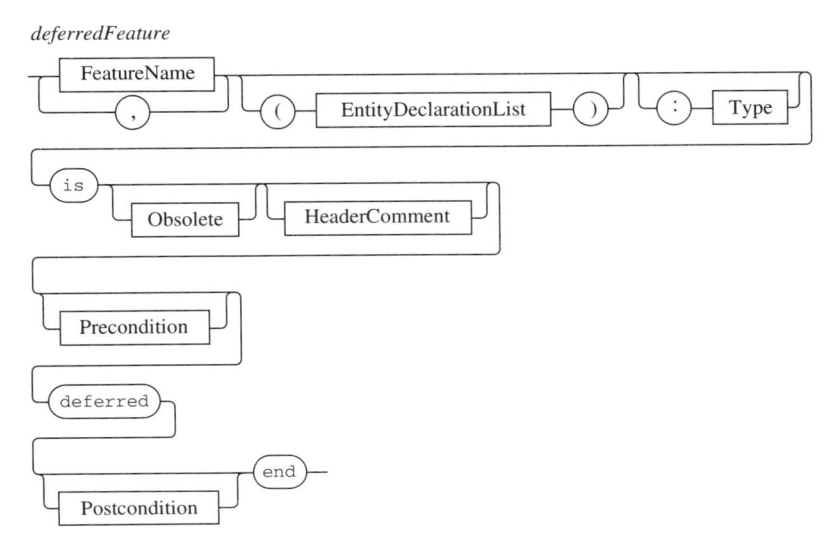

```
┌─ FeatureName ─┬─ ( ─ EntityDeclarationList ─ ) ─┬─ : ─ Type ─┐
│       ,       │                                 │             │
│               │                                 │             │
│  is ─┬─ Obsolete ─┬─ HeaderComment ─┐
│      │             │                 │
│  ┌─ Precondition ─┐
│  │                 │
│  ┌─ deferred ─┐
│  │             │
│  ┌─ Postcondition ─┐─ end ─┐
```

Syntax Diagram 32 Deferred feature syntax

plementation). An attribute may not be deferred, because it already has an implementation (formally the function returning its value).

3.6.2 Deferred Classes

As soon as a feature is left deferred, the enclosing class must be declared deferred. The deferred class syntax is presented in Syntax Diagram 33.

Conversely, a deferred class must have at least one deferred feature. Consider for example the kernel library class COMPARABLE encapsulating the notion of objects that may be compared according to a total order relation. It has a deferred function (*infix* "<") and a number of effective features defined after this function (see Example 3.35).

Whereas a class is the implementation of an ADT, a deferred class is a partial implementation of such an ADT (or even the ADT itself). Hence a deferred class may not be instantiated (see Example 3.36). It merely describes the common properties of a group of classes descendant from it. A deferred class may not have a **creation** part. Still, a deferred class defines a type (or a type pattern if it is a generic deferred class), and entities may be declared with this type.

Deferred classes are useful in structuring systems (see Section 3.6.4), but ultimately only their effective subclasses may be instantiated.

For the sake of conciseness, preconditions and postconditions are for the most part omitted in this listing.

This is related to the notion of abstract class found in various object-oriented language.

deferredClassDeclaration

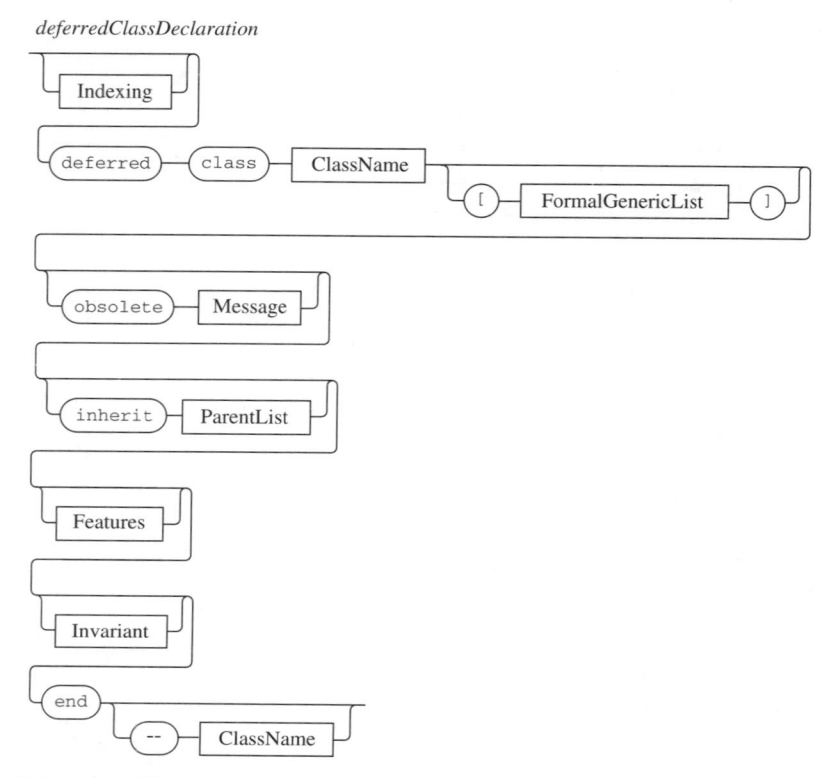

Syntax Diagram 33   Deferred class syntax

3.6.3 Inheritance and Deferred Classes

Beyond the feature adaptation mechanisms (renaming, exportation status, and redefinition; see Section 3.4) that are available for all kinds of features, a child class can change the deferred status of its parent features.

Effecting a Routine

This operation provides the inherited deferred feature with an implementation. No new syntax is required. The feature only needs to be present in a feature clause of the child class, with the same specification (name, signature, precondition, and postcondition) as inherited from its parent and with an implementation. Like any other function with no parameter, a deferred function may be implemented as an attribute.

If the deferred feature specification needs to be changed in the child class, the redefinition mechanism (as described in Section 3.4.2) must be used instead. Since routine overloading (*à la* Ada or C++) is not available in Eiffel, if

```
indexing
    description: "Objects that may be compared according to a
        total order relation"
    note: "descendants need only define the behavior of infix <"
deferred class COMPARABLE
feature
    infix "<" (other : like Current) : BOOLEAN is
            -- Is 'Current' less than 'other'?
        require
            other_not_void : other /= void
        deferred
        ensure
            asymmetric : Result implies not (other < Current)
        end
    infix "<=" (other: like Current): BOOLEAN is
            -- Is current object less than or equal to 'other'?
        do
            Result := not (other < Current)
        end
    infix ">" (other: like Current): BOOLEAN is
            -- Is current object greater than 'other'?
        do
            Result := other < Current
        end
    infix ">=" (other: like Current): BOOLEAN is
            -- Is current object greater than or equal to 'other'?
        do
            Result := not (Current < other)
        end
    min (other : like Current) : like Current is
            -- The smaller of 'Current' and 'other'.
        do
            if Current < other then
                Result := Current
            else
                Result := other
            end -- if
        end
    max (other : like Current) : like Current is
            -- The larger of 'Current' and 'other'.
        do
            if other < Current then
                Result := Current
            else
                Result := other
            end -- if
        end
invariant
    irreflexive_comparison: not (Current < Current)
end -- class COMPARABLE
```

Example 3.35

```
x : COMPARABLE    -- legal
!!x               -- illegal: COMPARABLE may not be instantiated
x := "Hello, world" -- legal: STRING inherits from COMPARABLE
```
Example 3.36

you mess up the feature signature, the compiler tells you what to do (either redefine the feature to take into account the new signature or correct it if it was a typo).

Merging Features Through Undefinition

*Undefining is possible provided the routine was not **frozen**.*

Undefining a feature allows a child class to wipe out the implementation of an effective routine (but not of an attribute) inherited from one of its parents. The syntax of an undefine clause is similar to that of a redefine clause (see Syntax Diagram 34), and just precedes it in the feature adaptation clause (Syntax Diagram 27).

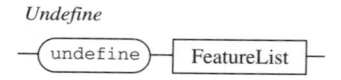

Undefine

─(undefine)─│ FeatureList │─

Syntax Diagram 34 Undefine

In Example 3.37, the feature *f* becomes a deferred feature in the class CHILD (which makes it a deferred class) while keeping the specification (name, signature, preconditions, and postconditions) it had in the class PARENT.

The usefulness of this undefining mechanism mainly concerns the merging of multiple inherited features, because a merge is valid only if at most one merged feature is effective.

```
      deferred class CHILD
      inherit
          PARENT
              undefine f
  5       end
      ...
```
Example 3.37

3.6.4 Deferred Classes: A Structuring Tool

Deferred classes may be used to factor out common properties of a set of classes into *abstract classes*. Some abstract classes appear naturally in the application domain, whereas other abstract classes are artificially manufactured as a convenient means for promoting code reuse. Consider for example the problem (discussed in depth in Chapter 9) of designing a linear algebra library around the notions of matrices and vectors.

A fundamental principle applied when designing this library is that the abstract specification of an entity is dissociated from any kind of implementation detail. Although all matrices, for example, share a common abstract specification, they do not necessarily require the same implementation layout. Obviously dense and sparse matrices deserve different internal representations. The same remark goes for vector entities.

The classes MATRIX and VECTOR are deferred classes: They provide no details about the way matrices and vectors shall be represented in memory. The specification of their internal representation is thus left to descendant classes. This does not imply that all features are kept deferred. Representation-dependent features are simply declared, whereas other features are defined— i.e., implemented—directly in MATRIX and VECTOR, as shown in Chapter 9.

3.7 Genericity and Inheritance

Genericity and inheritance are orthogonal concepts in Eiffel [99]. It is then interesting to see how they can be combined to foster versatile new possibilities for reusing software.

3.7.1 Heterogeneous Containers

A container class is a class that is able to store generic elements. Examples are the classes LIST[T], STACK[T], and ARRAY[T], etc., found in most Eiffel data structure libraries. This constraint is very difficult to express in a typeless language like Smalltalk. There is no simple way to forbid a particular kind of object from going into containers.

Getting back to our coffee machine example, imagine that a number of such machines are to be monitored to determine whether they need maintenance. We could design a class MANAGER (as in Example 3.38) that has a list of coffee machines (LISTE[COFFEE_MACHINE]; see Example 3.20). The ESPRESSO_MACHINE is a kind of COFFEE_MACHINE, so one can store both kinds of coffee machines in the list. It is thus a heterogeneous container, restricted to contain objects that are instances of COFFEE_MACHINE (or subclasses of COFFEE_MACHINE).

Thanks to dynamic binding, the right version of the feature *needs_maintenance* is applied to each element of the array in order to compute the total number of coffee machines that require maintenance. This routine (lines 14–25 of Example 3.38) may be written *without precise knowledge* of which objects

```
        class MANAGER
        feature
            machines : LISTE[COFFEE_MACHINE]
            add (new : COFFEE_MACHINE) is
 5              require
                    exist: new /= Void
                do
                    if machines = Void then
                        !!machines.make(new,Void)
10                  else
                        machines := machines.append(new)
                    end -- if
            end -- add
            total_needing_maintenance : INTEGER is
15              local m : like machines
                do
                    from m := machines
                    until m = Void
                    loop
20                      if machines.head.needs_maintenance then
                            Result := Result + 1
                        end -- if
                        m := machines.tail
                    end -- loop
25              end -- total_needing_maintenance
        end -- MANAGER
```

Example 3.38

really are in the heterogeneous container, provided they conform to COFFEE_MACHINE.

In a procedural language (such as C, Pascal, or Ada83), this function would have been written using a case statement discriminating among case selector values (encoding on the actual type of the considered object) to make the correct procedure call (the one from either COFFEE_MACHINE or ESPRESSO_MACHINE). The same kind of processing would then be repeated for each routine dealing with the heterogeneous container. The object-oriented solution, here based on the dynamic binding of the routine *needs_maintenance*, makes it possible to avoid such a duplication of code.

Once again, much more than the savings obtained during the design and the coding, the real savings appear during the maintenance phase of the software. Imagine that at this stage (maybe 10 years after the software is running in production mode), a new kind of COFFEE_MACHINE is adopted (e.g., a CAPPUCCINO_MACHINE), with a new means to compute its *needs_maintenance*. With the procedural language solution, we would have to locate and modify every routine dealing with the explicit type of a COFFEE_MACHINE (e.g., *needs_* *maintenance*). Then every modified module would have to be retested (both for the new functionality and for nonregression).

In contrast, in the object-oriented solution, once the CAPPUCCINO_MACHINE class has been implemented and tested, no other part of the software has to be modified (except perhaps for the routine dealing with the initialization of the container). Most notably, the class MANAGER does not need to be changed and hence retested. The maintenance phase is clearly where the object-oriented approach is the big winner.

3.7.2 Constrained Genericity

The other mechanism for combining genericity and inheritance is constrained genericity, which makes it possible to specify that a generic parameter must be a descendant of a certain class. For example, a generic MATRIX class would require its generic parameter T to be a descendant of the NUMERIC class with the declaration:

classMATRIX [T — > NUMERIC]

If the NUMERIC class features an infix "+" operation, then a generic MATRIX addition operation could be defined, based on the addition of the individual elements of the MATRIX (see Example 3.39).

```
    feature
        add (other: MATRIX [T]) is
                -- add other to Current matrix
            require
                not_Void: (other /= Void);
                same_size: (nrow = other.nrow) and (ncolumn = other.ncolumn)
            local
                i, j : INTEGER
            do
                from i := 1
                until i > nrow
                loop
                    from j := 1
                    until j > ncolumn
                    loop
                        put(item(i,j) + other.item(i,j), i, j)
                        j := j + 1
                    end -- loop on j
                    i := i + 1
                end -- loop on i
        end -- add
```

Example 3.39

```
class SORTABLE_ARRAY [T − > COMPARABLE]
inherit
    ARRAY [T]
creation
    make -- inherited from ARRAY
feature
    -- dealing with the sortable properties of the array
    is_sorted : BOOLEAN is
            -- is the array sorted
        do
            Result := is_sorted_range(lower, upper)
        end -- is_sorted
    quick_sort is
            -- sort the array in nondescending order in O(n log(n)).
        do
            if lower < upper then -- at least 2 items
                quick_sort_range(lower, upper)
            end -- if
        ensure
            sorted: is_sorted
        end -- quick_sort

    quick_sort_range(first, last: INTEGER) is
            -- sort elements first .. last into increasing order
            -- (quick sort algorithm)
        require range_not_empty: first <= last
    -- etc.
end -- class SORTABLE_ARRAY
```

Example 3.40

The class COMPARABLE was presented in Example 3.35.

The notion of constrained genericity encompasses the previously described notion of genericity (Section 3.2), which is actually an abbreviation for genericity constrained by ANY. Thus a LISTE[T] is equivalent to a LISTE[T − > ANY]. This constrained genericity mechanism enables the generic definition of powerful abstraction, such as a SORTED_LIST[T − > COMPARABLE]—that is, a sorted list of generic elements. The mere notion that the list is sorted implies that its elements can be compared, hence the constrained genericity.

Another example is to define an ARRAY in such a way that it can be sorted (see Example 3.40), e.g., to encapsulate the *quicksort* algorithm presented in Example 2.23 of Section 2.6.

Some examples of the use of this mechanism are described in the keyword-in-context (KWIC) index problem presented in Section 3.8.

3.8 Case Study: The KWIC System

We now illustrate the concepts introduced in this chapter by considering the KWIC index problem, inspired by R. Wiener [137] or B. Liskov [91]. It is a well-known case-study in the software engineering literature, so the reader is advised to compare the Eiffel solution to this problem to the CLU or the Ada83 one.

3.8.1 Presentation of the KWIC System

A KWIC index is a list of titles of books, research articles, and so on, arranged so that each title that contains a "key" word can be found easily. Associated with the title is the inventory number of the book. For example, consider the following titles:

```
The Hitch-Hiker's Guide to the Galaxy G. Adams 4242
Software Engineering with Ada and Modula-2 R. Wierner and R. Sincovec 6543
Object-Oriented Software Engineering with Eiffel J.-M. Jezequel 6789
The Evolution of the Universe: Part 1 C. Charlie 9834
```

The KWIC index for this list with the "key" words in the first column would be:

```
Ada and Modula-2                          Software Engineering with    6543
Eiffel                       Object-Oriented Software Engineering with  6789
Engineering with Ada and Modula-2                              Software 6543
Engineering with Eiffel                   Object-Oriented Software     6789
Evolution of the Universe: Part 1                                   The 9834
Galaxy                                   The Hitch-Hiker's Guide to the 4242
Guide to the Galaxy                              The Hitch-Hiker's     4242
Hiker's Guide to the Galaxy                           The Hitch-        4242
Hitch-Hiker's Guide to the Galaxy                               The     4242
Modula-2                         Software Engineering with Ada and     6543
Object-Oriented Software Engineering with Eiffel                       6789
Oriented Software Engineering with Eiffel                      Object- 6789
Software Engineering with Ada and Modula-2                             6543
Software Engineering with Eiffel                      Object-Oriented  6789
Universe: Part 1                             The Evolution of the      9834
```

In each title, words that are articles, prepositions, or trivial are called *nonkeywords*. In the KWIC index, each title appears as often as there are keywords matching it. The titles are aligned so that all the keywords occur in the first column. The portion of the title that appears before the keyword has been shifted to the end of the line. The inventory number of the title is printed to the right of the title.

Such a KWIC index is useful in finding books and articles. To find titles on a particular subject, you just have to search the KWIC index for keywords related to the subject and get the corresponding title by reading first the right part, and then the left one. You also have the inventory number. A typical KWIC index may contain thousands of titles.

3.8.2 The KWIC Object-Oriented Software

A software system to produce a KWIC index is given book descriptions (basically a title, list of authors, and inventory number, see the class BOOK of Example 2.2) and the list of nonkeywords as input. The system identifies possible keywords and creates entries for the KWIC index, alphabetizes the entries according to the keywords, and then prints the KWIC index. The list of nonkeywords may be modified from run to run by adding or deleting words.

An object-oriented analysis (presented in [137]) allows the identification of the following classes:

BOOK   This class is described in Example 2.2.

KWIC_ENTRY   This class is basically a line of the KWIC index.

KWIC   This class is made of KWIC entries. It can be built after a list of books and a list of nonkeywords.

WORDS   This class is a representation of a book title broken into an iterable sequence of words.

DRIVER   The user interface to the KWIC index.

In the following, we present only the core of a solution: the classes KWIC_ENTRY, KWIC, and WORDS, and a simple class DRIVER. These classes only use classes from the Eiffel Standard Library (e.g., ARRAY, STRING) and classes previously defined in this book (e.g., LISTE, SORTABLE_ARRAY), so they should run in any existing Eiffel environment. Still, the reader is welcome to complete the system to get more insight into his or her Eiffel environment, by using a HASH_TABLE of nonkeywords instead of a LISTE (for evident efficiency reasons) or by designing a real user interface.

3.8.3 The Class KWIC_ENTRY

The class KWIC_ENTRY is made of a book title broken into two parts around a cutting point. These two parts are called *left* and *right* (see the 9th line in Example 3.41). We want to produce an alphabetized list of the KWIC entries, so they should be comparable to each other. Hence KWIC_ENTRY inherits from COMPARABLE (5th line), and we have to define the *infix* "<" operator according to a lexicographical order (lines 27–34 in Example 3.41).

```
    indexing
        description: "a line of the KWIC index"
    class KWIC_ENTRY
    inherit
5       COMPARABLE
    creation
        make
    feature
        left, right: STRING -- left and right part of the kwic entry
10      inventory : INTEGER -- inventory number of the corresponding book
        make (a_title : STRING; cutting_point, invent : INTEGER) is
            -- kwic entry with the title broken around the cutting_point
        require
            not_void: a_title /= Void
15          positive_cutting_point: cutting_point > 0
            bounded_cutting_point: cutting_point <= a_title.count
        do
            inventory := invent
            left := a_title.substring(cutting_point,a_title.count)
20          if cutting_point > 1 then
                right := a_title.substring(1,cutting_point−1)
            else
                !!right.make(0)        -- empty right part
            end -- if
25      ensure
            -- right prepended to left is equal to a_title
        end -- make
    infix "<" (other : like Current) : BOOLEAN is
        -- does this entry alphabetically precede other?
30      require else
            not_void: other /= Void
        do
            Result := (left < other.left)
                or else ((left.is_equal(other.left)) and right < other.right)
35      end -- infix "<"
    end -- KWIC_ENTRY
```

Example 3.41

```
   indexing
       description: "Collection of KWIC entries"
       implementation: "sortable array, exporting the feature quick_sort"
   class KWIC
5  inherit
       SORTABLE_ARRAY[KWIC_ENTRY]
           rename
               make as array_make
           end
10 creation
       make
   feature
       make (library: LISTE[BOOK]; non_keywords: LISTE[STRING]) is
           local l : like library
15         do
               trivial_words := non_keywords
               array_make(1,0) -- initialized to empty
               from l := library
               until l = Void
20             loop
                   make_entries_from(l.head)
                   l := l.tail
               end -- loop
           end -- make
25     make_entries_from(a_book: BOOK) is
               -- make the KWIC entries corresponding to a book title
           require exist: a_book /= Void
           local
               new_entry : KWIC_ENTRY
30             seq : WORDS -- the sequence of words in the book title
               w : STRING -- the current word of the sequence
           do
               from !!seq.init(a_book.title) -- initialize the sequence
               until seq.off
35             loop
                   w := seq.word      -- get the current word
                   w.to_lower         -- convert to lowercase
                   if not trivial_words.has(w) then -- it is a keyword
                       !!new_entry.make(a_book.title,seq.start_position,
40                                       a_book.inventory)
                       force(new_entry,upper+1) -- append the new entry
                   end -- if
                   seq.next -- advance the sequence of words
               end -- loop
```

Example 3.42 (Lines 1–44)

```
45              end -- make_entries_from
            print_index is
                -- print the KWIC index, with the "key" words in the first column
                local
                    i, j : INTEGER
50              do
                    from i := lower
                    until i > upper
                    loop
                        print(item(i).left)
55                      from j := item(i).left.count
                        until j > 70 − item(i).right.count
                        loop
                            print(' ')
                            j := j + 1
60                      end -- loop
                        print(item(i).right)
                        print(" "); print(item(i).inventory); print("%N")
                        i := i + 1
                    end -- loop
65              end -- print_index
            feature {NONE} -- private features
                trivial_words : LISTE[STRING]
            end -- KWIC
```

Example 3.42 (Lines 45–68)

3.8.4 The Class KWIC

The class KWIC is made of KWIC entries that may be alphabetized. We will implement it as a SORTABLE_ARRAY[KWIC_ENTRY] (6th line in Example 3.42) that features a *quick_sort* procedure (see Example 3.40). A KWIC index is built after a list of books and a list of nonkeywords, so its creation procedure (*make*) accepts such parameters (13th line). It stores the nonkeyword list in a private attribute (called *trivial_words*) , and then for each book in the *library* book list, it makes the corresponding KWIC entries (lines 18–23).

The procedure *make_entries_from* (lines 25–45) creates as many KWIC entries as there are keywords matching words in the book title. It is based on a loop asking for successive words of the title and checking whether their lowercase forms are keywords. If so, the corresponding KWIC entry is made. The last procedure, *print_index*, is just a loop for printing all KWIC entries in the format defined in Section 3.8.1.

```
indexing
    description: "An iterable sequence of words in a STRING"
    implementation: "keeps a reference on the original string"
class WORDS
creation
    init
feature
    ref : STRING
    init (s : STRING) is
            -- init the iterable sequence of words
        require
            exist: s /= Void
        do
            ref := s
            next -- set the sequence on the first word
        end -- init
    word : STRING is
            -- a copy of the current word in the sequence
        require
            not_off: not off
        do
            Result := ref.substring(start_position,end_position)
        end -- word
    off : BOOLEAN is
            -- is the sequence of words exhausted?
        do
            Result := start_position > ref.count
        end -- off
    next is
            -- advance to the next word in ref
        require not_off: not off
        do
            from start_position := end_position + 1
            until off or else is_letter(ref.item(start_position))
            loop
                start_position := start_position + 1
            end -- loop
            if not off then
                from end_position := start_position
                invariant on_letter: is_letter(ref.item(end_position))
                variant ref.count − end_position + 1
                until end_position = ref.count or else
                    not is_letter(ref.item(end_position + 1))
```

Example 3.43 (Lines 1–43)

```
                    loop
45                      end_position:= end_position + 1
                    end -- loop
                end -- if
            ensure
                progress: start_position > old(end_position)
50          end -- next
        is_letter(c:CHARACTER): BOOLEAN is
                -- is c a lowercase or uppercase letter, a-z or A-Z?
            do
                Result := (c>='a' and c<='z') or (c>='A' and c<='Z')
55          end -- is_letter
        start_position : INTEGER -- of the current word within ref
        end_position : INTEGER -- of the current word within ref
    invariant
        ref_exist: ref /= Void
60      end_after_start: (not off) implies end_position >= start_position
        start_on_letter: (not off) implies is_letter(ref.item(start_position))
        end_on_letter: (not off) implies is_letter(ref.item(end_position))
        next_not_letter: end_position < ref.count implies
                              not is_letter(ref.item(end_position + 1))
65  end -- WORDS
```

Example 3.43 (Lines 44–65)

3.8.5 The Class WORDS

The class WORDS is an iterable sequence of the words present in a STRING. A *word* is a substring made of the letters *a* to *z* and *A* to *Z* only (see the function *is_letter*, lines 51–55 of Example 3.43).

For its implementation, it simply keeps a reference (*ref*) on the original string. The sequence must be initialized with the creation procedure *init*. It may be iterated with the procedure *next*, which advances to the next word (feature *word*) in the string.

3.8.6 The Class DRIVER

The class DRIVER is a simple example to exercise the KWIC problem. A real driver to this problem should provide a real user interface, deal with a book database, and have an intelligent way to manage the list of nonkeywords. In Section 4.3.3 we illustrate the input/output facilities available in the Eiffel Standard Library with a modified version of this class to deal with data read from a disk or standard input.

100 OBJECT-ORIENTED ELEMENTS

Instead, Example 3.44 uses hard-coded data to produce the KWIC index listing of Section 3.8.1.

Despite the high level of the language, the generated code is kept small and efficient; e.g., a stripped version of the executable code for this KWIC system (optimized compilation with the TowerEiffel compiler 1.4.3.0b) on a SPARC workstation is only 40,960 bytes large. See Appendix C for instructions on how to obtain the full source code of this example.

```
    indexing
        description: "exercise the KWIC problem with a simple example"

    class DRIVER
5   creation
        make
    feature
        library : LISTE[BOOK]
        non_kw : LISTE[STRING]
10      make is
            local
                k : KWIC
            do
                read_library              -- read the list of books
15              read_non_keywords         -- read the list of non_keywords
                !!k.make(library,non_kw)  -- build the KWIC
                k.quick_sort              -- sort it
                k.print_index             -- print it
            end -- make
20      read_library is
            -- put a number of books in the 'library' list.
            local
                b : BOOK
            do
25              !!b.make("The Hitch-Hiker's Guide to the Galaxy",
                        "G. Adams", 4242)
                !!library.make(b,Void)
                !!b.make("Software Engineering with Ada and Modula-2",
                        "R. Wierner and R. Sincovec", 6543)
30              library:=library.append(b)
                !!b.make("Object-Oriented Software Engineering with Eiffel",
                        "J.-M. Jezequel", 6789)
                library:=library.append(b)
                !!b.make("The Evolution of the Universe: Part 1",
35                      "C. Charlie", 9834)
                library:=library.append(b)
            end -- read_library
```

Example 3.44 (Lines 1–37)

```
        read_non_keywords is
            -- put a number of non_keywords in the 'non_kw' list.
        do
            !!non_kw.make("and",Void)
            non_kw := non_kw.append("of")
            non_kw := non_kw.append("or")
            non_kw := non_kw.append("part")
            non_kw := non_kw.append("s")
            non_kw := non_kw.append("the")
            non_kw := non_kw.append("to")
            non_kw := non_kw.append("using")
            non_kw := non_kw.append("with")
        end -- read_non_keywords
end -- DRIVER
```

Example 3.44 (Lines 38–51)

4
The Eiffel Environments

In This Chapter

- 4.1 System Assembly and Configuration
- 4.2 Assertion Monitoring
- 4.3 Overview of the Eiffel Standard Library
- 4.4 Interfacing with Other Languages
- 4.5 Garbage Collection

At this point you know enough about the Eiffel language to understand probably more than 95% of any Eiffel system. Eiffel programs do not exist in the void, so this chapter brings in environmental matters: system configuration and monitoring, an overview of the Eiffel kernel library, interfacing with external software, and controlling garbage collection.

4.1 System Assembly and Configuration

4.1.1 Assembling Classes

An Eiffel software system is the *assembly* of a number of software components, usually a mixture of off-the-shelf and ad hoc classes, with an occasional pinch of external software.

Assembling a system consists of telling the compiler where the relevant classes (and potential external software) are located, which one among them is the "root" class of the Eiffel program, and which creation feature of the root class is the program entry point. System assembly can be customized according to many options such as assertion monitoring level, debugging level, optimization level, garbage collection status, and tracing. These options may be specified at a system-wide level or, except for the garbage collection status, on a per cluster or even on a per class basis. This kind of specification of what to do with many software components is called an Assembly of Classes

104 THE EIFFEL ENVIRONMENTS

They contain roughly the same information, so some translators are even available.

in Eiffel (ACE). In the next sections of this chapter, we describe in further detail the various concepts involved in ACE. However, first we need notation to describe ACE. There are several variants of such notation, none of which is standardized yet by NICE. Two of them are:

LACE is the *language for assembling classes in Eiffel*. It has an Eiffel-like syntax, and deals with all the items mentioned previously. It is used in the environments sold by ISE or Tower Technology.

PDL/RCL provides the same kind of functionality, but it is divided into two parts: the *program description language*, which deals with the compilation management itself, and the *run-time control language*, which deals with execution options (assertion monitoring level, debugging level, etc.). PDL/RCL is used in the SiG Computer GmbH environments.

You don't need to be very proficient in their respective syntaxes, because usually the environment provides you with a template containing all of the default fields, which you simply customize for your application.

We overview the most frequently available mechanisms to configure Eiffel systems. Compiler vendors sometimes add several useful features (e.g., the ability to generate various executables at once, or the possibility of sharing precompiled code among many systems) that are not described here.

4.1.2 Generating an Application

The first part of an ACE deals with the notion of an application, that is, an Eiffel system. It allows you to specify the name of the generated executable program (or possibly the library) and where its entry point is located.

For example, if we consider the ACE corresponding to Example 2.1 (the "*Hello, world*" program), we would specify that the executable file should be called *hello*, that the root class is the class HELLO (found by default in a file called **hello.e**, and that the entry point is the feature *make*. This translates in LACE to:

```
system hello
root hello : make
```

which corresponds to the following PDL:

```
program hello
root hello : make
```

4.1.3 Specifying Clusters

An ACE description should allow you to specify which clusters contain the sets of classes used in your application. A cluster is not an Eiffel language-level notion. Any mechanism that allows you to group several related classes might be used. In most UNIX, Windows, or DOS systems, a cluster is usually a directory containing a set of files, themselves containing class descriptions.

For both LACE and PDL, cluster descriptions come after the keyword **cluster**. For example, here is a LACE fragment specifying that two clusters are used, a *local* one, which is the current working directory, and the *kernel* one, which is probably mandatory for most compilers, because it contains the Eiffel Standard Library classes.

$EIFFEL refers to the value of an environment variable.

```
cluster
    local: ".";
    kernel: "$EIFFEL/clusters/kernel";
```

The difference in the PDL version is that clusters are not given symbolic names:

```
cluster
    "."
    end
    "$EIFFEL/library/basic"
    end
```

4.1.4 Excluding and Including Files

By default, all class texts contained in files suffixed with ".e" are considered by the compiler for each specified cluster. This default rule may be modified in two ways:

- If some ".e" suffixed files do not contain relevant Eiffel classes, they can be *excluded* from the cluster, which translates to LACE with:

    ```
    exclude "file1"; "file2"; .. "filen";
    ```

    and to PDL with:

    ```
    exclude "file1", "file2", .. "filen".
    ```

- Conversely, if some relevant Eiffel classes are not stored in conventional files (e.g., because of some OS filename limitations), they still can be included in the cluster. With LACE, you may use the **include** keyword:

```
            include "file1"; "file2"; .. "filen";
```

whereas with PDL you may use a *find* clause to let the compiler look for specific classes in some files:

```
            find classname1 in "file1", classname2 in "file2".
```

4.1.5 Dealing with Class Name Clashes

In large projects in which you use several third-party libraries, it is highly possible that a class name clash will eventually happen. In some cases (e.g., if you don't have the sources of the libraries), it will be beyond your reach to change the source code to avoid such clashes. Both LACE and PDL provide an external way to *rename* conflicting classes, in much the same way as conflicting features are renamed with multiple inheritance.

In LACE, you may use an *adapt* clause within a cluster specification:

```
local : "."
  adapt
    cluster1:
      rename C as C1,
             D as D1;
    cluster2:
      rename C as C2;
```

Thus for all the classes of the *local* cluster, the classes C and D belonging to the cluster *cluster1* are known under the names C1 and D1, whereas the class C belonging to the cluster *cluster2* is known as C2.

In PDL, the renaming occurs within the original clusters of the conflicting classes, and a *use* clause specifies for which classes the new name is to be used (this is either an enumeration or the keyword **all** to specify it for all classes).

```
    "$DVP/cluster1":
      rename C as C1,
             D as D1
      use C1, D1 for [list of class]

    "$DVP/cluster2":
      rename C as C2
      use C2 for [list of class]
```

4.2 Assertion Monitoring

4.2.1 Rationale

Remember that Eiffel's modularity is based on the "programming by contract" principle. When you violate the preconditions of a class feature, you don't respect your part of the contract: There is an error in *your* code. It could be called a *domain error*. It is up to you whether you want a clean error message at run time (telling you where and why you have an error), or maximum efficiency, risking a dirty crash if your program contains a domain error.

Thus there are two mutually exclusive approaches to dealing with assertion checking:

- In the first case, you don't use assertion checking to bring you security at run time (i.e., software fault tolerance), but just to help you document and test your classes.

  Domain errors are much like type errors, because what you can do (and what you can't) with a class (the implementation of an ADT) is defined by the feature signatures *and* the class assertions (preconditions and invariants). However, the problem of checking domain errors is not (generally) achievable at compile time, and thus run-time checking is the poor man's solution.

  If your compiler is clever enough to detect some domain errors at compile time, then it saves you *testing* time (the same as for type errors). When you are confident that your program is correct and if you badly need full efficiency, just disable assertion checking.

- The second approach is to use assertions as a variant of defensive programming, to bring some kind of software fault tolerance. Software then may be built with the hypothesis that at least precondition checking is always enabled, and may be prepared to handle exceptions raised by precondition violations (see Section 5.1).

  In this case you should be careful about the performance penalties of assertion checking, at least until Eiffel compilers are clever enough to check assertions at compile time whenever possible.

4.2.2 Enabling Assertion Checking with LACE

Assertion checking can be enabled with `assertion(level)`, where *level* is one of the following keywords representing the level of monitoring:

no means that no assertion is to be checked.

require means that only preconditions are to be checked.

ensure means that *both* preconditions and postconditions are to be checked.

invariant means that class invariants also should be checked (see Section 2.5.3).

loop means that loop variants and invariants also should be checked (see Section 2.4.7).

check means that check instructions also should be executed (see Section 2.4.8).

all means everything should be checked (actually, it is equivalent to the level **check**).

Assertion monitoring is a subset of the compilation options that can be specified with LACE. Like other options, they may appear at any of the three following levels:

- At system-wide level with a top-level *default* clause,
- At cluster level with a cluster-level *default* clause, or
- On a per class basis, with an *option* paragraph in the cluster specification.

For example,

Remember that most Eiffel environments offer a user-friendly way to generate these ACEs.

```
system hello
root hello : make

default
  assertion(ensure); debug(no);
cluster

  local: "."
    default
      assertion(all); debug(all);
    end;

  kernel: "$EIFFEL/clusters/kernel"
    option
      assertion(invariant): ARRAY;
    end;
```

The same mechanism is used to enable *tracing* (a message is printed each time a routine is entered or exited) and *debug* code (that is, code enclosed in a *debug* instruction; see Section 2.4.9). The LACE keywords **trace** and **debug** are used in much the same way as the **assertion** keyword. The argument *no* means that no debug code is to be executed. A list of keys may be used to enable the execution of the corresponding debugging code:

```
debug("TRACE","RECURSIVITY").
```

The argument *all* allows all debugging code to be executed, whatever its key.

4.2.3 Enabling Assertion Checking with Run-Time Control Language

Enabling assertion checking and debugging code are not compile-time options specified with PDL, but run-time options specified with *run-time control language* (RCL). The advantage of this approach is that you don't have to recompile your Eiffel system if you just want to modify such options. The final code you get is not fully optimized, however, unless you specify "optimization: on" in your PDL file. In that case, you can no longer have assertion checking.

An RCL file is simply a list of *tags* (corresponding to the various assertion checking levels given previously) followed with a ":" and a list of class names or the keywords **none** and **all**. For example:

```
precondition: all
postcondition: ARRAY, STRING
loop_variant: none
loop_invariant: none
invariant: ARRAY
debug: none
debug_key: "TRACE","RECURSIVITY"
trace: KWIC_ENTRY
```

4.3 Overview of the Eiffel Standard Library

4.3.1 Purposes of the Eiffel Standard Library

Eiffel has a precise language definition that guarantees a first level of interoperability among various compilers. In practice, however, the compilers are dependent on a small set of classes called the Eiffel Standard Library in areas such as array and string manipulation, object copying and cloning, in-

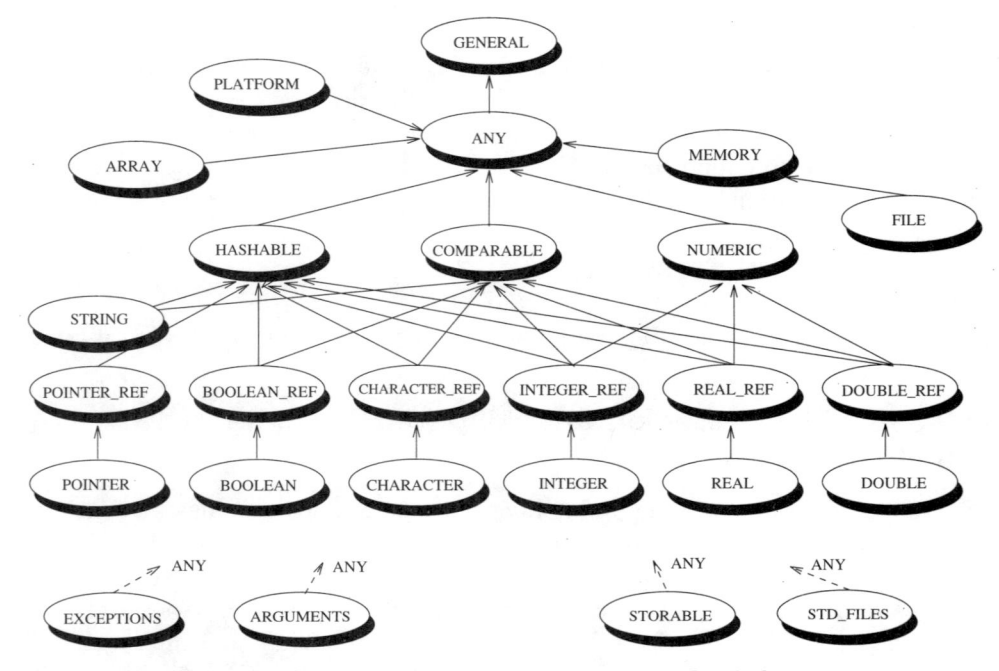

Figure 4.1 The inheritance relationships among standard classes

put/output, object storage, basic types, etc. For libraries and applications to be portable across compilers, these classes should present the same interface in each implementation. This is the purpose of the Eiffel Library Standard, which is standardized by NICE. This standard is revised on a yearly basis, in the spirit of preserving the technology investment of Eiffel users, while allowing for improvements. Each successive version of it is known as a *vintage*.

In this section we give an overview of Vintage 95 of the Eiffel Library Standard. Full details are available from NICE or from your Eiffel compiler vendor (see Appendix C).

4.3.2 Required Standard Classes

Twenty-six classes belong to the Eiffel Standard Library. These classes are partially ordered with the inheritance relationships according to Figure 4.1. Here is a brief description of them:

1. GENERAL encapsulates all platform-independent universal properties of objects (see Section 3.3.5).

2. ANY is an ancestor to all developer-written classes. ANY inherits from GENERAL and may be customized for individual projects or teams (see Section 3.3.5).

3. COMPARABLE encapsulates the notion of objects that may be compared according to a total order relation. It has a deferred function (*infix* "<") and a number of effective features defined after this function (see Section 3.6.2 and Example 3.35).

4. HASHABLE represents values that may be hashed into an integer index for use as keys in hash tables. It has a deferred function *hash_code*. Among others, BOOLEAN, CHARACTER, INTEGER, POINTER, and STRING are descendants of HASHABLE, thus hash tables have keys derived from these types.

5. NUMERIC is a deferred class encapsulating the notion of objects to which numerical operations (available in a commutative ring) are applicable (+, −, ∗, /, etc.) (see Section 3.7.2).

6. BOOLEAN represents truth values, with the usual Boolean operations, as described in Section 2.5.7. Some of its features are presented in Examples 2.18 and 2.19.

7. CHARACTER represents ASCII characters, with comparison operations. It was outlined in Section 2.3.4. This class inherits from COMPARABLE and HASHABLE.

8. INTEGER is for integer values (outlined in Section 2.5.7). This class inherits from COMPARABLE, NUMERIC, and HASHABLE.

9. REAL is for floating-point values (single precision) as outlined in Section 2.5.7. This class inherits from COMPARABLE, NUMERIC, and HASHABLE.

10. DOUBLE is for floating-point values (double precision) as also outlined in Section 2.5.7. This class inherits from COMPARABLE, NUMERIC, and HASHABLE.

11. POINTER represents references to objects meant to be exchanged with non-Eiffel software (see Section 4.4.2). Pointers are HASHABLE.

12. ARRAY implements sequences of values, all of the same type or of a conforming one, accessible through integer indices in a contiguous interval (see Section 3.2.3 and Example 3.22).

13. STRING implements sequences of characters, accessible through integer indices in a contiguous range. It was described in Section 3.1.5, with some of its features presented in Example 3.11. This class inherits from COMPARABLE and HASHABLE.

14. STD_FILES encapsulates commonly used input and output mechanisms. Most notably, the feature *io* of the class GENERAL is an instance of STD_FILES that may be used by any class to deal with basic input/output such as reading or writing integers, reals, or strings from or to standard input or standard output or standard error.

15. FILE is viewed as persistent sequences of characters (see Section 4.3.3).

16. STORABLE encapsulates the notion of objects that may be stored and retrieved along with all their dependents. This class may be used as an ancestor by classes needing persistency properties. It thus provides a primitive connection toward object-oriented databases.

17. MEMORY encapsulates facilities for tuning up the garbage collection mechanism. This class may be used either as an ancestor or as a supplier by classes that require its facilities (this is described in Section 4.5.3 in relation to garbage collection). Its interface appears later in this chapter as Example 4.6.

18. EXCEPTIONS encapsulates facilities for adapting the exception handling mechanism. It is described in Section 5.1 and its interface appears as Example 5.2.

19. ARGUMENTS encapsulates facilities for accessing command-line arguments (see Section 4.3.3).

20. PLATFORM encapsulates platform-dependent properties such as the number of bits in an INTEGER or a REAL.

In addition, the six classes BOOLEAN_REF, CHARACTER_REF, INTEGER_REF, REAL_REF, DOUBLE_REF, and POINTER_REF are available as the reference classes corresponding to the six basic types.

4.3.3 Using I/O Classes: An Example

The classes ARGUMENTS, FILE, and STD_FILE can be used to build a new driver for the KWIC system described in Section 3.8 (Example 4.1). This new driver inherits from the class DRIVER of Example 3.44 and redefines the procedures *read_library* and *read_non_keywords* to deal, respectively, with a file of books given as the first argument on the command line, and a file of nonkeywords given as the second argument on the command line or the standard input if the second argument is "-". These procedures deal with abnormal cases in reading their input files through exceptions.

4.3 OVERVIEW OF THE EIFFEL STANDARD LIBRARY

```
indexing
    description: "exercise the KWIC problem on a small database"
class FILEDRIVER
inherit
    DRIVER
        redefine read_library, read_non_keywords
        end
    ARGUMENTS
creation
    make
feature
    read_library is
        -- read book descriptions from the file whose name is given
        -- as argument(1). The format of a book description is:
        -- title %T authors %T inventory_number
        -- (%T is the <TAB> character in Eiffel)
    local
        f : FILE
        title, authors : STRING
        inventory : INTEGER
        b : BOOK
        tab_position1, tab_position2 : INTEGER
        new_head : like library
    do
        from !!f.make_open_read(argument(1))
        until f.end_of_file
        loop
            f.readline       -- read a line from f and leave it in 'laststring'
            tab_position1 := f.laststring.index_of('%T',1)
                                             -- get position of the first %T
            title := f.laststring.substring(1,tab_position1−1)
                                             -- extract title
            tab_position2 := f.laststring.index_of('%T',tab_position1+1)
                                             -- get position of the second %T
            authors := f.laststring.substring(tab_position1+1,
                tab_position2−1)     -- extract authors
            inventory := f.laststring.substring(tab_position2+1,
                                   f.laststring.count).to_integer
            !!b.make(title,authors,inventory) -- make a new book
            !!new_head.make(b,library) -- add it to the library
            library := new_head
        end -- loop
    rescue
        io.error.putstring(argument(1))
```

Example 4.1 (Lines 1–44)

```
45                    io.error.putstring(": read error%N")
                      -- print error message on STDERR & propagate the exception
                 end -- read_library
              read_non_keywords is
                 -- read a list of nonkeywords from the file whose
50               -- name is given as argument(2). If the name is '-',
                 -- then read from STDIN
                 local
                    f : FILE                              -- source of data
                    word : STRING                         -- to store non_keywords
55                  new_head : like non_kw
                 do
                    if argument(2).is_equal("-") then -- read from STDIN
                       f := io.input
                    else -- read from file argument(2)
60                     !!f.make_open_read(argument(2))
                    end -- if
                    from
                    until f.end_of_file
                    loop
65                     f.readword -- read a word and leave it in f.laststring
                       word := clone(f.laststring) -- clone the last word read
                       !!new_head.make(word,non_kw) -- add it to the list
                       non_kw := new_head
                    end -- loop
70                  rescue
                       io.error.putstring(argument(2))
                       io.error.putstring(": read error%N")
                       -- print error message on STDERR & propagate the exception
                 end -- read_non_keywords
75            end -- FILEDRIVER
```

Example 4.1 (Lines 45–75)

4.4 Interfacing with Other Languages

4.4.1 Declaring External Routines

Eiffel promotes the construction of software systems through the assembly of reusable software components, so it has to be possible to interface new Eiffel software with existing pieces written in other languages. Also, if Eiffel is to be used within the context of embedded systems, the problem of interfacing with the low-level functions (usually written in assembly language or C) must be dealt with.

As seen in Section 2.5, the routine body of an effective routine may be *external*, that is, not implemented within an Eiffel class. To specify that a

Other effective routines are internal, that is, they begin with **do** *or* **once***; see page 39.*

```
     sync is
          -- forces pending output to be written out immediately to the disk
          external
               "C"
5    end
```
Example 4.2

routine has an external implementation, one must use the keyword **external** instead of **do** or **once**. This keyword must be followed by a manifest string (that is, a string between double quotes) indicating the language in which the routine is written (e.g., "C"). The declaration of Example 4.2 can be used to make the UNIX system call *sync* available to an Eiffel system.

The actual implementation language is not that important, as long as it follows calling conventions that are compatible with the language specified in the manifest constant.

It is possible to refer to an external routine through a name other than its original name. This renaming is useful for giving a routine a new Eiffel name to follow naming conventions (see Section 6.6.2), or simply because the foreign name contains uppercase letters, or otherwise does not match Eiffel syntax (e.g., leading underscore). In such a case you may use an alias, that is, a syntactic clause introduced with the keyword **alias** and followed with a manifest string containing the original (foreign) name of the routine (e.g., *getpid* in Example 4.3). The syntax of an external routine body is presented in Syntax Diagram 35.

```
     pid : INTEGER is
          -- the id of the process executing this program
          external
               "C"
5         alias
               "getpid"
          end
```
Example 4.3

External

──(external)──│ LanguageName │──────────────────────────────────
                                 └──(alias)──│ ManifestString │──

LanguageName

──│ ManifestString │──

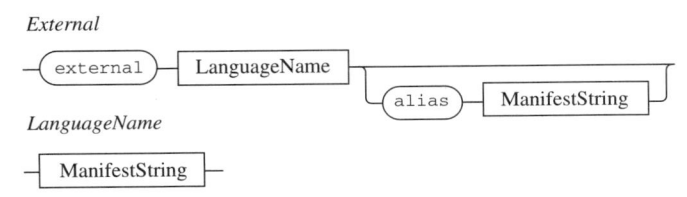

Syntax Diagram 35 External routine declaration syntax

4.4.2 Calling External Routines

Once they are given an Eiffel specification (a signature and possibly preconditions and postconditions), external routines may be called exactly like internal ones. The only caveat lies in the argument and result transmission: Their type must be common to Eiffel and the external language. Clearly, this depends on both the Eiffel implementation and the foreign language one.

If you are not concerned with this case (e.g., you use DOS or Windows 3.1), check with your compiler vendor.

In the simplest case where the foreign language is C on a 32-bit computer (which is the case for most UNIX systems, Windows95, or Windows NT), a given implementation of Eiffel might provide the following mappings:

Eiffel type	C type
INTEGER	int
REAL	float
DOUBLE	double
CHARACTER	char
POINTER	(void*)

The standard library classes STRING and ARRAY also provide (not yet standardized) features to facilitate the transmission of string and array parameters between Eiffel and C.

Consider for example the function *system* found in most UNIX, Windows, and DOS environments (see Example 4.4). It takes as its parameter a C string (a pointer to a memory zone ending with a NUL character), and gives it to the shell as input. In the TowerEiffel environment, a feature called *to_c* can be used to convert an Eiffel STRING to a C string. This feature is named *to_pointer* in the ISE environment. An Eiffel feature might then make use of features such as *pid* or *system* as shown in Example 4.5.

Routines that deal with reference type may be declared on the external side as expecting a pointer on anything (void* in C). As long as the foreign routine only stores or forwards the reference, no major problem will arise.

```
system (c_string:POINTER) is
    -- gives the c_string to the shell as input,
    -- just as if it had been typed as a command from a terminal
    external
        "C"
    end
```

Example 4.4

```
      foo is
          -- print the pid and list the
          -- directory
          local
5             command : STRING
          do
              io.putstring("This process number is: ")
              io.putint(pid); io.new_line
              command := "ls"
10            io.putstring("This directory contains:%N")
              system(command.to_pointer) -- to_c for TowerEiffel
      end -- foo
```

Example 4.5

To do anything more, the routine must access the internal structure of the object, using for instance the C Eiffel call-in library (CECIL) (provided with some Eiffel implementations) for the C language.

The CECIL library contains macros, functions, types, and error codes dealing with the view C programs have of Eiffel objects, and how to call (back) features on them. Their actual contents are not yet standardized by NICE, so you should check your vendor-specific documentation for more information.

4.4.3 The Address Operator

Eiffel provides an address operator $ with which you can obtain the address of features (both attributes and routines) from the enclosing class. This operator returns an object of type POINTER that is useful only for transmitting attribute or routine addresses to external software.

This mechanism can be used to implement callback to Eiffel routines from a user interface. The problem with this approach is that because the address of a feature is static by nature, you lose all the advantages of dynamic binding and jeopardize your program integrity.

4.4.4 Linking with External Software

Unless all of the external routines belong to the standard C library (*libc*), you must specify in your ACE file where to find their code.

With LACE, you may specify under an *external* clause the names of the object files (".o") and library files (".a") containing the external routines you need for the link:

```
external
  object: "filename.o $MYSOFT/mylib.a -ltermcap".
```

With PDL, you use two separate clauses for object files and library files:

```
link "filename.o"
lib  "$MYSOFT/mylib.a -ltermcap".
```

Most vendor environments allow their ACE files to drive one or several *makefiles* that could be needed to deal with the external file dependency management.

4.5 Garbage Collection

4.5.1 Definition

With many languages, programmers must explicitly reclaim heap memory at some point in the program by using a *free* or a *dispose* statement. Eiffel frees the programmer from this burden, by means of a garbage collector. The garbage collector's function [83] is to:

In practice, these two phases may be interleaved, because the reclamation technique is strongly dependent on the garbage detection one.

1. Find data objects that are no longer in use or distinguish the live objects from the garbage in some way (garbage detection).

2. Make their space available for reuse by the running program or reclaim the garbage objects' storage (garbage reclamation).

3. Optionally move objects in memory to enable memory compaction (i.e., defragmentation), thus improving the locality of reference.

An object is considered garbage and hence subject to reclamation if it is not reachable by the running program via any path of reference traversals. Live (that is, reachable) objects are preserved by the collector, ensuring that the program can never traverse a dangling reference into a deallocated object.

The set of live objects is thus the set of objects on any directed path of references from the root object, i.e. the instance of the root class created when the program starts. Any object that is not reachable from the root object is garbage (useless) because there is no legal sequence of program actions that would allow the program to reach that object. Garbage objects therefore can't affect the future course of the computation, and their space may be safely reclaimed.

A comprehensive overview of garbage collection is available in (139).

4.5.2 Interest for Software Correctness

Garbage collection is necessary for fully modular programming to avoid introducing unnecessary intermodule dependencies. If objects must be deallocated explicitly, some module must be responsible for knowing when other objects are no longer interested in a particular object. Thus, many modules must cooperate closely (liveness is a global property). This cooperation leads to a tight binding between supposedly independent modules, and introduces nonlocal bookkeeping into routines that might otherwise be locally understandable and flexibly composable. This bookkeeping inhibits abstraction and reduces extensibility, because when new functionality is implemented, the bookkeeping code must be updated.

The unnecessary complications and subtle interactions created by explicit storage allocation and deallocation are especially troublesome because programming mistakes often break the basic abstractions of the programming language, making errors hard to diagnose. Failing to reclaim memory at the proper point may lead to memory leaks; in other words, unreclaimed memory gradually accumulates until the program terminates or the swap space is exhausted. Reclaiming memory too soon can lead to very strange behavior, because an object's space may be reused to store completely different data while an old reference still exists.

These programming errors are particularly dangerous because they often fail to show up repeatably, making debugging very difficult (although products are available that can help). In the worst case, they don't show up at all until the program is stressed in an unusual way. For instance, if the allocator happens not to reuse a particular object's space, a dangling pointer may not cause a problem during the testing phase of the software. Later, perhaps long after delivery, the application may crash because of a special memory access pattern, or because of any other apparently undetermined reason. Similarly, some memory leaks (called slow leaks) may not be noticeable while a program is being used in normal ways—perhaps for many years—because the program terminates before too much extra space is used. If the code is incorporated into a long-running server program, however, the server will eventually exhaust the available memory and crash.

These problems lead many applications programmers to implement some form of application-specific garbage collection (e.g., reference counting) within a large software system. This obvious need for a reusable, bullet-proof garbage collection subsystem explains why garbage collection has to be part of any Eiffel implementation, and not left to the programmer.

4.5.3 The Cost of Garbage Collection

It was once widely believed that garbage collection was quite expensive relative to explicit heap management, but several studies [5, 151, 124] have shown that garbage collection is sometimes cheaper than explicit deallocation, and is usually competitive with it.

A well-implemented garbage collector should not slow running programs down by more than 10% (with respect to explicit heap deallocation).

Some programmers regard such a cost as unacceptable, but many others believe it to be a small price for the benefits in convenience, development time, and reliability. In the long run, poor program structures induced by manual garbage collection may incur extra development and maintenance costs, and may cause programmer time to be spent on maintaining inelegant code rather than optimizing time-critical parts of applications. Even for C and C++, several add-on packages exist to retrofit them with garbage collection [18].

Recent advances in garbage collection technology make automatic storage reclamation affordable for use in high-performance systems. Generational techniques reduce the basic costs and disruptiveness of collection by exploiting the empirically-observed tendency of objects to die young. Incremental techniques may even make garbage collection relatively attractive for real-time systems [47, 84, 123, 140].

Most Eiffel implementations come with such an incremental garbage collector, which can be activated and suspended at will.

4.5.4 Controlling the Garbage Collector

To control the garbage collector, you may inherit from (or use an instance of) the standard library class MEMORY (the interface of which is presented in Example 4.6), and call *collection_off* at the beginning of your application. Then, once in a while or each time you have some time to waste (e.g., during asynchronous I/O or in a reactive system main loop when no event is waiting to be processed), you may call the routine *collection_on* to ask for a partial garbage collection. The more frequently you call it, the less time it takes. An example of this process is presented in Chapter 6 and actual performance results are given in Section 7.4.1.

4.5.5 Finalization

Finalization is the ability to perform actions automatically when an object is reclaimed [65]. It is especially useful when an object manages an external resource such as a file or a network connection. For example, it may be important to close a file when the object dealing with it is reclaimed. Finalization thus can generalize the garbage collector so that other resources are managed in much the same way as heap memory and with similar program structure. This generalization makes it possible to write more general and reusable code,

```
indexing
    description: "Facilities for tuning the memory management system"
class interface MEMORY
feature
    full_collect
        -- Force an immediate garbage collection if garbage collection is
        -- enabled; otherwise do nothing.
    collection_off
        -- Disable the garbage collector.
    collection_on
        -- Enable the garbage collector.
    collecting : BOOLEAN
        -- Is garbage collecting enabled?
feature
    -- Finalization.
    dispose
        -- Called just before the garbage collector reclaims the object.
        -- This is only intended to enable cleaning of external resources.
        -- The object should not do remote calls on other objects since
        -- those may also be dead and have already been reclaimed.
        -- The current object is freed after the 'dispose' routine returns.
end -- MEMORY
```

Example 4.6

rather than having to treat certain kinds of objects very differently than normal objects.

An Eiffel class that requires finalization facilities can inherit from the standard library class MEMORY (see its interface in Example 4.6). It then may redefine the procedure *dispose* (which does nothing by default) to implement the finalization actions. However, because finalization occurs asynchronously (i.e., whenever the collector notices the object is unreachable and does something about it), the finalization code should be written with care. It should concentrate on cleaning external resources and should not do remote calls on other objects because those also may be dead and may have been reclaimed already.

5
Advanced Language Elements

In This Chapter
- 5.1 Exception Handling
- 5.2 Repeated Inheritance
- 5.3 Assignment Attempt
- 5.4 Other Issues of Typing
- 5.5 Parallelism

This chapter closes the Eiffel presentation with more advanced issues involving exception handling, repeated inheritance, typing problems, and parallelism. While the constructions and problems described in this chapter are not among the first things an Eiffel programmer needs to know, we present them here so as to complete our chapters on the language, thus giving you some awareness on the subject even if you just have an overview on it. Later on, you might find it useful to reread parts of this chapter when you need it.

5.1 Exception Handling

Until now, when something bad happened to an Eiffel program at run time, we just said that an exception was raised. In this section, we explain what happens next, and how the programmer can deal with such abnormal cases.

5.1.1 Causes of an Exception

We have already encountered some cases in which an exception might be raised:

- Assertion violation (see Section 2.5.3), which is only detected if the checking of the relevant assertion has been enabled by a compile-time or a runtime option.
- Illegal use of an object with a *Void* value. That is, calling a feature on a *Void* object or assigning it to an expanded object, either directly or through argument passing when calling a routine (Section 2.4.1).

The following events also raise an exception:

- Machine failure to carry out an operation (e.g., because no more memory is available or because of arithmetic overflow),
- Interruption or signal sent by the operating system,
- An exception raised by the software itself (see Section 5.1.4), or
- Failure of a called routine. If you call a routine that fails (does not repair the exceptional situation by itself), the exception is propagated to the calling routine.

Exceptions that originate in programming bugs (assertion violations or misuse of void values) are processed in the same way as "environment" exceptions (no more memory or interruptions). A limited tolerance of software faults (see Section 6.5.1) is thus allowed.

5.1.2 Default Handling of Exceptions

As outlined in Section 2.5.5, when an exception is raised in a routine, its rescue clause is invoked. If the routine does not have an explicit rescue clause, a default one is used instead. The action of this default rescue clause is to call the procedure *default_rescue*, which does nothing. This procedure is defined in the class GENERAL and thus is inherited by all classes. The interesting thing about this scheme is that the default rescue behavior can be changed on a per class basis if this routine is redefined (see Section 3.4.2).

When the failure that raised the exception has not been repaired (see Section 5.1.3), the routine is said to have failed. It then triggers the exception "routine failure" in the calling routine, and so on until the root creation procedure is reached. There, the system execution fails, and an exception history table is printed.

Imagine that you have deleted (by mistake) the 21st line (i := i+1) in the *quicksort_range routine*, thus jeopardizing the loop variant (Example 2.23). Even if by some miracle this error survived the initial debugging phases, when this algorithm is used in conjunction with a more complex system such as the KWIC problem of Section 3.8, you get the following type of error message:

```
Unhandled exception: Routine failure. Exiting program.
Exception history:
===============================================================================
Object                          Routine
Type of exception               Description                               Line
===============================================================================
#<SORTABLE_ARRAY[KWIC_ENTRY] 5f0c0> SORTABLE_ARRAY [COMPARABLE]:quicksort_range
Loop variant violated           ends_converging                             63
-------------------------------------------------------------------------------
#<SORTABLE_ARRAY[KWIC_ENTRY] 5f0c0> SORTABLE_ARRAY [COMPARABLE]:quicksort_range
Routine failure                                                             90
-------------------------------------------------------------------------------
#<SORTABLE_ARRAY[KWIC_ENTRY] 5f0c0> SORTABLE_ARRAY [COMPARABLE]:quicksort_range
Routine failure                                                             46
-------------------------------------------------------------------------------
#<KWIC 62000>                   KWIC:make
Routine failure                                                             19
-------------------------------------------------------------------------------
#<DRIVER 5f010>                 DRIVER:make
Routine failure                                                             18
-------------------------------------------------------------------------------
```

This approach is very useful, because the primary source of the error is immediately visible. Even if the application programmer does not bother to write his or her preconditions and postconditions properly, he or she still benefits from the library assertions (if compiled with the relevant option). Most notably, if the primary source of the exception is a precondition violation, the programmer can know immediately from the exception history table where and why he or she misused some library routine (that is, did not respect the associated contract). If the primary source of the exception is a postcondition violation, however, the errors lie in the library, and a bug report can be easily prepared from the information displayed. This clear separation and identification of responsibilities is invaluable when software is in its validation phase.

5.1.3 Trying to Repair Failures

Displaying the why and where of exceptions is always useful, but sometimes you cannot afford to see your program aborted because the triggered exception is benign (think of receiving operating system signals such as SIGALARM or SIGURG), or because you know how to circumvent it, or even because your software is of an embedded nature and aborting it is out of the question. In the latter case, the most straightforward solution is often to reset and restart the failing (sub)system. This effect can be obtained in a rescue clause with the **retry** instruction (the syntax of the *rescue* clause is presented in Syntax Diagram 36). The effect of a **retry** is to execute again the body of the routine. The routine then escapes failure.

*The **retry** keyword is allowed in a rescue clause only.*

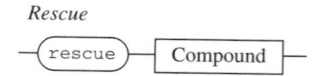

Rescue

──(rescue)──[Compound]──

Syntax Diagram 36 The syntax of the *rescue* clause

You need to be careful with this approach, however, because if the exception is raised again for the same reason, you might end in an infinite loop of restarting and exception handling. To avoid that, you can put a condition on whether or not you will try to execute your routine again. For example, you may want to try to send a network message at most n times before declaring yourself to have failed, as in Example 5.1.

If the rescue block is executed to the end without executing a **retry** (after n attempts in Example 5.1), the processing of the current exception terminates

```
   try_to_send (m:MESSAGE) is
     local
        attempts:INTEGER
     do
5       network_send(m)
     rescue
        attempts:=attempts+1
        if attempts<n then
           retry
10      end
        print ("failing to send message")
     end -- try_to_send
```

Example 5.1

and the routine *fails*; that is, the *routine failure* exception is propagated to the calling routine. Example 5.1 could be easily modified to try alternate methods if the first one used did not work, or to set a Boolean attribute to signal its inability to carry out the operation instead of failing. In rescuing from exceptions, take care to leave the current object in a consistent state (satisfying the invariant) before admitting failure, or to reestablish the routine precondition if the retry approach has been chosen.

5.1.4 User-Defined Exceptions

The kernel library class EXCEPTIONS allows the developer to raise an exception on purpose with the routine *raise (name)*. The name is a STRING describing the nature of the exception. Conversely, the name of the last developer-raised exception may be consulted through the feature *developer_exception_name* returning a STRING. Example 5.2 presents the interface of the class EXCEPTIONS as you could find it in an Eiffel kernel library.

```
    indexing
        description: "Facilities for controlling exception handling";
    class EXCEPTIONS
    feature
5       developer_exception_name : STRING
            -- Name of last developer-raised exception
        raise (name: STRING)
            -- Raise a developer exception of name 'name'
        die (code: INTEGER)
10          -- Terminate execution with exit status 'code'
        assertion_violation : BOOLEAN
            -- Was last exception due to a violated assertion
            -- or nondecreasing variant?
        exception : INTEGER
15          -- Code of last exception that occurred
        is_developer_exception : BOOLEAN
            -- Is the last exception originally due
            -- to a developer-defined exception?
        is_signal : BOOLEAN
20          -- Is the last exception due to an external event
            -- (operating system signal)?
    end -- EXCEPTIONS
```

Example 5.2

5.2 Repeated Inheritance

5.2.1 Definition

Because of multiple inheritance, it is possible for a class to be descendant of another one in more than one way; that is, *repeatedly* (see Figure 5.1). In both cases of Example 5.1, class D obtains the feature f of class A along two different paths. Whether D is getting one or two versions of f depends on how f is adapted along the various inheritance paths. If the original feature f is inherited under the same name along a number of inheritance paths, then f yields a single feature of D (sharing mechanism). On the other hand, any renaming of f would yield a supplementary feature of D (replication mechanism).

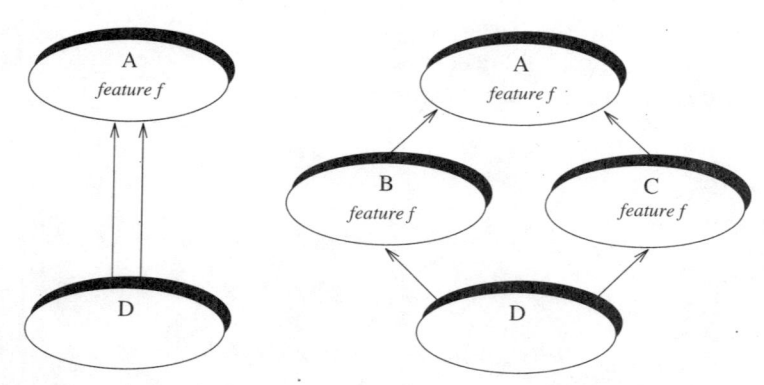

This principle also applies to attributes.

Figure 5.1 Two common cases of repeated inheritance

5.2.2 Conditions for Sharing

Many features inherited through multiple inheritance may be shared only if they have the same origin in an ancestor class A and if none of them is adapted (i.e., redefined, renamed, effected, or otherwise undefined) along the paths ranging from A to the considered class. This is as if the feature were directly inherited from A. This sharing mechanism is related to the merging of deferred features under multiple inheritance (see Section 3.6.3), only it doesn't require the shared features to be deferred.

If a class repeatedly inherits from an ancestor A and if no particular adaptation action is taken on the various inheritance paths, then each feature of A will yield just one feature, which is the intuitive expected behavior. This default-sharing behavior also explains why there is no problem in the fact that every Eiffel class implicitly inherits from the class ANY: Every explicit inheritance is also a case of repeated inheritance of the class ANY, which, unless special care is taken, is a case of sharing features.

5.2.3 Replication and Selection

To get two (or more) versions of a repeatedly inherited feature, it suffices to inherit them under different names.

Conversely, if sharing is not possible (e.g., due to redefinition) or not wanted, the situation is the same as for name clashes in the context of multiple inheritance. Hence, the solutions are the same:

- Merging of features (if they have the same signatures) through undefinition of all of them but one (see Section 3.6.3), and
- Renaming of the conflicting features, which yields replication in the context of repeated inheritance.

A new problem appears when the latter approach is used along with dynamic binding. Consider the second inheritance graph displayed in Figure 5.1 and the feature call x.f in Example 5.3.

Whether x.f refers to the version of *f* redefined in B or in C could have been ambiguous. In that case, Eiffel requires that the ambiguity be removed through a *select* subclause in the feature adaptation clause of D (see Syntax Diagram 37). The effect of this *select* subclause is to specify which

The syntax of the feature adaptation clause itself appeared in Syntax Diagram 27.

```
    local x : A
    do
       !D!x.make -- x has the dynamic type D
       x.f       -- which f is called?
5   end
```

Example 5.3

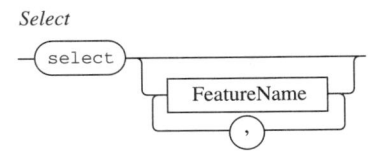

Syntax Diagram 37 The syntax of the *select* clause

```
        class D
        inherit
           B
              select
 5                f
              end
           C
              rename -- if C.f is different from B.f (redefinition)
                     -- one of them has to be renamed.
10                   -- It could have been the B's version as well.
                 f as c_version_of_f
              end
        end -- D
```
Example 5.4

version of the original feature is to be called in case of dynamic binding. In Example 5.4, the x.f instruction of Example 5.3 would call the version of *f* redefined in B.

5.2.4 Keeping the Original Version of a Redefined Feature

This characteristic is particularly true of creation routines.

Sometimes a routine is just slightly redefined, such as adding to the original only a few lines of code at the beginning, at the end, or both. While in Smalltalk you can use the *Super* object, or in C++ the PARENT::*foo()* notation, in Eiffel all the information dealing with the relations between a class and its ancestors is located within the *inheritance* clauses. This approach enforces a loose coupling between the inheritance hierarchy and the feature codes. In this way, it is much easier to modify an inheritance hierarchy because there is no need to check all the class features for calls on ancestor classes.

The Eiffel approach to isolate the code from any inheritance information has, however, a small drawback: Once a routine is redefined, the original version is lost. The only way out is to get two features from the original routine: one that is to be redefined and the other to be kept as the original version.

If you are responsible for the design of the parent class, you may anticipate such a need. You may provide multiple versions of the same routine body, with some versions frozen (not redefinable) as in Example 5.5.

Otherwise, you have to use repeated inheritance to get two versions of *foo*, and redefine one of them (see Example 5.6).

```
    class PARENT
    feature foo, frozen parent_foo is
        do
            ...
5       end
    end -- class PARENT
    ---------------------------------
    class CHILD
    inherit
10      PARENT
            redefine foo
        end
    feature foo is
        do
15          parent_foo
            ...
        end
    end -- class CHILD
```

Example 5.5

```
    class PARENT
    feature foo is
        do
            ...
5       end
    end -- class PARENT
    ---------------------------------
    class CHILD
    inherit
10      PARENT
            rename foo as parent_foo
                export {NONE} all -- to ensure that none of the new features
                    -- created by renaming is exported to the clients of CHILD
        end
15      PARENT
            redefine foo
            select foo -- in case of dynamic binding
        end
    feature
20      foo is
            do
                parent_foo
                ...
            end
25  end -- class CHILD
```

Example 5.6

5.3 Assignment Attempt

An assignment attempt is an operation of the form:

```
x ?= y
```

with *x* declared of (nonexpanded) type A and *y* of type B.

The purpose of this instruction is to deal with cases in which the assignment might be semantically legal (because the dynamic type of *y* conforms to A), but the normal assignment x := y may not be legal (for example, if B is not a subclass of A).

The assignment attempt thus looks at the dynamic type of *y*, performs the assignment if that type is compatible with that of *x*, and otherwise assigns to *x* a *Void* value. The value of *x* then can be tested against *Void* to determine whether the assignment succeeded (see Example 5.7).

```
      attempt (x : A; y : B) is
          do
              x ?= y
              if x = Void then
5                 -- assignment attempt did not succeed:
                  -- y is not conforming to the type of x
              else
                  -- assignment attempt succeeded:
                  -- we have now: x = y
10            end
      end -- attempt
```
Example 5.7

The assignment attempt feature is particularly useful when you "just know" (e.g., because of the program structure) that the object denoted by *y* is "of the right type," even if the static declaration of *y* is more general than that of *x*. This may be the case, for example, if *y* denotes an object retrieved from a file, a database, or a network connection.

The assignment attempt also may be used to implement a limited emulation of multiple dispatch. Related to the single dispatch available in Eiffel through dynamic binding, the multiple dispatch is the mechanism by which the choice of the most relevant feature to call does not depend on the receiver only, but also on the parameters of a feature (see Section 9.5.2).

5.4 Other Issues of Typing

Type checking a program ensures that the only operations that may be applied to an object are those that are defined for its type. If every entity x declared of a certain type A has to stick to this type, then type checking a program would consist of checking that for any call of the form $x.f$, the feature f is an exported feature of the class A.

What makes the object-oriented typing problem nontrivial is the presence of polymorphic aliasing, which at run time allows x to denote an object of type B, possibly different from A and statically unpredictable (because of the expressive power of the Turing machine; see Section 1.1.2).

The typing problem is then that the same object is accessible through names of two different types, which may have different rules with respect to which features are exported (see Section 3.4.3 on changing the export status of an inherited feature) and which feature arguments are permissible (see the covariance policy for redefinitions that is described in Section 3.4.2).

5.4.1 Changing Export Rules

The information hiding mechanism is orthogonal to the inheritance mechanism, so a feature hidden (or exported) by a class may be exported (or hidden) by any of its proper descendants (see Section 3.4.3). Consider a class BIRD exporting a feature *fly* to a class WRONG_USER. Assume that a BIRD's subclass OSTRICH decides to hide *fly* to WRONG_USER, and consider the class WRONG_USER presented in Example 5.8. The designer of the class OSTRICH has expressly removed *fly* from the list of operations applicable to such objects, so the last call *b.fly* in Example 5.8 should not be allowed.

```
     class WRONG_USER
     feature
         b : BIRD; Jane : OSTRICH
       wrong is
5        do
             !!b.make; !!Jane.make
             b.fly      -- legal because a BIRD can fly
             b := Jane  -- b now holds an OSTRICH
             b.fly      -- illegal statement because an OSTRICH can't fly
10       end
     end -- WRONG_USER
```

Example 5.8

5.4.2 Covariance Policy

The controversy concerning the use of either covariance or contravariance can be described as follows. In the record-based model proposed by Cardelli [27], an object is modeled by a record value, with fields that contain all the features of the object and with labels that correspond to messages that invoke the features. An object can be specialized to a different object in two different ways: either by adding new features or by redefining the existing ones.

The meaning of the subtyping relation is that a specialized object may be used wherever the object it specializes can be used. Thus, feature redefinition must be restricted if type safety is required. Consider the class PARENT (Example 5.9) and its subclass CHILD (Example 5.10). Here the problem comes down to defining which restrictions must be placed on the type of argument to *eat*, that is, 'FOOD' and 'CHILD_FOOD'. There are three possibilities:

no-variant rule: CHILD_FOOD must be equal to FOOD. There is no problem here.

This is the approach chosen in C++.

contravariant rule: CHILD_FOOD must be a superclass (ancestor) of FOOD. In the child class the types of arguments in redefined routines must be superclasses of types in the parent routine. The inheritance varies in the opposite direction, hence the name *contravariant*.

```
    class PARENT
    feature
        eat (arg: FOOD) is
            do -- some processing
5           end
    end -- PARENT
```
Example 5.9

```
    class CHILD
    inherit
        PARENT
            redefine eat end
5   feature
        eat (arg: CHILD_FOOD) is
            do
                arg.mill -- some new processing,
                         -- only available for CHILD_FOOD
10          end
    end -- CHILD
```
Example 5.10

covariant rule: CHILD_FOOD must be a subclass of FOOD. In the child class the types of arguments in redefined routines must be children of types in the parent routine. The inheritance varies in the same direction, hence the name *covariant*. In modeling real-world problems, it is often necessary to specialize related classes jointly. Consider the well-known example of HERBIVORES eating PLANTS. A COW is an HERBIVORE. GRASS is a PLANT. A COW eats GRASS but not other PLANTS, so the feature *eat* should be redefined covariantly in the class COW to accept a GRASS argument only.

This is the Eiffel approach. See Section 3.4.2.

At first, the contravariant rule seems theoretically appealing. Recall that polymorphism means that an entity can hold not only objects of its declared type, but also of any descendant (child) type. Dynamic binding means that a feature call on an entity will trigger the corresponding feature call for the *actual* type of the object, which may be a descendant of the declared type of the entity. With contravariance, we can assign an object of descendant type to an entity, and all feature calls will still work because the descendant can cope with feature arguments at least as general as those of the ancestor. In fact, the descendant object is in every way also a fully valid instance of the ancestor object: We are using inheritance to implement *true functional subtyping*.

If covariant typing is chosen without other considerations, however, then substitutability of an object by a specialized version is lost. Taking back the class definitions of Examples 5.9 and 5.10, assume now that the routine *eat* redefined covariantly in the class CHILD performs some new operation involving the calling of a routine *mill* on its argument **arg**, which is declared of type CHILD_FOOD. Assume also that *mill* is defined in CHILD_FOOD, but not in FOOD. Then the code presented in Example 5.11 is not valid.

```
    class BROKEN
    feature
        p : PARENT; c : CHILD
        x : FOOD;
5       wrong is
        do
            !!c.make; !!p.make; !!x.make;
            p.eat(x)    -- legal: the PARENT's version of eat is called
            p := c      -- p now holds a CHILD object
10          p.eat(x)    -- the CHILD's version of eat is called, which
                        -- tries to call the nonexistent feature x.mill
        end
    end -- BROKEN
```

Example 5.11

Contravariance thus would seem to be the "right" rule. However, besides being less natural (in the sense of real-world modeling) than the covariant one, it is indeed the source of many problems. The most surprising one appears with binary features such as comparisons. Consider again the class PARENT and its subclass CHILD. Imagine that for these classes we have defined a feature *equal*, which compares the current object with another object of the same type. Thus, *equal* has the functional type $(PARENT \times PARENT) \rightarrow Boolean$ in PARENT, but $(CHILD \times CHILD) \rightarrow Boolean$ in CHILD. If the contravariant rule is used, the type associated with *equal* for CHILD instances is not a subtype of *equal* for PARENT instances. As soon as this kind of feature is considered (and they are common), the contravariant rule prevents a subtyping relation between CHILD and PARENT. This problem would be quite unfortunate.

5.4.3 System-Level Validity

Experience with Eiffel (and other covariantly typed object-oriented languages such as O_2 [8]) shows that the difference between subclassing and true functional subtyping does not cause much problem in practice, because when you design a subclass that is not a true functional subtype of its superclass, you usually have a good reason to do so. If you have an OSTRICH class inheriting from a BIRD class (and changing the export clause related to *flying*), you would not write a routine to launch all birds from a cliff—an ostrich could be among them.

Thus a friendly language should not prevent you from building inheritance structures in which true functional subtyping is not respected, because unexpected special cases and exceptions always occur in the real world, even when you try to design inheritance structures that are as complete and regular as possible. Eiffel is committed to the building of better quality software, so it must ensure that the programmer is only performing type-safe manipulations. The *system-level validity* rule allows Eiffel systems to be fully type-safe, still modeling the problem domains in a natural way, where subclassing does not always conform to true functional subtyping.

Basically the *system-level validity* rule says that when a CHILD class inherits from a PARENT class, but is not a true functional subtype of PARENT because a certain feature *f* has a restricted export set or has been covariantly redefined, a CHILD object *c* can only be assigned to a PARENT entity *p* (either directly p := c or through parameter passing) *provided there is no risk that f is called on such a* p. This rule forbids such polymorphic assignment when the routine *f* might be called on a *p* entity anywhere in the same system (i.e., the set of classes making a given program). Thus, a class such as the BROKEN class presented in Example 5.11 would be rejected by the compiler. See [101] for a more formal description of the *system-level validity* rule.

5.5 Parallelism

5.5.1 Parallelism and Object-Oriented Languages

> To judge by the looks of the two parties, the marriage between concurrent computation and object-oriented programming appears an easy enough affair to arrange. This appearance is deceptive: The problem is a hard one. (B. Meyer)

Parallelism is often introduced in an object-oriented language through the idea that objects can be made active. Objects become concurrent activities communicating by sending messages: The object-oriented–message passing paradigm is mapped onto the communication structure of a parallel system. Object creation is assimilated to process creation. Such a notion of parallelism is implemented in POOL-T [2], where an object may have a "body," which is a local process that can execute in parallel with the bodies of all other POOL-T objects. Communications between objects are based on the remote procedure call (RPC) paradigm, and the POOL-T user has to control explicitly the concurrency structure.

Another way to introduce parallelism is by means of asynchronous operation calls. An object calling a feature of another object may continue its activities in parallel with the object executing the called operation. This is implemented in ABCL/1 [149], ELLIE [3], and ConcurrentSmalltalk [147].

Both ideas of active object and asynchronous operation calls are used to make an object-oriented language parallel either by integrating this parallelism directly into the design of a new concurrent programming language, or by extending existing sequential languages to handle parallelism (compiler directives or macros). The former approach leads to clear and unified support of conceptual models. ELLIE, PRESTO [12], POOL-T, and ABCL/1 are object-oriented languages in which a considerable number of structures are devoted to parallelism. Using the latter approach, we can find distributed extensions to Smalltalk [10] or to C++ [31] or the various common object request broker architecture (CORBA [111]) bindings existing for most sequential object-oriented and object-based languages (including Eiffel in the near future). This simple parallelism model does not meld well with inheritance, however, because synchronization constraints are hard to inherit in a context in which subtype substitutability is to be preserved. This problem is known as the *inheritance anomaly* [93] and is not easy to circumvent [98].

CORBA provides the mechanisms by which objects transparently make requests and receive responses.

Eiffel does not have an accepted standard and integrated way of dealing with concurrency issues. Instead, various proposals have been made, altering more or less the semantics of the language. These approaches are presented in the following sections by decreasing order of semantics difference with the sequential version of Eiffel.

5.5.2 The Eiffel // Approach

The Model of Concurrency

Caromel's model of concurrency [29] relies on a small set of basic concepts, which are often continuations of those existing in sequential programming. This model has been implemented as an extension of Eiffel and is named Eiffel //. The unification of module and type aspects into one construct (the class) is extended to encompass the notion of process. A *process structure* is a special class called PROCESS, and a *process* is an object instance of a class inheriting directly or indirectly from PROCESS (see Example 5.12). Any other object is a passive entity waiting for a call to execute its routines.

After creation and initialization, a *process object* executes its *live* routine. This routine describes the process *script* or *body*, the sequence of actions it executes over its life. When the *live* routine terminates, the process also *terminates*. The inheritance mechanism gives to any process the default behavior defined in the routine *live*. Requests to the process entry points are treated in a first in, first out (FIFO) order, one at a time. Redefinition may be used to override this default policy (see Section 3.4.2).

No Sharing of Objects

If two processes refer to the same object, routine calls to this object may overlap. This classic occurrence of shared data between processes must be solved through some kind of synchronization.

```
     indexing
         description: "Each heir of this class has process object instances"
     class PROCESS
     feature {NONE}
5        live is
             -- Process body (script)
             do
                 -- serve requests with a default FIFO policy
             end
10   end -- PROCESS
```

Example 5.12

In Eiffel //, each nonprocess object is a private object accessible by only *one* process. Only one thread of control has access to it: the process that directly or indirectly refers to it. A nonprocess may only belong to exactly one process context. Only processes may be shared; thus, if an object must be shared by several processes, the designer has to design it as a process.

This model ensures the absence of sharing. An object *argument* of communication between two process contexts is passed not by reference but by *copy* (deep copy of the object). A parameter of a communication can also be a process. In this case, parameter transmission is achieved by reference; this does not create shared objects, and it provides for dynamic process topology.

Communications

When an object owns a reference to a process, it can communicate with that process, or call one of its exported features. What is usually called a *process entry point* is unified with the basic concept of a feature. An instruction $o.f$ either reflects a classic feature call on the object o or an interprocess communication if o is a process. Moreover, the presence of polymorphism makes it possible to refer dynamically to a process while o is statically declared as a regular object. This possibility brings real benefits regarding reusability and design methodology for concurrent systems.

The semantics of the communication are based on the synchronous transmission of the feature parameter between the calling object and the called process. When an object o executing a statement *p.f(parameters)*, and p is dynamically a process, the following operations are triggered:

1. A specific exception *request* is raised in the context of p.
2. p is interrupted.
3. A handshake between p and o is established and an object of type REQUEST is sent from o to p, where it is stored in a list of *pending requests*.
4. p resumes its previous activity, and o executes its next statement.

The object transmitted (of type REQUEST) models the call to p, i.e., it describes the actual parameters of the call.

Processing Requests

Once the request is in the process context, it is processed by the *live* routine. The default FIFO policy of the live routine may be changed through redefinition when inheriting from PROCESS. When the process decides to serve a request it just selects one among the list, in mutual exclusion with potential other requests. Many basic routines—to retrieve information and to select and serve pending requests—are defined in the class PROCESS, and can be used readily when redefining the *live* routine.

Everything is under the programmer's control. If the programmer does not find the required selection, he or she just programs it. Although the model promoted is highly asynchronous, it may be *resynchronized* by limiting the number of pending requests in a process.

Synchronization

Between the request transmission and its processing, the caller does not wait but keeps executing; this is the *asynchronous* part of the request. A *built-in* synchronization mechanism called the *wait-by-necessity* principle is used. A process is synchronized—i.e., it waits—only when it attempts to use an *awaited object* or the result of a feature call that has not been returned yet.

The *reference* to an awaited object may be used freely. No wait is triggered by assigning it to another variable, or passing it as a parameter. A wait occurs only when one needs to access an *awaited object* itself, syntactically a dot notation or a transmission (a copy) to another process.

This principle can be related to the *future* concept found in several languages: Act 1 [89] and the primitive *Hurry*; Concurrent Smalltalk [148] with the *CBox* objects; and ABCL/1 [149] with the *future type message passing*. However, the important difference is that the Eiffel // mechanism is systematic and *automatic*, reflected by the absence of any special syntactical construction.

The only synchronization is a *data-driven* synchronization. There are no explicit synchronization dependencies among classes, so they remain *self-contained* modules.

5.5.3 The Parallel Eiffel Approach

Separate Objects

In Meyer's model of concurrent object-oriented programming [102], different objects may be "handled by" different processors. These processors are threads of control; they do not need to be different physical processors, but may be UNIX processes or even threads. Thus, the model applies to true parallelism (shared memory parallel computers and distributed memory parallel computers) as well as to quasi parallelism (coroutines). In particular, identical software may run as the "real system" in a truly parallel environment, and as a simulation of that system on a sequential processor.

The declaration:

```
x : separate A   -- A must be neither deferred nor expanded
```

states that objects corresponding to *x* will be handled by a different processor. The keyword **separate** is the only new keyword distinguishing parallel Eiffel from sequential Eiffel. A major consequence of this design decision is that there is no distinction between "active" and "passive" objects. There is no need for a built-in notion of "process." The equivalent notion is a separate object having only one exported routine (call it *live* if you want).

Asynchronous Feature Calls

Parallelism is obtained through asynchronous operation calls. Resynchronization after a parallel call is automatically made when it is needed. This is the same mechanism (*Lazy wait*, or *wait-by-necessity*) as in Eiffel // (presented in the previous section).

Semantics of Assertions

Because the "contract model" does not hold in the same way for a call handled by a different processor, preconditions must have different semantics. They serve as the basic synchronization mechanism. For a client object, failing to meet the routine precondition of a separate server object means that the conditions are not ripe yet for the routine body to execute. For example, if the server is a bounded buffer object, the impossibility of adding an item to the buffer may be temporary only. The call in this case would just block the client from progressing, releasing the server's processor for handling other requests that fortunately may produce effects that will make the precondition true.

Obvious consistency reasons (cf. class invariants) imply that calls must be mutually exclusive on a given object. A client may attempt to interrupt a competitor's call, however, raising an exception in the competitor or in the interrupter (depending on whether the interruption is successful).

Reserving Objects

Considering preconditions as wait conditions does not provide enough control if a client needs to reserve an object for a sequence of operations (because it could be interrupted between two calls by a competing client). The idea is thus to protect (i.e., hold on) a separate server for the full duration of a routine *r*: no feature call *f* on a separate object *server* is allowed unless *server* is a formal argument of the enclosing routine *r*. Conversely, if *server* is a separate

```
indexing
    description: "Encapsulation of access to bounded buffers"
class BUFFER_ACCESS [T]
feature
    put(q: separate BOUNDED_BUFFER [T]; x: T) is
            -- Insert x into q, waiting until q is not full
        require
            not_full: not q.full
        do
            q.put(x)
        ensure
            not_empty: not q.empty
        end -- put
    remove(q: separate BOUNDED_BUFFER [T]) is
            -- Remove an element from q, waiting until q is not empty
        require
            not_empty: not q.empty
        do
            q.remove
        ensure
            not_full: not q.full
        end -- remove
    item(q: separate BOUNDED_BUFFER [T]): T is
            -- The oldest element from q, waiting until q is not empty
        require
            not_empty: not q.empty
        do
            Result := q.item
        end -- item
end -- BUFFER_ACCESS [T]
```

Example 5.13

argument to the routine r, then the call to r would block until *server* becomes available.

A direct call to a separate object feature is not allowed, so all such calls are meant to be encapsulated in *access* classes (such as the BUFFER_ACCESS of Example 5.13). These access classes are synchronization agents that can reserve a set of separate objects for the benefit of a client operation.

This mechanism is powerful enough to foster simple, concise, and elegant solutions for classic concurrency problems (such as the *dining philosophers*). However, its implementation in distributed systems is costly.

5.5.4 The Parallelism Encapsulation Approach

The previous models of parallelism are based on a multiple instruction, multiple data (MIMD) programming model, which seems to match some kinds of

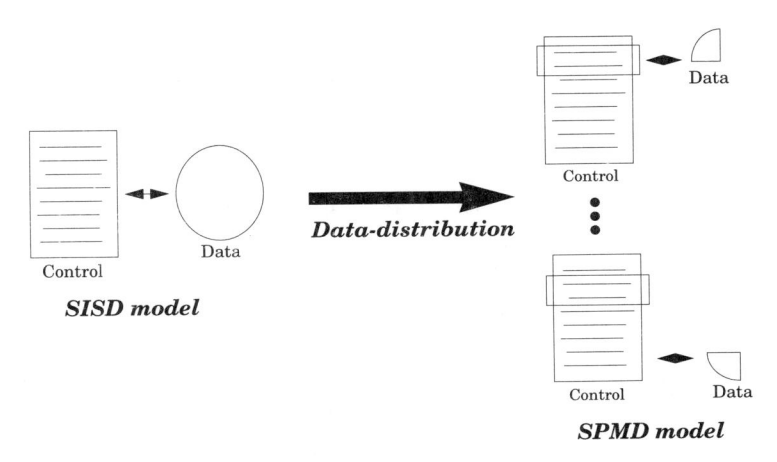

Figure 5.2 Principle of data distribution in SPMD mode

problems (such as operating systems and industrial process control) rather well. This model of parallelism is typically dedicated to handling functional parallelism: A given function is divided into some subfunctions that can be processed by new computational threads.

One of the most difficult obstacles to be worked around with this approach is to ensure that problems that are well-known in the protocol engineering community—such as deadlocks, livelocks, unspecified receptions, and so on— are properly dealt with. Because the cooperation between processes is explicitly coded, it is usually difficult to manage the overall communication structure. The reuse of software components could help to manage the complexity of concurrent programming. For example, synchronization constraints can be encapsulated in classes and reused (and customized) through inheritance [28, 35].

However, the definition of the concurrent processes is still determined by the subtask decomposition, which is application dependent and requires strong involvement from the user. Furthermore, the resulting processes are of heterogeneous nature, leading to difficult load balancing and scalability problems in the context of high-performance distributed computer systems. Also, the dynamic creation of processes necessitates the use of general and costly mechanisms such as object naming servers and object migration.

To override these drawbacks, a different model of parallelism may be used [78]. It is based on Valiant's block synchronous parallel (BSP) model [131], associated with a single program multiple data (SPMD) mode of execution (see Figure 5.2).

This model keeps the conceptual simplicity of the sequential instruction flow, while exploiting the fact that most of the problems running on high-performance parallel computers are data oriented and involve large amounts of data in order to generate scalable parallelism. A computation can be parallelized efficiently only if the cost of synchronization, communications, and other processing paid for managing parallelism is compensated for by the performance improvement brought by the parallelization. A satisfactory increase in speed will be obtained only if the size of the data structure is large enough, and this increase in speed will increase with the ratio of computation time to communication time.

A computation that fits the BSP model can be seen as a succession of parallel phases separated by synchronizations and sequential phases. Each process executes the same program, corresponding to the initial user-defined sequential program. However, when data parallelism is involved, only a subset of the data is used on a given processor: its own data partition. When control parallelism is involved, though, each processor runs a subset of the original execution flow (typically some parts of the iterations). In any case, the application programmer still views his or her program as a sequential one and the parallelism is derived from the data representation. The object-oriented message passing paradigm is no longer mapped onto actual interprocess communications.

These ideas have been implemented in an Eiffel parallel execution environment (EPEE) [78]. Data and control parallelism are totally encapsulated in regular Eiffel classes [63], without any extension to the language nor modification of its semantics. EPEE really is a library approach to parallelism. It may be seen as a kind of toolbox. It contains a set of classes providing the communication and location facilities used to build parallel classes. Common data distribution patterns and computation schemes are factored out and encapsulated in abstract parallel classes, which are to be reused by means of multiple inheritance. Reusable parallel components include parameterized general-purpose algorithms for traversing and performing actions on generic data structures.

Most current Eiffel compilers (e.g., ISE, Tower, SiG, Eon) rely on the C (or C++) language to produce intermediate code. Consequently, compiling Eiffel code for a parallel machine is not really an issue, because all parallel platforms provide at least a C compiler in their software environment. The EPEE toolbox includes cross-compilation tools that consist mainly of script files that deal with compiler flags and options correctly. Thus, any application designed with EPEE can be compiled for any target processor (as long as an Eiffel runtime system exists for this processor). EPEE also includes a highly portable communication library called parallel observable machine (POM), which provides sophisticated facilities for tracing a distributed execution [61]. This library is available for several platforms (e.g., Intel iPSC/2, Paragon XP/S, and networks of UNIX workstations) using various communication kernels or operating systems (e.g., BSD sockets, NX or SunMos primitives, or both). It greatly facilitates the porting of communicating applications across widely different architectures.

There are two levels of programming with EPEE: the class user (or *client*) level and the parallelized class designer level. The aim is that at the client level, nothing but performance improvements appear when running an application program on a parallel computer. Moreover, these performance improvements should be proportional to the number of processors of the parallel computer (linear speedup), which would guarantee scalability. A user of a library designed with EPEE must be able to handle distributed or shared objects just like sequential ones.

The problem is thus for the designer of the library to implement distributed objects using the general data distribution or parallelization rules, or both. While implementing these objects, the designer must ensure their portability and efficiency, and preserve a "sequential-like" interface for the sake of the user from whom distribution and parallelization issues must be masked.

Consequently, whenever an object already has a sequential implementation, its distributed counterpart must have exactly the same behavior. Each parallelized feature should leave a distributed object in the same abstract state as the corresponding sequential one. The goal is to ensure the transparency for the user (the application programmer), to preserve the global semantics of the aggregate (and most especially the semantics of its access), and to preserve its interface.

An application of this approach to a linear algebra library example is presented in Chapter 9.

Part III

Building Software Systems with Eiffel

6
From Analysis to Implementation

In This Chapter

- 6.1 Object-Oriented Methodology
- 6.2 Case Study: An SMDS Server
- 6.3 SMDS: Object-Oriented Analysis
- 6.4 Eiffel and Object-Oriented Design
- 6.5 SMDS: Object-Oriented Design
- 6.6 Implementation

An object-oriented software engineering process may make the best use of Eiffel. This chapter does not aim to provide a comprehensive guide to object-oriented software engineering—a full book would not be enough for it. Rather, we outline object-oriented software engineering processes and point out relevant bibliographical references. At the same time, we concentrate on specific guidelines to facilitate the translation from an OOAD to a maintainable Eiffel implementation.

6.1 Object-Oriented Methodology

6.1.1 The Object-Oriented Software Engineering Process

Despite their departure from conventional software engineering processes, object-oriented analysis and design (OOAD) methods can still be retro-fitted in classic models of software development, such as the waterfall model [120] or the V model introduced in Section 1.1.3. The usual progression is from analysis down to design down to implementation, and then up to unit testing, integration, and delivery. The analysis phase helps in building a relevant model of the real world through the identification of the classes and objects that form the vocabulary of the problem domain. The design phase facilitates identification of the hierarchy among classes and helps in depicting both static and dynamic models as well as logical and physical models of the system. During design, many of the objects and classes identified during analysis are retained and refined. The following phase consists of implementing each of the classes to conform to the static and dynamic design models. Once the implementation is finished, the work is only halfway done. A sound software engineering practice is to verify and validate (V&V) everything that is developed through the steps of unit, integration, and acceptance testing.

This classic model of software development is often characterized as being too rigid. Several variants address this issue, such as Boehm's spiral model [18], which is basically a risk-driven incremental prototyping approach. Each consecutive prototype may in turn follow the waterfall or the V model of software development.

Most object-oriented methods now make it possible to tackle the incremental, iterative, and evolutionary nature of software development. The various phases of analysis, design, and implementation use the same conceptual framework (based on objects) and have no rigid frontiers between them, so the object-oriented software engineering process can be called *seamless*. This term emphasizes the fact that there are no impedance mismatches between the phases, as is often the case in other software development methods such as the analysis (data flow diagrams) to design (structure charts) to programming gaps found in traditional structured analysis and design [118]. Seamlessness is so important for modern software systems because the main effort in software development (perhaps 80% or more) is spent not on new development but on maintenance of existing software. Therefore, the very role of analysis and design in software engineering is changing. Rather than addressing only the earliest stages of the software lifecycle, it is increasingly being viewed as the intellectual support needed across the entire software construction process.

Problem domain modeling together with seamlessness yields considerable benefits in terms of flexibility and traceability. These properties translate to better quality software systems (fewer defects and delays) that are much easier to maintain because a requirement shift may usually be easily traced down to the (object-oriented) code.

6.1.2 An Overview of Object-Oriented Methodology

Modern OOAD methods are the result of more than 10 years of experimentation and improvements rooted in the seminal works of Chen on the entity-relationship model [32], Jackson on JSD [73], Booch on object-based design with Ada [19], and so forth.

Despite the large number of already available OOAD methods (more than 20 are mentioned in a 1992 survey article [105]), several new methods keep popping up every year. Among the most popular methods are:

Berard, published in [11], covers many topics on object-oriented software engineering, including coverage of object-oriented domain and requirements analysis.

Booch, initially published in [21], is a kind of reference book on object-oriented design. It offers design notations and basic methodological principles, but only briefly covers analysis. It has, however, several case studies in Smalltalk, Object Pascal, C++, CLOS, and Ada83. The second edition [22] of Booch's method relies on the same notations, but incorporates some of the best ideas for analysis found in Wirfs-Brock's CRC and Jacobson's use cases, and in some ways is very close to OMT (see below).

Business object notation (BON), by Nerson and Walden [109], is a method and notation for high-level analysis and design of software systems. BON is focused on both the seamless development necessary to make large-scale reuse possible, and the software reliability needed to make reusable components accepted and used by the software industry. It is centered around the principles of *seamlessness, reversibility*, and *software contracting*.

Class-responsibility-collaboration (CRC), in which Wirfs-Brock [142, 143] presents a *responsibility-driven design* approach with the so-called *class, responsibility, collaboration* (CRC) technique.

Coad/Yourdon was published in [33] for the analysis part and in [34] for the design part. Both books contain concise and informative data so that novice software engineers can rapidly grasp the essence of OOAD.

Fusion, which Coleman *et al.* published in [49], is a second-generation object-oriented method building on successful components of many first-generation methods (OMT, Booch, CRC, ObjectOry, Meyer's design by contract), hence the name. This method was designed with the requirements of industrial software developers in mind (e.g., traceability, management.)

Hierarchical object-oriented design (HOOD), published in [59], is only object based and mainly directed toward an Ada83 implementation. It was developed by the European Space Agency and is quite popular in the European aerospace industry.

Object factory for software development (ObjectOry), the Jacobson's *use case* driven approach originally published in [74], is described in [75]. ObjectOry builds on 25 years (!) of object-based and object-oriented design in the telecommunications domain.

Object modeling technique (OMT), by Rumbaugh *et al.* [121] is described in depth below since we use it as the methodological support for the rest of this chapter.

OOSD, where deChampeaux [41] elaborates on basic ideas from [39]. It provides a fully integrated treatment of OOA and OOD, with a parallel computational model of one thread per object.

Real-time object-oriented modeling (ROOM), published in [122], addresses the needs of real-time object-oriented systems with an iterative and incremental development process. A single set of consistent graphical modeling concepts is used thoroughly. It emphasizes executable models for the early validation of requirements, architecture, and design combined with techniques for automatic generation of implementations.

Shlaer and Mellor method, published in [125], is often credited as the first object-oriented analysis method. Their complete approach [127] consists of addition to the structured analysis family, such as dynamic modeling with a state-transition driven approach.

Even if these methods use widely different notations and vocabulary, they basically all support the same concepts (modeling and object orientation). Recent methods tend to converge toward common principles on the software development process, through a continuous incorporation of the best and more successful ideas and cookbook recipes found in previous methods. This trend has been accelerated by recent moves in the industry, such as J. Rumbaugh and Y. Jacobson joining Rationale (G. Booch), effectively merging three of the most popular object-oriented methods.

The evaluation and comparison of methods has been the subject of various articles [40, 118, 105, 141] and reports [6, 132, 68]. Wilkie's book [138] summarizes and compares 11 popular analysis and design methods (e.g., Booch, Coad/Yourdon, CRC, HOOD, ObjectOry, OMT, Shlaer and Mellor) and gives several examples and case studies.

6.1.3 An Overview of OMT

In their book [121], Rumbaugh *et al.* propose a set of object-oriented concepts and a language-independent graphical notation, called the object modeling technique (OMT). This modeling technique can be used to analyze problem requirements, design a solution to the problem, and implement the solution in a target programming language or database. The OMT, which promotes an object-oriented approach, allows the same concepts and notations to be used through the entire software development process. The software developer does not need to translate into a new notation at each development stage, as is required by many traditional methods.

The OMT emphasizes that object-oriented technology is more than just a way of programming. It is a way of thinking abstractly about a problem using real-world concepts, rather than computer concepts. The OMT also places great emphasis on object-oriented constructs as models of real things, rather than as techniques for programming.

The OMT defines some boundaries between object-oriented analysis, design, and implementation phases. The first step, object-oriented analysis, is concerned with devising a precise, relevant, concise, understandable, and correct model of the real world. The purpose of object-oriented analysis is to model the problem domain so that it can be understood and serve as a stable basis for preparing the design step. The analysis model extends itself in three dimensions:

- The object model (based on classes, associations, and grouping constructs) shows the static structure of the real-world system through abstract or physical classes and their relationships.

- The dynamic model (based on events and states) shows the temporal behavior of the objects in the system.

- The functional model shows the constraints between the objects in the system (and between inputs and outputs).

The *design* phase starts with the output of the analysis phase and gradually shifts its emphasis from the application domain to the computation domain. The implementation strategy is defined, and trade-offs are made accordingly. Then the definition of classes is refined by collapsing the dynamic and functional analysis dimensions onto the object model. Auxiliary classes may be introduced at this stage to deal with complex relationship or implementation-related matters.

The output of the object-oriented design phase is a blueprint for the implementation. When the implementation is made with an object-oriented language such as Eiffel, it is basically an extension of the design process.

6.1.4 Eiffel and Object-Oriented Analysis and Design

> Eiffel is arguably the best commercial object-oriented language in terms of its technical capabilities (page 327 in the OMT book [121]).

Eiffel is the ideal language for implementing the object-oriented design obtained through OOAD methods such as the OMT, BON, Fusion, and others. Most modern methods even incorporate Meyer's *design by contract* ideas (where contract elements are expressed in terms of preconditions and postconditions and class invariants), whereas Eiffel is one of the few languages to properly integrate this paradigm with respect to inheritance (see Section 6.4.2).

For example, in the book describing Fusion [49], 42 pages are dedicated to the problem of mapping the design into an effective implementation. Implementation techniques for Fusion design concepts are discussed in a general way, with particular emphasis on C++ and Eiffel. Most of the Fusion design concepts directly map to Eiffel concepts, such as the contractual model of programming, assertions, exception handling, dynamic binding as the default rule, reference semantics and so on. The C++ implementation, however, requires lengthy considerations. For instance, memory management requires three lines for Eiffel vs. 3 pages for C++.

BON [109], also partly based on the ideas of *design by contract*, was cowritten by Jean-Marc Nerson, who was deeply involved in the design of Eiffel. BON is really an OOAD front end for Eiffel.

6.2 Case Study: An SMDS Server

To make this chapter more concrete we will use a case study from the telecommunications domain. We go step by step from the initial requirements to an Eiffel implementation. The OMT OOAD method is used for the descending part of the software life cycle in the V model. The ascending part (that is, V & V problems) is the topic of the next chapter.

6.2.1 An Overview of SMDS

Modern telecommunication networks are built around switching systems (SS) connected through high-speed communication lines. Upon entering the network, the data to be transmitted (either data, voice, pictures, video, etc.) are cut in small chunks called *packets*. These packets are directed toward their destinations through a number of switching systems, playing the same role as marshalling yards do for trains. To compute the path from a source to a destination and to transmit the data without undetected errors, these SS collaborate by exchanging messages (themselves cut into packets), following sets of rules known as *communication protocols*. Depending on whether the path between the source and the destination is computed once for all the packets of a communication, or independently for each packet, the network is said to be *connected* (e.g., X25 or ATM) or *connectionless* (e.g., the Internet Protocol, IP).

Switched multimegabits data service (SMDS) [9] is a connectionless, packet-switched data transport service running on top of connected networks such as the Broadband Integrated Service Digital Network (B-ISDN), which is based on the asynchronous transfer mode (ATM).

SMDS was designed to provide high-throughput and low-delay transmissions, and to be able to maintain them over a large geographical area. As a result, it can be used to interconnect multiple-node local-area network (LANs) and wide-area networks (WANs), and provide them with "any-to-any" service (a capability sometimes referred to as the *dial-tone for data*). SMDS also features multicasting (the ability to handle group addressing), E.164 addressing (SMDS addresses are like standard telephone numbers), support for key protocols used in LANs and WANs (TCP/IP, Novell, DECNet, AppleTalk, SNA, OSI), network scalability, SNMP-based network management, call blocking, and validation and screening for the secure interconnection of LANs.

SMDS relies on an overlay network with non-ATM switching to transfer connectionless messages [87]. This network consists of a set of interconnected *connectionless servers*. Clients who are willing to do connectionless traffic just have to access the nearest connectionless server using any available protocol, such as an ATM connection.

As a connectionless service, SMDS eliminates the need for carrier switches to establish a call path between two points of data transmission. Each switch reads the E.164 address included in SMDS packets, and then forwards them one by one over any available path to the desired endpoint. The benefit of this connectionless "any-to-any" service is that it puts an end to the need for precise traffic-flow predictions and connections only between fixed locations. With no need for a predefined path between devices, data can travel over the least congested routes in an SMDS network, providing faster transmission, increased security, and greater flexibility to add or drop network sites.

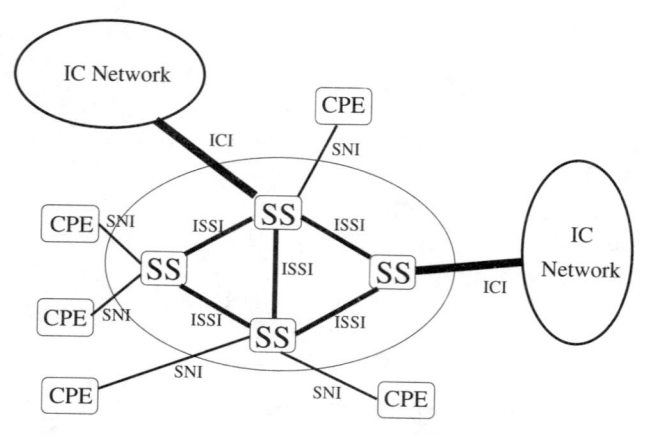

Figure 6.1 Architecture of an SMDS network

6.2.2 Problem Requirements

An SMDS network is based on a three-tiered architecture: a switching infrastructure made of SMDS servers (or switches, SS); a consumer premise equipment (CPE) delivery system made of subscriber network interfaces (SNIs); and an external network access system, independent carrier interface (ICI) (see Figure 6.1). Each SMDS server thus has to switch packets incoming from SNIs, ICIs, and interswitching system interface (ISSI) links. SMDS servers determine the route for an SMDS frame/packet (called an "L3_PDU") by examining the E.164 *destination address* field present in each packet.

SMDS can be supported by various lower level layers, such as ATM (AAL3/4 or even 5) or DQDB (see Figure 6.2). SMDS thus features a technology-independent interface, fostering fully portable SMDS servers. There is also a variant in which this technology independence is not respected. In the so-called high-performance SMDS, the segmentation and reassembly (SAR) of AAL3/4 cells is avoided by a *cut-through* routing that makes use of the message identifier (MID) field. This project should concentrate on building a portable SMDS server: *cut-through* routing then might be considered as yet another hardware-dependent optimization.

The advantage of building a portable SMDS server is the possibility of implementing it on an embedded system, while prototyping it on a standard UNIX workstation. It also makes it possible to use a high-level language to allow the programmer to concentrate on algorithmic optimization issues instead of C or assembly language fine-tuning and debugging.

Portability is not yet an established idea in the telecommunications world, where most systems are of a real-time nature and are finely tuned to get

SMDS Protocol Service Users

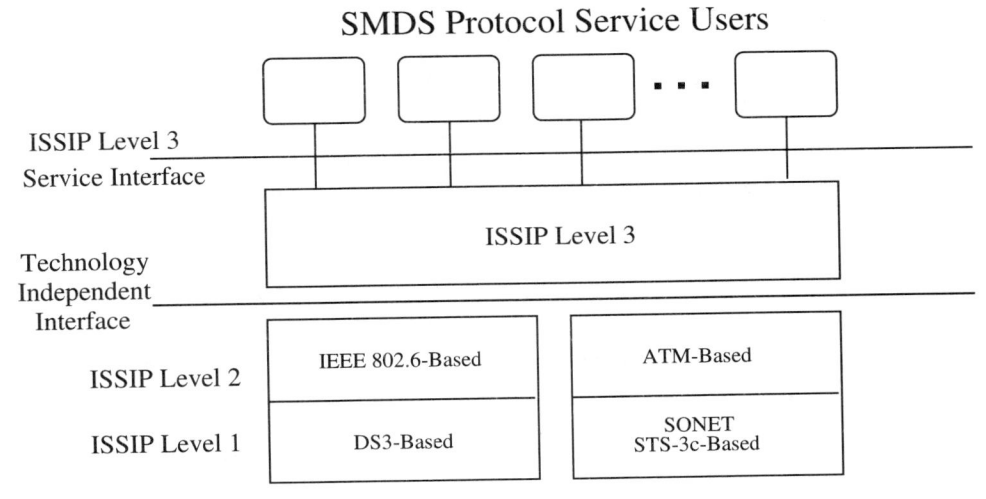

Figure 6.2 Architecture of an SMDS server

the best performances out of a given architecture. However, this is changing because the versatility of the new value-added telecommunication services induces huge software development costs that need to be paid off on more than one hardware generation (whose lifetime is becoming shorter and shorter).

The aim of this case study is to show how an OOAD method (the *object modeling technique* [121]) followed with an implementation in Eiffel may be used to build a highly evolutive and portable SMDS server, still respecting the (soft) real-time constraints of SMDS and featuring high-throughput and low-delay transmissions.

6.3 SMDS: Object-Oriented Analysis

6.3.1 The SMDS Server Problem Domain

The first step of the OMT is concerned with devising a precise, concise, understandable, and correct model of a relevant part of the real world. The purpose of object-oriented analysis is to model the problem domain so that it can be understood, and serve as a stable basis for preparing the design step. To do this, we must examine functional requirements (the 300 pages of Bellcore's document [9]), analyze their implications on the underlying model, and identify the assumptions made about the real world. We also must extract critical real-world domain information first, and defer details until later. The result of analysis should be an understanding of the problem in preparation for future design.

Note that the requirements for real systems are rarely as formal as protocol specifications; often they evolve together with the design and implementation of the system. An important point of OO development is to make the building of such systems possible. We don't need to understand the entire problem before starting to code—as long as we develop classes for the parts that we do understand.

An SMDS server (SS) is a collection of equipment that provides high-speed packet-switching in a network supporting SMDS. An SS is structured around the ISSI protocol stack. This stack is made of four levels:

The SMDS Protocol Service Users. This group of entities uses the level 3 SMDS services (see below) to support the transport of both network management and end-user data units:

- The *network management entity* (NME) supports inter-SS operations and management, such as loop-back testing, route testing, and administration of congestion information.

- The *local SNI mapping entity* (L-SME) provides a bridge between the subscriber protocol stack and the ISSIP stack.

- The *LEC-IC mapping entity* (L-IME) provides a bridge between the intercarrier protocol stack and the ISSIP stack of the local exchange carrier (LEC).

- The *LEC-LEC mapping entity* (L-LME) provides a bridge between two distinct LECs. It works the same way as the L-IME.

- The *group addressing mapping entity* (GARME) supports group address resolution (multicasting).

The ISSIP Level 3. As illustrated in Figure 6.3, level 3 is the core of the SMDS server. It provides a generic, connectionless, packet-switching service to the SMDS service users. To support this service, ISSIP level 3 provides packet forwarding, relaying, and receiving functions, as well as route management and congestion management. It is made of three cooperating entities, each managing its own protocol:

- The *data transport protocol* (DTP) supports packet forwarding (from the mapping entities toward the ISSI), relaying (from ISSI to ISSI), and receiving (from the ISSI toward the mapping entities) functions, as well as functions to support group addressing. For that, it asks

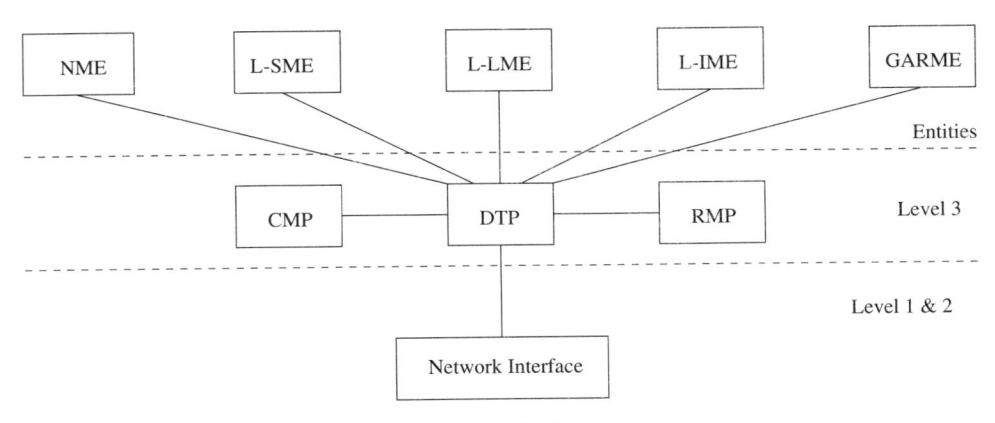

Figure 6.3 Internal architecture of an SMDS server

the RMP for routing information, and the CMP for congestion information. The DTP encapsulates (or extracts) each packet created by (or bounded to) the service users or the RMP or the CMP (see below) in (or from) a level 3 DTP (L3_DTPDU).

- The *routing management protocol* (RMP) maintains in each SS the correct topology of the network and calculates shortest paths from the host SS to other SSs in the network. It also maintains a routing table used to flood a group-addressed packet through a shortest path spanning tree rooted at the source SS. For that, the RMP exchanges routing management PDUs (through the DTP) with its peers in the other SSs. Most important among these RMPDUs are the link state advertisements (LSAs).

- The *congestion management protocol* (CMP) supports procedures for the generation, distribution, and receipt of congestion management PDUs containing explicit congestion notification (ECN) messages. These ECN messages allow a congested SS to inform other SSs in the network of its congested state so that they may take appropriate congestion control actions; that is, delete a percentage of the traffic directed toward the congested SS.

ISSIP Levels 1 and 2. These are the technology-dependent ISSIP levels. ISSIP level 2 enables the transport of variable-length packets (the L3_DTPDUs) between SSs, and supports such functions as bit-error detection, framing, and segmentation and reassembly (SAR). ISSIP level 1 provides the physical interface to the actual ISSI transmission path.

We are only interested in a portable and technology-independent SS, so the actual technology used for these levels is of little importance to us. It can be based on ATM or DQDB (IEEE 802.6) as defined in [9], or on any other technology providing the same level of service.

6.3.2 Object Modeling

The first step in analyzing the requirements is to define and construct an *object model*. The object model shows the static structure of the real-world system and organizes it into workable pieces. The object model must identify and describe real-world information through abstract or physical object classes, and their relationships to each other. The most crucial part is the top-level organization of the information domain into classes connected by the appropriate *association* abstractions. These association abstractions are relationships such as *generalization/specialization, aggregation, composition*, and *grouping*.

The following steps are suggested in [121] as a recipe to construct an object model in OMT.

- Identify real-world (classes of) objects. At this stage, an *object* is a concept, abstraction, or thing with clear boundaries and meaningful descriptions for a given application domain. Objects may be identified after the names appearing in the problem statement. In OMT diagrams, classes are represented as boxes labeled with the class name.

   In the case of the SMDS server, the main classes clearly appear in Bellcore's specifications. These are the service user entities (NME, LME, GARME); the global management entities (system manager, operator); the level 3 protocol managers (routing, congestion, and data transfer managers); and at the lower level, the interfaces to the communication lines. Also quite central in our object model are the various protocol data units (PDUs), i.e., the messages used by the protocol entities to communicate with their remote peers, and the service data units (SDUs), i.e., the user data.

- Prepare a data dictionary, describing in short definitions the meanings of the names associated with objects (or classes) in the context of the problem domain. See, for example, the definitions for the various SMDS top-level entities presented in the Section 6.3.1.

- Identify associations. An association is a physical or conceptual connection between classes. It is represented with a labeled link connecting two (or more) classes. The name of a binary association usually reads in a particular direction, but the binary association can be traversed in either direction. Associations may be identified through verbal sentences in the problem statement.

In our SMDS model, we can find for example the binary relationship *cooperate* between the DTE (data transfer) and the RME (routing), or the 1-to-N relationship *has a representation of* between an RME and the N models it has of its peer RME located in neighbor servers of the SMDS network.

Aggregation is a special kind of association. Aggregation is the "a-part-of" relationship (represented with a diamond) in which objects representing the *components* of something are associated with an object representing the entire *assembly*. The most significant property of aggregation is *transitivity* and *antisymmetry*. For example, an L3_DTPDU is made of (that is, aggregates) a header, an L3_payload, and a pad (near the center of Figure 6.4).

- Identify attributes and properties of objects and links. List them in the boxes representing the classes in the object diagram. For example, an L3_DTPDU header features a source address, a destination address, a length, and a service type (see Figure 6.4).

- Organize and simplify object classes using inheritance for generalization/specialization of abstractions. Inheritance can be regarded as a specialized association link among classes sharing a set of similarities. It is represented with a triangle on the object diagram. For example, the CMPDU (congestion packets), L3_SDU (management and user data), and RMPDU (routing packets) are the various kinds of L3_Payload that may be found in an L3_DTPDU (level 3 packet): They thus inherit from the L3_Payload.

- Iterate and refine the model. Figure 6.4 presents the full object model of the SMDS server. It is a rather complex picture, but considering that it is deduced from a 300-page specification, the fact that it still fits on a single sheet of paper is a good point for the conciseness and the expressiveness of the OMT object model notation.

6.3.3 Dynamic Modeling

A *dynamic model* shows the temporal (or time-dependent) behavior of the system and objects in it. There are two major concepts in dynamic modeling: the *state* of objects and the *event* modeling the external stimuli suffered by objects. A state is represented in Figure 6.5 as a rounded box, whereas an event is represented as a label on a transition between states (itself represented as an arrow).

162 FROM ANALYSIS TO IMPLEMENTATION

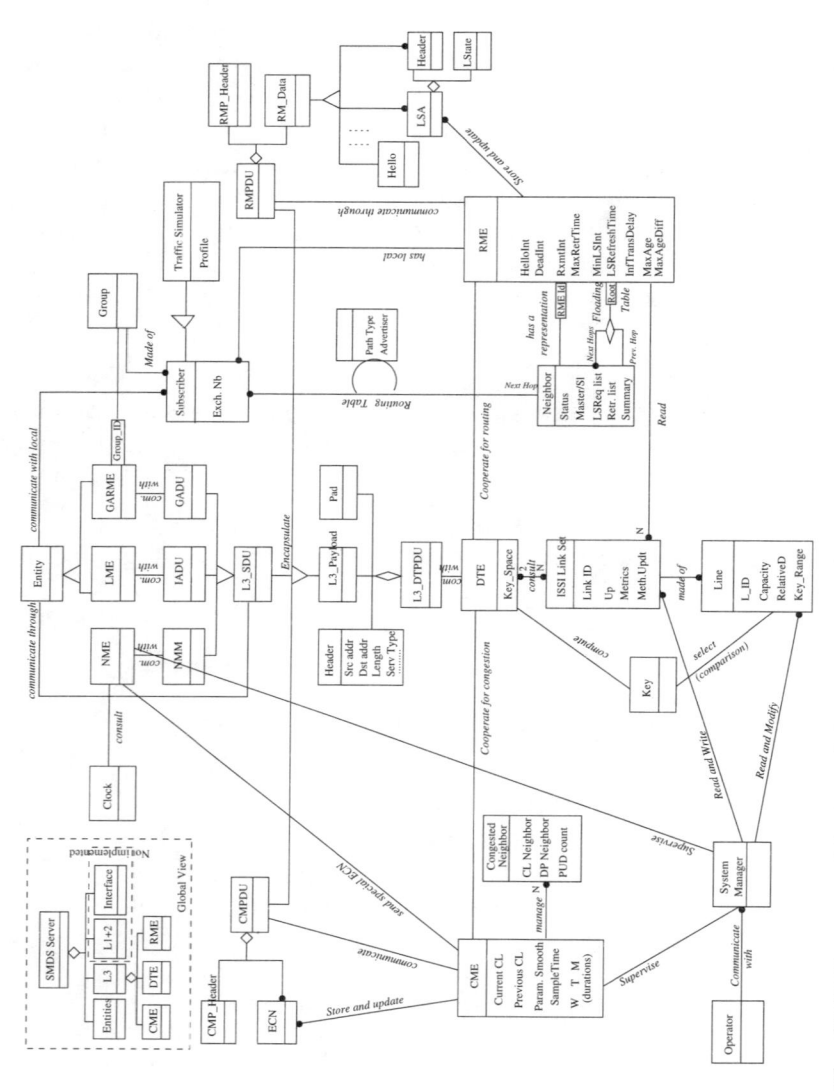

Figure 6.4 The SMDS server object model

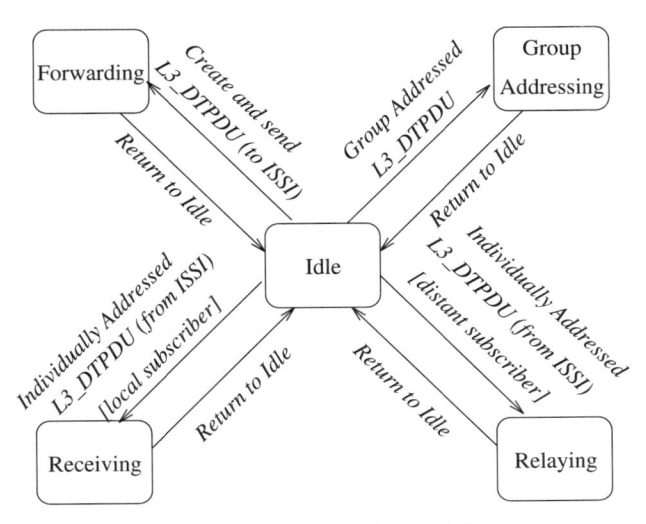

Figure 6.5 The data transfer entity dynamic model

The dynamic model emphasizes the use of events and states to specify control. Like other objects, events and states may be organized into generalization hierarchies to share both structure and behavior properties.

The process to begin the dynamic analysis is to look for events of external stimuli and responses, then summarize permissible event sequences for each object with a *state diagram*. Algorithm execution is not relevant during analysis; if there are no externally visible requirements, algorithms are part of implementation. For most applications, logical correctness depends on the sequences of interactions, not the exact times of interactions. Real-time systems, however, do have exact timing requirements on event interactions that must be considered during analysis.

When the problem domain deals with telecommunication protocols, most of the analysis work regarding the dynamic model is already done, because it is explicitly included in the requirements as the definition of the protocol. This definition is usually made of chunks of communicating finite state automata, extended with some private variables and watchdog clauses.

As a connectionless service, SMDS has relatively little contextual information. For example, the state diagram associated with the data transfer entity (see Figure 6.5) shows that it must come back to the *Idle* state before processing any of its events. An event is fully processed before the next one is dealt with. For such "flat" classes, the dynamic model merely consists of the listing of all acceptable events, whether they are external ones or timer triggered.

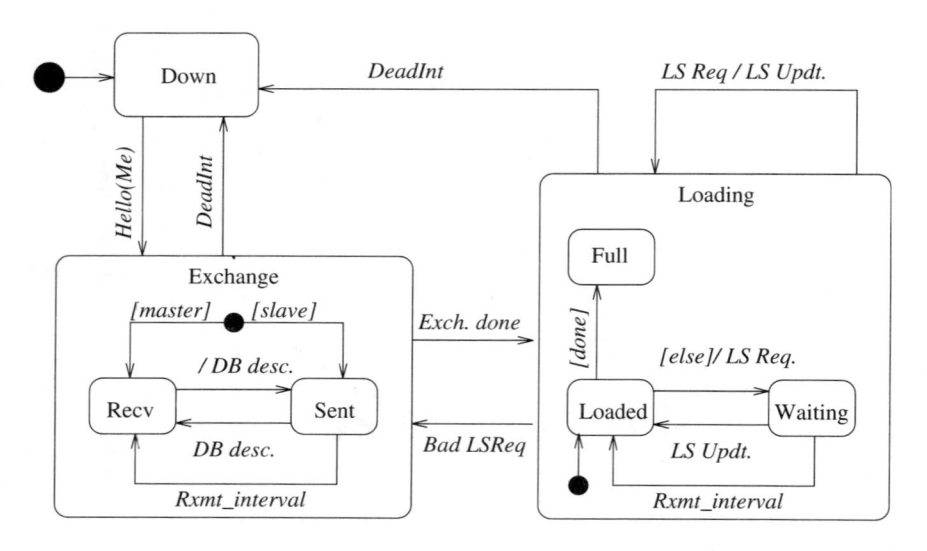

Figure 6.6 The neighbor dynamic model

Only satellite protocols, such as the Hello protocol of the RME must remember a state, in that case the adjacency level of each neighbor (see Figure 6.6).

6.3.4 Functional Modeling

The *functional model* provides the last view on the analysis model, completing the object model and the dynamic model. It shows how values are computed, without too much regard for sequencing or object structure. The functional model concentrates on functional dependencies, so data flow diagrams (DFDs) may be used to shed new light on the system being modeled. The processes on a DFD correspond to activities or actions in the state diagrams of the classes. The flows correspond to objects or attribute values in the object diagram.

Figure 6.7 shows a global view of the SMDS server, with the main entities (DTE, RME, CME, NME, LME, GARME, Operator) represented as actor objects (boxes), the internal databases (individual address routing table, group address routing table, LSReqList, neighbor) as data stores (pairs of parallel lines), and the main data flows (represented with arrows) between these objects.

Once the top-level DFD is completed, each process can be described with either its own DFD (see, for example, the process *RecLSReq* shown in Figure 6.8), or using any appropriate notation for simple functions. It is best to

6.3 SMDS: OBJECT-ORIENTED ANALYSIS   **165**

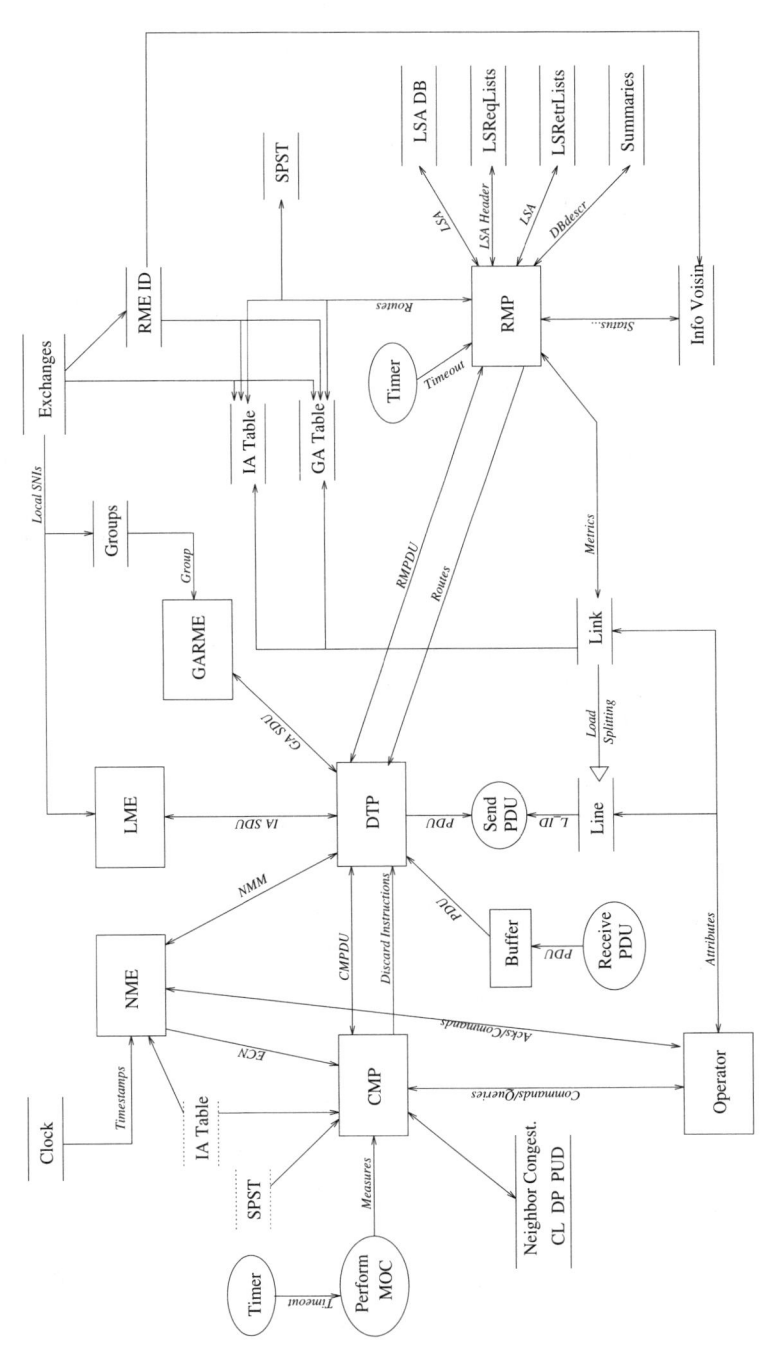

Figure 6.7 The SMDS server top-level data flow diagram

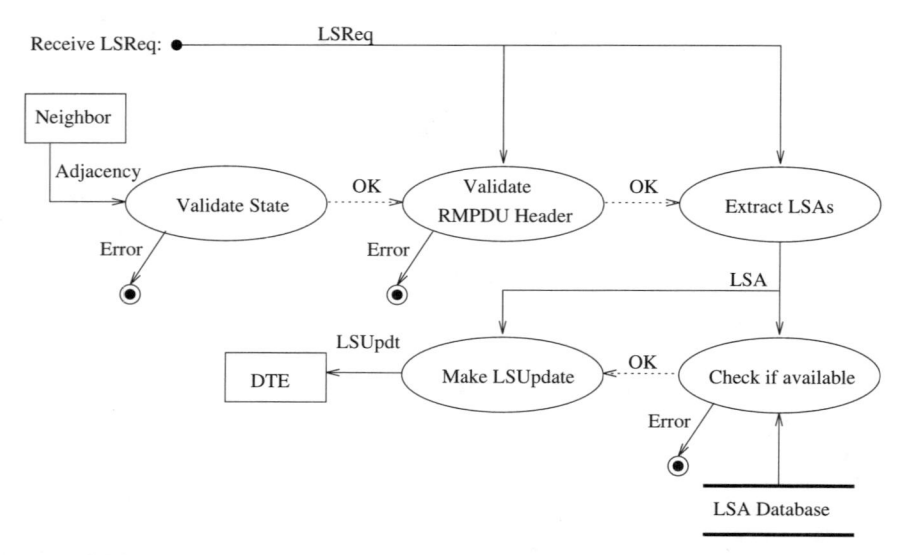

Figure 6.8 The *Receive Link State Request* process description

try to describe functions in a declarative way; e.g., using preconditions and postconditions that will be translated readily to Eiffel (thus providing the way to check the implementation against its specification). If, however, their control flow is too complex, function behaviors may be described using natural language, event tables, or even pseudocode. Still, it is a good idea to fit them out with Eiffel-style preconditions and postconditions when appropriate.

6.4 Eiffel and Object-Oriented Design

6.4.1 Introduction to Design Patterns and Idioms

The particular semantics of a given programming language influence design decisions. To ignore these influences may leave you with abstractions that do not take advantage of the language's unique features, or with mechanisms that cannot be implemented efficiently. The idea that object-oriented design is totally independent from the implementation language is a myth: Only people having one implementation language in mind say that.

An object-oriented designer may avoid some headaches by knowing that her or his implementation language is to be Eiffel, so we describe several design patterns that can serve as guidelines for any Eiffel-based design.

Design patterns and idioms are useful tools for guiding and documenting system design [55]. They capture the intent behind a design by identifying objects, their collaborations, and the distribution of responsibilities. Design patterns play many roles in the object-oriented development process. They provide a common vocabulary for design, they reduce system complexity by naming and defining abstractions, they constitute a base of experience for building reusable software, and they act as building blocks from which more complex designs can be built. Design patterns can be considered reusable microarchitectures that contribute to an overall system architecture [36]. A design pattern is both part of a system and a description of how to build that part of the system.

6.4.2 Design by Contract

In his seminal article [100] B. Meyer eloquently makes the case for the *design by contract* pattern of software construction, which is seen as a succession of documented contracting decisions. This *design by contract* approach has a sound theoretical basis in relation to partial functions, and provides a methodological guideline to build robust, yet modular and simple systems. In some ways, *design by contract* is the exact opposite of *defensive programming* [91], in which it is recommended that every software module be protected by as many checks as possible. Defensive programming makes it difficult to precisely assign responsibilities among modules, and has the additional malevolent side effect of increasing software complexity, which eventually leads to a decrease in reliability.

The *design by contract* approach prompts developers to specify precisely every consistency condition that could go wrong, and to assign explicitly the responsibility of its enforcement to either the routine caller (the client) or the routine implementation (the contractor). As it was first introduced in Section 2.5.3, assertions are the Eiffel mechanisms that enable the formalization of this contract between a client and a contractor. A contract carries mutual obligations and benefits: The client should only call a contractor routine in a state where the class invariant and the precondition of the routine are respected. In return, the contractor promises that when the routine returns, the work specified in the postcondition will be done, and the class invariant will be respected.

A party failing to meet the contract terms indicates the presence of a fault, or a bug. A precondition violation points out a contract broken by the client: The contractor then does not have to try to comply with its part of the contract, but may signal the fault by raising an exception. A postcondition violation points out a bug in the routine implementation, which does not fulfill its promises.

The Eiffel assertion mechanism is fully integrated into the type system through the inheritance mechanism. Redefinition is a semantics-preserving transformation. This mechanism provides the necessary semantics for subtyping and subclassing, and paves the way for the notion of *subcontracting*. That is, dynamic binding can be viewed through the perspective of a routine subcontracting its actual implementation to a redefined version. Clearly, the redefined routine must at least fulfill the contract of the original routine, and optionally do more (e.g., accepting cases that would have been rejected by the original contractor or returning a "better" result than originally promised). In Eiffel, these constraints are enforced at the language level (see Section 3.4.2), because preconditions and postconditions are automatically inherited by redefined features. They still can be modified, but only through the syntax **require else** and **ensure then,** making sure that preconditions may only be weakened (accept more) and postconditions strengthened (do more).

Contrary to, e.g., C++ where the redefinition is not harnessed.

6.4.3 Encapsulation and Information Hiding

One Abstraction per Class

The class is the unit of modularity in Eiffel. It is also the implementation of an ADT, which means that classes should be cohesive units representing complete abstractions.

Disassociated pieces of functionality should not be encapsulated in the same class. This encapsulation can happen when objects of the same class are involved in the algorithms for different system operations. Designing unrelated functionality in the same class loses the "real-world modeling" benefit of the object-oriented approach for that class.

One Class per Abstraction

In object-oriented software systems, functionality is distributed across the objects, but the same functionality should never be duplicated across a collection of objects. Functionality in a well-designed object-oriented system is tied to one class. Spreading functionality across a collection of objects makes change-control difficult. A change in one function may require changes to the other, but the reference is lost in the object-oriented structure.

Each individual class should serve a particular purpose. Object diagrams should be reviewed to check that the same functionality is not implemented by unrelated classes and that each class is coherent with strongly associated functionality.

Information Hiding

Beyond allowing us to present a controlled interface to the outside world, the encapsulation mechanism enables the underlying implementation of a class to be hidden. It should be used to keep the representation hidden and reduce the interface dependence on the representation. Easy replacement of representations to implement the same interface is then permitted, which is useful in design and especially for reuse.

Minimality of Class Interfaces

Each feature should serve a well-understood and accepted purpose, and thus be characterized by a well-defined contract (precondition, postcondition, and class invariant). Features should be orthogonal, that is, there should be no overlap of functionality across features. To keep the class interfaces as simple as possible, features that do not need to be exported should explicitly be kept private.

Beyond these common principles, there are several schools of thought about the problem of the size of class interfaces:

The minimalist school considers that the composition of functions should be left to the client and not the server. A class provides the primitive building blocks (i.e., atomic features), and users of the class group the primitives into useful compositions. For example, a *pop* feature of a STACK class should remove the top of the stack, and a *top* feature should select the top of the stack. Combining these two separate functions into one feature would restrict the usefulness and flexibility of the STACK interface. The STACK interface should include the two primitives *pop* and *top* only.

The pragmatic school considers that pure minimalism is too extremist, and admits that nonprimitive features that are still *pragmatically* useful to a class should be included (e.g., for ease of use or efficiency purposes). The class may then provide a combination of primitive features, but this is only valid when the primitives are also part of the provided interface. If it wouldn't have clashed with the "pure function" requirement (see Section 6.4.6), the feature *pop*, for example, would qualify for inclusion in the STACK interface under this pragmatic-minimalist rule.

The shopping list school considers that all *potentially* useful features should be included in the class interface, provided they respect the basic rules of minimality. The idea is that *one more feature will hurt no one—and may help someone tremendously* [103].

Whereas the pragmatic point of view is probably the most efficient for building stand-alone applications (such as our SMDS server), Meyer makes some good points about defending the shopping list approach when the design concerns reusable libraries [103]. This subject is discussed again in Chapter 8 (Section 8.1.2).

6.4.4 Modularity and Coupling

Macro Organization

The class is a necessary but insufficient vehicle for decomposition. For large systems, one of the worst organizations would consist of a flat collection of classes, through which developers would have to navigate to find what they needed. A better design principle is to ensure that the universe of classes is partitioned into loosely coupled subsystems, or clusters as managed by ACEs (see Section 4.1.1). Closely-coupled objects can be grouped in relevant clusters. They have client/server relationships, so the clusters can be structured according to usual principles such as partitioning and layering.

Minimize Object Interactions

The patterns of interactions for objects should be kept simple by constructing *interaction graphs* (as proposed in Fusion [49]). They should have a minimal number of objects and a minimal number of references. Minimizing the number of objects limits the dispersion of an operation implementation across the object collection. Minimizing the number of references makes designs more efficient. The fewer the references, the shorter the access paths needed to implement an algorithm.

Cycles in the interaction graphs denote mutual feature calls between objects (e.g., in SMDS the RME uses the DTE to talk to its remote peers, whereas the DTE uses the RME for routing information). Mutual feature calls require copies of object references across object collections, known as *aliasing*. If this is the key to an algorithm, as in some user interface protocols, the cycle length should be reduced to localize potential aliasing. Localized aliasing in small structures can be managed once documented.

Minimize Interface Dependencies

Mutual interface dependencies should be reduced as much as possible across object boundaries. A guide to help achieve this is given by the *law of Demeter* [88], which states that for each object, o, and each of its features, f, the objects that can be referenced are the:

- Object itself, that is, *o*;
- Object-valued attributes of *o*; and
- Arguments of *f*.

An object observing this law may only call the features of the objects that are immediately referenced.

6.4.5 Inheritance Structure

Implementation Inheritance and Delegation

The organization of object-oriented classes into class hierarchies is an aid to reuse. Classes can be tailored and specialized to produce new classes. However, reuse by inheritance is not always the best option. Classes can be extended through inheritance *or* delegation (also called composition). Deciding when to build new classes by inheritance and when to use delegation is an aspect of object-oriented design.

Inheritance should be used when the complete interface of the old class applies to the new class (*is-a* relationship). Delegation (*has-a* relationship), however, can be considered when a high proportion of code needs to be rewritten or when some of the features of the old class are irrelevant; that is, when the new class is not a true functional subtype of the old class (see Section 5.4.3). The places where true subtyping is violated should be documented as such. Building by composition allows the designer more control in the new class interface. The designer can decide which aspects of the old class are relevant and can be reused, and which parts can be effectively discarded.

This guideline also applies to the cases in which all you need is a module importation mechanism. Consider for example the class MATH as it appears in several Eiffel vendors' libraries. This class is merely a module encapsulating a number of mathematical constants (e.g., π) and functions (e.g., *sin, cos, tan*, etc.). If you need these functions in another class, you could make it inherit from MATH as in Example 6.1.

Inheritance then would be used as a module importation mechanism, and not at all as a subtyping facility. Although this is a valid use of the Eiffel inheritance mechanism, it feels wrong in a certain way, because this inheritance relationship does not relate to the problem domain but to implementation decisions.

In this kind of module importation problem, it might be better to be a client of the MATH module rather than its heir. Still, we would like to avoid the overhead of an extra indirection and of an extra attribute. The solution then is

```
      class HEIR_SHIP
          inherit MATH
      feature
          latitude, longitude : REAL -- current bearing of the ship
5         head_to(lat, long : REAL) : REAL is
              -- the head leading to the bearing (lat,long)
          do
              if long = longitude then
                  if lat > latitude then
10                    Result := 0
                  else
                      Result := 180
                  end
              else
15                Result := atan((lat-latitude)/(long-longitude))
              end
          end -- head_to
      end -- HEIR_SHIP
```

Example 6.1

to use a (private) expanded MATH object (such as *libm*), obtained through the following declaration:

```
feature {NONE}
    libm : expanded MATH
```

This object could be used as in Example 6.2.

The class MATH only declares constants and functions, so its instances have no attributes, and hence do not take space in memory. Furthermore, *libm* is an expanded object, so it is not subject to polymorphism, and all its features may be statically bound, and even in-lined by the compiler. You then can expect exactly the same space and time behavior for both Examples 6.1 and 6.2. In large software, you gain the additional benefit of the qualified call (*libm.atan*) telling you from which module the imported feature came from and the benefit of avoiding potential name clashes.

Complexity of the Inheritance Graph

You should not worry too much about the complexity of the inheritance graph. Keep it simple, but not simpler than necessary. In languages such as C++, multiple inheritance is poorly integrated (and may have a performance penalty), and thus design guidelines targeting an implementation in C++ tell you to develop shallow inheritance graphs.

```
class CLIENT_SHIP
feature
    latitude, longitude : REAL -- current bearing of the ship
    head_to(lat, long : REAL) : REAL is
            -- the head leading to the bearing (lat,long)
        do
            if long = longitude then
                if lat > latitude then
                    Result := 0
                else
                    Result := 180
                end
            else
                Result := libm.atan((lat-latitude)/(long-longitude))
            end
        end -- head_to
feature {NONE}
    libm : expanded MATH
end -- CLIENT_SHIP
```

Example 6.2

This is not necessary in Eiffel. Even if the inheritance graph leading to a class X is complex, there is no performance penalty. Finding a feature subject to dynamic binding can be done in constant time whatever the inheritance graph. This is possible because of the inheritance semantics in Eiffel, by which each class X inheriting from a set of other classes has an equivalent form, called its *flat* form, which can be expressed without *any* inheritance. It is the client's view on X, or what the user of class X needs to know about it: the complete description of its interface. Where that interface came from is of absolutely no significance. You might want to know all of its ancestor classes to understand its polymorphic behavior, but the way in which it is constructed from these classes is irrelevant.

Most Eiffel environments provide tools to show that.

6.4.6 Routines

Complexity of Routines

Each routine should be kept so short and simple that its mere name (aided by a comment at its header) is enough to understand its purpose, and that the reading of its contract is enough to know how to use it. Complicated or imbricated control structures (such as loops and switches), or both, should be avoided as much as possible. Dynamic binding should be relied on instead. In McCabe's terms [94], where the *cyclomatic complexity* of a software component is defined as the number of independent paths through it, a routine cyclomatic complexity should be as small as possible. Unless you are dealing with special cases (e.g., parsing user input), it should stay in the range of [0..2] (2 corresponds to an **if then else**). This minimal complexity will simplify the routine debugging and testing dramatically (see Section 7.1.3 on testing). The performance penalty of having large numbers of very short routines should not be feared. Eiffel type-checking rules require so much from the compiler that it is easy for it to *in-line* short routines each time it finds it useful.

Command-Query Distinction

Eiffel fosters a style of design that clearly separates commands from queries. A command is a procedure that may modify the state of an object. A query, however, should return information about an object without modifying its state. It can be an attribute or a *pure function*. A pure function is a function without side effects, such that $2 \times f(x) = f(x) + f(x)$. If a function is complex enough that it is not clear whether it is pure, this property can be specified explicitly with a postcondition as illustrated in Example 6.3.

> **ensure**
> pure_function: deep_equal(**Current**,old(deep_clone(**Current**)))

Example 6.3

In addition to the theoretical advantages of this command-query distinction, pure functions enable their use in assertions, and will facilitate the testing of classes.

Optional Behaviors

In an object-oriented system, dynamic binding should be used when we want to provide the user with a set of options tuning the behavior of the system. When this is not possible or not practical, behavior tuning can be provided within a routine through explicit tests on one or more entities that hold the values of the options. Whereas in traditional software these options are usually transmitted through routine arguments (e.g., FORTRAN mathematical subroutines frequently have half a dozen option parameters in addition to their operands), the encapsulation available in object-oriented languages allows a simpler approach to be chosen by means of separately *settable options*. The entities holding the option values no longer need to belong to the argument list of the routine, but can be attributes of the class. True operands then can be the only arguments of routines, whereas the tuning is factored out and dealt with at the object level (or even at the class level if *once* functions are used to provide class attributes). Depending on the scope of an option (class, object, or routine), a setting routine (or two if the option is Boolean) may be included in the class interface.

6.5 SMDS: Object-Oriented Design

We will now try to use these design guidelines with the object design of our SMDS case study. The OMT design phase starts with the output of the analysis phase and gradually shifts its emphasis from the application domain to the computation domain. There are two parts in the OMT object-oriented design. The first part is the *system design* phase, in which the analysis models are further elaborated, refined, and then optimized to produce a practical implementation strategy for a target environment. The second part is the *object design* phase, in which full object definitions about classes and associations are added for the final implementation. The output of the object-oriented design phase is a blueprint for the implementation.

6.5.1 System Design

During the system design there is a shift in emphasis from the application domain to the computation domain. First, the basic algorithms are chosen to implement each major function of the system. Based on these algorithms, the structure of the object model is then optimized for efficient implementation.

During the system design phase, the designers must make many design decisions about the organization of the system into components, and about object persistence, run-time concurrency, etc. The designers also must choose the implementation of control in software, handle boundary conditions, and set design trade-off priorities and alternatives. These points are detailed in the following paragraphs for the system design of our SMDS server.

Organizing the Systems into Components

For most real-world applications, the first step in system design is to divide the system into a number of components. These components should be rather autonomous and loosely coupled subsystems, featuring well-defined interfaces.

The main subsystems of our SMDS server are the three levels of the ISSI, the ICI, the SNI, and the network management interface (NMI) (see Section 6.2.1). In the following, we concentrate on the core of the SS, the part dealing with the communications between SMDS servers (that is, the ISSI). The other subsystems either will be implemented as stubs (SNI and NMI), or not at all (ICI). In future versions of this project they would actually be implemented, thus making our development process follow Boehm's spiral model [18].

To implement the lower levels of our SMDS server, we use a portable communication library called a parallel observable machine (POM) [61]. This library, ported on various parallel computer operating systems (including networks of workstations), greatly facilitates the porting of communicating applications across widely different architectures. It provides sophisticated features for observing distributed executions. It enables the generation, collection, and exploitation of execution traces and incorporates mechanisms for stamping events and for computing global dates. Since layer 3 is technology independent, the POM, which features an Eiffel interface, is then used as the underlying layers 1 and 2 for our SMDS server.

Identify Inherent Concurrency

The analysis model should reflect the real world, so all objects are concurrent. It is an important goal of system design to identify which objects must be active concurrently, and which objects can or must be folded in the same thread of control.

In the SMDS server, all interfaces to the external world (i.e., ISSIP levels 1 and 2 and the various external protocol stacks used by the SMDS service user entities) inherently work concurrently with the SS entities. The Eiffel garbage collector also might run concurrently to the SS entities (its incremental nature fosters a coroutine sort of behavior).

Allocate Subsystems to Processors and Tasks

According to the requirements for a portable SS, we use a general-purpose board (with a UNIX-like kernel) or a workstation driving a set of technology-dependent interface boards.

We leave open a possible evolution toward the use of connection parallelism [79] to improve the aggregate bandwidth of our SS.

Choose an Appropriate Persistent Object Store

Nearly all of the useful data are permanently stored in main memory. Only the initial configuration information used to initialize the server is stored in files.

Handle Access to Global Resources

We have no internal concurrent activities, so the remaining shared resource problems are dealt with by the on-board kernel.

Choose the Implementation of Control in Software

During analysis, all interactions are shown as events between objects; this closely matches a hardware implementation. We must now choose the way to implement control in software.

Our SS is mostly stateless at the main level, and all its entities process the events in an atomic way. No new event is taken into account before the current event has been completely processed. The core of the SS then may be an event dispatcher. It monitors all possible sources of events, serializes them, and dispatches them to the relevant entities for atomic processing. The behavior of these entities may be described with a state diagram, and they present a procedural control style.

The event dispatcher is implemented by *polling* the various event sources, with the following priorities:

1. Commands coming from the "system manager" or from the operator.
2. *Timer* expirations.
3. Message reception at one of the network interfaces (SNI, ICI, ISSI).

Furthermore, if no event is waiting to be processed (*Idle* period), the event dispatcher launches an iterative garbage collection if needed. However, because the garbage collector's work is shorter when it is called more often, a collection also may be forced if no idle period presents itself for some amount of time. This method should allow us to respect the (soft) real-time constraints of SMDS (see Section 7.4.1 for a confirmation).

Handle Boundary Conditions

Boundary condition design is concerned with the initialization, termination, and failure recovery of the system.

The initialization of our SS is implemented in the root class: COM. It creates the main entities and provides them with the references they need to establish the cooperations identified in the object model. For instance, the data transfer entity has a reference to the routing management entity, and conversely. The rest of the SS is then configured using the initialization files read on the disk, and the various network interfaces are set up by their driver entities. Once the initialization is completed, the SS enters the polling loop described in the previous section.

The termination may be required by the operator. Its effect is to finish the polling loop, clean up everything, and terminate the root creation procedure and thus the program.

```
    make is
            -- initialize and run this SMDS server
        do
            from initialize
5           until is_shutdown_required
            loop
                process_next_event
            end -- loop
            clean_up
10      rescue
            clean_up
            retry
        end -- make
```

Example 6.4

Failures in the SS should be reported by means of exceptions; dealing with fatal failures consists of handling otherwise unexpected exceptions (nonfatal errors are reported as warnings to the OPERATOR). The creation procedure then may be provided with a *rescue* clause to clean things up and restart the SS (see Example 6.4). This is a kind of warm boot, because everything restarts as if it were initialization time. The garbage collector will then recycle the resources associated with the overridden entities.

The SMDS protocols have been designed to deal with SS crashes (fail stop) and later recovery, so this simple mechanism also provides a limited amount of both hardware and software fault tolerance. It also can be disabled during the testing phases to get the standard exception history dumps (see Section 5.1).

Set Design Trade-off Priorities and Alternatives

Many studies in the literature identify bottlenecks in high-performance communication systems. Depending on the context in which their authors work, several approaches aimed at circumventing these bottlenecks have been proposed.

First, the PDU header processing speed determines an absolute limit on the global performance of the communication system. The system may not have a throughput per I/O board greater than the maximum PDU size divided by the header processing speed. This header processing speed then has to be optimized as much as possible. The introduction of parallelism has been considered at this level, but it generally does not pay off [43, 130] because of the limited intrinsic provision for concurrency in such kinds of processing. This tendency is even enforced with a "lightweight" protocol such as SMDS, which features a simplified header processing that leaves nearly no room for parallelization.

Another important source of performance loss is linked to data movement inside the system [150, 71]. To be efficient, an implementation should avoid copying packets from memory to memory because of its time cost (dynamic RAM bandwidth does not follow processing power). Also, for parallel implementations, data transfers between two separate nodes should be minimized because excessive internal communications can lead to link saturations and even to a global system slowdown. A good solution [23] is the use of a shared buffer in which all the packets are stored. The processing entities would only access the headers and trailers of these packets and would never deal with the data they include.

The execution environment also has a large influence on performance. The raw power of each processor determines the throughput of the system [71], and the bandwidth of the channels connecting the different nodes limits the global data flow.

The last bottleneck may be the interface between the processing system and the physical layer [23]. Its throughput should be sufficient not to limit the system. If the number of access points to the physical links is insufficient, they are considered to be shared resources. They can then be saturated if too many processing units try to use them at once.

All these points must be considered in the design of our SMDS server.

6.5.2 Object Design

During the object design phase, full object definitions about classes and associations are added for the final implementation. At the same time, operational interfaces and feature algorithms are specified to a reasonable detail level. The object design phase also adds internal objects for implementation convenience.

Combining the Three Models

At this stage, the definition of classes is refined by collapsing the dynamic and functional analysis dimensions onto the object model. We must convert the actions and activities of the dynamic model and the processes of the functional model into operations attached to classes in the object model.

We can associate an operation with each event received by an object. For instance, the operation *Receive LSReq* (Figure 6.8) deals with the event LSReq (Figure 6.6), and thus may be associated with the class NEIGHBOR.

Such an action of the state diagram may be expanded into a DFD in the functional model. The network of processes represents the body of the operation, whereas the flows are intermediate values. This diagram is to be converted into a linear sequence of steps in the implementation phase. The problem to be dealt with now is to determine the target object of the suboperations when it is not the same as the target of the enclosing operation. This problem can be solved with a set of rules such as:

- If a process extracts a value from an object (input flow, data store, or actor), this object is the target of the operation (e.g., *LSReq* is the target of the *Validate RMPDU Header* operation in Figure 6.8).

- If a process has an input flow and an output flow of the same type, then it is probably an object transformation. This object should be the target of the operation.

- If a process constructs a value from several inputs, the operation is a creation routine of the value's class (e.g., *Make LSUpdate* in Figure 6.8).

Designing Algorithms

Each operation that has been specified declaratively in the functional model now must be formulated as an algorithm.

Most of the algorithms used in our SS are quite simple and fully described with DFDs. There remains a small set of more complex algorithms to deal with problems such as the computation of the *shortest path spanning trees* (SPSTs) needed to update the routing tables. This kind of complex algorithm usually involves the introduction of auxiliary new classes, which must be integrated in the object model.

Consider also the problem of dealing with events such as *DeadInt*, which signals that a certain interval of time has elapsed without hearing from an SS neighbor, and thus that its state should be set back to *down* (see Figure 6.6). Such events usually are generated by hardware or operating system timers, but there is no easily portable way to deal with the many timers used in our SS. We thus decided to implement them in software, using a class TIMER featuring an expiration date and the object to ring when the date is reached. Each object that wants to use a timer service must inherit from a class RINGABLE and define its deferred feature *ring* (called by the timer) to perform the actions associated with the alarm processing.

The timers are stored in a priority queue (by increasing date of awakening) that is probed in the main event loop. On loading (or disabling), a timer inserts (or removes) itself in (or from) the queue, which is a TIMER class variable (the *once* function in Eiffel).

Design Optimizations

The analysis model should be semantically correct, but has no reason to describe an efficient implementation. One of the design tasks is to optimize this model to make the implementation more efficient, still preserving the clarity needed to ease the future maintenance of the system.

Design optimizations consist of:

- Adding redundant associations for efficient access. The analysis model is a transitive reduction over the associations between classes, so an object willing to access services provided by other objects may need to traverse several associations. For frequently traversed associations, this may induce a severe performance penalty that may be avoided with (redundant) direct associations.

  This is the case for the congestion management entity that must frequently read the spanning trees (class SPST) computed by the routing management entity. A new association connecting the congestion management entity and the SPST thus has been added to the object model. The same decision has been taken to set new associations between the network management entity and the routing management entity's routing table.

- Rearranging the computation for efficiency. Consider for example the reception of a packet. It involves the creation of an L3_DTPDU (the class modeling a packet), its processing within the SS, and its destruction afterward. Such a cycle is to be repeated hundreds or thousands of times per second, so we can achieve great performance improvements if we manage always to use the same L3_DTPDU object and avoid the creation/destruction cycles. This L3_DTPDU object will be created at boot time with the maximum allowed size, and will be filled with new content each time a real PDU is received from the lower levels. Actually, a second one is needed for the service user entities that are willing to send their own PDUs. The same holds for all kinds of messages circulating within the SS, which are basically references to the relevant part of the L3_DTPDU object with their own data access features. This mechanism also avoids any memory-to-memory copying of data.

- Saving derived attributes to avoid recomputation. With Eiffel, this decision may even be deferred to implementation time, because there is no syntactical difference between a parameterless function call and an attribute read.

Implementation of Control

The implementation of control in each class follows the decisions made in the system design phase:

- A *polling* loop in the SS root class.
- A procedural interface in the other classes. However, classes featuring an interesting state diagram (e.g., NEIGHBOR) have an explicit state variable (e.g., *Adjacency* in class NEIGHBOR) that is checked by the features implementing the state transitions. A user exception is raised when a transition is triggered from an improper state. In a telecommunications context it denotes a protocol error.

Adjustment of Inheritance

The class structure should be adjusted to increase reuse, both internal (i.e., among classes sharing something in the object model) and external (i.e., reusing library classes).

Design of Associations

The last step toward an implementable object model is to transform the association that still glues the object model to implementable object-oriented concepts. The efficient implementation of associations depends on their multiplicity and on whether they are inherently bidirectional.

- A one-way association (used in one direction only) may be implemented in the accessor as a mere attribute if it has a multiplicity "one," or as any instance of a relevant container class otherwise. Most associations qualified with an RME ID are implemented as hash tables (with the RME ID as a key), such as to NEIGHBOR or LSA_DB. Others are implemented as linked lists, e.g., *LSReqLists, LSRetrLists,* or Summaries).
- A two-way association may be implemented as attributes in both directions if the association has a relatively permanent nature (e.g., between the DTE and the RME, or between the CME and the DTE).

More complex associations may be implemented as distinct objects, thus reifying the relationship between instances of the classes. This is the case for the routing tables, which are both implemented as hash tables:

Individually Addressed The key is the destination address, providing access to the link type, the RME ID of the next hop on the outgoing path, and the cost of the path.

Group Addressed The key is the RME ID of the root SS (i.e., the one at the origin of the multicast) and it provides access to the RME ID of the SSs to which the multicast must be forwarded.

Determine the Representation of Object Attributes

Most classes are defined in terms of other classes, but eventually something must be defined in terms of primitive data types such as INTEGER or STRING.

For example, consider the representation of E.164 addresses within our SS. Such an address is formally defined as a six-digit BCD number. Within inter-SS exchanges, it is coded with 3 bytes.

We can make a class called E164_ADDRESS, and implement it as a BIT24 subclass. The only operations needed for these addresses are value comparison and hashing, though, so it is more efficient (and simpler) to implement it as an INTEGER-expanded heir for internal SS operations.

Packaging Classes into Clusters

Classes should be grouped into loosely coupled *clusters* that can be managed (for implementation and testing) by independent teams. An object model may consist of one or more clusters. A cluster provides an intermediate unit of packaging between an entire object model and the basic building blocks of classes and associations. Class name and association names must be unique within a cluster.

Our SS is organized around the following clusters:

CME: congestion management

COM: the SS root cluster

DAT: the packet class hierarchy

DTE: data transport

ENT: the SMDS service users (LME, GARME, NME)

OPE: operator (human interface) and SYSTEM_MANAGER

INT: the network interface (ISSI levels 1 and 2)

RME: routing management

SIM: the traffic simulators at the SNIs

SUP: the support cluster (e.g., timers).

It also uses the EiffelBase data structure clusters that are presented in Section 8.2.

The inheritance graph and the class interfaces (the short version of Eiffel classes) now can be extracted from the object design documents and packaged into their relevant clusters, ready for implementation.

6.6 Implementation

6.6.1 Introduction

Implementation is an extension of the design process. It may be accomplished using any programming language. However, using non-object-oriented programming languages requires much care and discipline to preserve the language itself, and thus it is more likely to violate the object-oriented concepts and produce inconsistent implementations. Object-based languages (e.g., Ada83, Modula-2) provide a better framework, but implementation of an object-oriented design is easiest with a full-blown object-oriented language. Even so, different languages vary in their support for object-oriented concepts. Each language represents a compromise among conceptual power, efficiency, and expressiveness of the object design. With Eiffel, the code should only be a simple translation of the design decisions. A CASE tool could be used to produce Eiffel class templates automatically from the OMT models. An integrated CASE tool (such as EiffelCase for the BON method [109]) could even allow you to swing back and forth seamlessly between the object model notations and Eiffel code, automatically reporting code changes in the object model and conversely.

The implementation should make the most efficient use of the available resources. In a software engineering context, another very important issue is that the understandability of the code also should be maximized to ease future maintenance. Clarity depends on good readability of the code, an accurate versioning system, and strong, up-to-date documentation.

Defining style and documentation guidelines contributes to that purpose. In Section 7.1.3 about testing, we will see that the most efficient technique for finding faults in a software system is still based on documentation and code inspections, hence the importance of having a uniform and readable style among projects, or even better at a company level. Good documentation and uniform, readable naming conventions are also of great importance if you plan to build libraries. Their users should be able to use them without digging in the code, and should not be bothered by varying policies among feature and class name forms.

Enforcing these kinds of standards at a company level is often a required step when implementing a quality assurance approach to pave the way for ISO 9000 or SEI/CMM certifications (see Section 1.1.3).

6.6.2 Style Guide

Some long-held style principles apply to Eiffel codes. The recommendations made in this section follow very closely those in Appendix A of [101]. We have adopted them in the SMDS case study, and tried to follow them in all of the examples of Eiffel codes in this book.

General Layout

The code should be laid out to show the structure of the program. Thus, the things that a reader might wish to find (e.g., the name of a feature) should be made prominent.

A consistent scheme of indentation should be used. The number of spaces for each level of indentation has to be chosen to make the code easy to read. Indentation must be sufficient to make the block structure clear, while avoiding lines that are too long. The precise definition of the layout is a matter of taste. The only really important thing is that the same conventions are used consistently.

- Major sections (the class header, creation block, each feature block, and the class invariant block) should start in column 1 and may be separated by a blank line if it enhances readability.

- Each block should be indented by a small fixed number of spaces (e.g., three) relative to the enclosing block.

Feature Layout

- If there is a feature block that is exported to all, then it must be first. The ANY keyword should be omitted.

- If a feature block is not exported, then it should be the last feature block and it should be written NONE rather than {}.

- Related features should be grouped within a feature block, with a comment giving a name for it (e.g., creation, access, status reporting). Creation procedures should come first.

- Logically related unique features should be defined together on the same line. Multiple attributes of the same type also may be defined together on one line.

Optional Semicolons and End *Keywords*

Semicolons should not be used except where they are mandatory; e.g., to remove ambiguity in an assertion clause beginning with an opening parenthesis or a prefix operator.

After each class name inside an inherit block, the **end** should only be present if there is a feature adaptation clause (such as rename or redefine).

Lexical Rules

All names should be meaningful but not excessively long. Local entity names (like loop indices), however, can be shorter (e.g., *i*). The name of a feature or the name of an entity should not include the name of its class.

The text should be in lowercase except for class names, reserved words, and comments. Multiple-word names should be underscored.

- Class names should be in capital letters.

- Keywords should be lowercase, but other reserved words should have their first letter capitalized (these include *Current, Result, Void, False,* and *True*).

- Comments should be in mixed case, conforming as much as possible to the usual conventions of your working language (e.g., English, French).

Most of the time, normal English rules should be followed with respect to spacing. Commas must be followed by (but not preceded by) a space, and a space precedes a '(' and follows a ')'. However colons and assignment operators (:= and ?=) may have a space before and after them.

Naming Conventions

Classes should be nouns, and uniform naming rules should be adopted to facilitate quick recognition and understanding of a feature role. Verbs in the imperative form should be used for commands (i.e., procedures such as *put*), nouns should be used for queries (functions and attributes such as *item* or *capacity*), and adjectives should be used for Boolean queries (prefixed with *is_* if there can be an ambiguity with a verb, as in *is_empty*). These rules enable program texts to look like grammatically correct English sentences, as in Example 6.5.

Feature names also should be used consistently across classes to provide what is sometimes called *ad hoc polymorphism*. For example, each container class featuring a function that tests for membership should name the function, e.g., *has*.

```
if my_container.is_empty then
    io.putstring("No more objects in ")
    io.putstring(my_container.name)
    io.new_line
end -- if
```

Example 6.5

6.6.3 Version Management

If Eiffel is used to build reusable software, reusable components have to be supported and maintained for at least several years. On this timescale, the use of version management tools is mandatory. Version managers should be used to deal with multiple revisions of classes. Commented-out and dead code should not be left lying around. Version managers also can automate the storage, retrieval, logging, identification, and merging of revisions.

One popular version management tool is the revision control system (RCS). It is freely available for most operating systems. Several other version management tools exist, either free or commercial, but they basically have the same types of functionality.

RCS allows the programmer to store and retrieve multiple revisions of text in a space-efficient way. Revisions can be retrieved according to ranges of revision numbers, symbolic names, dates, authors, and states. RCS logs all changes automatically (stamped with author, date and time data, and log message). It also can deal with access conflicts, maintain trees of revisions, and merge them back.

With RCS, each revision of a class may be identified automatically with name, revision number, creation time, and author. The identification is like a stamp that can be embedded at an appropriate place in the text of a class. The identification makes it simple to determine which revisions of which classes make up a given configuration.

To use this mechanism, an Eiffel class should feature a manifest string of the form "Id". RCS will replace this marker with a string of the form:

```
"$Id: hello.e,v 1.3 1995/03/20 17:03:42 jezequel $"
```

Markers expanded in more concise ways also exist.

With such a marker in the indexing clause of each class (see Section 6.6.4), you can always determine which revision you are working on. RCS keeps the markers up to date automatically. To propagate the markers into your object code, simply put them into constant string features (see Example 6.6).

A class revision can then be queried at run time (e.g., by test programs). An RCS command called *ident* also extracts such markers from any file, even object code and dumps. Thus, *ident* lets you find out which revisions of which classes were used in a given program.

You also may find it useful to put the marker Log inside a comment, preferably at the end of the class. This marker accumulates the log messages

```
        rcs_id : STRING is "$Id"
```
Example 6.6

associated with each revision. Thus, you can maintain the complete history of your class directly inside it.

6.6.4 Documentation and Indexing

Analysis and Design-Level Documentation

Within the maintenance phase of a software system life cycle, poor documentation costs even more than poor code. Analysis and design-level documentation should be available so the future maintenance team can understand the rationale behind the code. Most notably, all design decisions should be remembered, along with their motivations. If the context changes in the future, the maintenance team should be able to reverse a design decision with full knowledge of all its ramifications.

Clearly, the OMT diagrams developed at several stages of the software system life cycle are very useful for documenting a complex system. Ideally they should be made available in a computer-readable form (which is easy if a CASE tool is used) and stored along with the relevant subsystems. Enough resources should be allocated during the maintenance phase to keep them consistent with the actual evolving structure of the software system. Even better, if an integrated bidirectional CASE (such as EiffelCase for the BON method [109]) tool is used, this consistency between analysis and design information and the actual software system would be automatically maintained.

Code-Level Documentation

Implementation-related documentation that is not part of the code is usually so wrong or out of date that it does not help. The documentation has to be part of the code, integrated in the version management system, and then manipulated sensibly with browsing and extraction tools. With Eiffel you no longer need the kind of documentation in which each function gets a huge header with lots of asterisks that tell you who wrote the code, what day of the week it was, and everything that duplicates easily accessible information (like the names and types of the parameters and the name of the feature), and nothing whatsoever about what the feature actually does.

Most of the interesting information about a class is already present and made prominent in the class text: whether it is generic, its parents, its features and their specifications (signatures, preconditions, postconditions), and its class invariant. Widely available class abstractors (the various flavors of the *short* tools) can use this information to produce concise and relevant documentation. This documentation is often called the *flat-short* form of a class, because it produces a self-contained description of everything a client needs to know to use the class, and nothing more. That is, it deals with renaming and redeclaration. It also reconstructs full preconditions, postconditions, and class invariants by combining all the assertions from the ancestor classes. Finally, it removes all information that is not relevant to client classes, including nonexported features and routine implementations.

The only things that would need to be added would be a short description of the class purposes (e.g., extracted from the OMT class dictionary); version information; warnings that are applicable to the class users (such as whether a given routine or the full class has been made obsolete by a new release); or information about the space and time requirements of features; and possible bibliographical references for the algorithm used. This extra information may still be embedded in the class text, through comments occurring in specific places, and through *indexing* and *obsolete* clauses.

Comment Layout

To make the automatic extraction of comments possible, several conventions should be followed with respect to the layout of the relevant comments:

- Each routine should have a short comment that explains what it does. This comment should follow the keyword **is** on one or more new lines as necessary. The information already available in the routine specification (signature, preconditions, and postcondition) should not be repeated in this comment. It should not be necessary to look at the implementation to find out what a routine does.

- If an attribute needs a comment (e.g., it has a misleading name), the comment should follow either on the same line or, as for routines, on the following one.

- The **end** at the end of a class should be followed by a comment that recalls the class name.

- The **end** at the end of a routine definition should take the form **end --** followed by the routine name (unless the routine definition is all on one line in which case the comment may be omitted).

- With nested control structures the **end** at the end of a loop may be written **end -- loop** and at the end of an **if** may be written **end -- if**.

Indexing Clause

The *indexing* clause provides a powerful mechanism for cataloging classes under many criteria. It consists of a set of pairs (index, value), as described in Syntax Diagram 38.

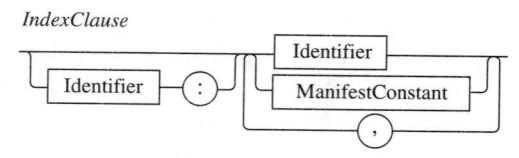

Syntax Diagram 38 Index clause syntax

Although indices are free identifiers, it is useful to define a small set of indices used consistently across all the classes of a given project or, still better, at the company level. The following indices are widely used in the Eiffel world:

description: associated with a short description of the class, coming for example from the OMT data dictionary elaborated during the object-modeling phase, and enriched in the design phase.

revision: associated with a version management-specific manifest string; e.g., "Id" for RCS.

implementation: associated with a list of keywords that describe implementation properties.

Other indices could be added to library classes to facilitate query-based automatic retrieval from eventual databases of software components.

Obsolete Clause

During the maintenance phase of a software system life cycle, a feature may become obsolete, because of a simplification in the implementation, a change in the class interface, or simply because a more meaningful name has been found for it. The *obsolete* clauses are then available to preserve the existing software without stifling the unavoidable process of evolution.

With the syntax described in Syntax Diagram 39, it is possible to declare either a routine to be obsolete (see Example 6.7) or the full class (the class obsolescence clause was described in Syntax Diagram 1 on page 20).

A feature declared *obsolete* can still be used normally, but any call to the feature will trigger a compile-time warning (the same holds for an obsolete class). An obsolete feature also will disappear from the short form of the class, and then should be slowly forgotten by clients. This approach provides for the seamless evolution of a software system, without breaking the existing one.

Obsolete

```
─( obsolete )─┤ Message ├─
```

Message

```
─┤ ManifestString ├─
```

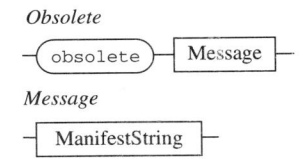

Syntax Diagram 39 Obsolete clause syntax

```
    sort(first, last: INTEGER) is
        obsolete "You should use quick_sort_range(first, last)"
        do
            quick_sort_range(first, last)
        end -- sort
```

Example 6.7

6.6.5 Implementation Strategy of the SMDS Server

The OMT system design allowed us to decompose our application in a set of loosely coupled clusters that are implemented as operating system directories (see Section 6.5.2). Each cluster should contain:

- The source code of the Eiffel classes belonging to it, plus possibly the source and object code of related external software (e.g., low-level interface modules written in C),

- A subdirectory called `RCS`, which holds all the versioning information (see Section 6.6.3),

- a subdirectory called `docs`, which holds the cluster-level documentation such as the OMT diagrams concerning this cluster,

- A subdirectory called `tests` which holds the test cases for this cluster, along with the necessary configuration and input files, and

- For library clusters, a subdirectory called `examples`, which holds the Eiffel source code of a set of pedagogical use case examples of the library classes.

Depending on the version management tool used in a project, the versioning information could be organized differently.

The output of the object-design stage gave us the class specifications, which consist of the inheritance relationships and the specifications (signature, preconditions, and postconditions) of each feature. For each class, a skeleton can then be generated (either manually or with the help of a CASE tool), thus enabling the Eiffel compiler to syntactically check the signature consistency among classes. The implementation then can proceed feature by feature. Provided the precondition holds, code must be written to satisfy the postcondition, using the algorithms chosen in the relevant object-design subphase and the various *programming in the small* correctness-enforcing Eiffel features (such as loop variants and invariants described in Section 2.4.7).

The order in which features are implemented is important and is discussed in relation to V & V issues in the next chapter.

7
From Implementation to Delivery

In This Chapter
- 7.1 Verification and Validation
- 7.2 Unit Testing of Eiffel Classes
- 7.3 Integration Testing
- 7.4 SMDS Server Acceptance Testing
- 7.5 The OMT/Eiffel Approach

"Errare humanum est, persevare diabolicum." Because they are human, even the best software engineers make errors. The worst sin would be to ignore this reality, so we now address verification and validation (V&V) issues with respect to Eiffel systems built according to the principles presented in the previous chapter. We take you where most of the OOAD methodologies leave you (descending down to the bottom of the V model), and try to help you safely climb the ascending branch, through unit testing, integration, acceptance testing, and future maintenance.

7.1 Verification and Validation

7.1.1 Introduction

For the reasons outlined in Section 1.1, large software systems are inherently complex. Statistics show that at the end of the implementation phase, most software systems have 1 to 3 bugs per 100 lines of code [135]. This bug rate does not change much with the programming language used (although you make a much larger system with 100 lines of Eiffel using powerful libraries than with 100 lines of assembly language). The software engineering answer to this problem is to V&V everything that is developed. Extensive V&V during software development is essential for building better software.

Verification is the evaluation of the software during each phase of its life cycle to ensure that it meets the requirements laid down in the previous phase. For example, the verification of an Eiffel routine implementation would consist of formally proving that it meets its specification—that is, provided its precondition is respected, the implementation implies the postcondition (and the class invariant). Even if such a fully formal specification exists for each routine, formal software verification is generally too tedious to do successfully on a large scale without machine aids. Automated formal verification tools, however, are quite limited by the size of the problems with which they are able to deal.

Validation refers to a process that aims at increasing our confidence that software meets its requirements. It usually relies on a combination of reasoning and testing, and encompasses unit, integration, and acceptance testing. These testing phases match the implementation, design, and analysis phases, as illustrated earlier in Figure 1.1.

The purpose of testing is to find out whether there are faults in a software system; this is different from *debugging*, which refers to the process of ascertaining *why* software fails. (In the IEEE standard terminology, *errors* represent human mistakes that can result in *faults* or *bugs* in a system; the execution of a faulty system produces *failures* [106].) The process of testing is to find the minimum number of test cases that can produce the maximum number of failures in the concerned system to achieve a desired level of confidence.

The costs of validation should not be underestimated. Testing-related activities may consume at least half of the total development cost of a software system [17, 146]. Even though the importance of testing is well known, few techniques are available for testing object-oriented systems. Most of the OOAD techniques proposed as of this writing do not really address V&V activities.

7.1.2 The Testing Process

Exhaustive testing is generally not possible because the input and output spaces of software systems are usually so large that the number of possible combinations that could require testing may be considered infinite for all practical purposes. As E. W. Dijkstra put it, *"Testing can determine the presence of faults, never their absence."* The only result that can be expected is a high level of confidence that the unit being tested operates correctly. In practice, the number of test cases actually required to achieve a high degree of reliability is small in proportion to the size of the possible input and output spaces [107]. A strategy is thus needed to drive the testing process efficiently. The testing activity can be divided roughly into five stages that are still applicable in an object-oriented context:

1. Identification of the testing criteria. Testing criteria define the goals for comparing a system to a specification. Some relevant testing criteria are *reliability*, *completeness*, *robustness*, *consistency*, and *usability*. Testability is a measure of the ease with which other criteria for testing can be established.

2. Identification of the target components for testing. In procedural systems, the components that were subject to testing were procedures and functions, clusters of procedures and functions, execution paths, and the complete application as a whole. However, in object-oriented systems there are new components that must be tested, such as effective and deferred classes and hierarchy among classes.

3. Generation of test cases, where each test case consists of test input and expected output. Test case generation is driven by the testing criteria discussed earlier. Of all the stages of testing, test case generation is the most time-consuming because it is not so prone to automation. The primary goal in test case generation is to produce test cases that can identify faults in an implementation. The number of admissible test cases for a given program design is huge, so the actual goal of test case generation is to generate the smallest number of test cases that will be effective in identifying the largest number of faults in a program.

4. Execution of test cases against the target components. Once the tests have been defined, it may be necessary to develop specific programs or environments to run the tests.

5. Evaluation to determine whether the tests have produced the expected results. If not, a bug report has to be issued. The Eiffel assertions (and specifically the postconditions, class invariants, loop variants, and invariants) can be of great help in automating bug detections (see Section 7.2.3).

7.1.3 Testing Techniques

The objective of pragmatic testing is thus to reduce the number of test cases and minimize the cost of testing without sacrificing its quality. Various pragmatic testing methods have been developed to test conventional software [13,

107]. Each of these methods specifies a strategy for generating and evaluating test cases to judge various aspects of software system quality. In the following paragraphs, we outline these various test case generation techniques and strategies and specifically state whether they are applicable to Eiffel systems in the context of design by contract.

Black-Box Testing

Black-box comparisons are based on the input and output alone without any consideration of the underlying implementations [107]. Black-box test cases thus are generated from the functional specifications of a software component. The black-box methods are subcategorized as random test case generation, partition-based test case generation, and cause-effect–based test case generation.

Random testing is the generation of test inputs randomly from the input space of the system. Although it is traditionally considered a weak method, its ease of generating test inputs and power of detecting failures have been noticed and explained by the fact that a small percentage of input space can be used to determine a good estimate of the reliability of the system. For random testing to be effective it must be easy to generate expected outputs, or to have an easy way to check that the system had a correct reaction. Eiffel class invariants and routine postconditions can be used for that purpose. A routine postcondition states that the routine must guarantee certain requirements at completion of any correct call. It thus provides a formal specification of what the routine should accomplish. The Eiffel run time makes it possible to check dynamically that the routine meets its specification (see Section 4.2).

Partition testing (input or output based) is used to reduce the number of test cases by partitioning the input or output spaces into equivalence classes and sampling test cases from each equivalence class. Partition-based test case generation techniques include input partitioning, output partitioning, boundary value analysis, and equivalence partitioning. However, beyond boundary testing—which requires that test cases be generated that are on and immediately around the boundaries of the input and output for a component—the partitioning criteria are not obvious and may require considerable expertise.

Cause-effect graph testing uses the functional specifications and the implemented solution to generate test cases in an exhaustive fashion [107].

Although this type of testing is not feasible for a complete system, it can point out ambiguities and incompleteness in a subset of solution (or problem) specifications and implementation. The exhaustive nature of this testing makes it particularly effective for detecting unanticipated side effects in critical subsystems.

White-Box Testing

White-box testing, the opposite of black-box testing, uses internal properties of the system as test case generation criteria [107]. Test cases are generated based on the possible execution paths in a program, without regard to the specification. The goal of white-box testing is to identify, for example, unintentional infinite loops, paths through the code that should not be allowed, and dead code. There are several dynamic paths in a program, so these paths can be partitioned and test cases can be generated from each partition.

There are different variations of white-box testing techniques based on the coverage criteria [107], which is a measure of the number and type of statements executed, as well as how these statements are executed. *Statement coverage* is simply the proportion of executable statements in the system that is exercised at least once. *Branch (or condition) coverage* is the proportion of binary decisions that take on a true and a false outcome at least once, and the proportion of exceptions that are raised at least once. *Multiple condition coverage*, or the proportion of clauses in the conditional tests within the program that produces all outcomes, is also useful.

It is very unlikely that 100% coverage of a system will be achieved with any of these coverage measures, because loops may have a varying number of iterations depending on the input space; there may be branches within the program that may only be executed during exceptional circumstances; there may be dead code (though with modern Eiffel compilers you are warned of it); and there may be paths through the program that are not feasible, because of the mutual exclusivity of two conditions [53, 110]. Another problem is illustrated by the small algorithm discussed in Section 1.1.2. For all practical purposes, you need an infinite number of test cases (one for each possible input number), so your test coverage will be 0%! Fortunately, not all programs are that pathological.

Path-based testing [94] is probably the most commonly used white-box testing technique. McCabe defines the *cyclomatic complexity* of a software component as the number of independent execution paths through it. This number can be used along with a graph of the control flow through the same piece of software to come up with a set of test cases that will cause executable statements to be executed at least once. One can make a strong intuitive argument that, if done correctly, McCabe's approach will bring a very high degree of coverage; i.e., at least statement coverage and, quite possibly, as much as multiple-condition coverage [11]. A disadvantage of this technique is that the effort in testing is proportional to the number of paths in the design. However, if you follow the design guidelines provided in Section 6.4.6, you'll end up with short Eiffel routines that have very low cyclomatic complexities. Then the testing of these routines can be made very easy, or even so trivial that it can be replaced with (manual) verification.

This is yet another argument for small and simple routines in Eiffel.

In traditional systems, these test cases must be augmented with additional test cases for exceptions and interrupts. Due to the disciplined nature of the exception mechanism available in Eiffel (see Section 5.1) there may only be a limited rupture of the flow of control when an exception is raised: The real cyclomatic complexity of a routine subject to exceptions only grows linearly with the number of instructions in the routine. Exception handling code does not bring additional complexity by itself, because it can only *retry* the execution of the routine, or propagate the exception.

In contrast, the dynamic binding mechanism makes path-based testing across feature boundaries extremely difficult, and impossible in practice.

State-Based Test Case Generation

A feature can change the state of an object based on different input data. If feature functionalities can be expressed in a state-based design (such as the OMT dynamic model), then classic state-based test case generation techniques can be applied to each feature for test case generation.

Inspections and Walkthroughs

Inspections and walkthroughs are manual or computer-assisted (through CASE tools) comparisons of software development products (analysis and design documents and actual code [50, 45]). To be efficient, these activities require that the documents and software be read and paraphrased by engineers other than the original developers. Walkthroughs are done by going through the various execution paths of a program. Inspections are usually done by comparing the target product to a checklist of design recommendations. Several studies made it clear that in conventional systems, inspections and walkthroughs efficiently assist in identifying faults early and thus improve the quality of the software applications [58] (see Table 7.1).

The dynamic structure of object-oriented system execution often makes it difficult to statically determine the execution flow. Therefore, new techniques and tool support are essential for performing walkthroughs on an object-oriented design or program. The inspection of analysis and design documents and the code reading inspections are, however, still very useful in detecting

Table 7.1 Comparison of testing efficiency

Testing type	Efficiency (defects found/hour)
Regular use	0.210
Black box	0.282
White box	0.322
Reading inspections	1.057

faults early in an object-oriented system, provided a set of basic rules (such as defined in Section 6.4) is defined at a project level. For example, if routines are kept as small as recommended in Section 6.4.6, the code inspection can become an actual *verification* that the postcondition is ensured by the routine body (even if the postcondition is a nonexecutable assertion). Clearly, this manual routine verification almost eliminates the need for intraroutine testing, which then should be reserved for special kinds of routines, such as routines dealing with user input.

Implementing a systematic code review process in software projects has a nonnegligible psychological side effect. Developers know that the first test their software will pass is a peer's reading inspection, so they tend to write software *that can be read easily* in order for them to avoid providing detailed oral explanations. This clarity will make future maintenance work considerably easier, and thus improve the overall quality of the software.

7.1.4 Specificities of Object-Oriented Testing

Very few of the numerous first-generation books on analysis, design, and implementation of object-oriented software explicitly address V&V issues. Despite this initial lack of interest, testing of object-oriented systems is receiving much more attention [15]. For example, it was the subject of a special issue of the *Communications of the ACM* in September 1994 (Vol. 37, No. 9). This special issue starts with a discussion of test case generation from OOAD products of OMT [116]. Object-oriented integration testing using message-feature pairs is discussed in [80] without, however, giving details on test case generation nor on the criteria that can be used for selecting message-feature pairs from all possible pairs. Discussions of cluster and class testing, test case management, and execution using a scripting language are found in [106]. An object-oriented testing approach integrated in the software development process is presented in [95]. The conclusion of this special issue covers the author's experiences with testing of object-oriented programs [7].

Several issues related to V&V and maintenance of object-oriented programs are given in [49, 11, 82]. There is also a discussion in [16] of how to align the development process with testing so that designs are testable and testing is maximally effective.

We outline the consequences the object-oriented approach has on three levels of testing: intrafeature testing, interfeature testing, and testing of class hierarchies.

Intrafeature Testing

An object-oriented routine body can be compared to a classic imperative routine, so most of the techniques developed for procedural testing still apply, as outlined in the previous section. This application has been confirmed by several studies; e.g., in [51] there is a description of how the McCabe cyclomatic testing method was used to ensure independent path coverage of features in a C++ system. Test cases were derived from the range of values expected by parameters to methods, boundary analysis of parameter values, and erroneous values to place the unit under stress. Other test cases were derived from the unit specification. Classes are validated in the order determined by a call graph of the project. The classes at the bottom of the graph are validated first, removing the requirement for test driver classes that emulate unvalidated parameter classes.

Interfeature Testing

A class is a mapping of the real world into code. More test cases thus may be derived intuitively, because of easy visualization of the model on which the class is based by the programmer and tester [130].

A class also can be considered as an abstract data type (ADT), and tested relative to the ADT specification. For example, in [52] an approach based on the algebraic specification of ADTs is used with Eiffel to build a set of tools for object-oriented testing (ASTOOT). Test cases consist of pairs of sequences of features along with a tag. The tag reflects whether the two sequences of features should leave an object in the same abstract state. The method depends heavily on the completeness of the ADT's specification (see [76] for more details). A class is said to be a correct implementation of an ADT if and only if for every pair of sequences of features applied to a pair of objects, the objects are put into observationally equivalent states (a user-supplied routine is used to check the equivalence of the two objects). ASTOOT consists of three components: the driver generator, the compiler, and the simplifier. The compiler and the simplifier combine to form an interactive test generation tool, which allows the user to generate a sequence of operations from an algebraic specification. The simplifier uses rewrite rules provided by the compiler to produce two equivalent sequences of operations that form a test case. The driver generator allows the execution of automatically or manually generated test cases.

A testing technique based on specifications representing the causal relations among various features of the classes is proposed in [82]. Two kinds of specifications are used. The method sequence specification (MtSS) of a class documents the correct causal order in which the features of the class can be invoked. The message sequence specification (MgSS) of a feature documents the causal order in which messages can be sent to different instances of classes (a simple regular expression formalism is used to represent causal order in both cases). The MtSS and MgSS of classes document the message-feature interaction and the correct sequence in which messages can flow through a system containing objects. The MtSS and MgSS can be incorporated easily as a part of many OOAD techniques so that for each class, the sequence specification can be captured. It is also possible to derive the sequence specification from OOAD products.

Testing of Class Hierarchies

As a factorization tool, inheritance should intuitively help the testing of class hierarchies. The features of the class that are provided by a parent class would only require minimal testing [134, 72]. However, one of the first papers addressing in depth the relationship between inheritance and testing was not so optimistic [115]. The authors describe the applicability of Weyuker's test adequacy criteria (described in [136]) to object-oriented systems. Their conclusion was that many of the well-tested parent class features would have to be retested in the context of subclasses, because the context of the features might have changed.

Fortunately, the testing of Eiffel class hierarchies is not that bad. First, the Eiffel inheritance mechanism is not "wild." It is harnessed by the notion of *design by contract* (see Section 6.4.2), which implies that a subclass must respect all the contracts of its ancestors. In Eiffel, a test set based on a routine specification should still be applicable to all its redefined versions [64]; this contradicts the premises of [115] holding for C++ or Smalltalk.

The suggested order of testing for an inheritance hierarchy of classes is (intuitively) from the top downward; that is, starting with the base classes, and continuing down the hierarchy. Testing must proceed by testing each feature in isolation, and then testing the interactions between the features. A test history associates a test case with the features it tests. A test history for a subclass is created by incrementally updating the test histories from the parent classes with information about the derived class's differences from the parent(s). From the new test history, reusable test cases from the parent class can be identified along with any attributes for which new test cases must be generated.

Still, inheritance of classes that maintain explicit states poses several open problems such as subtype substitutability and testing. A set of rules is provided in [82] for checking the consistency of inherited tests in the presence of single and multiple inheritance.

Finally, a good synthesis of the process of object-oriented testing can be found in [128]. The authors make a strong argument for "stateless" classes, or classes with features that can be combined in any order.

7.2 Unit Testing of Eiffel Classes

7.2.1 Class-Level Testing

The IEEE defines unit testing as the testing of individual hardware or software units or groups of related units. Usually the *unit* is tested in isolation by surrounding it with test stubs and drivers. Test stubs are replacements for the features called by the unit under test. Test drivers are replacements for the features that use the services provided by the unit under test.

In traditional (procedural) software systems, the chosen size of the unit tends to be the feature (function or procedure). However, in an object-oriented context, it is difficult to isolate a feature from its surrounding class and then to write test drivers and stubs (which themselves require testing) to replace the code removed, when the majority of the code required is already provided in the form of other features of the class or by other closely coupled classes belonging to the same cluster. The class therefore should be considered as the smallest unit for a test. In case of a cluster of strongly coupled classes, the smallest unit of the test could even be the cluster itself.

Testing methods designed for use with procedural style languages can be adapted for use with object-oriented systems, although they have to be applied to classes as a whole unit, rather than to individual features. Features are not tested in isolation, but the test cases simply concentrate on exercising each feature in turn to its maximum coverage. A test set is therefore created for each feature of a class, according to the testing strategy (i.e., the testing criteria) and using relevant testing tactics (as defined in the previous section, e.g., black-box random testing).

The individual feature test sets are grouped together at the class (or the cluster) level in one or more test sequences. Unit testing can then be conducted by applying these test sequences to one or more instances of the class being tested.

7.2.2 Test Development

Several approaches may be considered to implement test sequences, from the less intrusive to the more integrated. Each has its strong and weak points, so an adequate combination of these implementation techniques should be used to deal with the peculiarities of the class being tested.

Testing from the Client Perspective

Clearly, testing from the client perspective is the most elegant solution for black-box testing of effective classes (e.g., implementing ADTs). For each such class X to be tested, an X_DRIVER class can be developed to create an instance of X, to invoke its features with the appropriate parameters, to create the initial scenario for the test cases, to perform the sequence of test cases, and to validate any results. In the case of testing of tightly coupled classes or very small classes, a single test driver class could be used to test a full cluster.

The drawback of this approach is that the strong encapsulation available in Eiffel does not always allow a test driver to determine whether a given operation did its job correctly (e.g., if the correctness property could not be expressed as an executable assertion). Also, testing from the client perspective does not allow private features to be tested directly, and otherwise produces very little information on the coverage of the test cases.

Testing from a Subclass Perspective

An Eiffel class may not hide features to its children, so testing from a subclass perspective would allow private features to be tested directly. An X_TEST class may be derived from the class X (which is being tested) and get privileged access to all its features, as well as the capability to perform any relevant consistency checks. Testing from a subclass perspective also enables deferred classes to be tested. For each feature left deferred in X, an effective stub implementation could be provided in X_TEST.

However, if the class being tested is a generic class, it may be difficult or even impossible to provide relevant values for generic input parameters, and to check the generic results. A dedicated class would need to be used for testing X_TEST with actual generic parameters. If the X_TEST class is not generic, however, and if all classes being tested have a creation procedure called, for example, *self_test*, then a single test driver pattern could be used for all X_TEST classes (see Example 7.1).

The advantage of this solution is that no modifications are needed on the actual code of the class being tested. The drawback is that three parallel hierarchies of classes must be maintained and updated consistently: For each X

```
    class X_SELF_TEST_DRIVER
    creation
        make
    feature
5       make is
            -- exercise the X self test capability
        local unit: X_TEST
        do
            !!unit.self_test
10      end -- make
    end -- X_SELF_TEST_DRIVER
```
Example 7.1

there are a class X_TEST and a class X_SELF_TEST_DRIVER, even if this latter class could be generated automatically for nongeneric classes.

Embedded Tests

Just as the class is sometimes compared to an integrated component, the solution to this problem also comes from the hardware field, where basic test suites are packaged with VLSI reusable components; standard built-in test capability is provided to automatically exercise the component. Otherwise, this approach has the same advantages and disadvantages that the previous one had with respect to genericity and test drivers.

A new advantage is that the test code is automatically inherited by subclasses—although it can be redefined if needed. Specific testing code becomes dead code in the delivered version of the software, and is thus eliminated as a compile-time optimization available in most Eiffel compilers.

7.2.3 Test Execution and Evaluation

Test execution and evaluation correspond to the actual running of the tests to check whether they produce the expected results. If not, a bug report has to be issued.

For that, all test drivers must be compiled, instantiated, and run, either through a shell script or through another Eiffel class (a kind of META_DRIVER class). During the driver executions, all assertions should be monitored by the Eiffel run time (see Section 4.2). If a failure is detected (either through an assertion violation or a specific test), an exception should be raised and the exception history should be printed to help localize the fault and produce a bug report.

Results from the test runs also could be verified by simple file comparison with the expected results. This technique is cumbersome, however, because of the time required to generate the expected output exactly. Still, in some cases it can be an easier technique to use, rather than to develop self-verifying test cases.

7.2.4 Life-Cycle and Nonregression Testing

Life-cycle testing addresses issues such as when to stop testing (reliability testing), whether existing test cases are sufficient to detect certain kinds of faults (mutation testing), or whether an old feature has been changed during software maintenance (autoregression testing). Autoregression testing has been used extensively on conventional software. It is fully applicable here, and quite facilitated if META_DRIVER classes are used in each cluster to automatically exercise all test cases with a single entry point, such as the routine *make* of the class META_DRIVER.

7.3 Integration Testing

7.3.1 Integration Strategies

Integration is an activity whereby the software components identified at the design stage and checked during unit testing are assembled. Integration is a key phase in software construction. At this stage many projects fall behind schedule and suffer large cost overruns.

The IEEE defines integration testing as the testing phase in which software components, hardware components, or both are combined and tested to evaluate the interaction between them. The interface between the components is the focus of the testing process. Integration must be carefully prepared. The order in which the parts are integrated must be designed carefully, and an integration test strategy must be adopted. If all units were integrated simultaneously, integration testing would result in an attempt to test the resulting whole at once (sometimes called "big bang" testing). With the exception of very small, noncritical systems, nonincremental integration testing is not advisable. Incremental testing, on the other hand, dictates that after each unit (that is, a class or a cluster of strongly coupled classes) has been tested in isolation, it should be integrated, one at a time, into the system, testing the overall system while integrating it. There are many different approaches to incremental testing, such as top-down, bottom-up, and sandwich [107]. Incremental testing is almost always preferable to nonincremental testing [11].

7.3.2 Incremental Integration

The strategy adopted for the SMDS server integration is guided by the client-server relationships among classes (which roughly correspond to the call graphs found in procedural languages); these relationships are outputs of the OMT design phase. The classes at the bottom of the graph that are called by other classes, but that do not call any themselves, are tested first. The testing then continues up the graph using the previously validated classes in the testing of other classes. If the testing is conducted in this manner, the resources that would have been used for writing and testing the test stubs replacing the called classes are saved.

However, the call graph of a complex system is seldom a tree. In our SMDS server, for example, the level 3 classes (congestion, data transfer, and routing management entities) have mutual feature calls. It is thus necessary to choose an integration order among them, and replace lately integrated classes with stub classes. For example, the STUB_CME (Example 7.2) contains the function *is_ok_for_sending_to* that is queried by the DTE when it has to send a user L3_DTPDU. The stub version of this function always answers *yes*, whereas the real one relies on a complex congestion management algorithm to make its decision. Stub procedures simply print information messages on the standard output.

The output of the object-design stage gave us the class specifications, consisting of the inheritance relationships and the specification (signature, pre-

```
        indexing
            description: "Entity dealing with the congestion in the network, %
                    %and monitoring it within the SS"
        class STUB_CME
5       inherit
            RINGABLE
        creation
            make

10      feature {ANY}
            make (shared_pdu : L3_DTPDU) is
                require
                    pdu_exist: shared_pdu /= Void
                do
15                  !!my_cmpdu.make_from(shared_pdu)
                ensure
                    cmpdu_exist: my_cmpdu /= Void
                end -- make
```

Example 7.2 (Lines 1–18)

```
            set_links (the_dte : DTE) is
20              require
                    dte_exist: the_dte /= Void
                do
                    dte := the_dte
                end -- set_links
25          process_CMPDU is
                    -- process the new CMPDU aliased my_cmpdu
                    -- May come from either the DTE or from myself
                do
                    io.putstring("process_CMPDU stub called%N")
30              end -- process_CMPDU
            is_ok_for_sending_to (destination : INTEGER) : BOOLEAN is
                    -- Whether the next PDU may be sent by the DTE
                do
                    Result := True
35              end -- is_ok_for_sending_to
            IA_Table_Recalculated is
                    -- Tell the CME that the IA routing table has been changed,
                    -- and that its internal data structures have to be reset
                do
40              end -- IA_Table_Recalculated
        feature {OPERATOR}
            process_request (r : OPER_REQUEST) is
                    -- process an operator request
                do
45                  io.putstring("process_request stub called%N")
                end -- process_request
            perform_MOC is
                    -- Measures of congestion on ISSI links
                do
50              end -- perform_MOC
            -- etc.
        feature {TIMER}
            ring is
                    -- call back by a timer upon ringing
55              do
                end -- ring
        feature {NONE}
            my_dte : DTE -- Link to the DTE
            my_cmpdu : CMPDU -- Local PDU, which is physically included in
60                              -- the globally shared L3_DTPDU
        end -- STUB_CME
```

Example 7.2 (Lines 19–61)

conditions, and postconditions) of each feature. A skeleton class then can be generated for each class, and the Eiffel strong encapsulation mechanism ensures that clearly defined interfaces exist between them. This can be syntactically checked with the Eiffel compiler. All signature discrepancies should be caught *before* the integration phase begins.

Conducting the phases of implementation, unit testing, and integration in an incremental way makes it possible to have these activities merged. The idea is to progressively replace stub features with the real implementations, and then test them class by class. After a class is implemented, it is tested separately to validate its internal consistency, according to the method presented in Section 7.2. It is then added to the system in lieu of its stub class, and the system is tested against this new set of functionalities. The preconditions of Eiffel features are used to monitor the correctness of the values passed across objects.

This merged process has the additional benefit of circumventing the difficulty of writing test stub classes that model the responses of real classes accurately without actually having to write the classes themselves. There is, of course, an exception; when dealing with external stimuli, it is likely to be more cost-effective to write the test stubs for unit testing. This choice has to be made by the tester, and must be based on the resources required to write the stub as opposed to using the original class.

Test drivers also still have to be written, using high-level information on the expected reaction of the subpart of the system being integrated. One can write several scenarios in which several subsystems cooperate, for example, using the scenarios developed for the dynamic model of the system during the OMT analysis phase. Each of the subsystems must be used in a well-defined manner and scenario-based testing helps to ensure that at the highest level these subsystems function properly. In addition, scenario-based test sequences are useful in testing the end-user classes. These test sequences also can be used as system-level test cases. The scenarios between the system and the user are captured for testing the major interactions and information exchanges. Scenarios must be constructed for normal situations first and then for exception situations. Thus, for each kind of functionality supported at interface classes, one can generate several scenario-based test sequences.

7.3.3 Assembling the SMDS Server

The SMDS server is built and tested incrementally, according to the principles discussed in Section 7.2. The test bed is a bunch of UNIX workstations communicating through an Ethernet LAN. We are not interested in performances at this stage, so the low bandwidth of Ethernet is not a problem.

The order of integration considered in the following paragraphs is dictated by the call graph, and highly reflects the layered structure of the SMDS server software.

Support Modules These are general-purpose support modules (e.g., timer handling or spanning tree algorithms) that can be implemented and tested separately. A great deal of effort should be devoted to making them as general and bug-free as possible, because they are likely to be reused in future applications.

Lower Levels We start the SMDS server implementation with the class INTERFACE, which deals with the network interface. It is validated with the sending and receiving of L3_DTPDUS, and by checking that read and write accesses to the various PDU fields are made correctly. There is no integration testing at this stage because it is the only cluster implemented.

DTE Once the lower level works, we can attack the level 3, starting with the DTE. To prepare its integration tests, we write a DTE_DRIVER class playing the role of an SMDS service user entity. The integration test consists of having two partially implemented SMDS servers (INTERFACE + DTE + DTE_DRIVER) exchanging messages.

LME The DTE_DRIVER is then replaced with a real LME, which is driven by a TRAFFIC_SIMULATOR. The validation test is the same as for the DTE, but now the system is somehow more "real" because a TRAFFIC_SIMULATOR communicates with a distant peer via the LME, the DTE, the INTERFACE, and the Ethernet. This test, however, needs some kind of a routing table in the SMDS servers, which is hard-coded in a STUB_RME heir class called FIXED_RME.

GARME The GARME implementation proceeds in the same way. It is connected to the TRAFFIC_SIMULATOR and tested with a FIXED_RME. This step might have been interchanged with the previous one.

NME The NME and its client, the OPERATOR, are implemented with the same pattern as for the LME and the TRAFFIC_SIMULATOR. The integration test also uses the FIXED_RME, which allows the OPERATOR to exchange NME-specific PDUs (*route_test*, *loop_back* ...) with its peers.

RME The RME is the most complex part of our SMDS server. It is implemented incrementally. Following the NEIGHBOR state diagram shown in

Figure 6.6, we replace several related stub features with the real ones. In a first stage, we consider the features dealing with the *Hello* packets, then with the *DBdescr* ones, and finally with the *LSReq*, *LSA*, and *LSAck* packets.

Once the adjacency protocol has been implemented and tested, the computation of the routing tables can be considered. This computation uses shortest path spanning tree algorithms that have been implemented and tested with the support modules. To test the overall result, we have to create various (logical) topologies of connected SMDS servers using several workstations and check that the routing tables are properly computed and consistent among the various SMDS servers of our test bed network.

Other Modules The STUB_CME should be replaced with an actual CME, and the TRAFFIC_SIMULATOR with a real subscriber interface (e.g., to an IP network) to obtain a real SMDS server. These steps are not described here, because they are not necessary to start acceptance and performance testing.

7.4 SMDS Server Acceptance Testing

Once the integration tests of the SMDS server are completed, we can start the final phase of SMDS server development—the acceptance tests. The goal of the acceptance testing process is to check how closely a software system conforms to its initial requirements. A client will accept or reject the delivered software product based on the results of this acceptance testing process. Acceptance testing consists of both qualitative and quantitative tests. Qualitative tests try to check whether the SMDS server behaves according to its specifications. Quantitative tests give information about the overall performance of the SMDS servers.

7.4.1 Qualitative Tests

Test Case Generation for Robustness

So far we have mainly concentrated on test case generation techniques for checking the correctness of the target classes. It is also important to generate test cases to test the robustness of the classes. Robustness testing can be minimized at the class level through the use of preconditions, but it is still useful to check whether the system is robust against external input/output. One way to test the robustness is to generate negative test cases or dirty test cases [13]. A negative test case is a test case with invalid data so that the target code can identify and raise exceptions.

Real-Time Constraints

Eiffel frees the programmer from the burden of explicitly reclaiming heap memory, thanks to a garbage collector (see Section 4.5). However, we must ensure that the garbage collector does not take over the processor for too long, thus violating real-time constraints.

Most Eiffel implementations come with an incremental garbage collector that can be activated and suspended at will. On our SMDS server, we used the ISE EiffelBench environment, and we made measurements that determined that the garbage collector's work takes less time when it is called often, and that it globally needs less than 1% of the computation time. So, with frequent iterative garbage collections, its work duration has a Gaussian-like distribution with an average of 3 ms. As a result, our SMDS server launches an iterative collection each time it is otherwise idle (not to penalize packet processing), but if a working period is too long, a collection is forced so the optimal interval between two collections is respected, and the collecting time never exceeds 10 ms and has a probability of 99.9% to be under 7 ms. Despite the use of a high-level environment, the SMDS real-time constraints have been met (particularly the 10-ms *HelloInt* timer, which is the strictest).

In addition to limiting the garbage collector monopolization of the processor to short periods, the shifting of memory management processing to idle periods allows time savings during active periods. Our server then has a higher ability to absorb traffic peaks.

Stability Testing

The purpose of stability testing is to check whether the SMDS server software is stable enough to run for a long time without problems.

This test involves several SMDS servers (e.g., 20), each one implemented on a different workstation, running for several days (e.g., one week). Once their "adjacency" is established with all of their neighbors (the state diagram of Figure 6.6 is in the *Full* state), we check that it is never broken down (no *DeadInt* event) while moderate traffic is exchanged between the SMDS servers.

Dynamic Reconfiguration Testing

The purpose of dynamic reconfiguration testing is to check whether the SMDS network reconfigures itself properly in case of an SMDS server failure, and whether it is restored once the faulty SMDS server resumes.

In a first stage, we can check that routing tables are properly recomputed when another SMDS server fails (i.e., stops to answer messages). This test is implemented at the network management level, where the status of the routing tables can be made available to the operator.

In a second stage, we monitor the behavior of the SMDS network when more than one SMDS server fails, and how it evolves when the failure rate grows. This stage is implemented with more and more frequent random failures in the SMDS server.

Header Processing Speed

We first determine the internal performance limits of our SMDS server. The significant figures are the speed of header processing in different contexts: emission (packet received from an SNI and then injected in the SMDS network), reception (PDU incoming from an ISSI link and delivered to an SNI), and switching of traffic (from an ISSI link to another one).

For these specific measures, we use a specialized SMDS server, where the lower layers are simulated (we use a SIMULATED_INTERFACE instead of the class INTERFACE described in Section 6.5.2). An emission only consists of incrementing a counter. As for reception, the server is always told that a PDU is ready to be read and the reception is simulated (a fixed set of predefined PDUs is used). The measures consist of performing continual operations on the server and computing their mean durations (which is more realistic than exploring the assembly language listing to add up individual times of machine language instructions on a given path of the header processing).

The measurements in Table 7.2 have been made on a Sun SPARC20 workstation. These tests involve no network connection, so the results are directly proportional to the processing power of the processor.

The performance figures in Table 7.2 show that the internal speed of a sequential server is sufficient to reach gigabit flow rates on a standard processor: the slower operation reaches 3.29 Gb/s with 64k PDU.

Thus the bottleneck in such a system is not likely to be localized in the header processing but in the interface with the network. We have to measure the maximal data flow rate of a real server to confirm that.

Table 7.2 Header processing speed in an SMDS server

Kind of processing	Headers processed/s	Mean processing time
SNI to ISSI	5025	199 us
ISSI to SNI	8093	124 us
Switching (ISSI to ISSI)	5347	187 us

7.4 SMDS SERVER ACCEPTANCE TESTING

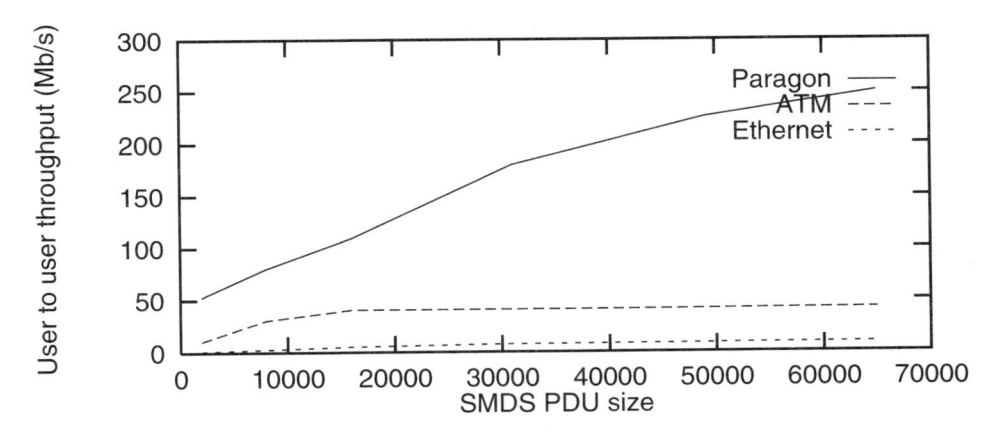

Figure 7.1 Maximal data flow rate of an SMDS server

Flow Rate Measurement

We want to determine the maximal data flow rate of our SMDS server for a set of representative physical network technologies. We measure a one-way, user-to-user, actual data flow rate through two SMDS servers communicating through a unique link. This measure takes into account the header processing, the operating system, the segmentation and reassembly overheads, and the actual data transmission between the two users. This experiment has been done with a range of PDU sizes, which allows us to get information on both the latency and the throughput of the network (see Figure 7.1).

The Ethernet (maximum bandwidth 10 Mb/s) and ATM experiments were led on SPARC workstations, with Fore System SBA-200 SBus interface boards in the latter case (maximum bandwidth 100 Mb/s). To experiment with a higher bandwidth, we also used the internal network of a parallel computer, the Intel Paragon XP/S. This computer is made of 56 processing nodes, linked by high-speed communication channels (having a maximum bandwidth of 640 Mbs/s for 64K messages) in a 2D grid topology. Each node of this machine has, in addition to the main processor (i860), a co-processor dedicated to communication with the other nodes. This parallel computer enables the simulation of large SMDS networks in a real context of multimegabit communication lines.

In any of these cases, the physical network bandwidth and the internal processing speed of our SMDS server both widely exceed the server maximal unidirectional flow rate. Thus, in our system there is a bottleneck located in the lower layers of the protocol (probably due to some inefficiencies at the network-server interface, to segmentation and reassembly, and to operating system overhead). The classic solution to this problem is to multiply access points to the network (see [60] for more details).

7.5 The OMT/Eiffel Approach

7.5.1 Effort Breakdown

The building of our server may be broken down into five main phases, following the V model of the software life cycle. The breakdown of the effort among these phases is described in Table 7.3.

The object-oriented approach, together with the incremental integration of the software, made it possible to greatly reduce the relative cost of the integration phase, which is usually much more costly and frequently exceeds all expectations (the nightmare of project managers).

Table 7.3 Effort breakdown among the phases of the software life cycle

Analysis	35%
Design	20%
Implementation and unit testing	25%
Integration testing	5%
Acceptance testing	15%

7.5.2 Coding Statistics

After the software is fully written, we may try to evaluate its size (without the test-related classes). The newly written code has 65 classes (totaling 7800 lines of code), unevenly distributed among 10 clusters:

CME: 1 class / 167 lines (not fully implemented).

COM: 1 class / 177 lines.

DTE: 1 class / 324 lines.

OPE: 1 class / 179 lines.

SIM: 2 classes / 297 lines.

INT: 3 classes / 373 lines.

ENT: 4 classes / 529 lines.

SUP: 12 classes / 833 lines.

RME: 23 classes / 3041 lines.

DAT: 17 classes / 1906 lines.

Most classes have between 100 and 150 lines of code (with the coding style described in Section 6.6.2). Some support classes are smaller, and the DTE is larger, with 300 lines.

The 65 classes contain 455 features, and the mean number of arguments per routine is 1.3.

7.5.3 Reuse

The main reuse source comes from ISE's EiffelBase library (see Section 8.2). The SMDS server software uses 54 classes of this library (totaling 11860 lines). The reuse rate equals 45% of the classes and 60% of the lines of codes.

Reuse also may work the other way around. Most of the classes specifically written for the SMDS server implementation may be reused for several related projects such as for support classes that are not tied to the particular SMDS protocols. Specific components, such as the RME, could be reused with little modification in SMDS-related implementations. For example, the OSPF Internet gateway protocol (RFC 1247) uses the same routing protocols.

Consider also the problem of simulating the behavior of a very large SMDS network. Instead of creating a single SMDS server on a workstation, we could create several hundreds or thousands of SMDS servers, with a simulated network interface and an event-driven simulation engine. This SMDS network simulator could be implemented easily, reusing most of the clusters developed so far. These clusters could be considered to be an SMDS simulation library.

8

Building Libraries: The Case of Data Structure Libraries

In This Chapter
- 8.1 Library Design
- 8.2 The EiffelBase Library
- 8.3 The **Tower***Eiffel* Booch Components
- 8.4 The SiG Library

Building a high-quality class library requires detailed domain knowledge and considerable development effort. There will be medium- or long-term payoffs if multiple applications are developed using abstractions from this domain. In this chapter we discuss several specific aspects of library design. We then outline three different designs for general-purpose data structure libraries (arguably among the software components with the most potential for reuse) that have led to commercial products: EiffelBase (from ISE), **Tower**Eiffel *Booch components (from Tower Technology), and the SiG library (from SiG). References for the corresponding vendors are listed in Appendix C.*

8.1 Library Design

8.1.1 Introduction

Building libraries of reusable components is a demanding and time-consuming undertaking. Object-oriented technology is an *enabling* technology for building such libraries. A language such as Eiffel, which features strong encapsulation mechanisms, inheritance, polymorphism, and dynamic binding, is a powerful tool for building reusable software components because it fosters a software construction method based on the paradigm of *real-world modeling*. Reusability does not come for free once you adopt Eiffel, however. Reusability must be a design goal, and enough resources should be allocated for it.

Reuse is not a new idea in software engineering (see, for instance, [96]). However, attempts to go beyond the reuse of source code and the reuse of personnel (i.e., reuse of the know-how of a given software engineer) are plagued by a set of well-identified problems such as the lack of reuse frameworks and the lack of flexibility of older software components. Also often underestimated are psychological and management-related problems. These problems include the "not invented here" syndrome, the lack of reward mechanisms for reusing code, and the conflict between the quick and dirty design of a component (e.g., if it is badly needed to meet a deadline) and the high quality (both in design and documentation) needed for making it reusable.

Reuse of class libraries actually can occur only if reuse is concretely profitable. That is, it must be easier, more efficient, and less costly to reuse software components from a class library than to rebuild them from scratch. However, the cost analysis for reuse should not be limited to the initial development phase of a software system, but should encompass its *full life cycle*, including its maintenance phase (sometimes spanning several years and several times the initial cost of the system).

These remarks allow us to express a set of external quality factors for Eiffel class libraries. These sometimes competing quality factors should be maximized for reuse to pay off:

Complete The library should provide facilities that are useful to many possible applications.

Efficient This goal is concerned with providing easily assembled components (efficient in compilation resources) that impose minimal run time and memory overhead (efficient in execution resources) and that are more reliable than hand-built mechanisms (efficient in developer resources).

Safe and reliable Assertions should be used extensively throughout the library to provide the user with the benefits of design by contract. The library ideally should come with test drivers that allow the library users to test it in their environment.

Easy and intuitive to use Clear and consistent organization should make it easy to identify and select appropriate components for a given need. Library use should follow intuitive and easy-to-remember patterns.

Extensible Adding new facilities or integrating new components while preserving the architectural integrity of the library should be possible and easy.

Platform- and compiler-independent The library should rely on the Eiffel Standard Library to be portable across compilers and architectures.

These goals cannot be achieved separately. On the contrary, they can only be met if several design principles are followed in a consistent way across the entire library.

Building a high-quality class library requires detailed domain knowledge and considerable development effort. It will bring a medium- or long-term payoff if multiple applications are developed using abstractions from this domain.

8.1.2 Domain Analysis

Object-oriented analysis is an initial step that allows the design of an implementable solution for a specific problem (see Section 6.3). Building reusable components requires a broader perspective, because reusable components should not only satisfy the immediate needs of the current system, but those of the future as well. Thus, the model of the real world—built as the first step of the object-oriented analysis—should be extended beyond the immediate problem domain to deal with classes and objects that are common to a range of software systems [21]. This commonality may come from the fact that a range of systems is to be built within a given application domain (e.g., telecommunications, MIS, and banking), or that they use common parts (e.g., graphical user interfaces and database interfaces) or general-purpose resources (e.g., data structures and mathematical operations).

This extended real-world modeling activity, often called *domain analysis*, is only useful if many related systems are to be built so that the cost of the domain analysis can be amortized over the cost of all the systems. Berard [11] define domain analysis as:

the process of identifying, collecting, organizing, and representing the relevant information in a domain based on the study of existing systems and their development histories, knowledge captured from domain experts, underlying theory, and emerging technology within the domain.

Domain analysis is a specific activity that can hardly be integrated in the normal life cycle of a given software system because the construction of reusable components has specific requirements (application independence, flexibility, and increased quality assurance). These requirements make reusable components more expensive to produce than other components; this expense may not be accounted for in project budgets and schedules. Domain analysis is also a difficult activity, because it requires software engineers who are able to deal with abstractions but are still highly proficient in the specific application domain and familiar with object-oriented concepts and ideas.

The process of domain analysis basically broadens the scope of a single system analysis. In [117], Prieto-Diaz enumerates the following steps as a basis for an object-oriented domain analysis effort:

1. Define the domain as narrowly and as quantitatively as possible. Check to see whether it is economically justified to invest in reusable components for this domain.

2. Scope the domain by listing the types of applications considered. Check that future applications within the domain will still have a high probability of presenting the same characteristics.

3. Generate or collect information, either through deduction from underlying common principles or through generalization from a representative sample of the applications found in the defined domain.

4. Analyze and abstract the collected information to yield the types of objects that are to be considered for reuse within the defined domain. Prepare a nomenclature.

5. Construct analysis models, or work on the classification of objects. You may want to use a *shopping list* approach [103] to determine which features are *potentially* useful to a client of the class library.

6. Define reusability guidelines regarding the reusable components, and demonstrate effective reuse examples. Make recommendations for incorporating the reusable objects into current and future projects.

There is no such thing as a perfect library. Perfection is not something of this world. The overall quality of a class library is only a trade-off between competing design decisions. Several iterations of this process are probably needed after confrontations with applications using the resulting class library have occurred. The obsolescence concept that exists in Eiffel (see Section 6.6.4) is of great help here in smoothing the transition between successive versions of the class library.

Further reading on domain analysis and library design can be found in [117, 20, 126, 11, 49, 103].

8.1.3 Design Patterns and Frameworks

One of the hardest parts of using any large class library is learning which mechanisms it embodies. If the competing technical and organizational requirements are tackled in complete isolation from one another, the class library will surely end up with little sharing of naming, policies, usage patterns, or implementation. It will then lead to an abundance of concepts that intimidate the eventual clients of a library, and so inhibit its reuse.

Software design patterns (such as those introduced in Section 6.4) are of great help in providing higher levels of description for libraries. As abstractions, patterns often cut across other common software abstractions like procedures and objects, or combine more common abstractions in powerful ways [36]. A simple pattern is the use of one object as an iterator that nondestructively visits every element of a collection object. The term *pattern* applies both to the thing (e.g., a collection class and its associated iterator) and the directions for making a thing. In this sense, software patterns can be likened to a dress pattern: The general shape is in the pattern itself, though each pattern must be tailored to its context.

A framework consists of a collection of classes together with many patterns of collaboration among instances of these classes. It provides a model of interaction among several objects that belong to classes defined by the framework. To use a framework, first study the collaborations and responsibilities of several classes [143].

In practice, developers generally start by using the most obvious classes in a new library. As they grow to trust certain abstractions, they move incrementally to the use of more sophisticated classes. Eventually, developers may discover a pattern in their own tailoring of a library set of classes, and so add it to the library as a primitive abstraction.

To illustrate the importance of design patterns and frameworks in large class libraries, let us now outline a set of patterns that occur in three data structure libraries. Although the following patterns exist in all these libraries, they are sometimes implemented quite differently.

Basic Abstractions

A container is an abstract data type in which one may store objects of a given type and expect to find them again at some later time. In most of the cases in which arrays, linked lists, and related data structures are used in conventional software, all that is really needed is this simple functionality of a container.

Reference Semantics and Equality

In Eiffel, as in every language using reference semantics, the question of the meaning of equality is not straightforward (see Section 2.4.2). Usually a distinction is made between the *identity* and *equality* of objects. Two entities are *equal* if they refer to objects in the same state. Two entities are *identical* if they refer to the same object. In Eiffel, identity is tested using =, and equality corresponds to the features *equal* or *is_equal*, which are available from the class ANY (by default these functions determine field-by-field equality, but may be redefined in any class to account for more specific notions of equality).

A general problem arises for any feature that must compare an external item and an item in a container (e.g., the function *has* encountered in several places in this book). Which of the two interpretations should be used in reference comparisons: identity or equality? There is no universal answer. Assume, for example, that a car rental agency has a data structure containing references to car objects representing real-life cars. When searching the list you may at different times need to answer two different kinds of questions:

- Is this the car that needs to be repaired?
- Does this car correspond to what my client requested?

Identity is appropriate when answering questions of the first kind; object equality (with a suitable redefinition of *equal* to account for a reasonable notion of duplicate) is appropriate for the second.

Solving this problem consistently across the class library is an important design pattern, because it would be unacceptable for a library user to deal with varying policies on the semantics of comparison routines. Actually, each one of the three libraries presented in the following sections has its own consistent solution for handling this pattern.

Iterators

Clients of container classes often need to traverse them to apply a certain action or compute a function on some or all of their items. In the Eiffel context, an *iterator* may be defined as an object that controls the process of accessing all objects in a collection. It is also a simple pattern. Again, several solutions are used to implement this pattern in the Eiffel data structure libraries presented in the following sections.

8.1.4 Producing Class Libraries

Building and managing a class library is similar to building and maintaining another object-oriented software system. The main difference is that the clients of the system are not end users, but are themselves software developers. The design and implementation guidelines presented in Sections 6.4 and 6.6 thus should be followed even more rigorously than for internal systems.

In addition to being of high quality from the point of view of the library provider, class libraries must inspire confidence in their users. Purchasing a library from a third party is like purchasing parts (such as engines) for building a plane. To be usable, a class library must feature very precise specifications, and provide the means for the client to test it against the specifications. Such a client also is entitled to watch or otherwise control the quality of the manufacturing process (compare the various SEI or ISO 9000 certification processes).

With Eiffel, the precise specifications of a library are available as a direct consequence of the *design by contract* paradigm, and they are documented with the always up-to-date short forms of the classes belonging to the library.

The solution to allowing a client to test the correctness of the library is to ship the test cases bundled with the library. This solution is facilitated if the classes contain self-tests, as described in Section 7.2.2. The library classes then can be easily tested during the initial client's evaluation, under various operating system configurations, various compilers, or even various levels of optimizations. This practice would provide a marketing edge to the class library vendors who implement it, because a potential user would feel much safer with a class library that could be auto-tested in his or her environment.

Finally, a quality assurance system can be built after the design and implementation guidelines presented in Chapter 6. It will increase user confidence in the development and maintenance processes used to produce the class library.

8.1.5 Conclusion

Making a profit by selling high-quality reusable class libraries for dedicated application domains is an activity that is still in its infancy. Although it has still to overcome numerous problems, most of them are of a managerial nature. Indeed, a language such as Eiffel addresses most of the technical issues relative to the construction and the use of such libraries because it was initially designed for this very purpose. Several Eiffel class libraries already exist for various application domains such as graphical user interfaces, database interfaces, linear algebra (see Chapter 9), and general-purpose data structures. This last application domain is described in the following sections.

8.2 The EiffelBase Library

Most of this section is taken from (103) and is reproduced here with Meyer's kind authorization.

EiffelBase, a product of ISE, is a library of reusable components covering data structures and algorithms. It is the result of a long-term systematic effort to classify the fundamental patterns and structures of computer science in a Linnaean manner. EiffelBase relies heavily on Eiffel-specific constructions, in particular assertions (preconditions, postconditions, and class invariants), *design by contract*, constrained genericity, and repeated inheritance.

8.2.1 Overview

All classes that describe containers are descendants of the deferred class CONTAINER. A container can be studied from three viewpoints: access, storage, and traversal.

The *access* criterion affects how the clients of a container can access its items. For example, in a stack or queue, only one item is accessible at any given time, and clients do not choose that item; in contrast, clients of an array or hash table must provide an index or, more generally, a key with which to access an item.

The *storage* criterion affects how the items are put together. For example, some containers are finite and others are potentially infinite. Among finite structures, some are bounded and others are unbounded.

The *traversal* criterion affects how, if in any way, the items of a container can be traversed. A traversal is a mechanism that makes it possible to examine each item of a container once, in a clearly specified order. For example, some containers can be traversed sequentially, in one direction or two. Tree structures lend themselves to preorder, postorder, and breadth-first traversals.

Figure 8.1 shows the CONTAINER inheritance structure. For each one of these criteria the EiffelBase libraries offer a single-inheritance hierarchy of deferred classes. The top of the access hierarchy is the class COLLECTION, the top of the storage hierarchy is the class BOX, and the top of the traversal hierarchy is the class TRAVERSABLE. These three classes are heirs of the most general class, CONTAINER.

8.2 THE EIFFELBASE LIBRARY

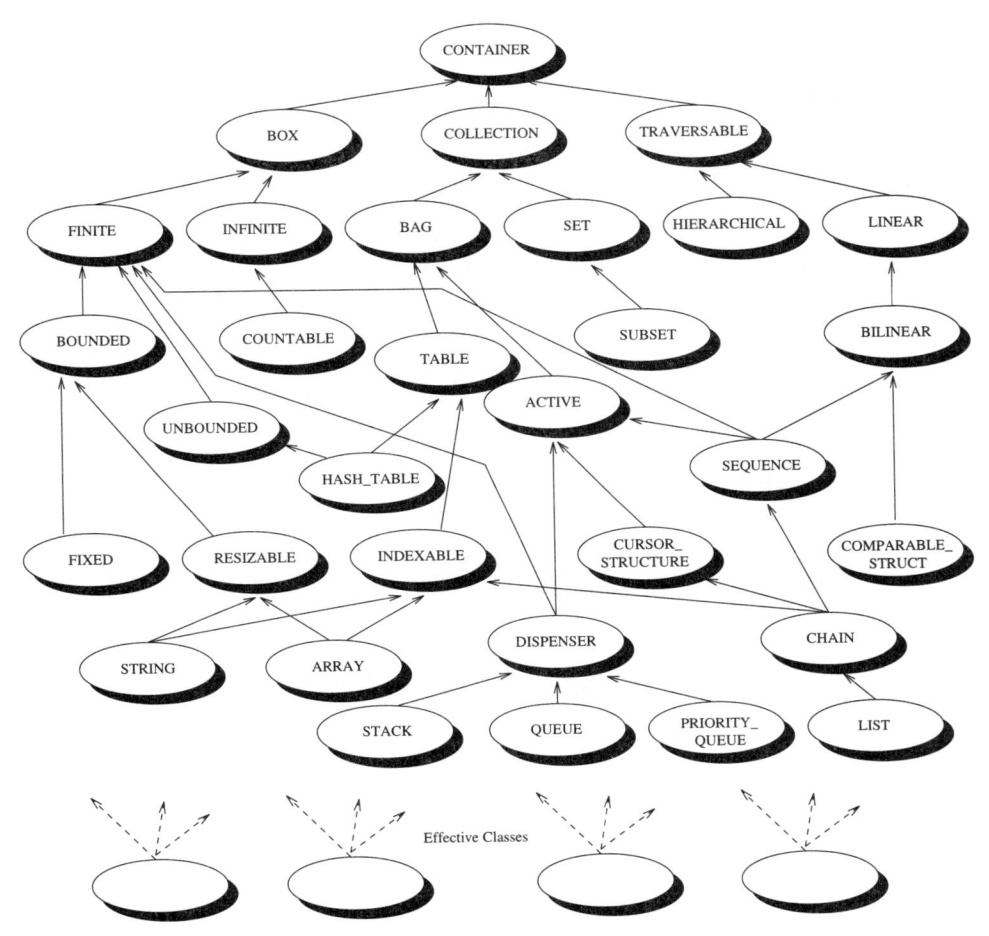

Figure 8.1 (Partial) inheritance structure of the EiffelBase library

The technique for building a class that describes a specific form of container is to pick one class from each of these three hierarchies and to combine these classes through multiple inheritance, yielding a class that is fully characterized by its access, storage, and traversal properties. This process causes many occurrences of repeated inheritance because all such classes will be descendants of CONTAINER through several paths.

Only a few features, defined in CONTAINER, are applicable to all container objects: membership testing, emptiness testing, and routines to change and query the object comparison mode (see its interface in Example 8.1).

```
     indexing
         description:    "Data structures of the most general kind"
     deferred class interface
         CONTAINER [G]
5    feature -- Access
         has (v: G): BOOLEAN
                 -- Does structure include 'v'?
                 -- Reference or object equality, based on 'object_comparison'
             ensure
10               not_found_in_empty: Result implies not empty
     feature -- Status report
         empty: BOOLEAN
                 -- Is there no element?
         object_comparison: BOOLEAN
15               -- Must search operations use 'equal' rather than '='
                 -- for comparing references? (Default: no, use '='.)
         changeable_comparison_criterion: BOOLEAN
                 -- May 'object_comparison' be changed?
     feature -- Status setting
20       compare_objects
                 -- Ensure that future search operations will use 'equal'
                 -- rather than '=' for comparing references.
             require
                 changeable_comparison_criterion
25           ensure
                 object_comparison
         compare_references
                 -- Ensure that future search operations will use '='
                 -- rather than 'equal' for comparing references.
30           require
                 changeable_comparison_criterion
             ensure
                 reference_comparison: not object_comparison
             end
35   feature -- Conversion
         linear_representation: LINEAR [G]
                 -- Representation as a linear structure
     end -- class CONTAINER
```

Example 8.1

8.2.2 Design Patterns

Reference Semantics and Equality

The meaning of equality for the items of a container is configurable in EiffelBase on a per container basis. This technique relies on two option-setting procedures, *compare_references* and *compare_objects*, which are defined in the class CONTAINER. Clients of a container may use the calls *c.compare_references* and *c.compare_objects* to switch between the two modes for the container attached to *c*. The mode selected through one of these calls will remain in effect for all search operations on this container until another call changes the setting. The default, in the absence of any call, is *compare_references*. To find out what mode is in effect on *c*, use the Boolean expression *c.object_comparison* the value of which is true if and only if the current search mode for *c* compares objects (default: false).

Objects as Machines

The idea is to look at containers as machines with an internal state, with commands (procedures) to change the state, and queries (functions) to read it. This approach yields a simple and efficient interface for container objects, but poses several problems if multiple state modifying iterators are needed on a single container.

Iterators

In EiffelBase, iterators are considered to be *clients* of the container classes. From the ADT point of view, an ITERATOR is an object that can iterate over TRAVERSABLE objects, on which it can perform repeated actions and tests according to several predefined control structures such as "if," "until," and others (see an extract of the ITERATOR interface in Example 8.2).

Various specialized versions of the deferred class ITERATOR are available to deal with the various specializations of the class TRAVERSABLE (e.g., a LINEAR_ITERATOR iterates over a LINEAR object, see Figure 8.2).

EiffelBase iterators may be used either through inheritance or as explicit independent objects. In the first case, objects that are willing to iterate over their clients just have to inherit from the appropriate subclass of ITERATOR and redefine either or both of the *test* and *action* features to perform the actual tasks on each item of the client (the iteration itself is called with the relevant routine; e.g., *do_all*). If more than one iteration is needed on a client, it is possible to inherit more than once from ITERATOR and get several versions of the *action*, *test*, and iteration routines (Section 5.2 describes the conditions

BUILDING LIBRARIES: THE CASE OF DATA STRUCTURE LIBRARIES

```
    indexing
        description:        "Objects that are able to iterate over TRAVERSABLE"
    deferred class ITERATOR [G]
    feature -- (extracts)
5       target: TRAVERSABLE [G]
        test: BOOLEAN is
                -- Test to be applied to item at current position in 'target'
        set (s: like target) is
                -- Make 's' the new target of iterations.
10  feature -- Cursor movement
        forall: BOOLEAN is -- Is 'test' true for all items of 'target'?
        exists: BOOLEAN is -- Is 'test' true for at least one item of 'target'?
        do_all is -- Apply 'action' to every item of 'target'.
        do_if is -- Apply 'action' to every item of 'target' satisfying 'test'.
15      do_until is -- Apply 'action' to every item of 'target' up to
                    -- and including first one satisfying 'test'.
        -- etc. with do_while, until_do, while_do
    feature -- Element change
        action is
20              -- Action to be applied to item at current position in
                -- 'target'. For iterators to work properly, redefined
                -- versions of this feature should not change the
                -- traversable's structure.
    end -- class ITERATOR
```

Example 8.2

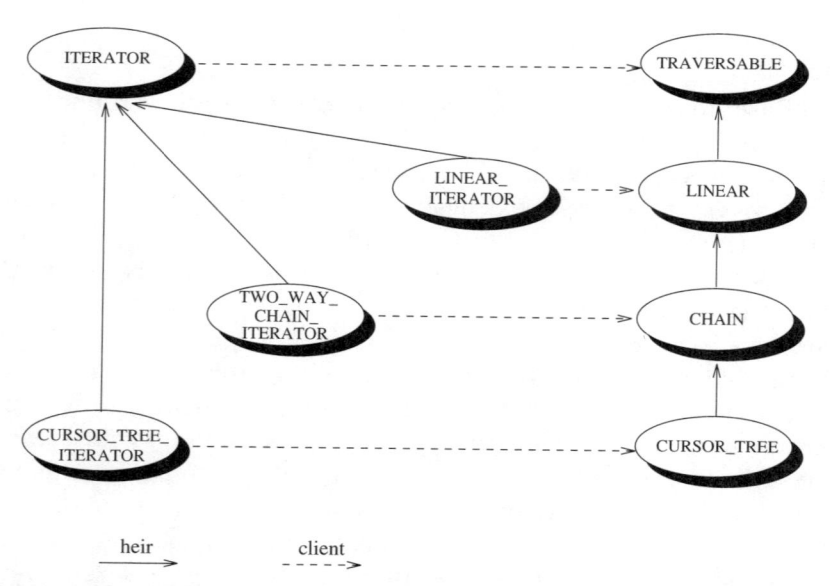

Figure 8.2 Inheritance structure of the iteration classes

```
     class SQUARE [G]
     inherit
         LINEAR_ITERATOR [G –>NUMERIC]
             redefine action end
5    feature
         action is
             -- replace item with item^2
             do
                 target.put(target.item*target.item)
10           end
     end -- SQUARE
```

Example 8.3

in which feature duplications and sharing are possible). This repeated inheritance technique, however, may be a bit cumbersome if more than a few iteration schemes are necessary for a given client class. In that case, explicit iterator objects might provide the needed flexibility. These iterator objects are kinds of *agents* that know how to *do* things (here iterate) to other objects. Example 8.3 defines an agent to square the (numerical) elements of a LINEAR collection. This agent can be used as in Example 8.4 to square each element of a double-linked list of integers.

```
     squarelist (l: TWO_WAY_LIST[INTEGER]) is
         require
             not_void: l /= Void
         local
5            square_iterator: expanded SQUARE[INTEGER]
         do
             square_iterator.set(l) -- attach the iterator to l
             square_iterator.do_all -- square each item in l
         end
```

Example 8.4

8.2.3 Containers: The Access Hierarchy

The access hierarchy has the class COLLECTION, a direct heir of CONTAINER, as its top. In addition to their general container properties, collections are characterized by their ability to have items added to them and removed from them.

Collections are further divided, according to their access mechanisms, into various categories such as bags (and their variants, active and cursor structures) and tables.

Procedures *put* and *extend* add an item to a collection. At the level of the class COLLECTION these procedures are synonymous. The procedure *fill* takes an arbitrary container as an argument and fills the current collection with the items of the other container.

The procedure *prune* removes an occurrence of a given item from a collection. The procedure *prune_all* removes all occurrences of an item. In both cases, the criterion used to determine what constitutes an occurrence follows from the current setting of *object_comparison*, as affected by the procedures described previously. The procedure *wipe_out* removes all items from a structure.

Addition and removal are not always possible. All the addition procedures have the property *extendible* as part of their precondition; all the removal procedures have *prunable* as part of their precondition. The two queries *extendible* and *prunable* are Boolean-valued features of the class.

The class SET introduces the feature *count*, which represents the number of items of a finite set. Its heir SUBSET introduces features corresponding to set theory's basic operations on subsets of a given set: the queries *is_subset* (subset inclusion), *is_superset*, and *disjoint*, and the procedures *intersect* (intersection), *merge* (union), *subtract*, and *symdif* (symmetrical difference).

Tables and Active Structures

Two major kinds of bags are tables and active structures, which are represented by the classes TABLE and ACTIVE. They differ in the way occurrences of items are added and accessed, as represented in particular by the signatures of the two basic procedures *put* and *item*:

- In a table, there is a key associated with each item. As a result the class has two generic parameters. It is declared as TABLE[G,H], where G represents the type of items and H the type of keys. Examples of tables are arrays (where the keys are integers), hash tables (where the keys are strings or other hashable values), and strings (which are conceptually similar to arrays of characters). There is no constraint on H in the class TABLE, but there will be in the descendants of TABLE such as INDEXABLE and HASH_TABLE.

- An active structure, as represented by the class ACTIVE and its descendants, is characterized by the existence, at each stage of its life, of a "current position" that may have an associated "current item." The basic access and modification operations apply to the current position. Examples of active structures include stacks (where the current position is always the position of the latest insertion, the stack's "top") and lists (which have an associated cursor that various procedures can move forward and backward, and where the current position is the cursor's position).

Cursor Structures

An important special case of active structure is the notion of cursor structure, represented by the class CURSOR_STRUCTURE.

A cursor structure is an active structure in which the current position is known through a marker, or cursor. Various operations will make it possible to move the cursor. At the level of the CURSOR_STRUCTURE there is only *go_to*, but descendants introduce *forth*, *back*, and others for linear structures such as lists, as well as *up* and *down* for hierarchical structures such as trees.

Cursors are in fact already present conceptually in ACTIVE structures, because there is a notion of current position, which can be visualized as a fictitious cursor marking a certain item of the structure. The novelty with CURSOR_STRUCTURE is that the cursor now becomes an object on its own.

As declared in CURSOR_STRUCTURE, the cursor is of the type CURSOR, another deferred class that has various descendants. In simple structures such as ARRAYED_LIST (lists implemented by arrays) the cursor may be implemented as an integer, but more elaborate forms of cursors are possible. To preserve simplicity and abstraction, however, all cursors are viewed by clients as being of the type CURSOR.

Dispensers

Another common case of active structures is the dispenser. This name comes from an analogy with a simple real-life dispenser, such as an unsophisticated vending machine that has just one button and delivers just one product. Similarly, a dispenser is a container in which you may at any given time access, remove, or replace at most one item—the current item. You do not choose that item—the "machine" (the dispenser) chooses it for you. So when you insert an item you have no control over where it goes into the container, or when you will get it back.

The two most common kinds of dispensers are the stack, in which the current item is the one inserted most recently, and the queue, in which the current item is the oldest one inserted and not yet removed.

Sequences

The third major variant of the notion of active structures is the sequence. A *sequence* is a linear structure with a notion of current position. The class SEQUENCE serves as ancestor to such classes as LIST and CIRCULAR_CHAIN.

The basic notion of sequence allows for insertion at the end only. Variants such as DYNAMIC_LIST and DYNAMIC_CHAIN support insertion at any position.

Kinds of Tables

The class INDEXABLE describes tables in which each item is identified through a unique integer. The two most common examples are arrays and strings, represented by the classes ARRAY (a generic class, declared as ARRAY[G] and representing arrays of items of an arbitrary type) and STRING, which represents character strings.

Finally, a hash table is a table in which the keys can be hashed; hashing a key means deriving an integer from it, so that the items can be kept in an array in which the hashed key serves as index. The requirement that keys must be hashable is expressed by constrained genericity: The class is declared as

$$\text{class HASH\_TABLE}[G, H-> \text{HASHABLE}],$$

meaning that the type used as a second actual parameter in any generic derivation must be a descendant of HASHABLE.

8.2.4 Containers: The Storage Hierarchy

The storage hierarchy has the class BOX, a direct heir of CONTAINER, as its top. In addition to their general container properties, boxes are characterized by how many items they may contain and whether this property may be changed.

BOX has two heirs: FINITE and INFINITE. These containers hold finite and infinite quantities of items.

Infinite Containers

In practice the only effective descendants of INFINITE are descendants of its heir COUNTABLE, which describes countable structures (those with items in one-to-one correspondence with the integers), and more precisely of COUNTABLE_SEQUENCE, which inherits from COUNTABLE, ACTIVE, and LINEAR. The current cases are:

- The class PRIMES, which describes prime numbers.
- The class RANDOM, which describes pseudorandom number sequences.

COUNTABLE has a deferred feature i_th, such that $c.i\_th\ (i)$ is the ith item of a countable structure such as the set of primes or a pseudorandom sequence.

Bounded, Unbounded, Fixed, and Resizable Containers

The class FINITE has heirs BOUNDED and UNBOUNDED. In a bounded container there is, at any given time, an upper limit to the number of items that can be inserted (through the *put* operation); the limit is represented by the feature *capacity*, an integer query that usually is implemented as an attribute. An unbounded container has no such limit.

The class BOUNDED itself has two heirs: FIXED and RESIZABLE. In a fixed container, the capacity is hardwired at creation time (normally it will be an argument of the creation procedure). In a resizable container, procedures are available to change the *capacity* on request.

- An instance of the class INFINITE is a structure that is intrinsically infinite. An example is the set of prime integers.

- An instance of the class UNBOUNDED is a structure that is finite, but with no upper limit on the number of items it may contain. An example is a linked list (a list in chained representation).

- An instance of the class RESIZABLE is a finite structure that at any time has such an upper limit, but with mechanisms available to change that limit if necessary.

8.2.5 Containers: The Traversal Hierarchy

The traversal hierarchy has the class TRAVERSABLE, a direct heir of CONTAINER, as its top. In addition to their general container properties, traversable structures are characterized by one or more traversal mechanisms.

A traversal mechanism defines an ordering of all the items of a container and makes it possible to apply an arbitrary operation to all these items in the order thus defined.

Traversable Structures

The class TRAVERSABLE introduces only a few features. The procedure *start* starts a traversal. The Boolean query *exhausted* indicates whether the latest traversal is complete. Internally, a traversal will use a cursor, so that traversable structures share some properties with instances of CURSOR_STRUCTURE described in Section 8.2.3. The equivalent features will be merged in common descendants through the sharing facility of repeated inheritance. In particular, *off* is false if and only if there is no item at the current cursor position. If *off* is not false, *item* gives the item at the cursor position.

Linear and Bilinear Structures

The class LINEAR describes structures. It features the procedure *forth* as a deferred procedure that advances the cursor to the next position. The procedure *finish*, which brings the cursor to the last item if any, is also deferred.

Although still deferred, the class LINEAR effects the general container query *has*, using an algorithm that searches for an item in a linearly traversable container by traversing the container until it either finds the item or runs out of items. Descendants of LINEAR may, because of their specific properties, offer more efficient searching algorithms, in which case they will redefine *has* to override this default.

A bilinear structure is a linear structure that can be traversed in both directions. As a consequence, the class BILINEAR (an heir of LINEAR) provides the deferred procedure *back* along with *forth*. The class BILINEAR plays an essential role as ancestor of the sequence.

Hierarchical Structures

Hierarchical containers are structured as trees. The class HIERARCHICAL has remarkably few features:

- *c.back* will move to *c*'s predecessor (parent).
- *c.forth (i)* will move to the ith successor (child) of *c*. Note the presence of an argument to *forth*.

More elaborate traversal mechanisms such as preorder or postorder may be found in the descendants of the class TREE and in the classes of the iteration library.

8.3 The Tower*Eiffel* Booch Components

Most of this section is from "Tower Technology," and is reproduced here with Rock Howard's kind authorization.

The **Tower***Eiffel* Booch components are available as a joint product of Rational Software Inc. and Tower Technology Corp. They represent the combination of Booch's OOAD approach [21] with the ideas and techniques for object-oriented software development introduced by Eiffel, particularly *design by contract*. Having evolved from the Ada and C++ versions that are widely used around the world, the **Tower***Eiffel* Booch components are a mature library. The Eiffel version is more than a simple port from C++. Rather, it was carefully redesigned to take advantage of Eiffel's unique features. Many of the features that were important to the C++ Booch components are handled by the Eiffel run-time system. For example, the STORAGE_MANAGER and POOL classes were not necessary because of the automatic memory management that is included with every Eiffel system. Similarly, the EXCEPTION class was not needed because Eiffel systems supply that functionality directly.

The current version of the components is compatible with the Eiffel Standard Library from NICE (see Section 4.3), and thus should be completely compiler independent.

8.3.1 Overview

The **Tower***Eiffel* Booch components (TEBC) are organized into one of three major categories:

- Structures: data structures,
- Agents: agents that act on structures, and
- Support: low-level classes used to build the other classes.

Almost all classes in the **Tower***Eiffel* Booch components library begin with "BC_". This prefix is often omitted here.

Data Structures

Figure 8.3 displays the inheritance graph for the TEBC data structures. All of the classes with a dotted rectangle are generic. The classes marked with a triangle are abstract (i.e., deferred). Most of these classes have concrete descendants coming in dynamic, unbound, and bound forms. If the access to structure is mostly random and not too much resizing takes place, use the dynamic form. It is very fast because it uses an array as its underlying mechanism but can resize itself as necessary. The unbound form uses a linked list as its underlying mechanism. The bound form uses a fixed-size array for its mechanism. The data structure name indicates which of the forms is utilized. For example, BAG_D is dynamic, BAG_U is unbounded, and BAG_B is bounded. The deferred class BAG is the common abstract ancestor of these classes (i.e., you cannot create instances of BAG—you must choose a concrete descendant). It is possible to create new low-level forms and easily create new versions of the various high-level data structures to utilize your custom form.

When viewed in terms of inheritance, the data structures of the **Tower***Eiffel* Booch components come in three basic flavors—simple, iterated, and indexed. The simple classes are support classes. Of these, PAIR and CURSOR are used most often. The others are used by the data structure classes and are rarely, if ever, used directly.

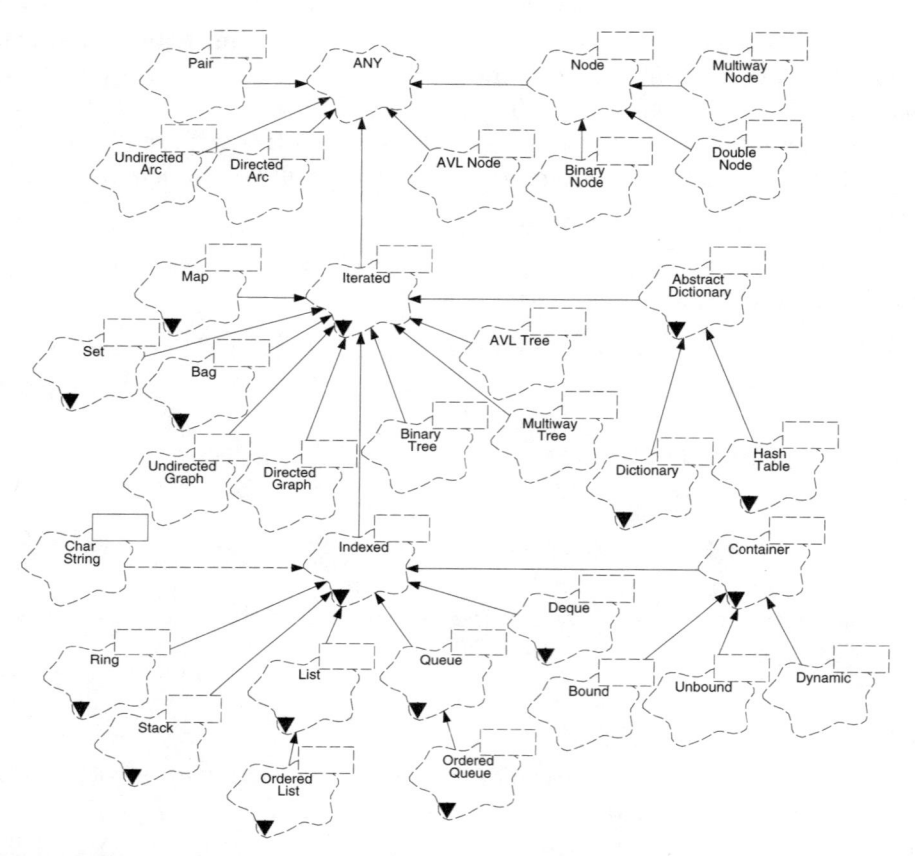

236 BUILDING LIBRARIES: THE CASE OF DATA STRUCTURE LIBRARIES

Figure 8.3 Inheritance graph for the TEBC data structures

The classes that descend from ITERATED are full-fledged container-style classes that are used to hold and manage multiple items. All concrete classes that are derived from ITERATED can return an iterator. The class named ABSTRACT_DICTIONARY and its descendants, DICTIONARY and HASH_TABLE, are support classes that are used to implement the various versions of BAG, MAP, and SET. The user of this library is advised to use BAG, MAP, and SET instead of DICTIONARY and HASH_TABLE because they are somewhat simpler to use and much simpler to subclass.

The classes that descend from INDEXED provide CURSORS that are descendants of ITERATOR that can traverse both backward and forward over the elements being contained. BC_CHAR_STRING is a descendant of both BC_INDEXED and the class STRING from the Eiffel kernel cluster. It allows the user to treat character strings as collections of characters.

        my_stack.copy_contents_of(my_queue)
        my_queue.copy_contents_of(my_stack)

Example 8.5

Even among these categories, there can be several classes with functional variations. In particular, there are ordered lists and ordered queues, which are ordered according to some ordering agent, and simple lists and queues, which are ordered according to the order in which the items were added to the structure. There are directed and undirected graphs. Trees can be binary, multiway, or balanced.

There are some high-level operations for adding the elements of one iterated data structure to another iterated structure. These operations can reduce effort in transforming a group of objects from one form into another. For example, reversing a queue can be done as in Example 8.5.

8.3.2 Design Patterns

Agents

Container classes are often searched, sorted, or transformed. All of these actions require tests to be performed against objects. It is easy to design an Eiffel container that defines a set of such tests and requires contained objects to provide them. The design gets more complex when the test criteria may change from time to time during an application run. Examples of classes that may have more than one ordering are common. Imagine a collection of employees. Sometimes their records are sorted according to hiring date, but other times they are sorted in alphabetical order.

A simple Eiffel "solution" (adopted in the KWIC case study, with the class SORTABLE_ARRAY[T]; see Section 3.8) is to rely on repeated inheritance to allow the renaming and redefinition of the key testing features that are used by the container class. In practice, this doesn't work out well because there is no easy way to "reselect" on the fly. Whichever version of a testing feature (e.g., "<") is chosen at compile time for a class is "it" for the duration! Coding the test feature with an inspect statement that switches based on a "current mode" setting is a kludge at best.

In the **Tower***Eiffel* Booch components, a set of agents is defined to encapsulate the ability to compare or judge objects. Agents are objects that do things, but remember very little. Often they are simply a single function. By encapsulating the idea of "less than" in an agent, a single class could be ordered according to several criteria. Developers who use the library can easily redefine the ideas of equality, ordering, and validity by creating subclasses of

For users of Smalltalk, COMPARATOR is the same as a sort block and VALIDATOR is much like the select block.

the agents EQUALITY_JUDGE, COMPARATOR, and VALIDATOR. Agents allow redefinable searching, sorting, transforming and filtering of containers. In the previous example, two different orderings of EMPLOYEE can be generated by creating two different descendants of COMPARATOR (the sorting agent).

The **Tower***Eiffel* Booch components thus include tool classes that act as agents. Naming conventions make it easy to use them. For example, an agent that sorts is called a SORTER. The feature to make it sort is called *sort*. (To sort a range of items in an indexed collection, use *sort_range*.) Agents include the following families of classes:

- Iterators: for stepping forward through iterated data structures.
- Cursors: Iterators that also can step backward or move to arbitrary locations within an indexed data structure.
- Sorters: for ordering collections. There are bubble sorters, heap sorters, quicksorters, shaker sorters, and other sorters. The name for each type of sorter ends with _SORTER.
- Matchers: for locating patterns within structures. There is an assortment of different pattern matching algorithms.
- Filters and transformers: for altering collections one item at a time.
- Selective and rejective iterators: for iterating over items with specified qualities.
- Finders: for locating items within collections. Finders can use sequential or binary search algorithms.

Two Levels of Abstractions

The **Tower***Eiffel* Booch components were built with the assumption that users who make subclasses will probably need to understand the source code to some degree. For this reason, a set of primitive collections was used. The primitive classes are not meant to be subclassed and have complex implementations, but they allow for clean readable code in the classes where they are used.

For example, when an object is placed in a stack, the source code simply shows its reference being added to one end of a primitive container. In this way, the design of STACK is kept understandable and efficient. You can extend STACK, or the other nonprimitive **Tower***Eiffel* Booch components, without necessarily understanding the nitty-gritty details of the incorporated primitive classes.

Iterators

Every data structure in **Tower***Eiffel* Booch components has an iterator. Iterators are extremely useful, but if you add or remove items while the iterator is working, the results can be unpredictable. Users should avoid modifying the structure of the collection while iterating through it. Changing the state of an object in the collection while iterating is not problematic—just don't add or remove them. Rehashing or reordering objects, or both, in containers during iteration also could have unpredictable results.

Reference Semantics and Equality

One of the major advantages of object-oriented programming is that it can accurately represent the problem domain. This representation can get lost in the complications that typically ensue from copying objects in software where the real-world analog would not be copied. Also, when there are several copies of what is conceptually a single object wandering around a system, each copy must be kept meticulously up-to-date. The processing to do this, along with the allocation, initialization, and destruction of the extra copies, can be expensive and certainly adds to the complexity of the software. In C++ Booch components, when an object is added to a collection, a copy of the object is made and placed in the collection. When the destructor for the collection is called, it calls the destructors for the copies in the collection.

The Eiffel version does not make copies of objects when they are put into a container. Eiffel Booch components simply hold a reference to the object within the container. Destructors are not a concern because Eiffel is a language with garbage collection. As long as there is a reference to the object inside the collection, the object is safe from the garbage collector.

A collection that doesn't make copies is said to have "reference semantics." C++ Booch components use "copy semantics." Using "copy semantics" with Eiffel Booch components simply entails copying (or more likely cloning) an object and putting the copy or clone of the object into the data structure instead of the original object.

A simple collection like STACK is not affected much by the decision to use reference semantics because internally it uses integers as an index. The consequences become more of a concern with a sophisticated collection such as a SET that uses a hash table for its implementation. Once you put an object in a hash table, it is very important that the hash code does not change, because the object could be lost from the table. When this is a problem, the **Tower***Eiffel* Booch components include two different hash tables. One type, DICTIONARY, uses a hash code that depends on the identity, not the state of the object. This identity is taken from the feature *object_id* defined in GENERAL, and thus available in all classes. The object id is an integer, and no two nonbasic objects have the same object id. It makes an acceptable hash code if the number of buckets (or hash chains) is a relatively large prime. HASH_TABLE uses the feature *hash_ code* which depends on the state, not the identity.

When using structures that are based on DICTIONARY, uniqueness is determined using references. Thus, a set based on a DICTIONARY will hold only one reference to a given object. It will, however, hold another reference to an equal but distinct object. The structures based on DICTIONARY are MAP, SET, and BAG.

When using structures that are based on HASH_TABLE, uniqueness is determined using *is_equal*. Thus, a set based on HASH_TABLE will hold references to only one of two equal objects added to the set. The structures based on HASH_ TABLE are IE_MAP, IE_SET, and IE_BAG. IE_ stands for *is_equal*, the feature used to determine uniqueness. These containers will only hold hashable items.

Danger is associated with using data structures based on HASH_TABLE. The hash code depends on the state, so if the state is changed the object can be "lost." One way to ensure that this doesn't occur is to add a copy of the object to the container instead of the original. Another way is to use the analogous structure based on DICTIONARY instead of a container based on HASH_TABLE.

All data structures also have features called *is_member* and *has_member_ equal_to*, which search for elements using identity and equality, respectively.

8.3.3 Architecture of the Library

Several important patterns are essential to the architecture of the **Tower***Eiffel* Booch components; these encompass the following issues:

- Time and space semantics,
- Idioms for iteration, and
- Protocol for agent usage.

Thanks to this set of familiar patterns, it is not necessary for a developer to comprehend the entire subtlety of a library as large as the **Tower***Eiffel* Booch components, just as it is not necessary to understand the details of how a microprocessor works in order to program a computer in a high-order language.

In both cases, however, the raw power of the underlying implementation can be accessed if necessary, but only if the developer is willing to absorb the additional complexity. These patterns serve as the soul of this library's architecture. The more one knows about these mechanisms, the easier it is to discover innovative ways to use existing components rather than fabricate new ones from scratch.

Each abstraction in this library can be considered from the perspective of its two kinds of clients: clients that use an abstraction by declaring instances of it and then manipulating those instances, and clients that subclass an abstraction to specialize or augment its behavior. Designing in favor of the first client leads to the hiding of implementation details and focusing on the responsibilities of the abstraction in the real world. Designing in favor of the second client requires certain implementation details to be exposed, but not too much, so that the fundamental semantics of the abstraction are not violated. This represents a very real tension of competing requirements in the design of the **Tower***Eiffel* Booch components.

Another architectural principle for this library is that a clear distinction is made between policy and implementation. In a sense, abstractions such as queues, sets, and rings represent particular policies for using lower-level structures such as linked lists or arrays. For example, a queue defines the policy whereby items can only be added to one end of a structure and removed from the other. A set, on the other hand, enforces no such policy requiring an ordering of items. A ring does enforce an ordering, but sets the policy that the front and the back of its items are connected. There is thus an opportunity for exploiting the representations common among the classes in this library. Organizing such lower-level abstractions is the purpose of a globally accessible cluster called "support." It is therefore used for those more primitive abstractions on which different policies can be formulated. This cluster is also used to collect the classes needed in support of the library's common mechanisms. By exposing this cluster to library builders, the library's requirement for extensibility is supported. In general, application developers need only concern themselves with the classes found in the structures and tools categories. Library developers and power users, however, may wish to make use of the more primitive abstractions found in the support cluster, from which new classes may be constructed, or through which the behavior of existing classes may be modified.

The last principle central to the design of this library is the concept of building families of classes, related by lines of inheritance. For each kind of structure, several different classes are provided, united by a shared interface (in the form of an abstract base class), but with several concrete subclasses, each having a slightly different representation, and therefore having different time and space semantics. In this manner, the library's requirement for completeness is supported. A developer can select the one concrete class with time and space semantics that best fit the needs of a given application, yet still be confident that, no matter which concrete class is selected, it will be functionally the same as any other concrete class in the family. This intentional and clear separation of concerns between an abstract base class and its concrete classes allows a developer to select one concrete class initially, and later, as the application is being tuned, replace it with a sibling concrete class with minimal effort (the only real cost is the recompilation of all uses of the new class). The developer can be confident that the application will still work, because all sibling concrete classes share the same interface and the same basic behavior. Another implication of this organization is that it makes it possible to copy, assign, and test for equality among objects of the same family of classes, even if each object has a radically different representation.

In a very simple sense, an abstract base class thus serves to capture all of the relevant public design decisions about the abstraction. Another use of abstract base classes is to cache common state information that might otherwise be expensive to compute. It can convert an $O(n)$ computation to an $O(1)$ retrieval. The cost of this style is the required cooperation between the abstract base class and its subclasses, to keep the cached result up-to-date.

The various concrete members of a family of classes represent the forms of an abstraction. Basically there are two fundamental forms of most abstractions that any developer must consider when building a serious application. The first of these is the form of the representation, which establishes the concrete implementation of an abstract base class. Ultimately, there are only two meaningful choices for in-memory structures: The structure is stored on the stack or it is stored on the heap. These variations are called the bounded and unbounded forms of an abstraction in **Tower***Eiffel* Booch components:

Bounded: The structure is stored on the stack and thus has a static size at the time the object is constructed.

Unbounded: The structure is stored on the heap, and thus may grow to the limits of available memory.

The bounded and unbounded forms of an abstraction share a common interface and behavior, so they are direct subclasses of the abstract base class for each structure.

In practice, the range of time and space semantics offered by the bounded and unbounded support classes is insufficient for some purposes. Specifically, the bounded form is space-inefficient for sequences such as strings, because this form must be instantiated for the longest expected sequence, thereby wasting a tremendous amount of storage in all shorter sequences. Similarly, the unbounded form is time-inefficient for sequences, because searching for an item or inserting an item in the middle of the sequence may require traversing its entire underlying linked-list structure. For this reason, a third representation form is introduced, with the following responsibilities:

Dynamic: The structure is stored on the heap as an array, the length of which may shrink or grow in multiples of some chunk size.

In this manner, the dynamic support class is a middle ground between the time efficiency of the bounded form (because items may be indexed directly) and the space efficiency of the unbounded form (because we only allocate storage for as many items as necessary).

To be precise, each of these three forms exhibits the following space complexity:

Bounded: $O(size \times size_{reference})$, where $size$ is provided on instantiation, and $size_{reference}$ is the size of a reference.

Dynamic: $O(n \times size_{reference})$, where n is a multiple of a chunk size, provided on template instantiation.

Unbounded: $O(3 \times size \times size_{reference})$.

The following rules of thumb are provided to guide developers in selecting one of these concrete forms:

- Dynamic: Almost always the best choice.
- Unbound: Best for structures that use lots of insertion and deletion other than at the front or back of the collection.
- Bounded: Almost never appropriate because it has almost the same performance as dynamic, but with the dangers of a fixed size. Supplied for very specific uses in multithreaded applications.

8.3.4 Outline of Some Tower*Eiffel* Booch Components

Bags A Bc_BAG is a collection of items. Unlike a set, a bag may contain duplicate items. A bag actually has only one reference to each unique item. Duplicates are counted, but not stored with the bag. There are four different types of Bc_BAG:

Bc_bag_d, which uses Bc_dictionary_d. Reference equality determines uniqueness.

Bc_bag_u, which uses Bc_dictionary_u. Reference equality determines uniqueness.

Ie_bag_d, which uses Bc_hash_table_d. *is_equal* determines uniqueness.

Ie_bag_u, which uses Bc_hash_table_u. *is_equal* determines uniqueness.

All versions of Bc_bag are iterated using a Bc_bag_iterator. Bound versions of Bc_bag are not included because they are not generally useful.

Deques A deque denotes a sequence of items in which items may be added and removed from either end of the sequence. There are three effective types of queues: dynamic (Bc_deque_d), bound (Bc_deque_b), and unbound (Bc_deque_u). To iterate a Bc_deque, get a cursor by using the feature named *cursor*. It will return a Bc_cursor that can do everything that a Bc_indexed_iterator can do, and more.

Graphs A graph can be thought of as a reference to a vertex. The vertex can be connected to several arcs, each of which ends at a vertex. Each vertex and each arc is associated with an object. The generic parameter *V_ITEM* is the type of the vertex item. The generic parameter *A_ITEM* is the type of the arc item. Cycles are permitted and more than one graph can refer to the same vertex. This class gives the user the ability to move among the vertices and create new vertices and arcs. The user is not permitted to directly affect the state of arcs and vertices. All of this is done with a graph. A graph is said to be *directed* if some of the arcs connected to a vertex are considered inbound and others are considered outbound. A graph is said to be *undirected* if arcs connected to a vertex are not considered inbound or outbound. There are two types of graphs: the Bc_directed_graph and the Bc_undirected_graph.

Lists Bc_list represents a list and can be iterated using a Bc_cursor. Unlike the C++ Booch Components, this implementation of a list does not allow structural sharing. There are three effective types of lists: dynamic (Bc_list_d), bound (Bc_list_b), and unbound (Bc_list_u). To iterate a Bc_list, get a cursor by using the feature named *cursor*. It will return a Bc_cursor that can do everything that a Bc_indexed_iterator can do, and more.

Maps Bc_map is a collection of key/value pairs. There are four effective versions: Bc_map_d, Bc_map_u, Ie_map_d, and Ie_map_u.

İe_map_d and İe_map_u are also collections of key/value pairs, but these classes use *is_equal* to determine equality as opposed to simple reference comparison. Bc_map_iterator is the iterator for Bc_maps.

Queues A queue denotes a sequence of items in which items may be added from one end and removed from the opposite end of the sequence. There are six effective types of queues: dynamic (Bc_queue_d), bound (Bc_queue_b), and unbound (Bc_queue_u), and their three ordered counterparts, in which items are inserted in an order Bc_ordered_queue_*x*. To iterate a Bc_queue, get a cursor by using the feature named *cursor*. It will return a Bc_cursor that can do everything that a Bc_indexed_iterator can do, and more.

Rings A ring is a sequence in which items may be added and removed from the top of a circular structure. This structure has no beginning or ending, so a client can mark one particular item to designate a point of reference in the structure. There are three effective types of rings: dynamic (Bc_ring_d), bound (Bc_ring_b), and unbound (Bc_ring_u). To iterate a Bc_ring, get a cursor by using the feature named *cursor*. It will return a Bc_cursor that can do everything that a Bc_indexed_iterator can do, and more.

Sets Bc_set denotes a collection of items drawn from some well-defined universe. Unlike a bag, a set may not contain duplicate items. There are four different types of Bc_sets:

Bc_set_d, which uses Bc_dictionary_d. Reference equality determines uniqueness.

Bc_set_u, which uses Bc_dictionary_u. Reference equality determines uniqueness.

İe_set_d, which uses Bc_hash_table_d. *is_equal* determines uniqueness.

İe_set_u, which uses Bc_hash_table_u. *is_equal* determines uniqueness.

Bc_set_iterator is used to iterate through all of the forms of Bc_set.

Stacks A stack denotes a sequence of items in which items may be added and removed from one end. Again, there are three effective types of stacks: dynamic, bound, and unbound.

String Bc_character_string is provided for developers who wish to use a character string in the same manner as the rest of the Booch components. It permits the use of all of the tools such as pattern matching and expression matching on a character string.

To iterate a BC_CHARACTER_STRING, get a cursor by using the feature named *cursor*. It will return a BC_CURSOR that can do everything that a BC_INDEXED_ITERATOR can do, and more.

Support The structures and tools that comprise the **Tower**_Eiffel_ Booch components are all built from more primitive support abstractions. In general, application developers need only concern themselves with the higher level abstractions of structures and tools. Library developers and power users, however, may wish to make use of the more primitive support abstractions, from which new structures and tools can be constructed, or through which the behavior of existing classes can be modified. The support classes include:

Primitive Containers BOUND, DYNAMIC, UNBOUND (all generic [Element_T]).

Dictionaries DICTIONARY, HASH_TABLE (both generic [Key_T, Value_T]).

Simple Agents EQUALITY_JUDGE, JUDGE_BY_IS_EQUAL, JUDGE_BY_REF, COMPARATOR, COMPARE_BY_COMPARABLE, VALIDATOR (all generic [Element_T]).

Abstract Ancestors ABSTRACT_DICTIONARY[Key_T, Value_T], and ITERATED, INDEXED, CONTAINER, READER, WRITER, TESTER, TOKEN (all generic [Element_T]).

Iterators ITERATOR, CURSOR (both generic [Element_T]) ABSTRACT_DICTIONARY_ITERATOR, DICTIONARY_ITERATOR, HASH_TABLE_ITERATOR (all generic [Key_T, Value_T]).

Nodes NODE, DOUBLE_NODE, BINARY_NODE, MULTIWAY_NODE, AVL_NODE (all generic [Element_T]) and PAIR [Key_T, Value_T].

Trees A binary tree is a rooted collection of nodes and arcs, in which each node has two children and in which arcs may not have cycles or cross-references (as in graphs). AVL trees are a form of balance tree (following the algorithm of Adelson, Velskii, and Landis) that only exposes operations to add, remove, and search for items. There are three types of trees: BC_AVL_TREE, BC_BINARY_TREE, and BC_MULTIWAY_TREE. Each tree has its own special iterator. The BC_BINARY_TREE_ITERATOR and the BC_MULTIWAY_

TREE_ITERATOR use a form of Lindstrom scanning. AVL_TREE enforces an ordering of the items in the tree, so the AVL_TREE_ITERATOR visits the items in order.

8.4 The SiG Library

8.4.1 Overview

Most of this section is from "SiG Computer GmbH," and is reproduced here with Michael Schweitzer's kind authorization.

SiG offers a data structure library bundled with its compiler. However, third parties have reported that this library can be compiled with other Eiffel compilers without many problems. The SiG library expressly embraces the philosophy *small is beautiful*. The idea is that a carefully selected collection of optimally programmed classes is preferable to a bag full of everything one can think of. Another key idea in the design of the SiG library is that classes should be implementations of abstract data types (ADTs), and only that. The names of classes implementing lists, for example, should not advertise that they are lists implemented with arrays or with two-way linked nodes, because the *abstractness* of the ADT concept would be lost. The implementations of the SiG library classes were chosen carefully by the class designers, and are hidden as much as possible from the user. In situations in which it is not possible to achieve time efficiency and space efficiency with the same implementation, two abstractions are created (e.g., LIST and SHORT_LIST) and documented (in this case, the former optimizes time efficiency and the latter is to be used when one has many short lists and space begins to be a problem).

Most of the data structure library fits in the CONTAINER cluster. This cluster actually contains two different abstractions: the *containers* and the *iterators*. These abstractions live in a sort of symbiosis with each other.

The container classes are classified along three important and orthogonal properties:

Unique Can the same object occur more than once in the container?

Ordered Are the objects in the container kept in sorted order? (This, of course, only makes sense if the type of the contained objects has a total order—i.e., conforms to COMPARABLE). This property can have an influence on the performance of the search routine and also on the behavior of the iterators.

Keyed Does one search for an object in the container by asking for the object itself? Or does one search for an object by giving a *key*, with which the object was presumably stored in the first place?

The cluster CONTAINER deals with these three properties of containers as follows:

- A container object is initialized with a *make* routine that takes a BOOLEAN argument *only_once*. If *only_once* is set to *true*, then the container will make sure that it never contains duplicates. Otherwise, duplicates are allowed.

- For each kind of container there is a sorted version and an unsorted version. The sorted version has a name beginning with SORTED_.

- The classes in which objects are searched for directly are called collections; those in which one searches using a key are called tables.

Thus there are altogether four basic types of container classes: collections, sorted collections, tables, and sorted tables.

8.4.2 Design Patterns

Reference Semantics and Equality

In most data structure clusters, "equality" means value equality—i.e., it is tested using *is_equal*. Because of the value equality semantics, the collections are provided with a feature *found_item* and the tables with a feature *found_key*. If after a search *found* is true, then *found_item* is bound to the item that was found to be *is_equal* to the searched item (which is different from =). Similarly, after a table search that was successful, *found_key* is bound to the key that was found.

General-Purpose Containers

The basic operations of the ADT container are presented in Example 8.6.

The semantics of the operations *add* and *remove* do, of course, depend on the uniqueness property of the container. If the container was created in unique mode, then *add* will change nothing if the object x is already in the collection or if the key k already occurs in the table. It is, however, not an error to call *add* repeatedly for the same object; *add* simply ignores the second and all further such calls.

Similarly, in unique mode, *remove* removes the one and only copy of x if x occurs in the container at all. In nonunique mode, however, just one copy of x

```
    class COLLECTION [G]
    feature
        count : INTEGER -- how many items herein
        empty : BOOLEAN
        found : BOOLEAN -- whether last call to found was successful
        found_item : G -- last item found
        protected : BOOLEAN -- whether at least one iterator is active
        make(only_once: BOOLEAN) is
            -- make a new collection allowing or not duplicate
        inside (it : ITERATOR) : BOOLEAN is
            -- is the iterator still inside the container?
            require not_void: it /= Void
        item (it : ITERATOR) : G is
            -- The element in this iterator window
        iterator : ITERATOR
            -- a new iterator able to traverse this container
        add (x: G) is
        -- add x to the collection, according to the creation mode
        remove (x: G) is
        -- remove x from the collection, according to the creation mode
        search (x: G) is
            -- look for x in the collection, set found and found_item
    end -- COLLECTION [G]
```

Example 8.6

is removed; there is no way to control which one. If the given element was not in the container, then *remove* simply does nothing.

All containers in the cluster are dynamic. That is, they grow and shrink as needed. Hence there is no attribute *full* in these classes. The inheritance hierarchy of the container cluster is presented in **Figure 8.4**.

Iterators

In the SiG library an iterator is a data structure that allows one to visit all the objects in a container one after the other—each one exactly once. An iterator object belongs to one particular container object and possesses some intimate knowledge about "its" container, which enables it to carry out this traversal. A container is also aware of any iterators associated with it (there may be several). This mutual knowledge between containers and iterators is the reason for the "symbiosis" referred to in Section 8.4.1. The basic operations of the ADT iterator are presented in Example 8.7.

In addition, there is an extended kind of iterator for the sorted containers: It can traverse the container in the reverse direction. These two-way iterators have two additional operations, *last* to go to the "last" object in the container

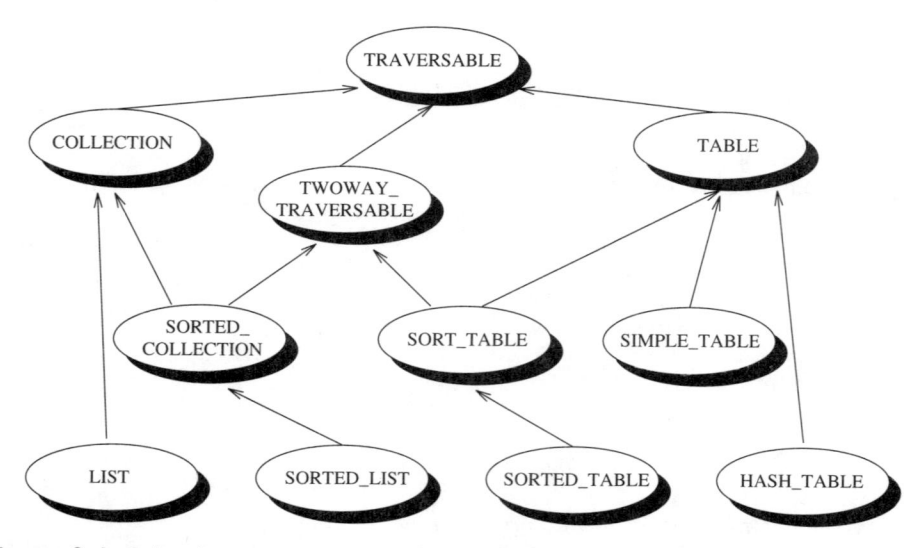

Figure 8.4 Inheritance structure of the container classes

and *back* to go to the "previous" object. A typical use of an iterator for a container *c* is shown in Example 8.8.

Here the iterator takes over the role of the iteration index *i* for an array iteration. There is no need to call `it.first` explicitly because the call to `c.iterator` does this automatically.

Multiple Iterators on the Same Container

There can be arbitrarily many iterators running over a container at the same time. All iterators are independent of one another, so they cannot interfere with each other.

An iterator could get quite confused if someone went about removing or adding objects from its container while it was in the process of traversing the container. For this reason, each iterator "logs in" to its container when it begins a traversal with *first* or *last* and it "logs out" again when it has reached

```
    class ITERATOR
    feature
        first  -- go to "first" object in container
        forth  -- go to "next" object in container
        stop   -- break off traversal
        finished : BOOLEAN  -- have we seen them all or stopped?
    end  -- ITERATOR
```

Example 8.7

```
     local
         c : COLLECTION [G]
         it : ITERATOR
     do
5        from it := c.iterator
         until it.finished
         loop
             if c.item (it) = ... then
                 it.stop
10           else
                 do_something_with (c.item (it))
             end -- if
             it.forth
         end -- loop
15   end -- example
```

Example 8.8

the last (or first) element or has been stopped with *stop*. A container will then decline to do an *add* or *remove* as long as some iterator is in progress. More precisely, one of the preconditions of *add* and *remove* is that no iterator is active. The attribute *protected* gives information about whether there is an active iterator.

Short Containers

The container classes described so far were designed to optimize speed. They can be comparatively wasteful of space in situations in which one has several containers with few elements. For this purpose there is a second category of containers: the "short" containers. They have names beginning with SHORT_, such as SHORT_LIST. They have the same syntax and semantics as their "long" cousins but are implemented to optimize use of memory. The price to pay is in the speed of many operations. As a rough guide one can say that the "short" containers should be used when they are only to contain a few dozen objects. There the loss in efficiency is not very noticeable and the savings in space can be considerable.

8.4.3 Other Abstractions Related to Containers

Special Kinds of Containers

In addition to the four basic container types mentioned in Section 8.4.1, there are some containers with somewhat deviant or restricted semantics. There is often a need to represent a one-to-one mapping between two sets, neither of which is of type INTEGER. For this purpose one uses the ADT *dictionary*—often also called *associative array*. Its *indices* can be of almost any type.

The container cluster offers for this purpose the class DICTIONARY [G, K]. The *index*, or *key*, has to have a type conforming to HASHABLE but can otherwise be arbitrary—for example, STRING. If d is of the type DICTIONARY, then the object associated with a *key* k is d.at(k). In all other respects a DICTIONARY is like other kinds of containers. In particular, it has the procedures *add* and *remove* as well as iterators for visiting all elements in the dictionary.

If one needs to represent a one-to-many mapping, the CONTAINER cluster offers the class CATALOG. A CATALOG is similar to a DICTIONARY but it associates with each key an entire list of objects. The function call c.at(k) returns not just a single object but rather an entire list of objects. The procedure call c.add (x,k) adds the object x to the list associated with key k (creating the list, if there was previously no list associated with k). Correspondingly, the call c.remove (x,k) removes the object x from the list associated with key k (if x was there; otherwise it does nothing).

CATALOG is a deferred class and has effective descendants for each of the kinds of lists that can be associated with keys. These include LIST_CATALOG, where the lists are of the type LIST, and SORTED_CATALOG, where the lists are of the type SORTED_LIST. There are also two "short" variants, in which the lists are of the type SHORT_LIST and SHORT_SORTED_LIST.

Further container classes with semantics that are more restrictive than those of the general containers are:

- STACK Stacks operate on the *last in, first out* (LIFO) principle. In other words, *remove* has no argument; it removes the object that was most recently added using *add*. The function *item* returns the element that was most recently added (and would be removed by a succeeding call to *remove*). There is no *search* routine.

- QUEUE Queue operates on the *first in, first out* (FIFO) principle. Thus, *remove* removes the element that has been in the queue the longest. This is the same element that is returned by the function *item*. Queues also have no routine *search*.

- PRIORITY_QUEUE A priority queue is a self-organizing container. The element "at the front" of the queue is the element with the highest priority. There are two kinds of priority queues. One of them accepts elements conforming to COMPARABLE and sorts them according to their inherent order. The other accepts an element and a priority (conforming to COMPARABLE) and sorts according to the priority member of the pair.

Thus, the function *item* for a priority queue will return the element with the *highest* priority currently in the queue. This is also the element removed by a succeeding call to *remove*. The procedure *add* always inserts an element at a position appropriate to its priority.

These special container classes are not provided with iterators, because the semantics of these ADTs would not normally involve traversing the containers. Moreover, their *make* routines do not have the argument *only_once*, because the question of uniqueness is irrelevant.

Implementation of the Container Classes

The ADTs available in the CONTAINER cluster are implemented in the following way:

- Collections are implemented by LIST.
- Sorted collections are implemented by SORTED_LIST.
- Tables are implemented by SIMPLE_TABLE and HASH_TABLE.
- Sorted tables are implemented by SORTED_TABLE.

With the exception of SIMPLE_TABLE, these implementations were chosen because they should be the most efficient for most applications. Normally one should never need to replace them by others. The HASH_TABLE is much more efficient for large tables but unfortunately does not fit smoothly into this general scheme, because its creation procedure *make* takes two arguments instead of one. In many situations in which one might at first think of using HASH_TABLE one should also consider using DICTIONARY.

In addition, four classes—SHORT_LIST, SHORT_TABLE, SHORT_SORTED_LIST, and SHORT_SORTED_TABLE—are implemented to optimize space requirements at the cost of speed. Otherwise their behavior is identical to that of the corresponding long versions.

Other Related Clusters

Along with the basic data structure cluster, some related clusters are available:

GRAPH Cluster A graph is defined by the classes VERTEX and EDGE. It may have weighted edges (WT_GRAPH) or unweighted edges (GRAPH). Iterators are provided to visit the edges emanating from a vertex (EDGE_ITER), or all the vertices of a graph in breadth-first order (BREADTH_ITER), depth-first order (DEPTH_ITER), or topological order (TOP_ITER).

The MATCHER Cluster The MATCHER class is a pattern matcher that can build and activate an automaton to search for patterns in text. Effective descendants search for text using the Rabin-Karp algorithm (RK_MATCHER), the Knuth-Morris-Pratt algorithm (KMP_MATCHER), and the Boyer-Moore algorithm (BM_MATCHER). Others search for regular expressions (RE_MATCHER) and lists of keywords (KEYWORD_MATCHER). TXT_MATCHER is an iterator that searches for multiple occurrences of a pattern in an array of strings, using any of the matcher classes.

The SORTER Cluster This cluster contains only one class, the class SORTER with only one exported feature, *sort*. This class plays the role of a sorting *agent* for collections implemented as arrays.

9

Building a Parallel Linear Algebra Library with Eiffel

In This Chapter
- 9.1 Introduction
- 9.2 Encapsulating Distribution
- 9.3 Replicated and Distributed Matrices
- 9.4 Dealing with Multiple Representations
- 9.5 Making Parallel Libraries Efficient
- 9.6 Conclusion

In this last chapter, we show how Eiffel can be used as an enabling technology to master a very complex problem: the building of a parallel linear algebra library allowing an application programmer to use distributed computing systems in a transparent way.

9.1 Introduction

Distributed computing systems (DCSs)—also called distributed memory parallel computers or *multiprocessors*—consist of hundreds or thousands of processors and are now commercially available. An example of this kind of DCS is the Intel Paragon supercomputer, a distributed-memory multicomputer with an architecture that can accommodate more than a thousand nodes connected in a two-dimensional rectangular mesh (see Figure 9.1). Its computation nodes are based on Intel i860 processors, and communicate by passing messages over a high-speed internal interconnect network. These kinds of multiprocessors provide orders of magnitude more raw power than traditional supercomputers at lower costs. They enable the development of previously infeasible applications (called *grand challenges*) in various scientific domains, such as materials

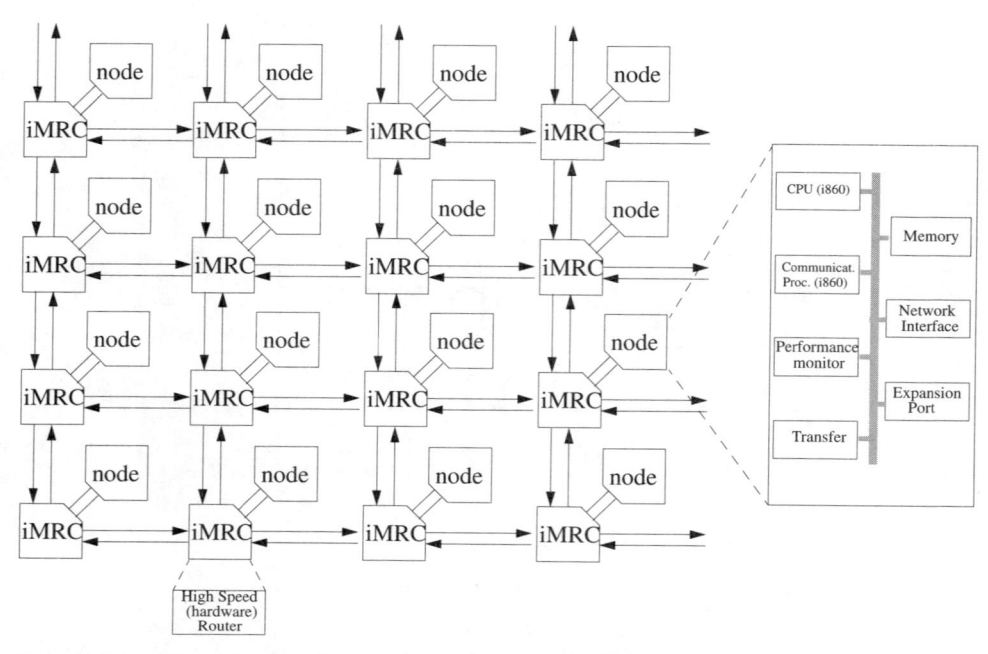

Figure 9.1 The architecture of the Intel Paragon XP/S supercomputer

science (for the aerospace and automobile industries), molecular biology, high-energy physics (Quantic chromodynamic), and global climate modeling.

Although the physical world they model is inherently parallel, scientific programmers used to rely on sequential techniques and algorithms to solve their problems, because these algorithms (e.g., the N-body problem) often present a better computational complexity than possible direct solutions. Their interest in concurrency only results from their desire to improve the performance of sequential algorithms applied to large-scale numerical computations [112]. Scientific programmers are generally reluctant to cope with the manual porting of their applications on distributed computing systems, because the average user will not move from an environment in which programming is relatively easy to one in which it is relatively hard unless the performance gains are truly remarkable and unachievable by any other method.

Programming is hard on parallel machines for two reasons. First, the standard sequential algorithms familiar to most users are often ill-suited to parallel computation. With 45 years of algorithm development for sequential machines, it should not be surprising that finding parallel algorithms achieving the same purpose would take time. A second factor that makes programming hard is the typical parallel programming interface that makes the architecture of the underlying machines visible to the user. Scientific programmers soon discovered how tedious it was to write parallel programs in a dialect that made the user responsible for creating and managing distribution and parallel computations and for explicit communication between the processors.

Tedious programming is not the only problem caused by machine-specific programming interfaces. A deeper problem is that the programs written for a parallel machine used to be architecture-specific, and need to be reprogrammed each time a new architecture emerged. Even worse, if the programmer wishes to run a program on different parallel architectures, multiple versions of the source used to be required. This is particularly problematic for corporate users contemplating a transition to parallelism for a production code. The conversion would be expensive in terms of programming manpower and the investment would ultimately not be protected. They might have to redevelop the program for their next machine or even the next generation of the same machine. For this reason, the independent software vendors, who produce science and engineering applications that are widely used in the commercial sector, resist moving to parallelism. Without these applications, parallelism would be doomed to be an interesting but unsuccessful experimental technology.

In this chapter, we show how Eiffel can be used to override these drawbacks. The idea is to build easy-to-use parallel object-oriented libraries permitting an efficient and transparent use of distributed computers. We use the EPEE framework (see Section 5.5.4) to encapsulate the tricky parallel codes in object-oriented software components that can be reused, combined, and customized in confidence by application programmers. In this context, we use a kind of parallelism known as *data parallelism*, encapsulated within purely sequential Eiffel classes, using the single program multiple data (SPMD) programming model. We define a set of methodological rules to help a programmer design and exploit parallel software components within this framework. We illustrate our approach with the example of Paladin, an object-oriented library devoted to linear algebra computation on distributed computing systems.

9.2 Encapsulating Distribution

9.2.1 Polymorphic Aggregates

The SPMD model is mostly appropriate for solving problems that are data-oriented and involve large amounts of data. Thus this model fits well application domains that deal with large, homogeneous data structures. Such data structures are commonly referred to as *aggregates*. Typical aggregates are large containers such as lists, sets, trees, graphs, arrays, matrices, and vectors.

Most aggregates admit several alternative representation layouts and thus must be considered as *polymorphic* entities, or objects that assume different forms and have forms that can change dynamically. Consider the example of matrix aggregates. Although all matrices can share a common abstract specification, they do not necessarily require the same implementation layout. Obviously dense and sparse matrices deserve different internal representations. A dense matrix may be implemented quite simply as a two-dimensional array, whereas a sparse matrix requires a smarter internal representation, based for example on lists or trees. Moreover, the choice of the most appropriate internal representation for a sparse matrix may depend on whether the sparsity of this matrix is likely to change during its lifetime. This choice also may be guided by considerations of the way the matrix is to be accessed (e.g., regular vs. irregular, nonpredictable access), or by considerations of whether memory space or access time should be primarily saved.

The problem of choosing the most appropriate representation format of a matrix is even more crucial in the context of distributed computation, because matrix aggregates can be partitioned and distributed on multi-processor machines. Each distribution pattern for a matrix (e.g., distribution by rows, by columns, by blocks) then can be perceived as a particular implementation of this matrix.

When designing an application program that deals with matrices, the choice of the best representation layout for a given matrix is a crucial issue. Paladin, for example, encapsulates several alternative representations for matrices (and for vectors as well, though this part of Paladin is not discussed here), and makes it possible for the application programmer to change the representation format of a matrix at any time during a computation. For example, after a few computation steps, an application program may need to convert a sparse matrix into a dense one, because the sparsity of the matrix has decreased during the first part of the computation. Likewise, it may sometimes be necessary to change the distribution pattern of a distributed matrix at run time to adapt its distribution to the requirements of the computation. Paladin thus provides a facility to redistribute matrices dynamically, as well as a facility to transform dynamically the internal representation format of a matrix (see Section 9.4).

9.2.2 One Abstraction, Several Implementations

To implement polymorphic aggregates—whether they are distributed or not—using the facilities of EPEE, we propose a method based on the dissociation of the abstract and operational specifications of an aggregate. The fundamental idea is to build a hierarchy of abstraction levels. Application programs are written in such a way that they operate on abstract data structures, the concrete implementation of which is defined independently from the programs that use them.

Eiffel provides all the mechanisms we need to dissociate the abstract specification of an aggregate from the details relative to its implementation. The abstract specification can be easily encapsulated in a class with an interface that determines precisely the way an application programmer will view this aggregate.

The distribution of an aggregate is usually achieved in two steps. The first step aims at providing transparency to the user. It consists of performing the actual distribution of the aggregate on the processors of a distributed computer, while ensuring that the resulting distributed aggregate can be handled in an SPMD program just like its local counterpart in a sequential program. The second step mostly addresses performance issues. It consists of parallelizing some of the features that operate on the distributed aggregate.

One or several distribution patterns must be chosen to spread the aggregate over a distributed computing system. We opted for a data parallel approach, so each processor will only own a part of the distributed aggregate. The first thing to do is thus to implement a mechanism ensuring a transparent remote access to nonlocal data, while preserving the semantics of local accesses.

When implementing distributed aggregates with EPEE, a fundamental principle is a location rule known as the *owner write rule*, which states that only the processor that owns a part of an aggregate is allowed to update this part. This mechanism is commonly referred to as the *Exec* mechanism in the community of data parallel computing. Similarly, the *Refresh* mechanism ensures that remote accesses are dealt with properly. Both mechanisms have been introduced in [25], and described formally in [4]. The EPEE toolbox provides various facilities for implementing these mechanisms, as illustrated in the following sections on the implementation of distributed matrices.

9.2.3 Matrices and Vectors in Paladin

Paladin is built around the specifications of the basic entities of linear algebra: matrices and vectors.

The abstract specifications of matrices and vectors are encapsulated in the classes MATRIX and VECTOR. Both classes are generic and thus can be used to instantiate integer matrices and vectors, real matrices and vectors, and complex matrices and vectors.

The classes MATRIX and VECTOR are deferred classes: They provide no details about the way matrices and vectors shall be represented in memory. The specification of their internal representation is thus left to descendant classes. This does not imply that all features are kept deferred. Representation-dependent features are simply declared, whereas other features are defined—i.e., implemented—directly in MATRIX and VECTOR, as shown in Example 9.1.

In the following we focus mainly on the content of the class MATRIX. The class VECTOR is designed in a very similar way. The class MATRIX simply enumerates the features that are needed to handle a matrix object, together with their formal properties expressed as assertions (e.g., preconditions, postconditions, and invariants), as illustrated in Example 9.1.

For the sake of conciseness and clarity, the class MATRIX that we consider here is a simplified version of the real class implemented in Paladin. The class includes some of the most classic linear algebra operations (sum, difference, multiply, and transpose) as well as more complex operations (such as triangular system solvers, etc.). It also encapsulates the definition of infix operators that make it possible to write in application programs an expression such as $R := A + B$, where A, B, and R refer to matrices.

The resulting class can be thought of as a close approximation of the ADT of a matrix entity [1, 26]. A matrix is mainly characterized by its size, stored in attributes *nrow* and *ncolumn*. Routines can be classified in two categories: accessors and operators.

```
    deferred class MATRIX [T–>NUMERIC]
    feature -- Attributes
        nrow: INTEGER      -- Number of rows
        ncolumn: INTEGER -- Number of columns
5
    feature -- Accessors
        item (i, j: INTEGER): T is
            -- Return current value of item(i, j)
            require
10              valid_i: (i > 0) and (i <= nrow)
                valid_j: (j > 0) and (j <= ncolumn)
            deferred
            end -- item
        put (v: T; i, j: INTEGER) is
15          -- Put value v into item(i, j)
```

Example 9.1 (Lines 1–15)

```
        require
            valid_i: (i > 0) and (i <= nrow)
            valid_j: (j > 0) and (j <= ncolumn)
        deferred
20      ensure
            item (i, j) = v
        end -- put

      row (i: INTEGER): VECTOR [T] is
25          -- Returns i'th row of matrix
        require
            valid_i: (i > 0) and (i <= nrow)
        do -- ...
        ensure
30          Result_not_void: (Result /= Void)
        end -- row
      column (j: INTEGER): VECTOR [T] is
            -- Returns j'th column of matrix
        require
35          valid_j: (j > 0) and (j <= ncolumn)
        do -- ...
        ensure
            Result_not_void: (Result /= Void)
        end -- column
40    diagonal (k: INTEGER): VECTOR [T] is
            -- Returns k'th diagonal of matrix
        require
            valid_k: (k > –nrow) and (k < ncolumn)
        do -- ...
45      ensure
            Result_not_void: (Result /= Void)
        end -- diagonal
      submatrix (i, j, k, l: INTEGER): SUB_MATRIX [T] is
            -- Returns submatrix as defined by arguments
50      do -- ...
        ensure
            Result_not_void: (Result /= Void)
        end -- submatrix

55 feature -- Operators
      trace: T is do ... end
      random (min, max: T) is do ... end
      add (B: MATRIX [T]) is do ... end
      mult (A, B: MATRIX [T]) is do ... end
60    LU is do ... end
      LDLt is do ... end
      Cholesky is do ... end
      -- ...
end -- class MATRIX
```

Example 9.1 (Lines 16–64)

Accessors

Accessors are the features that permit one to access a matrix in read or write mode. Paladin provides routines for accessing a matrix at different levels. The basic routines *put* and *item* give access to an item of the matrix. The implementation of accessors depends on the format chosen to represent a matrix object in memory. Consequently, in the class MATRIX, both accessors *put* and *item* are given a full specification (signature and preconditions and postconditions), but are left deferred.

Higher level accessors allow the user to handle a row, a column, or a diagonal of the matrix as a vector entity, and a rectangular section of the matrix (function *submatrix*). Assume that A is a newly created 5×5 integer matrix. The following code illustrates the use of the accessor *submatrix* to fill a section of A with random values (originally all items are set to zero).

$$A = \begin{pmatrix} 0 & 0 & 0 & 0 & 0 \\ 0 & 0 & 0 & 0 & 0 \\ 0 & 0 & 0 & 0 & 0 \\ 0 & 0 & 0 & 0 & 0 \\ 0 & 0 & 0 & 0 & 0 \end{pmatrix} \xrightarrow{A.\text{submatrix}(2,4,2,5).\text{random}} \begin{pmatrix} 0 & 0 & 0 & 0 & 0 \\ 0 & 6 & 1 & 9 & 6 \\ 0 & 2 & 7 & 2 & 8 \\ 0 & 7 & 3 & 5 & 1 \\ 0 & 0 & 0 & 0 & 0 \end{pmatrix}$$

An important feature of accessors is that most of the time they imply no copy of data. They simply provide a "view" of a section of a matrix. Thus, modifying this view is equivalent to modifying the corresponding section. Views necessitate special implementations, which are encapsulated in the classes ROW, COLUMN, DIAGONAL, SUBMATRIX, and SUBVECTOR.

The set of multilevel accessors actually provides the same abstractions as the syntactic short cuts frequently used in books dealing with linear algebra, such as [57]. Assuming that A is an $n \times m$ matrix, the expression $A.submatrix$ (i, j, k, l) is equivalent to the notation $A(i:j, k:l)$. Likewise, $A.row(i)$ and $A.column(j)$ are equivalent to $A(i,:)$ and $A(:,j)$, respectively.

Operators

Operators of the class MATRIX are high-level routines used for performing computations implying a matrix as a whole and possibly other arguments (i.e., other matrices or vectors). Paladin provides accessors at different levels (item, vector, and submatrix), so defining new operators is not a difficult task. Any algorithm presented in a book can be reproduced readily in the library.

Although the class MATRIX encapsulates the abstract specification of a matrix object, this does not imply that all features must be kept deferred in this class. Unlike the accessors *put* and *item*, operators such as *trace*, *random*, and

```
            trace: T is
                require
                    is_square: (nrow = ncolumn)
                local
                    i: INTEGER
                do
                    from i := 1 until i > nrow loop
                        Result := Result + item (i, i)
                        i := i + 1
                    end -- loop
                end -- trace
```

Example 9.2

add are features that generally can be given an operational specification based on calls to accessors and other operators. Consequently, the implementation of an operator (e.g., the *trace* of a matrix, which is the sum of its diagonal elements; see Example 9.2) does not directly depend on the internal representation format of the aggregate considered, because this representation format is masked by the accessors.

The organization of the class VECTOR is quite similar to that of MATRIX. In addition to the basic features (attribute *length*, accessors *put* and *item*, etc.), this class contains routines that perform scalar-vector, vector-vector (*saxpy*), and matrix-vector (*gaxpy*) operations.

9.3 Replicated and Distributed Matrices

9.3.1 Sequential Implementation of a Matrix

Once the abstract specification of an aggregate has been encapsulated in a class, it is possible to design one or several descendant classes (i.e., classes that inherit from the abstract class), each descendant encapsulating an alternative implementation of the aggregate. This implementation can either consist of the description of a representation format to store the aggregate in the memory of a monoprocessor machine, or it can be the description of a pattern to distribute the aggregate on a distributed system.

In the following, we show how the mechanism of multiple inheritance helps to design classes that encapsulate fully operational specifications of matrix objects. We first illustrate the approach by describing the design of the class LOCAL_MATRIX, which encapsulates a possible implementation for local—i.e., nondistributed—matrix objects. In this class we specify that an object of

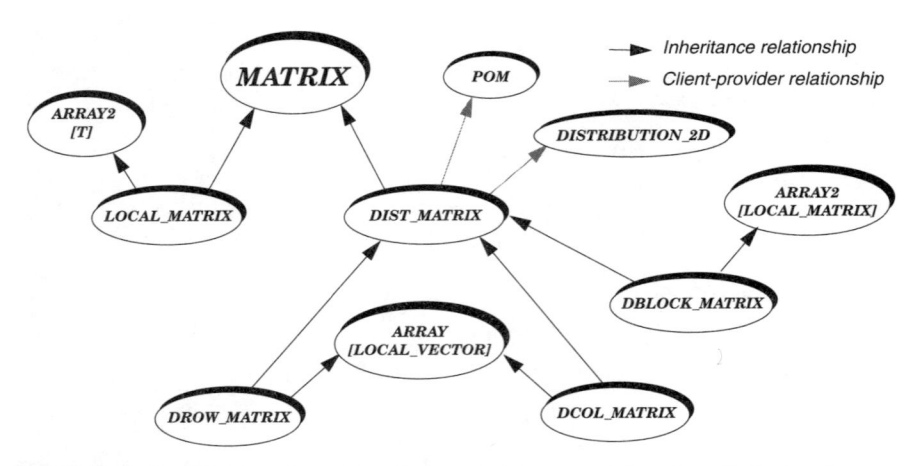

Figure 9.2 Inheritance structure for matrix aggregates (partial view)

the type LOCAL_MATRIX must be stored in memory as a traditional bidimensional array.

The class LOCAL_MATRIX simply combines the abstract specification inherited from MATRIX together with the storage facilities provided by the class ARRAY2 available in most Eiffel libraries (see also Figure 9.2). The text of LOCAL_MATRIX is readily written, because of the mechanism of multiple inheritance. The design effort only involves combining the abstract specification of the class MATRIX with the implementation facilities offered by ARRAY2, and ensuring that the names of the features inherited from both ancestor classes are matched correctly. In Example 9.3, while the features *item* and *put* get their implementation directly from the class ARRAY2, the attributes *height* and *width* of the class ARRAY2 are matched with the attributes *nrow* and *ncolumn* of the class MATRIX through *renaming*.

See Section 3.4.1 for a discussion of renaming.

A library designed along these lines may be augmented easily with new classes describing other kinds of entities such as sparse matrices and vectors, or symmetrical, lower triangular, and upper triangular matrices. Adding new representation variants for matrices and vectors simply comes down to adding

```
    class LOCAL_MATRIX [T–>NUMERIC]
    inherit
        MATRIX [T]
        ARRAY2 [T]
5           rename height as nrow, width as ncolumn end
    creation
        make
    end -- class LOCAL_MATRIX
```

Example 9.3

new classes in the library. Moreover, each new class is not built from scratch, but inherits from already existing classes. For the designer of the library, providing a new representation variant for a matrix or a vector usually consists of assembling existing classes to produce a new one. Very often this process does not imply any development of new code.

Unlike the abstract class MATRIX, the class LOCAL_MATRIX is a concrete (or effective) class, which means that it can be instantiated. It is thus possible to create objects of the type LOCAL_MATRIX in an application program, and to invoke on these objects some of the accessors and operators defined in MATRIX.

This possibility assumes that no operator has been left deferred in the class MATRIX.

9.3.2 Distribution of Matrices in Paladin

The Paladin approach to the distribution of matrices is quite similar to that of high-performance FORTRAN (HPF) [67]. The main difference is that HPF is based on weird extensions of the FORTRAN 90 syntax (distribution, alignment, and mapping directives), whereas Paladin only uses normal constructions of the Eiffel language.

Distributed matrices are decomposed into blocks, which then are mapped over the processors of the target distributed computing system. Managing the distribution of a matrix implies a great amount of fairly simple but repetitive calculations, such as those that aim at determining the identity of the processor that owns the item (i, j) of a given matrix, and the local address of this item on this processor. The features for doing such calculations have been encapsulated in a class DISTRIBUTION_2D, which allows the partition and distribution of 2-D data structures. The class DISTRIBUTION_2D is actually designed by inheriting two times from a more simple class DISTRIBUTION_1D. Hence, a class devoted to the distribution of 3-D data structures could be built just as easily.

The application programmer describes a distribution pattern by specifying the size of the index domain considered, the size of the basic building blocks in this domain, and how these blocks must be mapped on a set of processors. The definition of the mapping function has intentionally been left out of the class DISTRIBUTION_2D and encapsulated in a small hierarchy of classes devoted to the mapping of 2-D structures on a set of processors (see class MAPPING_2D in Example 9.4).

Paladin includes two effective classes that permit mapping of the blocks of a distributed matrix either row-wise or column-wise on a set of processors. In the class ROW_WISE_MAPPING, for example, the feature *map_block* is implemented as shown in Example 9.5.

The keyword **expanded** in the first line of this code implies that instances of the class ROW_WISE_MAPPING are value objects. Any attribute declared as

```
deferred class MAPPING_2D
feature
    map_block (bi, bj, bimax, bjmax, nproc: INTEGER): INTEGER is
            -- Maps block(bi, bj) on a processor whose identifier
            -- must be in the range [0, nproc]
        require
            bi_valid: (bi >= 0) and (bi <= bimax)
            bj_valid: (bj >= 0) and (bj <= bjmax)
        deferred
        ensure
            (Result >= 0) and (Result < nproc)
        end -- map_block
end -- class MAPPING_2D
```

Example 9.4

being of type ROW_WISE_MAPPING can be handled directly as an object of the type ROW_WISE_MAPPING.

The implementation of COLUMN_WISE_MAPPING is very similar to that of ROW_WISE_MAPPING. Any user could easily propose alternative mapping policies (e.g., random mapping or diagonal-wise mapping). The only thing a user must do is design a new class that inherits from MAPPING_2D and that encapsulates an original implementation of the feature *map_block*.

Figure 9.3 shows the creation of an instance of DISTRIBUTION_2D. The creation feature takes as parameters the size of the index domain considered, the size of the building blocks for partitioning this domain, and a reference to an object with a type that conforms to—i.e., is a descendant of—MAPPING_2D. The instance of DISTRIBUTION_2D created in Figure 9.3 will thus permit one to manage the distribution of a 10×10 index domain partitioned into 5×2 blocks mapped column-wise on a set of processors. Figure 9.3 also shows the resulting mapping on a parallel architecture providing four processors.

Each distributed matrix must be associated at creation time with an instance of DISTRIBUTION_2D, which serves as a distribution template for this matrix. The distribution pattern of a matrix can either be specified explicitly (in which case a new instance of DISTRIBUTION_2D is created for the matrix), or

```
expanded class ROW_WISE_MAPPING
inherit MAPPING_2D
feature
    map_block (bi, bj, bimax, bjmax, nproc: INTEGER): INTEGER is
        do
            Result := (bi * (bjmax + 1) + bj) \\ nproc
        end -- map_block
end -- class ROW_WISE_MAPPING
```

Example 9.5

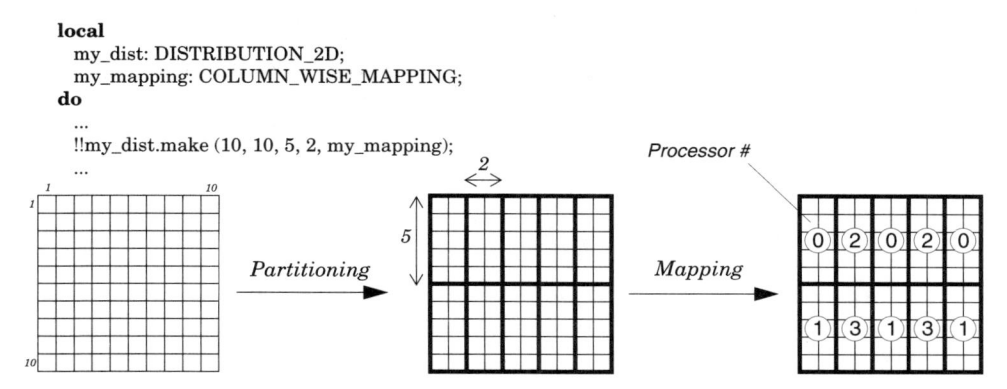

```
local
   my_dist: DISTRIBUTION_2D;
   my_mapping: COLUMN_WISE_MAPPING;
do
   ...
   !!my_dist.make (10, 10, 5, 2, my_mapping);
   ...
```

Figure 9.3 Example of a distribution allowed by class DISTRIBUTION_2D

implicitly by passing either a reference to an already existing distributed matrix or a reference to an existing distribution template as a parameter. Several distributed matrices thus can share a common distribution pattern by referencing the same distribution template.

9.3.3 Implementation of Distributed Matrices

The accessors *put* and *item* declared in the class MATRIX must be implemented in accordance with the *Exec* and *Refresh* mechanisms introduced in Section 9.2.2. This implementation is achieved in a new class DIST_MATRIX that inherits from the abstract specification encapsulated in the class MATRIX (see Example 9.6).

The accessor *put* is defined to conform to the *owner write rule*: when an SPMD application program contains an expression of the form M.put(v, i, j) —with M referring to a distributed matrix—the processor that owns item (i, j) is solely capable of performing the assignment. In the implementation of the feature *put*, the assignment is thus conditioned by a locality test using the distribution template (feature *dist*) of the matrix (see lines 20–25 of Example 9.6).

The accessor *item* must be defined so that remote accesses are properly dealt with: When an SPMD application program contains an expression such as v := M.item(i, j), the function *item* must return the same value on all the processors. Consequently, in the implementation of the feature *item*, the processor that owns item (i, j) broadcasts its value so that all the other processors can receive it (see lines 16–19 of Example 9.6). The invocation M.item(i, j) thus returns the same value on all the processors implied in the computation (the communication primitives are provided by the class POM of the EPEE toolbox).

Remember that all processors in an SPMD program run the same code as long as there is no explicit test on the processor identity.

```
indexing
    description: "Abstract matrix distributed along a template"

deferred class DIST_MATRIX [T–>NUMERIC]
inherit
    MATRIX [T] -- Abstract specification
feature -- Creation
    make (rows, cols, bfi, bfj: INTEGER; alignment: MAPPING_2D) is
        deferred end
    make_from (new_dist: DISTRIBUTION_2D) is deferred end
    make_like (other: DIST_MATRIX) is deferred end
feature -- Distribution template
    dist: DISTRIBUTION_2D
feature -- Accessors
    item (i, j: INTEGER): T is
            -- element (i,j) of the Matrix, read using the Refresh mechanism
        do
            if dist.item_is_local(i, j) then
                Result := local_item (i, j) -- I am the owner
                POM.broadcast (Result) -- so I send the value to others
            else -- I'm not the owner, I wait for the value to be sent to me
                Result := POM.receive_from (dist.owner_of_item (i, j))
            end -- if
        end -- item
    put (v: T; i, j: INTEGER) is
            -- write the element (i,j) of the Matrix, the Owner Write Rule
        do
            if dist.item_is_local(i, j) then
                local_put (v, i, j) -- Only the owner writes the data
            end -- if
        end -- put

feature {DIST_MATRIX} -- Communication features
    POM: POM

end -- DIST_MATRIX [T]
```

Example 9.6

This implementation of the features *put* and *item* deals with the distribution of data, but it does not deal with the actual *access* to local data. This problem must be tackled in the local accessors *local_put* and *local_item*; their implementation is closely dependent on the format chosen to represent a part of the distributed matrix on each processor. There may be numerous ways to store a distributed matrix in memory (e.g., the distributed matrix may be dense or sparse), so both features *local_put* and *local_item* are left deferred in the class DIST_MATRIX. They must be defined in classes that descend from

```
    indexing
        description: "Matrix distributed by blocks"

    class DBLOCK_MATRIX [T–>NUMERIC]
5   inherit
        DIST_MATRIX [T]
        ARRAY2 [LOCAL_MATRIX[T]]
            rename
                make as make_table,
10              put as put_block, item as local_block
            end
    feature -- ...
    end -- class DBLOCK_MATRIX [T–>NUMERIC]
```
Example 9.7

DIST_MATRIX and that encapsulate all the details relative to the internal representation of distributed matrices.

The class DBLOCK_MATRIX presented in Example 9.7 is one of the many possible descendants of DIST_MATRIX (see Figure 9.2). It inherits from DIST_MATRIX as well as from ARRAY2[LOCAL_MATRIX], and therefore implements a dense matrix distributed by blocks as a 2-D table of local matrices. Each entry in this table references a building block of the distributed matrix, stored in memory as an instance of LOCAL_MATRIX (see Figure 9.4). A void entry in the table means that the local processor does not own the corresponding block matrix. In DBLOCK_MATRIX, the local accessors *local_put* and *local_item* are defined to take into account the indirection caused by the table.

The class hierarchy that results from this approach is clearly organized as a layering of abstraction levels. At the highest level, the class MATRIX encapsulates the abstract specification of a matrix entity. The class DIST_MATRIX

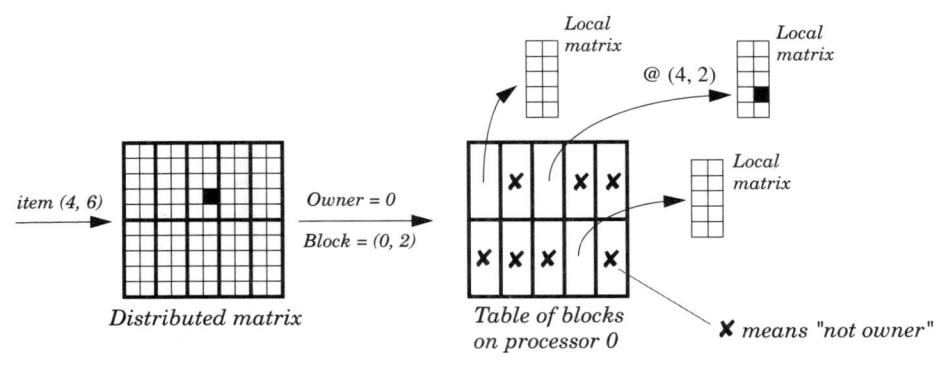

Figure 9.4 Internal representation of a matrix distributed by blocks

corresponds to an intermediate level, where the problem of the distribution of a matrix is solved, while the problem of the actual storage of the matrix in memory is deferred. At the lowest level, classes such as DBLOCK_MATRIX provide fully operational specifications for distributed matrices.

Besides DBLOCK_MATRIX, the class hierarchy of Paladin includes two classes, DCOL_MATRIX and DROW_MATRIX, that encapsulate alternative implementations for row-wise and column-wise distributed matrices. In these classes, distributed matrices are implemented as tables of local vectors. This kind of implementation fits well application programs that perform many vector-vector operations. Other kinds of distribution patterns or other kinds of representation formats could be proposed. One could for example think of exotic distribution patterns based on a decomposition into heterogeneous blocks or on a random mapping policy. One could also decide to provide an implementation ad hoc for triangular or band-distributed matrices. With the object-oriented approach, the extensibility of a class hierarchy such as that of Paladin has virtually no limit. It is always possible to incorporate new classes seamlessly in a preexisting class hierarchy.

9.4 Dealing with Multiple Representations

9.4.1 Interoperability

One of the major advantages of this class organization is that it ensures the interoperability of all matrices and vectors. A feature declared (and possibly implemented) in the class MATRIX is inherited by all the descendants of this class. Hence a feature such as *cholesky*, which performs a Cholesky factorization, can operate on any matrix that satisfies the preconditions of the feature: The matrix must be square symmetrical definite positive. This feature therefore operates on a local matrix as well as on a distributed one. In the library, a parallel version of the Cholesky algorithm is actually provided for distributed matrices, but this optimization remains absolutely transparent for the user who keeps using the feature the same way.

Interoperability also goes for algorithms that admit several arguments. For example, the class MATRIX provides an infix operator that computes the sum of two matrices (A and B) and returns the resulting matrix R. The user may write an expression such as $R := A + B$ while matrix R is duplicated on all processors, A is distributed by rows, and B is distributed by columns. Interoperability ensures that all internal representations can be combined transparently.

9.4.2 Dynamic Redistribution

Complementary to the interoperability of representation variants, a conversion mechanism is available for adapting the representation of a matrix or vector to the requirements of the computation. A row-wise distributed matrix, for example, can be "transformed" dynamically into a column-wise distributed matrix, assuming that this new representation is likely to lead to better performances in some parts of an application program. The conversion mechanism therefore acts as a redistribution facility.

An algorithm that permits a programmer to redistribute a matrix can be obtained quite simply using the communication facilities provided by the class POM and the distribution facilities provided by the class DISTRIBUTION_2D. Such a redistribution facility was implemented as shown in Example 9.8 in the class DBLOCK_MATRIX.

```
    redistribute (new_dist: DISTRIBUTION_2D) is
        require
            new_dist_valid: (new_dist /= Void)
            compat_dist: (dist.bfi = new_dist.bfi) and (dist.bfj = new_dist.bfj)
5       local
            bi, bj, source, target:   INTEGER
            tmp_matrix:   DBLOCK_MATRIX [T]
        do
            !!tmp_matrix.make_from (new_dist)
10          from bi := 0 until bi > dist.nbimax loop
                from bj := 0 until bj > dist.nbjmax loop
                    source := dist.owner_of_block (bi, bj)
                    target := tmp_matrix.dist.owner_of_block (bi, bj)
                    if (source = POM.my_node) then
15                      -- Send block matrix to target
                        local_block (bi, bj).send (target)
                    end -- if
                    if (target = POM.my_node) then
                        -- Receive block matrix from source
20                      tmp_matrix.local_block (bi, bj).recv_from (source)
                    end -- if
                    bj := bj + 1
                end -- loop
                bi := bi + 1
25          end -- loop
            dist := tmp_matrix.dist
            area := tmp_matrix.area
        end -- redistribute
```

Example 9.8

In this code, a temporary instance of DBLOCK_MATRIX named *tmp_matrix* is created according to the desired distribution pattern. Block matrices are then transferred one after another from the current matrix to *tmp_matrix*. Once the transfer is over, the attribute *dist* of the current matrix is reassociated with the new distribution template. Its former distribution template then can be collected by the garbage collector of the run-time system, unless this template is still used by another distributed matrix. Likewise, the attribute *area*, which refers to the table of block matrices of the current matrix, is reassociated to refer to the table of *tmp_matrix*. The former block table then can be collected by the garbage collector also. When the feature *redistribute* returns, the current matrix has a distribution corresponding to the pattern described by *new_dist* and its internal representation relies on the newly created table of block matrices.

Note that this implementation of the feature *redistribute* can only redistribute a matrix if the source and the target distribution patterns have the same block size (see the precondition in the code of the feature *redistribute*). The code of the feature *redistribute* reproduced here is actually a simplified version of the code implemented in DBLOCK_MATRIX. The real code is more flexible (a matrix can be redistributed even if the size of blocks must change during the process). It does not rely on a temporary matrix but directly creates and handles a new table of block matrices. Moreover, the garbage collection is performed on the fly. On each processor the local blocks that are sent to another processor are collected by the garbage collector immediately after they have been sent. Data exchanges also are performed more efficiently: The sequencing constraints imposed by the *Refresh/Exec* model in the former code are relaxed so that the resulting implementation of *redistribute* allows more concurrency. The real code encapsulated in the feature *redistribute* is thus more efficient than the code reproduced above, but it is also longer and more complex; thus we preferred to reproduce a simpler implementation of *redistribute* here.

Whatever the actual complexity of the algorithm encapsulated in the feature *redistribute*, it does not show through the interface of the class DBLOCK_MATRIX. From the viewpoint of the application programmer, an instance of DBLOCK_MATRIX can be redistributed quite simply. Consider the small SPMD application program of Example 9.9.

Imagine that in this application the requirements of the computation impose that matrices *A* and *B* be distributed differently in the first part of the concurrent execution. However, the second part of the computation requires that *A* and *B* have the same distribution. Then the redistribution facility encapsulated in the class DBLOCK_MATRIX can be used to achieve the redistribution.

```
    local
        A, B: DBLOCK_MATRIX [DOUBLE]
    do
        !!A.make (100, 100, 5, 2, ROW_WISE_MAPPING)
5       !!B.make (100, 100, 7, 3, COLUMN_WISE_MAPPING)
            ...(1)...
        B.redistribute (A.dist)
            ...(2)...
    end
```

Example 9.9

Other classes of Paladin (e.g., DIST_MATRIX, DCOL_MATRIX, and DROW_MATRIX) also encapsulate a version of the feature *redistribute*. Its implementation fits the characteristics of their distribution pattern.

9.4.3 Matrix-Type Conversion

Eiffel, like most statically typed object-oriented languages, does not allow for objects to change their internal structure at run time. Once an object has been created, its internal organization is in a way "frozen." Thus, in Paladin, there is no way one can transform an object of the type LOCAL_MATRIX into an object of the type DBLOCK_MATRIX. However, we can go around this constraint and propose a close approximation of "polymorphic" matrices using the only really polymorphic entities available in Eiffel: references.

Whenever we need to change the internal representation of a matrix aggregate, the conversion must be performed in three steps. At first, a new matrix aggregate must be created, with a dynamic type that conforms to the desired internal representation. Next, data must be "transferred" from the original aggregate into the new one. Finally, the reference associated with the original aggregate must be reassociated with the newly created one. This conversion procedure is illustrated in Example 9.10.

Assume that in an application program a local matrix is created and associated with reference M (Example 9.10).

After some computation (part 1) it becomes necessary to transform this local matrix into a distributed one. An instance of the type DBLOCK_MATRIX is created and associated with a temporary reference N. The information encapsulated in the original local matrix is copied into the distributed one using the routine *convert*. Once the copy is complete, the attribute M is reassociated with the newly created matrix because of a polymorphic assignment, so that the programmer can still refer to the matrix using the attribute M in the remaining part of the application program. The computation goes on using the distributed matrix (part 2). The conversion process is illustrated in Figure 9.5.

```
     local
         M, N: MATRIX [DOUBLE]
     do
         !LOCAL_MATRIX[DOUBLE]!M.make (...)
5        ...(1)...
         !DBLOCK_MATRIX[DOUBLE]!N.make (...)
         N.convert (M)
         M := N
         ...(2)...
10   end
```

Example 9.10

Conceptually, the feature *convert* performs a copy from the source matrix into the target one. It simply requires that both matrices have the same size. In the class MATRIX, the feature *convert* can be given a very simple implementation, based on two nested loops and calls to the accessors *put* and *item*. However, this implementation, which does not depend on the internal representation formats of the source and target matrices, should only be considered as a default implementation. Better implementations of *convert* can be encapsulated in descendants of the class MATRIX using some of the optimization techniques discussed in Section 9.5.1.

This method of changing the type of an aggregate requires that a new object be created. This requirement is acceptable, because the Eiffel garbage collector ensures that the object corresponding to the "obsolete" representation of the aggregate will be collected after the conversion is over. Actually, the main problem with this conversion mechanism lies in the lack of transparency for the application programmer, who must explicitly declare a temporary ref-

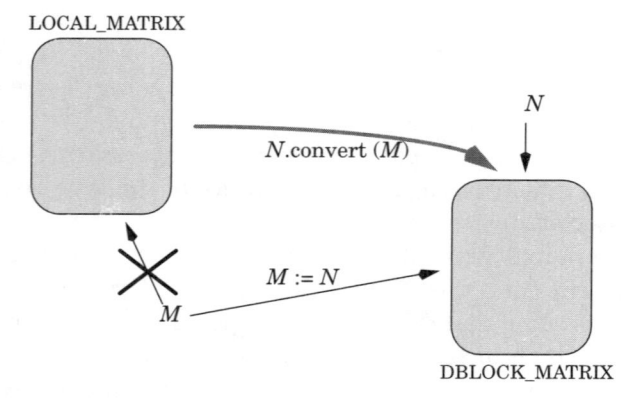

Figure 9.5 Example of matrix conversion

erence, create a new aggregate of the desired dynamic type, invoke the feature *convert* on this object, and eventually reassign the reference bound to the original object so that it refers to the new object.

9.4.4 Polymorphic Matrices

The features *redistribute* and *convert* together provide a satisfactory approximation of *polymorphic matrices*. In Paladin, these features are made available to the application programmer. Yet, they also could be invoked automatically within the library whenever an operator requires a particular distribution pattern of its operands. For example, any operator dealing with a distributed matrix could be implemented so as to systematically redistribute this matrix according to its needs before beginning the actual computation. If all operators in Paladin were implemented that way, the application programmer would not have to care about distribution patterns anymore, because all matrices would be redistributed transparently as and when needed. Yet, redistributing a matrix—or changing its type—is a costly operation, so that this approach would probably lead to concurrent executions in which most of the activity would consist of redistributing matrices or vectors. The best approach is probably an intermediate one between manual and automatic redistribution.

9.5 Making Parallel Libraries Efficient

9.5.1 Optimization Techniques

The techniques presented in the previous sections permit one to achieve the transparent distribution of an aggregate. From the viewpoint of an application programmer, there is no fundamental difference between the services offered by a distributed aggregate and those offered by a local, sequential, one. It is possible to handle larger aggregates, however, because the total memory offered by a distributed computing system usually amounts to several times that of a monoprocessor machine. Nevertheless, the flow of control of all features is still sequential, so that not much performance can be expected yet. To get better performance, it is necessary to redefine those operators of the distributed aggregate that can be considered critical (that is, computation-intensive ones). The method involves using the facilities provided by the EPEE toolbox again, but this time the goal is to optimize the operators.

The optimization techniques involved at this level are rather classic: most of them result from the work on the semiautomatic compilation of sequential imperative languages like FORTRAN and C for distributed systems. These techniques are:

Discarding useless Refresh/Exec When redefining an operator, if it can be statically deduced from the distribution pattern of the aggregate considered that data is locally present, this data then can be accessed directly. This optimization saves the useless tests and communications that are otherwise implied by the *Refresh* and *Exec* mechanisms. Likewise, when it can be decided locally that remote data have not been updated between two remote readings, then a *Refresh* operation can be saved using a temporary variable.

Restricting iteration domains So far, each processor must mark every step of an iteration, although only those steps that have to do with local data could be considered. Operators can be redefined to mark in an iteration only those steps that have to do with local data. In the best case, the size of an iteration domain—and consequently the duration of its execution—can be divided by the number of processors implied in the computation.

Optimizing index transformations Accessing an element of a distributed aggregate is usually a costly operation, because of the many calculations that are needed to locate this element. The features that compute index transformations usually can be encapsulated in a class (as shown in Section 9.3.2 in the example of the class DISTRIBUTION_2D), so it is possible to perform most of the index computations once and for all, and to store the results in private tables. Index conversion tables are created and filled in when a new distributed aggregate is created. These tables make it possible to locate an item quickly. They do not need to be updated, unless the aggregate with the distribution pattern that they describe is redistributed dynamically. With this optimization technique, the cost of an index conversion is only that of an indirection. The use of index conversion tables thus reduces index conversion times, at the expense of memory consumption.

Data vectorization In most modern parallel architectures, the cost of communication decreases every time a long message is preferred to many short ones. This observation led to many techniques for assembling several basic data elements in a single message (e.g., direct communication, data coalescing, data aggregation, and data vectorization). In EPEE, all these techniques can be used transparently, because data exchanges are encapsulated in classes and thus remain hidden to the user. *Data vectorization* is the technique of transmitting a large part of an aggregate instead of several smaller parts.

Dynamic redistribution Sometimes an operation requires a special distribution to be parallelized efficiently. The distribution is fully encapsulated within the class, so it is not a problem to dynamically redistribute the data to better suit the operation.

For example, the algorithm associated with the feature *trace* in the class MATRIX (see Example 9.2) is purely sequential and hence does not take into account the possible distribution of the matrix considered. We can redefine the operator *trace* in the class DIST_MATRIX, providing the feature with an algorithm that better fits the characteristics of a distributed matrix. The computation of the trace is performed in two steps. In the first step, each processor computes locally a partial trace for the items it owns. The locality test reduces the iteration domain so that each processor only deals with local diagonal items. The second step of the algorithm is a classic SPMD reduction.

The parallelization of features such as *add* is more complex. The feature *add* takes a matrix as a parameter and adds this matrix to the current one. It thus can be invoked to add two matrices of equal size A and B, just by introducing the expression A.add(B) in an application program. It was implemented quite simply in the class MATRIX, based on two nested loops and the accessors *put* and *item*. However, this default implementation is purely sequential, and therefore quite inefficient if either A or B or both matrices turn out to be distributed. We encapsulated in the class DBLOCK_MATRIX another operator, *add_dblock*, that also computes the sum of two matrices, but only if both matrices are distributed by blocks and if all blocks have the same size (see Example 9.11).

Instead of relying on the basic scalar accessors *put* and *item*, the algorithm of *add_dblock* is expressed directly in terms of block matrix operations. The iteration domain is reduced by locality tests so that each processor only performs local calculations. Communications, when they cannot be avoided, are naturally vectorized because the data exchanged are now block matrices instead of scalar elements.

Vectorizing data access is not profitable to communications only. Restructuring the algorithms encapsulated in the class MATRIX and its descendants so that they perform block matrix operations in their inner loops globally enhances the performance of Paladin, because it reduces memory swapping and cache defaults on most modern processors. Providing multilevel accessors to an aggregate therefore has an interesting consequence: it enhances the performances of operators by better exploiting the memory architecture and by reducing the cost of data exchanges between the processors of a distributed computing system.

```
            add_dblock (B: DBLOCK_MATRIX [T]) is
              require
                B_valid:      (B /= Void)
                same_size:    (nrow = B.nrow) and (ncolumn = B.ncolumn)
5               same_dist:    (dist.bfi = B.dist.bfi) and (dist.bfj = B.dist.bfj)
              local
                bi, bj, source, target:   INTEGER
                Bs_block:     LOCAL_MATRIX
              do
10              from bi := 0 until bi > dist.nbimax loop
                  from bj := 0 until bj > dist.nbjmax loop
                    source := B.owner_of_block (bi, bj)
                    target := owner_of_block (bi, bj)
                    if (source = POM.my_node) then
15                    -- Send B's block matrix to target
                      B.local_block (bi, bj).send (target)
                    end -- if
                    if (target = POM.my_node) then
                      -- Receive B's block matrix from source
20                    Bs_block.recv_from (source)
                      -- Add B's block to local block
                      local_block (bi, bj).add (Bs_block)
                    end -- if
                    bj := bj + 1
25                end -- loop
                  bi := bi + 1
                end -- loop
              end -- add_dblock
```

Example 9.11

At this stage, this approach does *not* lead to an explosion of the number of features in the library. Indeed, for each operation only a few distribution combinations can lead to an optimized parallel solver (e.g., the matrix-matrix sum). If the object distributions do not fit them, one can either use the default (inherited) algorithm or (dynamically) *redistribute* one or several of the involved objects to select an efficient solver.

9.5.2 Preserving User Friendliness

With the optimization techniques discussed in Section 9.5.1, each operator declared in the class MATRIX may be given several alternative implementations, each implementation being devoted to a particular representation or distribution pattern of the operands. It is obviously not desirable to have the application programmer specify explicitly which version of an operator is the most appropriate to mark every computation step in an application program.

See Section 3.5.2 for a discussion of dynamic binding.

The object-oriented answer to this problem lies in the dynamic binding of features to objects. This mechanism is available in all object-oriented languages, and ensures the transparency of features dispatching for parameterless features such as *trace*.

The problem is more complex for operators that admit several operands. Let us consider the feature *add* again. Remember that the feature *add* was given a default sequential implementation in the class MATRIX, but that DBLOCK_MATRIX encapsulates another feature *add_dblock* that is especially devoted to the computation of the sum of two matrices distributed by blocks. It is most important to understand why we did not simply overwrite the feature *add* in DBLOCK_MATRIX. It only permits the programmer to compute the sum of matrices distributed by blocks, so the algorithm of the feature *add_dblock* cannot just replace that of the feature *add*, which computes the sum of any matrices, be they represented the same way or not. The service they offer to the application programmer is not exactly equivalent in both operators, so *add* and *add_dblock* must remain available simultaneously in DBLOCK_MATRIX. This does not mean that the application programmer must be responsible for selecting which of these two operators is the most appropriate to sum up two matrices. Ideally, the selection of the most appropriate algorithm should be performed automatically at run time based on the dynamic types of the operands. Such a mechanism of *multiple dispatching* is provided by some object-oriented languages (e.g., CLOS [54] and Cecil [30]), but not by Eiffel—neither by Modula-3, Ada95, or C++ (whose *function overloading* mechanism is just syntactic sugar because it only considers the *static types* of the parameters). Anyway, one can emulate multiple dispatching by performing explicit tests on the dynamic type of operands. The idea is to redefine the feature *add* in the class DBLOCK_MATRIX to test the dynamic type of the matrix operand (see Example 9.12).

If the test shows that the dynamic type of the argument does not conform to the type DBLOCK_MATRIX, then the default algorithm inherited from the class MATRIX—and renamed as *add_default* in the inheritance statement of the class DBLOCK_MATRIX—is invoked. If the argument is recognized as being a matrix distributed by blocks, however, and if its basic building blocks have the same size as the blocks of the current matrix, then the optimized parallel algorithm *add_dblock* can be invoked. In both cases, the cost of the tests performed to select one or the other algorithm is negligible compared to the complexity of the algorithms that perform the actual matrix summation.

```
class DBLOCK_MATRIX [T–>NUMERIC]
inherit
    DIST_MATRIX [T]
        rename add as add_default -- Keep the default sequential operator
    end
    DIST_MATRIX [T]
        redefine add
        select add -- in case of dynamic binding
    end
    ...
feature -- Optimized operators
    add (B: MATRIX [T]) is
        local
            tmp_B : DBLOCK_MATRIX [T]
        do
            tmp_B ?= B
                -- tmp_B = B if B conforms to 'DBLOCK_MATRIX'
                -- tmp_B = Void otherwise
            if (tmp_B /= Void)
                and then (dist.bfi = tmp_B.dist.bfi) -- Do matrices have
                and then (dist.bfj = tmp_B.dist.bfj) -- same block size?
            then
                add_dblock (tmp_B)
            else
                add_default (B)
            end -- if
        end -- add
    ...
end -- class DBLOCK_MATRIX
```

Example 9.12

For the application programmer, however, the full transparency of the feature dispatching is ensured, as illustrated in the small application program of Example 9.13.

CLOS offers multiple dispatching but it is dynamically typed.

There are other techniques to emulate multiple dispatching with a language such as Eiffel or C++ (e.g., implementation of binary multimethods based on a technique of reverse delegation), but none of these techniques is fully satisfactory either. No object-oriented language combining such features as static type checking, data encapsulation, and multiple dispatching is widely available yet.

9.5.3 Implementation Efficiency

The object-oriented approach leads naturally to the design of quite complex class hierarchies, and the question of their efficient implementation arises nat-

```
        local
            A, B, C: MATRIX [DOUBLE]
        do
            !LOCAL_MATRIX!A.make (...)
            !DBLOCK_MATRIX!B.make (...)
            !DBLOCK_MATRIX!C.make (...)
            ...
            B.add (A)           -- 'add_default' is selected
            B.add (C)           -- 'add_dblock' is selected if B and C
                                -- have the same block size. Otherwise
                                -- 'add_default' is selected
        end
```

Example 9.13

urally. Efficiency is a crucial issue here, because the main rationale for using distributed computing systems lies in the exploitation of their ever-growing computational power. If we were to end up with a parallel code running slower than the (best) equivalent sequential code, we would clearly have missed the point. Fortunately, this is not so.

We have seen in Section 4.5 that using an automatic garbage collector does not cost much more than relying on manual memory management. Note that with our approach, all object migrations are fully encapsulated in relevant classes: An object cannot really "move," it can just be redistributed. Thus we can get rid of a global naming system, which is usually very costly both in communications and synchronizations. Furthermore, since every object exists on every node (be it duplicated or split across the distributed computer), the standard Eiffel garbage collector performs correctly, thus avoiding the need for a costly distributed garbage collector. In EPEE, garbage collection facilities are exploited most efficiently. On each processor of the distributed computing system, the garbage collection can be disabled during computations and incrementally enabled while the local process is idle, waiting for a message to be received. Hence, the garbage collector behaves like a coroutine and allows the effective overlapping of garbage collection over communications.

The cost of feature dispatching is paid only when some dispatching is actually required. Consider a matrix *M* declared as being of the type DBLOCK_MATRIX. DBLOCK_MATRIX has no descendant in the current state of the class hierarchy, so *every* feature invoked on *M* can be identified statically. The general dynamic dispatching mechanism of Eiffel is thus discarded at compile time and feature invocations result in simple procedure calls.

Modularity in object-oriented programming is often presented as a major obstacle to code optimization. The clear semantics of the language enables Eiffel compilers to perform advanced optimizations based on a system-wide analysis, and to identify new features that can be statically bound (i.e., transformed into simple procedure calls) instead of dynamically dispatched. It is also sometimes possible to avoid the overhead of feature calls with in-line expansions, and to eliminate features that are never called. Modern Eiffel compilers perform such optimizations automatically. Most of the modularity overhead is thus safely saved.

Once an Eiffel compiler has produced an intermediate code, state-of-the-art compiling techniques are used by a back-end (a standard C compiler in most Eiffel systems) to perform optimizations such as loop merging and common subexpression elimination. Experiments show that with current Eiffel compilers (e.g., TowerEiffel) the execution time of an Eiffel-written numerical algorithm is usually only 5% to 15% longer than that of an equivalent hand-written C algorithm.

We measured the execution times of parallel algorithms dealing with double-precision distributed matrices on the Paragon XP/S parallel computer. To avoid the undesirable side effect of memory swapping, we only considered matrices that easily fit in the memory of a single node (i.e., matrix size no larger than 1000×1000).

Figure 9.6 shows the performances obtained against the number of processors used (from 1–10 nodes) for a parallel implementation of the *Cholesky* factorization algorithm on distributed symmetrical definite positive square matrices distributed by columns. In each case, speedups are nearly proportional

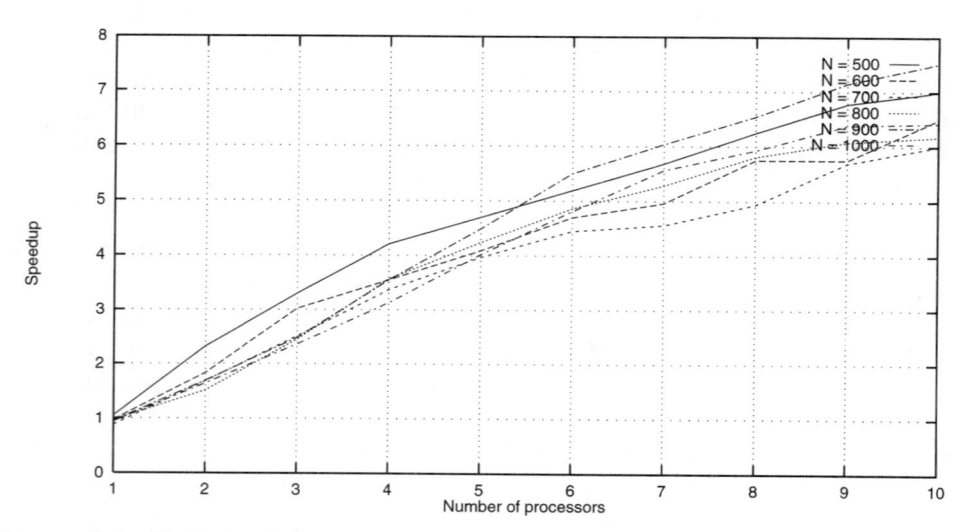

Figure 9.6 Cholesky factorization of $N \times N$ dense matrices distributed by columns

to the number of nodes used, which confirms the interest in this approach for programming massively parallel systems. In addition, provided your problem is large enough, the execution time of your program is inversely proportional to the number of processors used.

9.5.4 Reuse of External Optimized Libraries

As outlined in Section 4.4, Eiffel allows a class hierarchy to be interfaced with facilities provided by precompiled modules or libraries. The notion of code reuse is not limited to the reuse of classes. The encapsulation mechanism also permits the programmer to provide external code with an object-oriented interface. Precompiled external modules and libraries thus can be reused in an object-oriented context, even if they were not originally designed in an object-oriented way (this is actually the way Lapack.h++ [133] and ScaLAPACK++ [44] are designed).

Consider the BLAS kernel [86], which consists of a series of basic linear algebra subroutines and is primarily devoted to FORTRAN programming. This kernel is generally implemented on each parallel machine by the designers of this machine and, most of the time, this implementation is performed directly in assembly language in a machine-dependent way. Consequently, the performances observed when calling a BLAS routine are sometimes—e.g., on the Intel Paragon XP/S—far beyond those one could obtain from an equivalent hand-coded program written in a high-level language (or even with C). It was highly desirable to benefit from such performances in Paladin. Yet, it would not have been acceptable if the interfacing of the Paladin classes with the BLAS kernel had been achieved at the expense of the flexibility, extensibility, and ease of use of Paladin, just because the BLAS routines can only deal with matrices and vectors represented as FORTRAN arrays. Fortunately, the mechanisms of encapsulation, dynamic binding, and the emulation of multiple dispatching (described in Section 9.5.2) made it possible to interface some of the Paladin classes with the BLAS kernel transparently, without jeopardizing the consistency and the extensibility of the whole class hierarchy.

The representation format implemented in the class LOCAL_MATRIX should be compatible with that of FORTRAN arrays. Some of the operators inherited from MATRIX were redefined in LOCAL_MATRIX so that BLAS routines are now invoked whenever possible, that is, when the BLAS kernel is available on the target machine and when all the operands implied in an operation have a FORTRAN-compatible representation. For example, whenever the product of two instances of LOCAL_MATRIX must be computed, the BLAS subroutine general matrix multiply (GEMM) can be invoked transparently to perform the computation instead of the default Eiffel routine defined in the class MATRIX.

Table 9.1 Performances of a Paladin matrix-matrix product on the Paragon XP/S

Matrix size	Nb. Proc.	Mflops
400 × 400	1	45.71
400 × 400	4	121.90
800 × 800	4	159.75
1200 × 1200	16	540.85
2000 × 2000	40	1155.23
2800 × 2800	56	1599.42

By interfacing some of the Paladin classes with the BLAS kernel, the global performances of this library on the Paragon XP/S have been significantly improved without altering the transparency offered to the application programmer. Table 9.1 shows the performances observed when computing a double-precision Paladin matrix-matrix product (with matrices distributed by blocks) on the Paragon XP/S running the OSF/1 operating system. This table clearly shows that Eiffel does not prevent the programmer from getting the best performance out of this supercomputer.

9.6 Conclusion

An object-oriented library is built around the specifications of the basic data structures with which it deals. The principle of dissociating the abstract specification of a data structure (its ADT) from any kind of implementation detail enables the construction of reusable and extensible libraries of parallel software components. Using this approach, we have shown in this chapter that Eiffel is versatile enough to enable an efficient and easy use of distributed computing systems. The distributed data structures of a parallel library such as Paladin enable any programmer to write an application program that runs concurrently on a distributed computer. Encapsulation allows us to hide data distribution and code parallelization within class accessors that are redefined according to the distribution pattern, without any alteration of the class interface. The parallelization can proceed in a seamless way. The programmer first designs a simple application using only local aggregates. The resulting sequential application then can be transformed into an SPMD application, just by changing the type of the aggregates implied in the computation. For large computations, we have shown that the overhead brought about by the higher level of Eiffel remains negligible. By interfacing the internals of Paladin with the BLAS kernel, we have shown that Eiffel makes it possible to benefit from highly optimized machine code libraries and provide the best performances without sacrificing the high conceptual level of the user's point of view. Using the same framework, Paladin could be extended to deal with sparse computations and control parallelism.

Although the Paladin approach hides a lot of the tedious parallelism management, the application programmer still remains responsible for deciding which representation format is the most appropriate for a given aggregate. Hence, when transforming a sequential program into an SPMD one, the programmer must decide which aggregate shall be distributed and how it shall be distributed. This may not always be an easy choice. Finding a "good" distribution may be quite difficult for complex application programs, especially because a distribution pattern that may seem appropriate for a given computation step of an application may not be appropriate anymore for the following computation step. Dynamically redistributing aggregates as and where needed (as is possible in Paladin) might be a way to go around this problem. The redistribution could be controlled by the user, or even encapsulated with the features that require special distributions to perform an operation efficiently. On this topic the object-oriented approach has an important edge over HPF compilers that can only bind features to objects statically, thus producing very inefficient code if the dynamic redistribution pattern is not trivial.

Part III

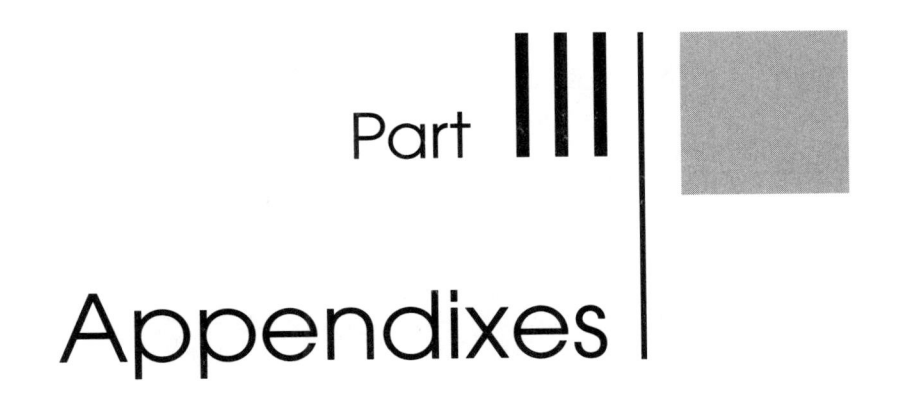

Appendixes

Appendix A | Glossary

ACE (assembly of classes for Eiffel), a specification of what should be done with many software components. See Section 4.1.1.

ADT An Abstract Data Type is the knowledge of a mathematical model of a thing, associated with a set of abstractly defined operations.

Agent Algorithmic abstractions encapsulated in objects. They do things (e.g., sorting), but remember very little. Agents allow redefinable searching, sorting, transforming, and filtering of containers.

Ancestor A class from which another class (called its heir, or its subclass) inherits. It is called a *superclass* in Smalltalk, or a *base class* in C++.

Assertion Either a comment or a Boolean expression that may be tagged with an identifier. See Section 2.4.7.

Attribute A named property of an object holding a part of its abstract state. It is called a *field* in procedural languages, a *data member* in C++, and an *instance variable* in Smalltalk.

Class A template description that specifies properties and behavior for a set of similar objects. It is the implementation of an abstract data type, which defines the data structures, features, and interfaces of software objects.

Client An object that uses the services provided by another object, which is called its *supplier* or its *server*.

Cluster A logical construct for grouping classes. An operating system notion such as a directory may be used to implement the logical cluster. Clusters enable an Eiffel system to be partitioned into manageable pieces. They provide an intermediate unit of packaging between the entire system and the basic building blocks of classes. Class names must be unique within a cluster.

Container class A class with instances that are collections of other objects (e.g., list, stack, hash table).

Contract Governs the relationship between client objects and supplier objects. It spells out the precise definitions of obligations and benefits for both clients and suppliers by means of a set of assertions that encompass feature preconditions and postconditions and class invariants.

Deferred class   A class having at least one *deferred feature*. A deferred class (*abstract class* in C++) may not be instantiated. It merely describes the common properties of a group of classes that descend from it. See Section 3.6.2.

Deferred feature   A specification (i.e., a name, a signature, and preconditions and postconditions) of a feature, but no implementation (*Pure virtual function* in C++). See Section 3.6.1.

Delegation   A mechanism by which an object can issue a request to another object in response to a request made to it; the operation is thus delegated. Delegation can be used as an alternative to the module extension aspect of inheritance.

Dynamic binding   A rule stating that the dynamic type of an entity determines which version of a *feature* is applied. Dynamic binding allows the choice of the actual version of a feature to be delayed until run time. Whenever more than one version of a feature might be applicable, dynamic binding ensures that the version most directly adapted to the target object is selected. The static constraint on the entity's type ensures at least one such version. See Section 3.5.2.

Encapsulation   A packaging mechanism by which external aspects of an object are separated from its implementation. Encapsulation enables information hiding.

Entity   A name used in the text of an Eiffel program to handle objects. There are four kinds of entities: attributes of classes, local entities of routines (including *Result* for functions), formal routine arguments, and *Current*, denoting the current object. See Section 2.3.

Feature   Features of an object are either *attributes* or *routines*. They are part of the definition of classes. The routines are the only means for modifying the attributes of an object, hence the encapsulation properties of an object. An object communicates with another through a request, which identifies either the attribute to be read or the routine to be performed on the second object. The object responds to a request by possibly changing its attributes or by returning a result.

Feature specification   Reflects the abstract data type view of a routine, i.e., its *signature* and *preconditions* and *postconditions*.

Garbage collection   The automatic reclamation of unused computer storage. See Section 4.5.

Genericity   The ability to define parameterized modules, called *generic classes*. A generic class is parameterized with formal generic parameters representing arbitrary types. See Section 3.2.

Inheritance   A relationship between classes. Every inheritance relationship has parents called *ancestors* and children called *subclasses*, and attributes and routines that are inherited. Inheritance allows for the definition and implementation of a new class by combination and specialization of existing ones. It is a mechanism for sharing commonalities (in terms of attributes and routines) between these classes, thus allowing for classification, subtyping, and reuse. See Section 3.3.

Instance   An *instance* of a *class* is an *object* belonging to this class.

Interface   The view an object offers to a set of its clients. Eiffel objects may present different interfaces to different clients.

Class invariants should not be confused with loop invariants.

Invariant   A *class invariant* characterizes properties that any of its *instances* must respect at any observable time; i.e., both on entering a routine (thus strengthening its *precondition*) and on exiting it (thus strengthening its *postcondition*). See Section 2.5.3.

Iterator   An object that controls the process of accessing all objects in a collection.

Kernel library   The Eiffel Kernel Standard Library offers several features in areas such as array and string manipulation, object copying and cloning, input/output, object storage, and basic types. It has the same interface for every Eiffel compiler, so it allows libraries and applications to be portable across compilers. See Section 4.3.

Loop invariants should not be confused with class invariants.

Loop invariant   Characterizes what a loop is trying to achieve, without describing how. It is a Boolean expression that must be true at the loop boundaries, just before the termination condition is evaluated. See Section 2.4.7.

Loop variant   A positive integer expression that is decreased by at least one at each iteration of a loop. By definition, it cannot go below zero, thus the number of iterations of a loop with a variant is bounded and then the loop eventually terminates. See Section 2.4.7.

Mixin   A deferred class used to specify a common functionality or interface for a number of subclasses.

Module   Characterized by a well-defined interface and by information hiding. The interface should be small and simple for modules to be as loosely coupled as possible. The principle of modularity is the key to support modifiability, reusability, extensibility, and understandability. In Eiffel, the unit of modularity is the *class*.

Object   An encapsulation of some state together with a defined set of operations in that state. It embodies an abstraction characterized by an entity in the real world. Hence, it exists in time, it may have a changeable state, and can be created and destroyed. Each object could be viewed as a computer (endowed with memory and a central processing unit) that can provide a set of services. The interface of an object is the set of *features* that can be requested by other objects; it gives the external view of the object.

Polymorphism   The possibility for an *entity* to be able to assume different forms, or to refer to various objects, not necessarily having the same type (provided they conform to the entity static type). See Section 3.5.1.

Postcondition States the property that a routine must guarantee at completion of any correct call. See Section 2.5.3.

Precondition States the conditions under which a routine may be called. The routine caller must guarantee this condition when calling the routine, or else the routine work cannot be done. See Section 2.5.3.

Routine Describes computations applicable to an object. It may be either a function—if it returns a result—or a procedure. Eiffel routines are called *methods* in Smalltalk and *member functions* in C++.

Signature The name and potential list of argument and result types of a feature.

Subclass A class that inherits from another class; its *ancestor*. A subclass is called a *derived class* in C++.

Supplier An object that provides a service to a *client*.

Appendix B | Lexical and Syntactic Elements

B.1 Manifest Constants

A manifest constant is a literal value present in the text of the class. It has a type, deduced from the context, which is one of the following:

Boolean There are only two Boolean constants, **True** and **False**. Both are instances of the kernel library class BOOLEAN, which is the implementation of the abstract data type *boolean*, with the usual associated features (logical AND, OR, etc.).

Character ASCII characters enclosed in single quotes. For example, 'a' is the lowercase letter *a*, 'A' is the uppercase letter *A*. The character '%' is a metacharacter that changes the meaning of the character it precedes. It is used to represent a nonprintable character, such as newline [NL], or backspace [BS], a quote, or the percent itself (see Table B.1).

Any character also may be denoted with the sequence '%/n/', where *n* is its ASCII code (decimal).

Again, these characters are instances of the kernel library class CHARACTER.

Integer An *integer constant* is a sequence of characters made of decimal digits (0–9) and of optional underscores (_). It may be prefixed with a negative sign (–). If any underscore is present, then there must be 3 digits to the right of every underscore, and there must not be any consecutive group of 4 digits. The underscores are meant to enhance readability, as in: 3_789_641_370. Integers are instances of the kernel library class INTEGER. The number of bits used to implement integers is system dependent. It is defined in the kernel library class PLATFORM.

Table B.1 Special characters in Eiffel

ASCII name	Eiffel code	ASCII name	Eiffel code
NL	%N	@	%A
CR	%R	^	%C
BS	%B	"	%"
FF	%F	'	%'
HT	%T	%	%%
NUL	%U	\	%H

Real and Double REAL and DOUBLE classes are floating-point implementations (in, respectively, single and double precision) of a real number abstract data type, with the usual mathematical features associated with this notion. Floating-point literal constants may be used with both types. The syntax of a floating-point constant is described in Syntax Diagram 40. Examples of floating-point constants are 3.14159265453 or 1.0 or 1. or 1E1 or 1e1 or 10e-1.

This is the usual syntax of Pascal, Ada, C, etc.

Bit sequences A bit sequence constant is a sequence of 0 or 1 followed by a *b* or *B*, with no intervening characters. Example: 00010011B.

String The syntax of a manifest string is a sequence of character values (including special characters prefixed with %) enclosed in double-quote char-

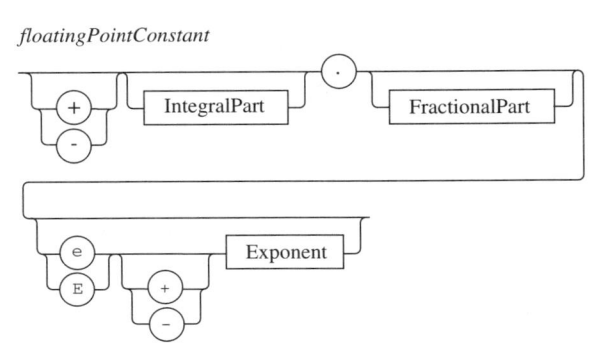

floatingPointConstant

Syntax Diagram 40 Floating-point constants

ManifestArray

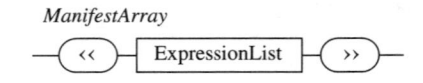

$\langle\langle$ — ExpressionList — $\rangle\rangle$

Syntax Diagram 41   Manifest array syntax

acters. This sequence may be split across a set of lines using the character % as a merger. Example:

```
"This is a%
    % manifest string split %
    % across 3 lines"
```

Strings are instances of the kernel library class STRING.

Array   A manifest ARRAY is much like a manifest STRING, except that it allows for sequences of objects other than characters (see its syntax in Syntax Diagram 41). It is an instance of the kernel library class ARRAY, which is provided with initial contents.

This library class has features, among others, that directly access the ith element of the sequence, both for reading (*item(i)*) and for writing (*put(new_value,i)*). More details are provided in Section 4.3.

For example, $<< 2, 3, 5, 7, 11 >>$ is a manifest array of integers initially holding the sequence of the five first prime numbers, whereas $<<>>$ is an empty manifest array.

Elements in the manifest array do not need to be of the same type, nor be manifest constants.

B.2   Reserved Words

Eiffel reserved words are:

Instructions

alias	all	and	as	check
class	creation	debug	deferred	do

else	**elseif**	**end**	**ensure**	**expanded**
export	**external**	**false**	**feature**	**from**
frozen	**if**	**implies**	**indexing**	**infix**
inherit	**inspect**	**invariant**	**is**	**like**
local	**loop**	**not**	**obsolete**	**old**
once	**or**	**prefix**	**redefine**	**rename**
require	**rescue**	**retry**	**select**	**strip**
then	**true**	**undefine**	**unique**	**until**
variant	**when**	**xor**		

Basic types

BITS	BOOLEAN	CHARACTER	DOUBLE
INTEGER	REAL	STRING	

Special identifiers

Current **Result**

There is also a set of universal features (defined in the class GENERAL) with which you should avoid clashes. These features are not really reserved words because you can redefine them.

Universal features

clone	*deep_clone*	*deep_equal*	*default_rescue*
equal	*generator*	*io*	*out*
print	*tagged_out*	*void*	

B.3 Syntax Diagrams

The Eiffel syntax diagrams are summarized here in alphabetical order. Every construct is included, except for the manifest constants described in Section B.1. Syntax diagrams are read from left to right. The lines may loop back on themselves, indicating that a construct may be repeated. A rectangle surrounds a construct that is defined in another syntax diagram (this construct is called *nonterminal*). A circle or ellipse denotes a literal string that appears exactly as stated.

296 LEXICAL AND SYNTACTIC ELEMENTS

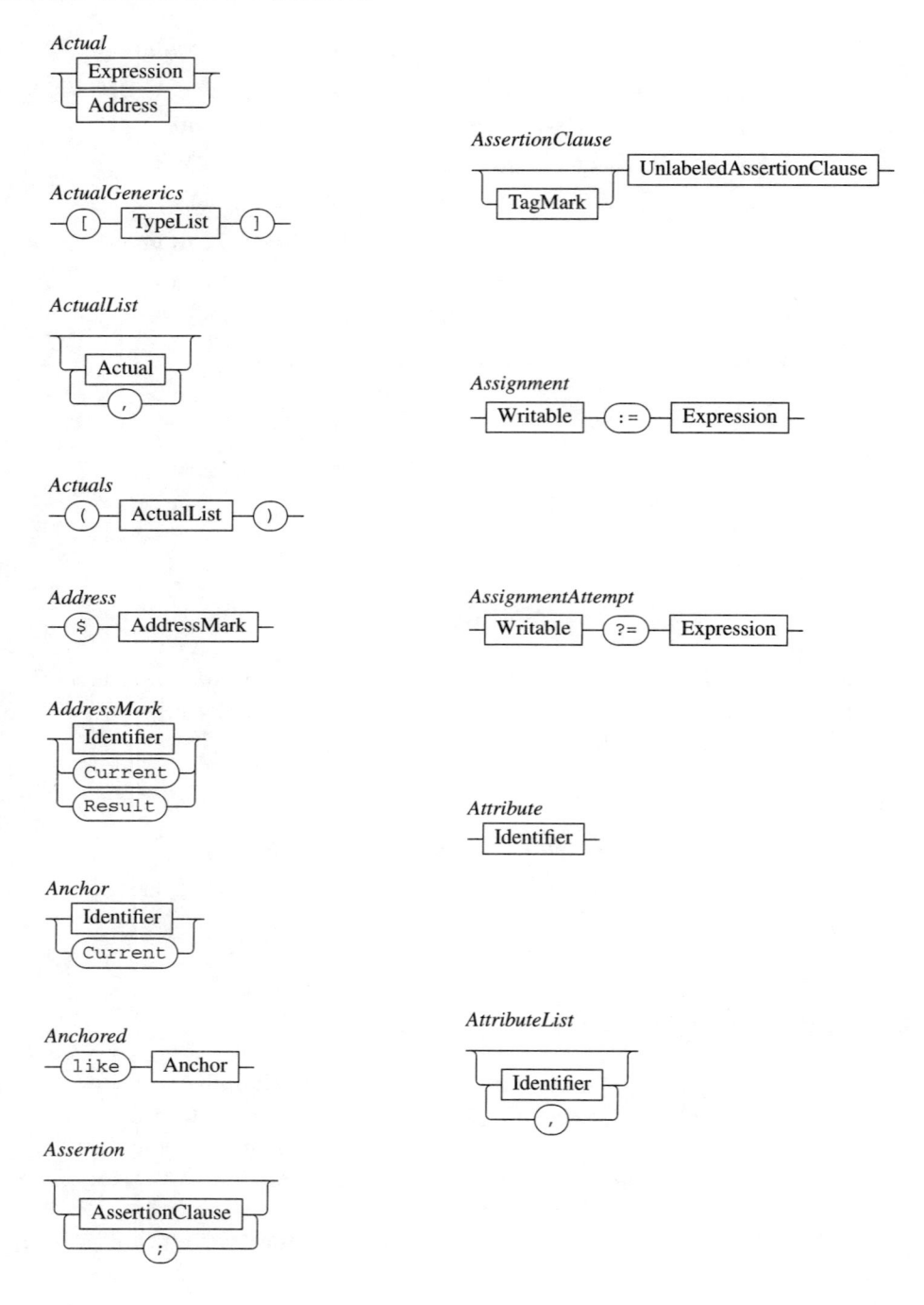

Actual
- Expression
- Address

ActualGenerics
— [— TypeList —] —

ActualList
{ Actual , … }

Actuals
— (— ActualList —) —

Address
— $ — AddressMark —

AddressMark
- Identifier
- Current
- Result

Anchor
- Identifier
- Current

Anchored
— like — Anchor —

Assertion
{ AssertionClause ; … }

AssertionClause
— [TagMark] — UnlabeledAssertionClause —

Assignment
— Writable — := — Expression —

AssignmentAttempt
— Writable — ?= — Expression —

Attribute
— Identifier —

AttributeList
{ Identifier , … }

B.3 SYNTAX DIAGRAMS

Binary
- +
- -
- *
- /
- <
- >
- <=
- >=
- //
- \\
- ^
- and
- or
- xor
- and then
- or else
- implies

BinaryExpression
Expression — InfixOperator
Expression

BitConstant
BitSequence

BitType
BIT — Constant

BooleanConstant
- true
- false

BooleanExpression
Expression

Call
ParenthesizedQualifier — CallChain

CallChain
UnqualifiedCall
.

CharacterConstant
' — Character — '

CharacterInterval
CharacterConstant — .. — CharacterConstant

Check
check — Assertion — end

Choice
- Constant
- Interval

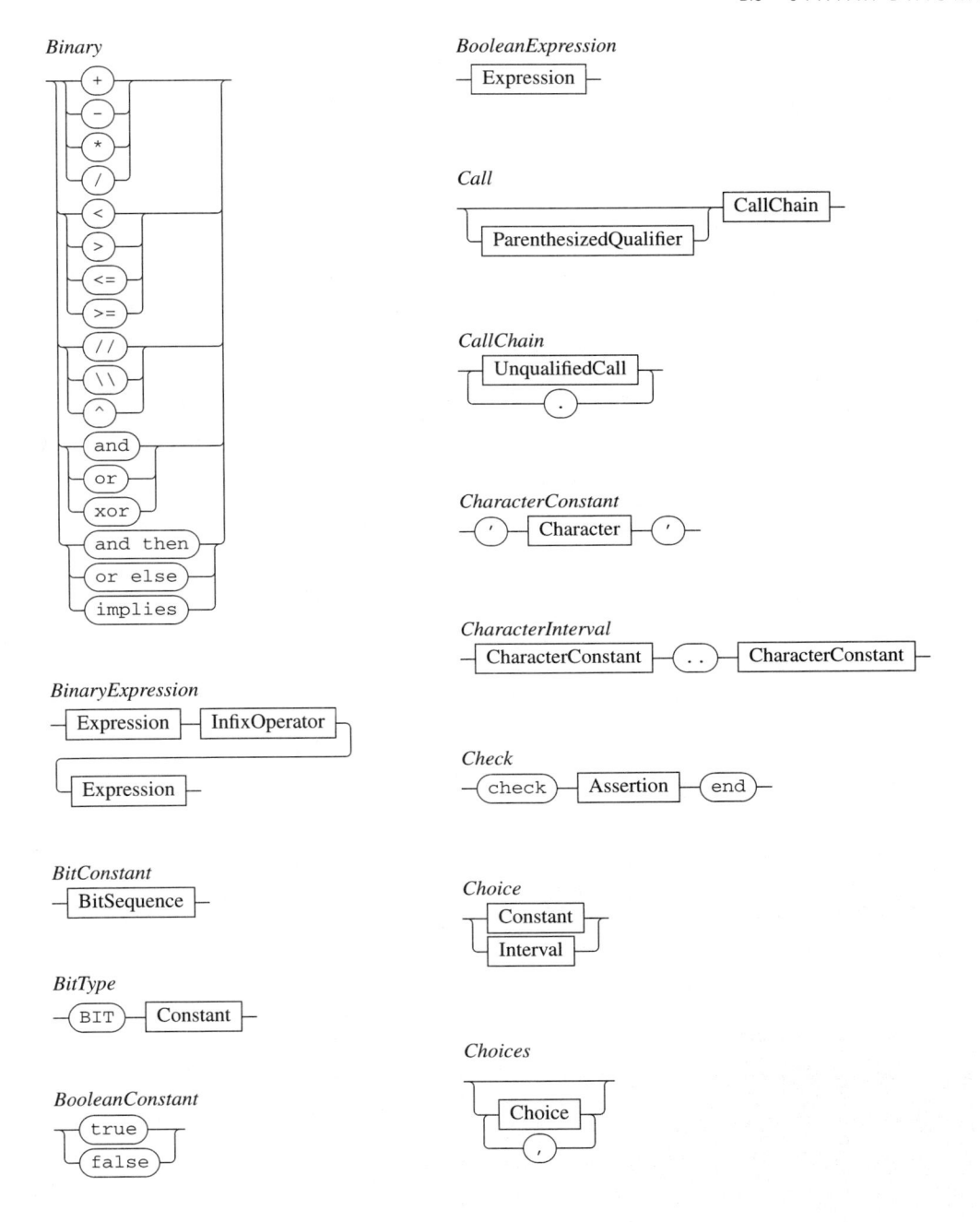

Choices
Choice
,

298 LEXICAL AND SYNTACTIC ELEMENTS

ClassDeclaration

- Indexing
- ClassHeader — FormalGenerics
- Obsolete
- Inheritance
- Creators — Features
- Invariant
- end — -- — ClassName

ClassHeader

- HeaderMark
- class — ClassName

ClassList

- ClassName
- ,

ClassName
- Identifier

ClassType
- ClassName — ActualGenerics

ClassTypeExpanded
- expanded — ClassType

Clients
- { — ClassList — }

Comment
- -- — SimpleString
- CommentBreak

CommentBreak
- NewLine — BlanksOrTabs — --

Comparison
- =
- /=

Compound
- Instruction
- ;

Conditional
- if — ThenPartList — ElsePart — end

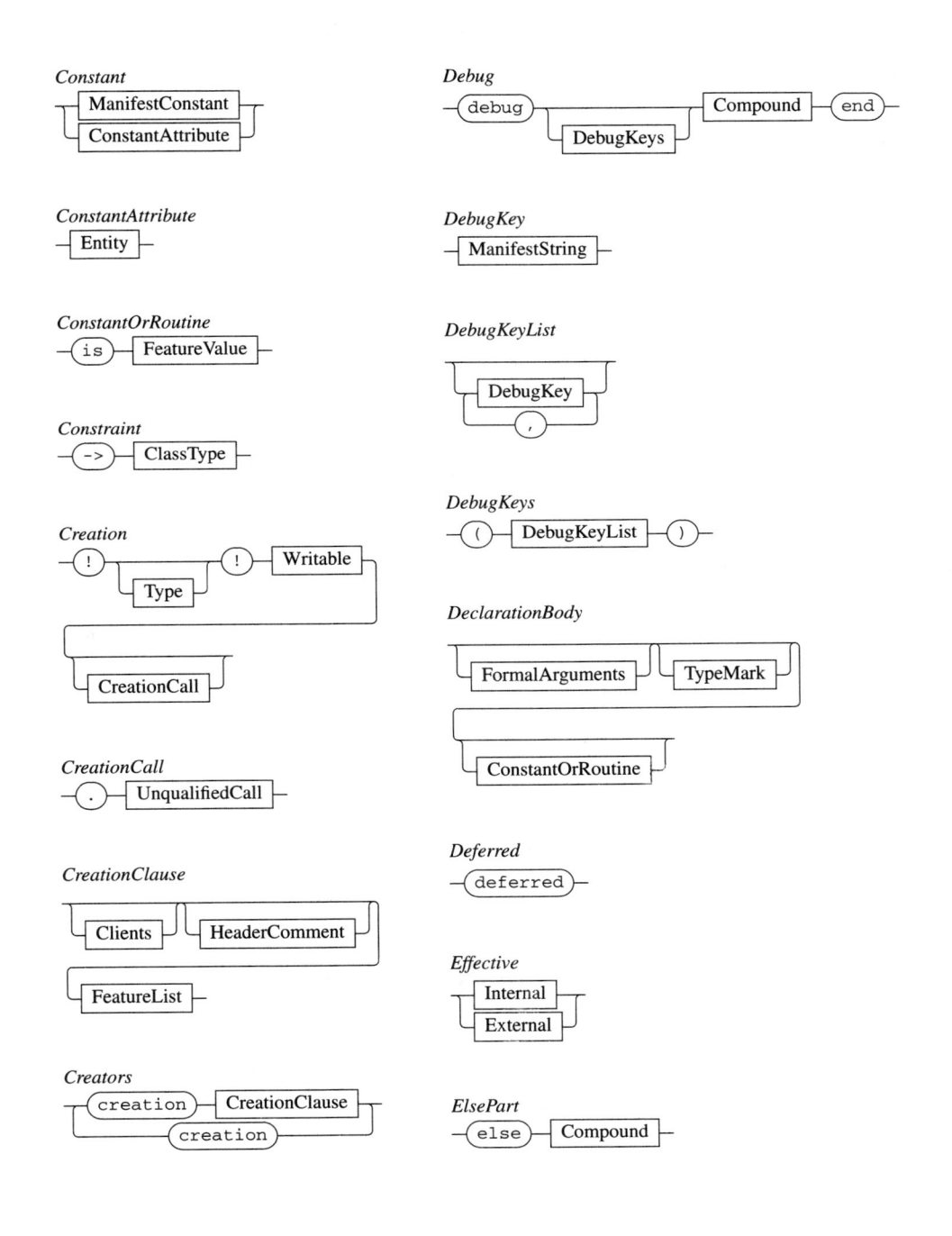

B.3 SYNTAX DIAGRAMS

Constant
- ManifestConstant
- ConstantAttribute

ConstantAttribute
- Entity

ConstantOrRoutine
- `is` FeatureValue

Constraint
- `->` ClassType

Creation
- `!` [Type] `!` Writable
- CreationCall

CreationCall
- `.` UnqualifiedCall

CreationClause
- Clients HeaderComment
- FeatureList

Creators
- `creation` CreationClause
- `creation`

Debug
- `debug` [DebugKeys] Compound `end`

DebugKey
- ManifestString

DebugKeyList
- DebugKey (`,` DebugKey)*

DebugKeys
- `(` DebugKeyList `)`

DeclarationBody
- FormalArguments TypeMark
- ConstantOrRoutine

Deferred
- `deferred`

Effective
- Internal
- External

ElsePart
- `else` Compound

LEXICAL AND SYNTACTIC ELEMENTS

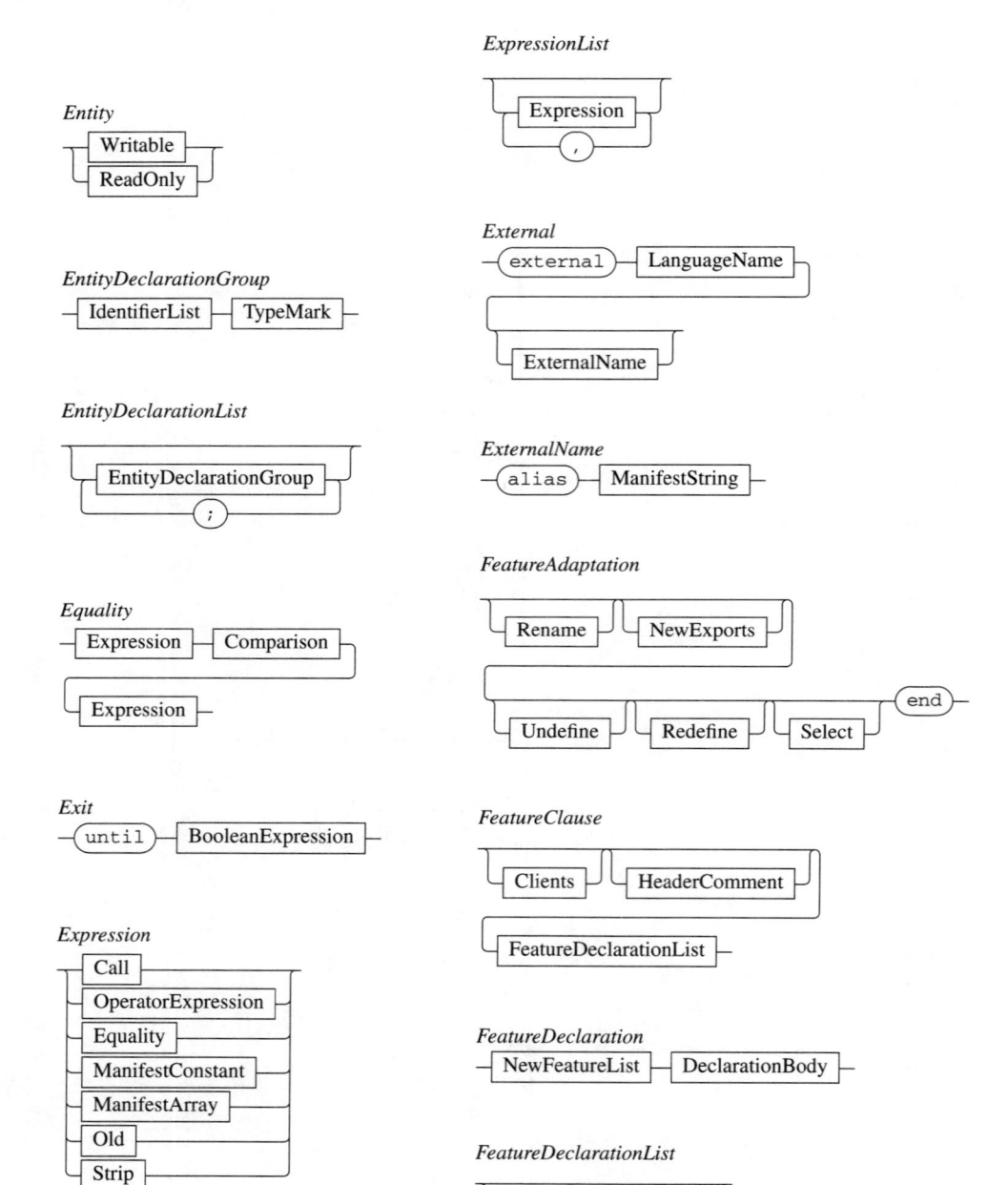

Entity
- Writable
- ReadOnly

EntityDeclarationGroup
- IdentifierList — TypeMark

EntityDeclarationList
- EntityDeclarationGroup
- ;

Equality
- Expression — Comparison
- Expression

Exit
- `until` — BooleanExpression

Expression
- Call
- OperatorExpression
- Equality
- ManifestConstant
- ManifestArray
- Old
- Strip

ExpressionList
- Expression
- ,

External
- `external` — LanguageName
- ExternalName

ExternalName
- `alias` — ManifestString

FeatureAdaptation
- Rename — NewExports
- Undefine — Redefine — Select — `end`

FeatureClause
- Clients — HeaderComment
- FeatureDeclarationList

FeatureDeclaration
- NewFeatureList — DeclarationBody

FeatureDeclarationList
- FeatureDeclaration
- ;

B.3 SYNTAX DIAGRAMS

FeatureList
- FeatureName (,)

FeatureName
- Identifier
- Prefix
- Infix

FeatureSet
- FeatureList
- all

FeatureValue
- ManifestConstant
- Unique
- Routine

Features
- feature FeatureClause
- feature

Formal
- Identifier

FormalArguments
- (EntityDeclarationList)

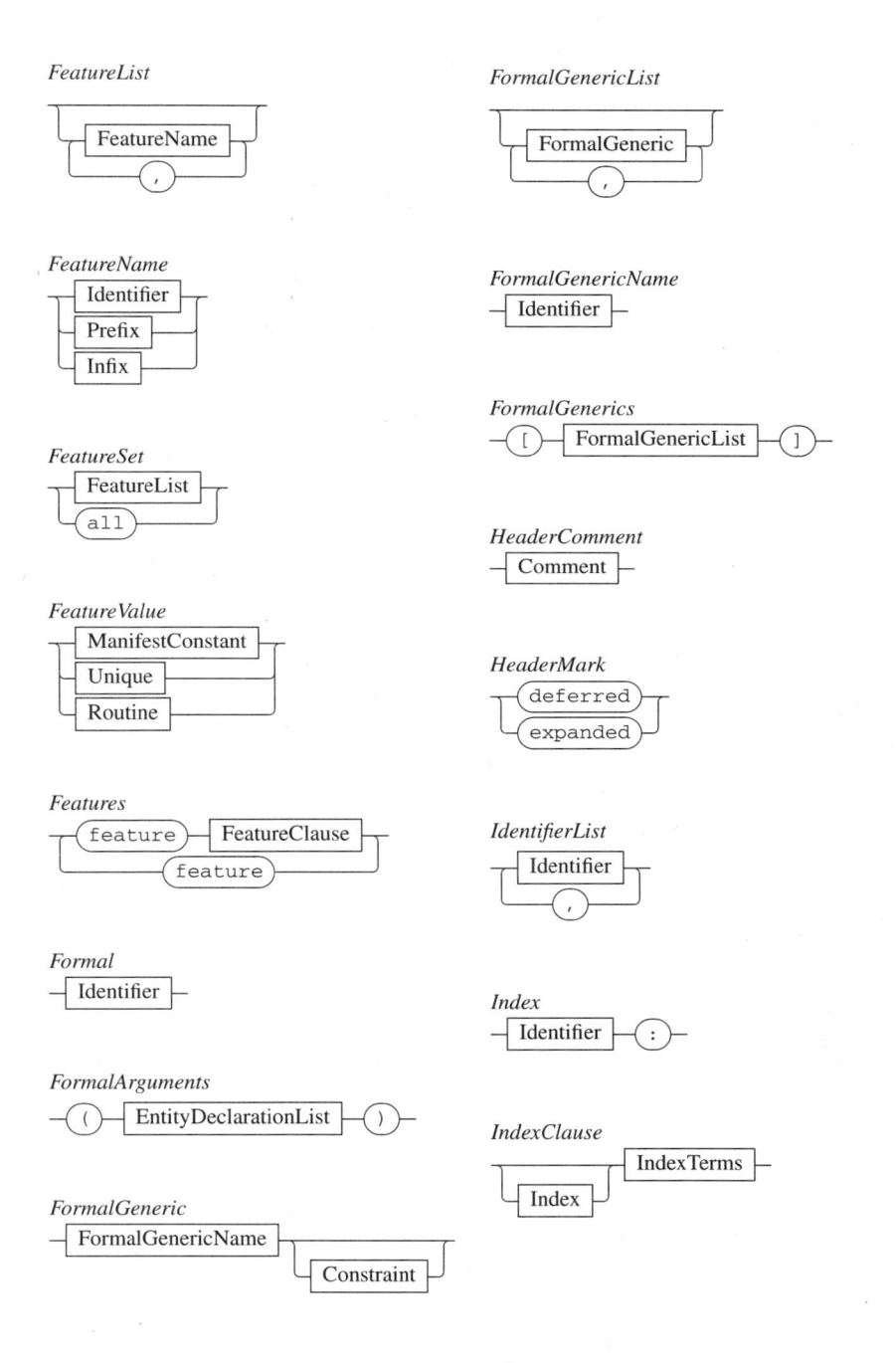

FormalGeneric
- FormalGenericName Constraint

FormalGenericList
- FormalGeneric (,)

FormalGenericName
- Identifier

FormalGenerics
- [FormalGenericList]

HeaderComment
- Comment

HeaderMark
- deferred
- expanded

IdentifierList
- Identifier (,)

Index
- Identifier :

IndexClause
- Index IndexTerms

IndexList
IndexClause { ; }

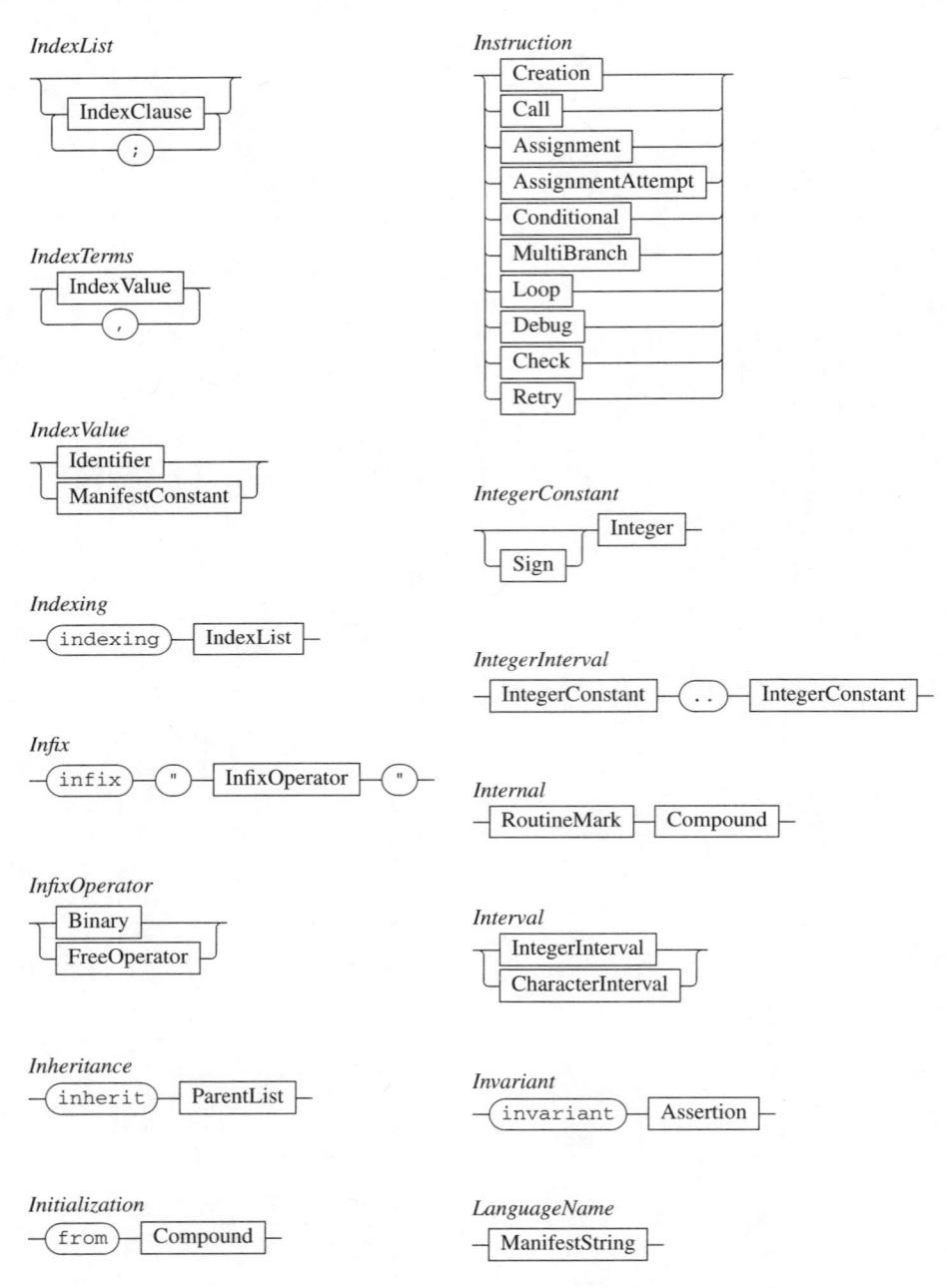

IndexTerms
IndexValue { , }

IndexValue
- Identifier
- ManifestConstant

Indexing
`indexing` IndexList

Infix
`infix` " InfixOperator "

InfixOperator
- Binary
- FreeOperator

Inheritance
`inherit` ParentList

Initialization
`from` Compound

Instruction
- Creation
- Call
- Assignment
- AssignmentAttempt
- Conditional
- MultiBranch
- Loop
- Debug
- Check
- Retry

IntegerConstant
[Sign] Integer

IntegerInterval
IntegerConstant .. IntegerConstant

Internal
RoutineMark Compound

Interval
- IntegerInterval
- CharacterInterval

Invariant
`invariant` Assertion

LanguageName
ManifestString

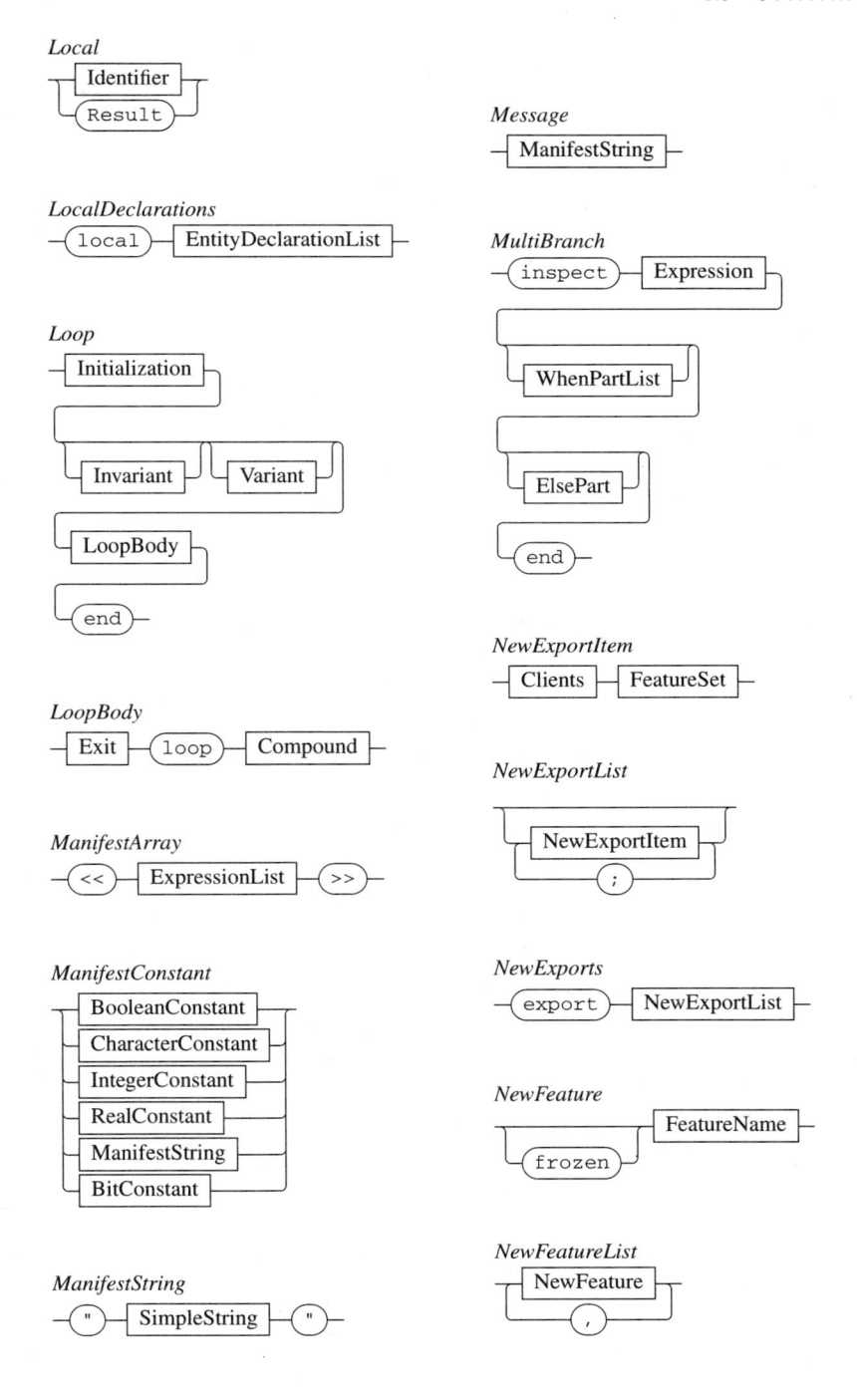

B.3 SYNTAX DIAGRAMS

Local
- Identifier
- Result

LocalDeclarations
- local → EntityDeclarationList

Loop
- Initialization
- Invariant — Variant
- LoopBody
- end

LoopBody
- Exit → loop → Compound

ManifestArray
- << → ExpressionList → >>

ManifestConstant
- BooleanConstant
- CharacterConstant
- IntegerConstant
- RealConstant
- ManifestString
- BitConstant

ManifestString
- " → SimpleString → "

Message
- ManifestString

MultiBranch
- inspect → Expression
- WhenPartList
- ElsePart
- end

NewExportItem
- Clients → FeatureSet

NewExportList
- NewExportItem
- ;

NewExports
- export → NewExportList

NewFeature
- frozen → FeatureName

NewFeatureList
- NewFeature
- ,

LEXICAL AND SYNTACTIC ELEMENTS

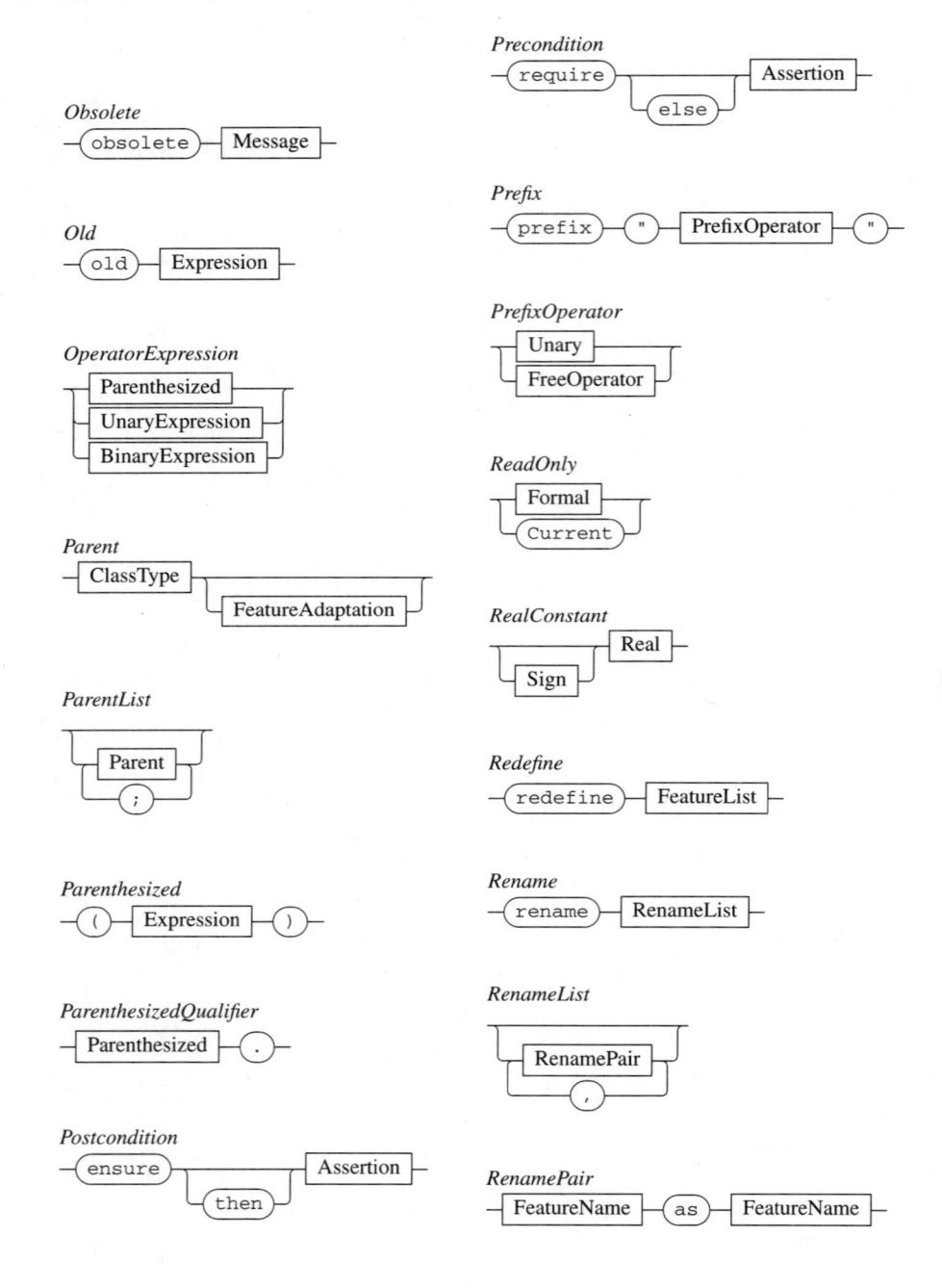

Obsolete

─(obsolete)─[Message]─

Old

─(old)─[Expression]─

OperatorExpression

├─[Parenthesized]─┤
├─[UnaryExpression]─┤
└─[BinaryExpression]─

Parent

─[ClassType]─┬─────────────────┬─
               └─[FeatureAdaptation]─

ParentList

─┬─[Parent]─┬─
 └────(;)───┘

Parenthesized

─(( )─[Expression]─( ))─

ParenthesizedQualifier

─[Parenthesized]─(.)─

Postcondition

─(ensure)─┬─────────┬─[Assertion]─
            └─(then)─┘

Precondition

─(require)─┬─────────┬─[Assertion]─
             └─(else)─┘

Prefix

─(prefix)─(")─[PrefixOperator]─(")─

PrefixOperator

├─[Unary]─┤
└─[FreeOperator]─

ReadOnly

├─[Formal]─┤
└─(Current)─

RealConstant

─┬─────────┬─[Real]─
 └─[Sign]─┘

Redefine

─(redefine)─[FeatureList]─

Rename

─(rename)─[RenameList]─

RenameList

─┬─[RenamePair]─┬─
 └──────(,)─────┘

RenamePair

─[FeatureName]─(as)─[FeatureName]─

B.3 SYNTAX DIAGRAMS

Rescue
── rescue ── Compound ──

Retry
── retry ──

Routine
── [Obsolete] ── [HeaderComment] ──
── [Precondition] ──
── [LocalDeclarations] ──
── RoutineBody ──
── [Postcondition] ── [Rescue] ──
── end ──

RoutineBody
── Effective ──
── Deferred ──

RoutineMark
── do ──
── once ──

Select
── select ── FeatureList ──

Sign
── + ──
── − ──

Strip
── strip ── (── AttributeList ──) ──

Tag
── Identifier ──

TagMark
── Tag ── : ──

ThenPart
── BooleanExpression ── then ── Compound ──

ThenPartList
── ThenPart ──
── elseif ──

Type
── ClassType ──
── ClassTypeExpanded ──
── FormalGenericName ──
── Anchored ──
── BitType ──

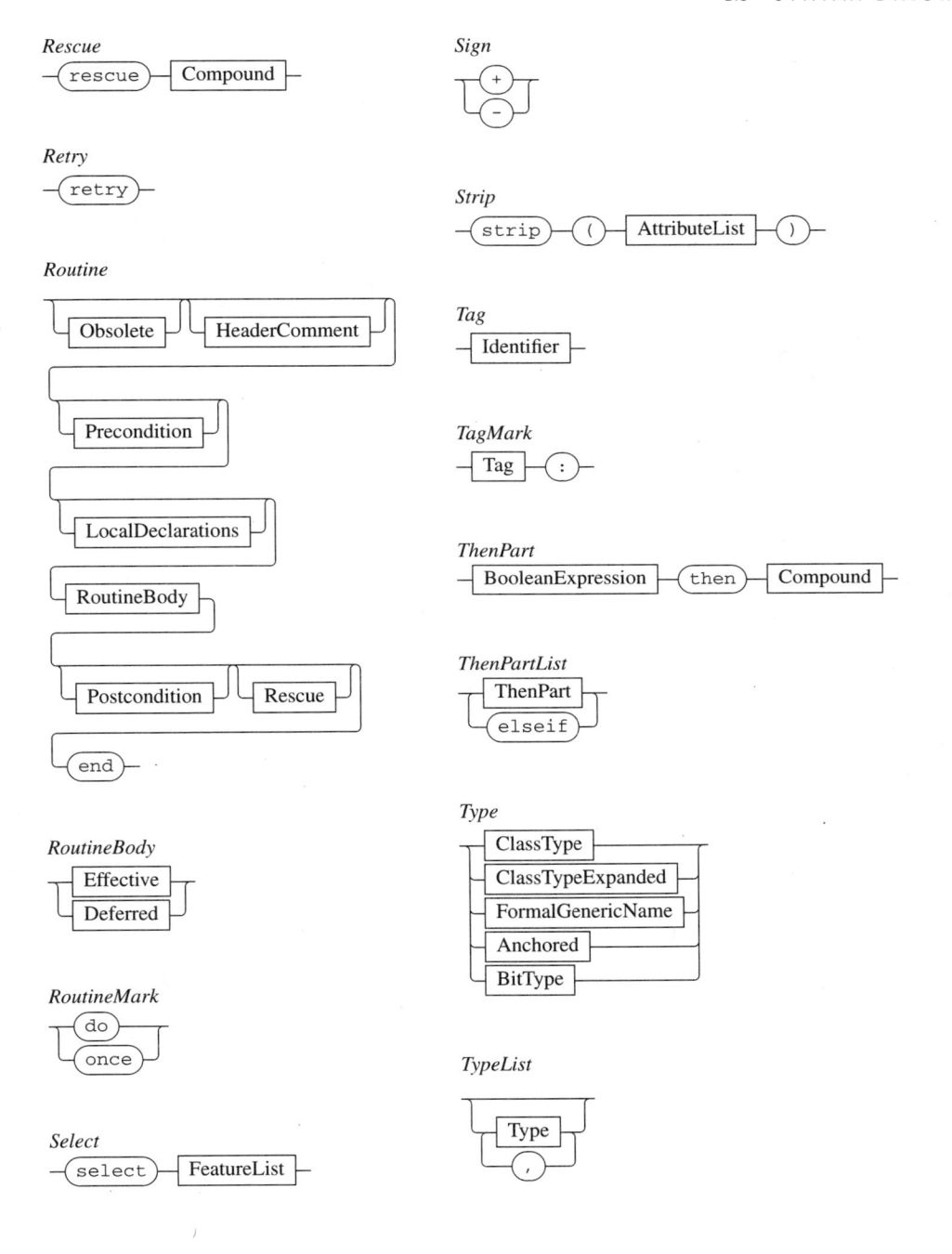

TypeList
── Type ──
── , ──

TypeMark
─(:)─[Type]─

Unary
─(not)─
─(+)─
─(-)─

UnaryExpression
─[PrefixOperator]─[Expression]─

Undefine
─(undefine)─[FeatureList]─

Unique
─(unique)─

UnlabeledAssertionClause
─[BooleanExpression]─
─[Comment]─

UnqualifiedCall
─[Entity]─
         └─[Actuals]─

Variant
─(variant)─┬─────────────┬─[Expression]─
           └─[TagMark]─┘

WhenPart
─[Choices]─(then)─[Compound]─

WhenPartList
─(when)─[WhenPart]─
  └─(when)─┘

Writable
─[Identifier]─

Appendix C | Eiffel Contact List

C.1 Eiffel Vendors

There are at least four independent sources of Eiffel products. They are listed in Sections C.1.1 through C.1.4.

C.1.1 Interactive Software Engineering, Inc.

This company is Eiffel's birthplace and sells the *ISE Eiffel 3 software development environment*, which contains:

- EiffelBench, a visual workbench for object-oriented development. It provides for edition, browsing, incremental compilation (melting ice technology), cross-development, source-level debugging, etc. EiffelBench is available for major platforms including SCO-ODT, Sun, IBM RS6000, 88K-Open, Silicon Graphics, Hewlett-Packard, Fujitsu, Pyramid, DEC/Alpha OSF1, MIPS, Windows, PS/2 AIX, Linux, and NEXTSTEP.
- EiffelBuild, Eiffel's graphical user interface (GUI) application and interface builder.
- EiffelCase, the analysis and design workbench based on the BON method.
- Various class libraries such as EiffelBase, the library of fundamental data structures and algorithms (see Section 8.2); EiffelLex for lexical analysis; EiffelParse for parsing; EiffelNet for exchanging objects over a network; EiffelStore, the library for database access (relational or object-oriented); and EiffelVision, the GUI library.

Since the summer of 1995, ISE has made available by FTP (ftp://ftp.coast.net/SimTel/win3/eiffel) a free personal Eiffel system for Windows, FREE EIFFEL FOR WINDOWS. It is a simple environment with a tty-based interface, which, although probably not suitable for the development of production systems, is more than enough to become familiar with the Eiffel language and the Eiffel approach to constructing quality software. It includes in particular the following features:

- Full implementation of the Eiffel language except *external* construct.
- No limitation as to the size of the systems that you may produce and compile.
- Comes with more than 150 reusable classes from the EiffelBase library.
- Based on ISE's Melting Ice compilation technology. The libraries are pre-compiled; user-contributed classes are "melted," that is to say the compiler generates directly interpretable code, avoiding C and machine-code generation.
- Introductory on-line documentation.
- Menu-driven textual interface allowing compilation (melting), and a number of browsing and documentation facilities: short and flat forms, access to ancestors of a class, access to descendants of a class, access to the clusters of a system, to all the redefinitions of a feature, etc.
- Allows the execution of the generated output on another PC (whether or not it runs FREE EIFFEL FOR WINDOWS) by copying a couple of files.

For more information, contact:

Interactive Software Engineering, Inc.
270 Storke Road, Suite #7
Goleta, CA 93117 USA
Telephone: 805-685-1006
Fax: 805-685-6869
e-mail: info@eiffel.com
WWW http://www.eiffel.com/

C.1.2 Tower Technology Corporation

Tower Technology Corporation was established in 1992 by the merger of two object-oriented technology companies who shared a vision of supplying high-performance Eiffel compilation systems to meet the needs of professional software developers. It sells the following Eiffel products:

- An Eiffel 3 programming environment, with a high-performance compiler, browsing and project management tools, automatic documentation generation, and a multilanguage source-level debugger. The supported platforms include Sun, HP, NeXTStep, OS/2, Linux, and Windows.

- Various class libraries, including Tower (kernel of basic data structures), the *TowerEiffel* Booch components (see Section 8.3); TowerEiffel Motif components (expressly designed to hook up with TowerEiffel X-Designer); and TowerEiffel/O2 Interface.

For more information, contact:

Tower Technology Corp.
1501 W. Koenig Lane
Austin, TX 78756 USA
Telephone: (512) 452-9455
Fax: (512) 452-1721
e-mail: info@twr.com
WWW http://www.cm.cf.ac.uk/Tower/

C.1.3 SiG Computer GmbH

SiG Computer GmbH in Braunfels (Germany) produced the first commercially available Eiffel 3 compiler. SiG also released Eiffel/S 1.3, a popular Eiffel/S environment encompassing a compiler and a data structure library (see Section 8.4). Eiffel/S is available for major UNIX systems and for MS-DOS and Windows.

For more information, contact:

SiG Computer GmbH
zu den Bettern 4
35619 Braunfels
Germany
Phone +49 6472 2096 Fax +49 6472 7213
e-mail: eiffel@eiffel.de
WWW http://www.sigco.com

C.1.4 Eon Software

Eon/Eiffel is an implementation of the Eiffel language. It is a shareware product for MS-DOS and Linux and a commercial product for UNIX machines.

The beta copy is available via ftp only from:

```
site: ftp.demon.co.uk
dir: /pub/eiffel/eon-eiffel
```

For more information, contact:

Eon Software
19 Stapleton Road
Headington
Oxford, OX3 7LX
United Kingdom
Telephone: +44 (0)1865 741452
e-mail: eon@eonsw.demon.co.uk

C.2 Eiffel Forums

C.2.1 NICE

The main forum dealing with Eiffel is the Nonprofit International Consortium for Eiffel (NICE).

NICE (Nonprofit International Consortium for Eiffel)
45 Hazelwood
Shankill
Co Dublin
Republic of Ireland
TEL: +353 1 282 3487
e-mail: nice@twr.com

C.2.2 *Eiffel Outlook*

Since 1991, *Eiffel Outlook* has been the leading source of information of concern to the international Eiffel community. The journal serves all Eiffel users, from beginners to seasoned professionals, with comprehensive news, technical features, and case studies that provide in-depth insight into actual applications of Eiffel. Each issue includes updates on offerings from Eiffel vendors and news from NICE. *Eiffel Outlook* is an unmatched tool for staying up-to-date on the very latest happenings in the Eiffel world.

Although published by Tower Technology Corp., the contents of *Eiffel Outlook* are chosen and edited by the independent team of Jim McKim and Richie Bielak, long-standing experts in the Eiffel world. Together they continue the tradition of serving the needs of the entire Eiffel community in an independent and effective manner.

C.2.3 Eiffel World

"Eiffel World" is a newsletter published by ISE (see above) for the international Eiffel community.

C.2.4 Journal of Object-Oriented Programming

Rock Howard has a regular column on Eiffel in the *Journal of Object-Oriented Programming*.

C.2.5 USENET

The following USENET news-groups have interesting material about Eiffel:

- **comp.lang.eiffel**
- **comp.object**
- **comp.software-engineering**

C.2.6 Frequently Asked Questions (with Answers)

Roger Browne maintains a listing of frequently asked questions (FAQ) about Eiffel. This question-and-answer list is posted monthly to the USENET news groups **comp.lang.eiffel**, **comp.answers**, and **news.answers**.

Please send corrections, additions, and comments to Roger Browne: e-mail: **rogerb@eiffel.demon.co.uk**

The FAQ is abstracted and condensed from the posts of many contributors to **comp.lang.eiffel**, and is supplemented by information from vendors. You can receive the latest copy by anonymous file transfer from:

```
ftp.cm.cf.ac.uk    /pub/eiffel/eiffel-faq
rtfm.mit.edu       pub/usenet/news.answers/eiffel-faq
```

or by sending an e-mail message to **archive-server@cm.cf.ac.uk** with the following message body:

```
send Eiffel eiffel-faq
```

A hypertext version of the FAQ is also available through the WWW at:

```
http://outback.eiffel.com/faq/faq_index.html
```

C.2.7 Mailing Lists

Several public mailing lists deal with Eiffel-related topics. Among them are:

Eiffel in Education The list is primarily intended for teachers in universities and other educational institutions, who are using or considering ISE

Eiffel for their curriculum. It is expected to include discussions of curriculum organization, the proper role of Eiffel, pedagogical issues, technical issues, libraries, student reactions, and textbooks.

To subscribe to the list, send a message to:

`education-request@eiffel.com`.

Send list submissions to `education@eiffel.com`.

The Eiffel Patterns Project This mailing list is being produced by Eiffel programmers who are working together on a volunteer basis to generate a catalog of object-oriented design patterns expressed in Eiffel.

Send subscription requests to:

`e-patterns-request@cbr.dit.csiro.au`

Send list submissions to `e-patterns@cbr.dit.csiro.au`. An FTP archive relating to the list is maintained at `ftp://cbr.dit.csiro.au/pub/SEG/e-patterns`.

C.2.8 World Wide Web

A vendor-independent WWW page on Eiffel can be found at:

`http://www.cm.cf.ac.uk/CLE`

Also see C.3 for the author's WWW page.

C.3 Getting More Information About This Book

The author maintains a World Wide Web server with information related to this book that might be of interest to you. Its HTTP address is:

`http://www.irisa.fr/pampa/EPEE/book.html`

This WWW server should provide you with up-to-date pointers to other Eiffel pages (from vendors and others) and contain an *errata* for this book. On this WWW server you can also find the source code of all of the examples presented in this book, such as:

- The generic class LISTE[T],
- The class SORTABLE_ARRAY[T] with its two binary search functions (iterative and recursive), the quicksort and mergesort routines, and other goodies,
- The KWIC system in full.

These codes should be usable with any Eiffel compiler, because they rely on the Eiffel Standard Library only.

Bibliography

[1] H. Abelson, G. Jay Sussman, and J. Sussman. – *Structure and Interpretation of Computer Programs*. – The MIT Press/McGraw-Hill, Cambridge, MA, 1985.

[2] P. America. – Pool-T: A parallel object-oriented programming. – In A. Yonezawa, editor, *Object-Oriented Concurrent Programming*, pages 199–220. The MIT Press, Cambridge, MA, 1987.

[3] Birger Andersen. – Ellie language definition report. – *SIGPLAN Notices*, 25(11): 45–64, November 1990.

[4] Françoise André, Jean-Louis Pazat, and Henry Thomas. – Pandore: A system to manage data distribution. – In *ACM International Conference on Supercomputing*, June 11–15, 1990.

[5] A. W. Appel, J. R. Ellis, and Kai Li. – Real-time concurrent collection on stock multiprocessors. – In *SIGPLAN'88 Conf. on Prog. Lang. Design and Implementation*, pp. 11–20, June 1988.

[6] P. Arnold, S. Bodoff, D. Coleman, H. Gilchrist, and F. Hayes. – An evaluation of five object-oriented development methods. – Technical Report, HP Laboratories, June 1991.

[7] T. R. Arnold and W. A. Fuson. – Testing in a perfect world. – *Communications of the ACM*, 37(9):78–86, September 1994.

[8] François Bancilhon, C. Delobel, and Paris Kanellakis, editors. – *Building an Object-Oriented Database System: The Story of O2*. – Morgan-Kaufmann, 1992.

[9] Bellcore. – Generic requirements for SMDS networking. – Technical Report TA-TSV-001059, Bell Communication Research, 1992.

[10] John K. Bennett. – The design and implementation of Distributed Smalltalk. – In *OOPSLA'87 Proceedings*, October 1987.

[11] Edward V. Berard. – *Essays on Object-Oriented Software Engineering*. – Prentice Hall, Englewood Cliffs, NJ, 1993.

[12] Briand N. Bershad, Edward D. Lazowska, and Henry M. Levy. – Presto: A system for object-oriented parallel programming. – In *Software—Practice and Experience*, February 1988.

[13] Boris Bezier. – *Software Testing Techniques*, 2nd ed. – Van Nostrand Reinhold, New York, 1990.

[14] R. Bielak and J. McKim. – The many faces of a class: Views and contracts. – In *Proc. TOOLS 11*, pp. 153–161, August 1993.

[15] R. V. Binder. – Testing object-oriented systems: A status report. – *American Programmer*, 7(4):23–28, April 1989.

[16] R. V. Binder. – Design for testability. – *Communications of the ACM*, 37(9):89–101, September 1994.

[17] B. W. Boehm. – The high cost of software. – In Ellis Horowitz, editor, *Practical Strategies for Developing Large Software Systems*. Addison-Wesley, Reading, MA, 1975.

[18] Hans-Juergen Boehm and Mark Weiser. – Garbage collection in an uncooperative environment. – *Software—Practice and Experience*, 18(9):807–820, September 1988.

[19] Grady Booch. – *Software Engineering with Ada*. – Benjamin Cummings Publishing Co., Menlo Park, CA, 1983.

[20] Grady Booch. – *Software Components with Ada*. – Benjamin Cummings Publishing Co., Menlo Park, CA, 1987.

[21] Grady Booch. – *Object Oriented Design with Applications*. – Benjamin Cummings Publishing Co., Menlo Park, CA, 1991.

[22] Grady Booch. – *Object-Oriented Analysis and Design with Applications*, 2nd ed. – Benjamin Cummings Publishing Co., Menlo Park, CA, 1994.

[23] T. Braun and M. Zitterbart. – Parallel XTP implementation on transputers. – In *The 1991 Singapore International Conference on Networks*, pp. 91–96. G. S. Poo, September 1991.

[24] Jean-Pierre Briot and Pierre Cointe. – Programming with explicit metaclasses in Smalltalk-80. – In *Proceedings OOPSLA'89, ACM SIGPLAN Notices*, pp. 419–432, October 1989.

[25] David Callahan and Ken Kennedy. – Compiling programs for distributed-memory multiprocessors. – *The Journal of Supercomputing*, 2:151–169, 1988.

[26] L. Cardelli and P. Wegner. – On understanding types, data abstraction, and polymorphism. – *ACM Computing Surveys*, 17(4):211–221, 1985.

[27] Luca Cardelli. – A semantics of multiple inheritance. – *Information and Computation*, 76:138–164, 1988.

[28] D. Caromel. – Concurrency and reusability: From sequential to parallel. – *Journal of Object-Oriented Programming*, 3(3):34–42, September 1990.

[29] D. Caromel. – Towards a method of object-oriented concurrent programming. – *Communications of the ACM*, 36(9):90–102, September 1993.

[30] C. Chambers. – Object-Oriented Multi-Methods in Cecil. – In *Proceedings of the European Conference on Object-Oriented Programming (ECOOP'92)*, 1992.

[31] Rohit Chandra, Anoop Gupta, and John L. Hennessy. – Cool: a language for parallel programming. – In D. Gelernter et al., editor, *Languages and Compilers for Parallel Computing*. The MIT Press, Cambridge, MA, 1990.

[32] P. P. S. Chen. – The entity-relationship model: Toward a unified view of data. – *ACM TODS*, 1(1):9–36, March 1976.

[33] Peter Coad and Edward Yourdon. – *Object-Oriented Analysis*, 2nd ed. – Prentice Hall, Englewood Cliffs, NJ, 1991.

[34] Peter Coad and Edward Yourdon. – *Object-Oriented Design*. – Prentice Hall, Englewood Cliffs, NJ, 1991.

[35] J.-F. Colin and J.-M. Geib. – Eiffel classes for concurrent programming. – In J. Bezivin *et al.*, editor, *TOOLS 4*, pp. 23–34. Prentice Hall, Englewood Cliffs, NJ, 1991.

[36] J. O. Coplien. – Generative pattern languages: An emerging direction of software design. – *C++ Report*, 6(6), July-August 1994.

[37] O. J. Dahl and C. A. R. Hoare. – *Structured Programming*. – Academic Press, San Diego, 1972.

[38] O. J. Dahl, B. Myhrhaug, and K. Nygaard. – Simula 67 common base language. – Technical Report, Oslo: Norwegian Computing Centre, 1970.

[39] Dennis de Champeaux. – Object-oriented analysis and top-down software development. – In P. America, editor, *Proceedings ECOOP '91*, LNCS 512, pp. 360–376, Geneva, Switzerland, July 1991. Springer-Verlag, Berlin.

[40] Dennis de Champeaux and Penelope Faure. – A comparative study of object oriented analysis methods. – *Journal of Object-Oriented Programming*, 5(1):21–32, April 1992.

[41] Penelope Faure, Dennis de Champeaux, Doug Lea. – *Object-Oriented System Development*. – Addison-Wesley, Reading, MA, 1993.

[42] E. W. Dijkstra. – *A Discipline of Programming*. – Prentice Hall, Englewood Cliffs, NJ, 1976.

[43] C. Diot. – *Architecture pour l'implantation hautes performances des Protocoles de communication de niveau transport.* – PhD thesis, Institut National Polytechnique de Grenoble, January 1991.

[44] J. Dongarra et al. – An object-oriented design for high-performance linear algebra on distributed memory architectures. – In *Proceedings of the Object-Oriented Numerics Conference (OON-SKI'93)*, 1993.

[45] E. P. Doolan. – Experience with Fagan's inspection method. – *Software—Practice and Experience*, 22(2):173–182, February 1992.

[46] Geoff Dromey. – *The Development of Programs from Specifications.* – Addison-Wesley, Reading, MA, 1987.

[47] J. R. Ellis, K. Lil, and A. W. Appel. – Real-time concurrent collection on stock multiprocessors. – Technical Report 25, Digital Systems Research Center, Palo Alto, CA, February 1988.

[48] B. H. Liskov et al. – *CLU Reference Manual*, memo 161 edition. – Computation Structures Group, Laboratory for Computer Science, MIT, Cambridge, MA, July 1978.

[49] Derek Coleman et al. – *Object-Oriented Development—The Fusion Method.* – Prentice Hall, Englewood Cliffs, NJ, 1994.

[50] M. E. Fagan. – Design and code inspections to reduce errors in program development. – *IBM System Journal*, 15(3):182–211, 1976.

[51] S. P. Fiedler. – Object-oriented unit testing. – Technical Report, *Hewlett-Packard Journal,* April 1989.

[52] P. G. Frankl and R. Doong. – Tools for testing object-oriented programs. – In *Proc. of the 8th Pacific NorthWest Conference on Software Quality*, pp. 309–324, 1990.

[53] P. G. Frankl and E. J. Weyuker. – An applicable family of dataflow testing criteria. – *IEEE Transactions on Software Engineering*, 14(10):1483–1498, October 1988.

[54] R. Gabriel *et al.* – CLOS: integrating object-oriented and functional programming. – *Communications of the ACM*, 34(9), 1991.

[55] Erich Gamma, Richard Helm, John Vlissides, and Ralph E. Johnson. – Design patterns: Abstraction and reuse of object-oriented design. – In O. Nierstrasz, editor, *Proceedings ECOOP'93*, LNCS 707, pp. 406–431, Kaiserslautern, Germany, July 1993. Springer-Verlag, Berlin.

[56] A. Goldberg and D. Robson. – *Smalltalk-80: The Language and Its Implementation*. – Addison-Wesley, Reading, MA, 1983.

[57] G. H. Golub and C. F. Van Loan. – *Matrix Computations*. – The Johns Hopkins University Press, Baltimore, MD, 1991.

[58] R. B. Grady. – *Practical Software Metrics for Project Management and Process Improvement*. – Prentice Hall, Englewood Cliffs, NJ, 1992.

[59] Hood Working Group. – *HOOD Reference Manual Issue 3.0*. – European Space Agency, 1989.

[60] F. Guerber, J.-M. Jézéquel, and F. André. – Conception et implantation d'un serveur SMDS sur architectures modulaires. – Technical Report 885, IRISA, November 1994.

[61] F. Guidec and Y. Mahéo. – POM: A virtual parallel machine featuring observation mechanisms. – Internal Publication 902, IRISA, January 1995.

[62] John Guttag. – Abstract data types and the development of data structures. – *CACM*, 20(6):396–404, June 1977.

[63] F. Hamelin, J.-M. Jézéquel, and T. Priol. – A multi-paradigm object oriented parallel environment. – In H. J. Siegel, editor, *Int. Parallel Processing Symposium IPPS'94 Proceedings*, pp. 182–186. IEEE Computer Society Press, April 1994.

[64] M. J. Harrold, J. D. McGregor, and K. J. Fitzpatrick. – Incremental testing of object-oriented class structures. – In *Proc. of the 14th International Conference on Software Engineering*, pp. 68–80. ACM Inc., May 1992.

[65] B. Hayes. – Finalization in the collector interface. – In *Proc. Int. Workshop on Memory Management*, Number 637 in Lecture Notes in Computer Science, pp. 277–298, Saint-Malo, France, September 1992. Springer-Verlag, Berlin.

[66] C. A. R. Hoare. – Monitors: An operating systems structuring concept. – *CACM*, 17(10):549–557, 1974.

[67] HPF-Forum. – High performance FORTRAN language specification. – Technical Report Version 1.0, Rice University, May 1993.

[68] D. Hsieh. – Survey of object-oriented analysis/design methodologies and future case frameworks. – Technical Report SRI-CSL-92-04, SRI International, March 1992.

[69] Watts Humphrey. – *Managing the Software Process*. – Addison-Wesley, Reading, MA, 1989.

[70] J. Ichbiah. – *Reference Manual for the ADA Programming Language.* – ANSI/MIL-STD 1815a, January 1983.

[71] M. Ito, L. Takeuchi, and G. Neufeld. – A multiprocessor approach for meeting the processing requirements for osi. – *IEEE Journal on Selected Areas in Communications*, 11(2), February 1993.

[72] T. J. Cheatham and L. Mellinger – Testing object-oriented systems. – In *Proc. of the 18th ACM Annual Computer Science Conference*, pp. 161–165, New York, 1990. ACM Inc.

[73] M. A. Jackson. – *System Development.* – Prentice Hall, Englewood Cliffs, NJ, 1985.

[74] Ivar Jacobson. – Object oriented development in an industrial environment. – In *Proceedings OOPSLA'87, ACM SIGPLAN Notices*, pp. 183–191, December 1987.

[75] Ivar Jacobson, Magnus Christerson, Patrik Jonsson, and Gunnar Overgaard. – *Object-Oriented Software Engineering – A Use Case Driven Approach.* – Addison-Wesley/ACM Press, Reading, MA, 1992.

[76] P. Jalote. – Testing the completeness of specifications. – *IEEE Transactions on Software Engineering*, 15(5):526–531, May 1989.

[77] C. Jard and M. Raynal. – The rudiments of object distribution in distributed systems. – In *Second Int. Conf. on Computers Inf. Sciences*, Istanbul, 1987.

[78] J.-M. Jézéquel. – EPEE: an Eiffel environment to program distributed memory parallel computers. – *Journal of Object-Oriented Programming*, 6(2):48–54, May 1993.

[79] J.-M. Jézéquel. – Parallélisation d'un routeur xtp. – In *Actes du colloque CFIP'93 sur l'ingénièrie des protocoles*, Montreal. Hermès, September 1993.

[80] P. C. Jorgenson and C. Erickson. – Object-oriented integration testing. – *Communications of the ACM*, 37(9):30–38, September 1994.

[81] Ian Joyner. – A critique of C++. – In *TOOLS Pacific, International Conference on Technology of Object-Oriented Languages and Systems,* Australia. An extended version is also available as ftp://ftp.desy.de/pub/c++/misc/c++.critique.ps, 1992.

[82] S. Kirani. – *Specification and Verification of Object-Oriented Programs.* – PhD thesis, University of Minnesota, 1994.

[83] D. E. Knuth. – *The Art of Computer Programming,* Vol. 1: *Fundamental Algorithms.* – Addison-Wesley, Reading, MA, 1968.

[84] E. K. Kolodner and W. E. Weihl. – Atomic incremental garbage collection. – In *Proc. Int. Workshop on Memory Management*, Number 637 in Lecture Notes in Computer Science, pp. 365–387, Saint-Malo, France, September 1992. Springer-Verlag, Berlin.

[85] W. LaLonde and John Pugh. – Subclassing $\neq$ subtyping $\neq$ is-a. – *Journal of Object-Oriented Programming*, 3(5):57–62, January 1991.

[86] C. Lawson, R. Hanson, D. Kincaid, and F. Krogh. – Basic linear algebra subprograms for FORTRAN. – *ACM Transactions on Math. Software*, 14:308–325, 1989.

[87] J.-Y. Le Boudec, A. Meier, R. Oechsle, and H. L. Truong. – Connectionless data service in an ATM-based customer premises network. – *Computer Networks and ISDN Systems*, 26(4):1409–1424, July 1994.

[88] Karl J. Lieberherr and Ian M. Holland. – Assuring good style for object-oriented programs. – *IEEE Software*, 6(6), 38–48 September 1989.

[89] H. Lieberman. – Concurrent object-oriented programming in Act 1. – In A. Yonezawa, editor, *Object-Oriented Concurrent Programming*, pp. 9–35. The MIT Press, Cambridge, MA, 1987.

[90] B. H. Liskov and S. N. Zilles. – Programming with abstract data types. – *SIGPLAN Notices*, 9(4):50–59, April 1974.

[91] Barbara Liskov and John Guttag. – *Abstraction and Specification in Program Development*. – The MIT Press/McGraw-Hill, Cambridge, MA, 1986.

[92] Barbara Liskov and Jeannette M. Wing. – A new definition of the subtype relation. – In O. Nierstrasz, editor, *Proceedings ECOOP'93*, LNCS 707, pp. 118–141, Kaiserslautern, Germany, July 1993. Springer-Verlag, Berlin.

[93] Satoshi Matsuoka and Akinori Yonezawa. – Analysis of inheritance anomaly in object-oriented concurrent programming languages. – In G. Agha, P. Wegner, and A. Yonezawa, editors, *Research Directions in Concurrent Object Oriented Programming*. The MIT Press, Cambridge, MA, 1993.

[94] T. McCabe. – A complexity measure. – *IEEE Transactions on Software Engineering*, pp. 309–320, December 1976.

[95] J. D. McGregor and T. D. Korson. – Integrating object-oriented testing and development processes. – *Communications of the ACM*, 37(9):59–77, September 1994.

[96] M. D. McIlroy. – Mass-produced software components. – In P. Naur, J. M. Buxton, and B. Randell, editors, *Software Engineering Concepts and Techniques (1968 NATO Conference of Software Engineering)*, NATO Science Committee 1976.

[97] Merriam-Webster. – *Webster's 7th Collegiate Dictionary, in Electronic Form (xwebster, by Niels Mayer).* – Merriam-Webster, Springfield, MA, 1963.

[98] José Meseguer. – Solving the inheritance anomaly in concurrent object-oriented programming. – In O. Nierstrasz, editor, *Proceedings ECOOP'93*, LNCS 707, pp. 220–246, Kaiserslautern, Germany, July 1993. Springer-Verlag, Berlin.

[99] B. Meyer. – *Object-Oriented Software Construction.* – Prentice Hall, Englewood Cliffs, NJ, 1988.

[100] B. Meyer. – Applying "design by contract." – *IEEE Computer (Special Issue on Inheritance & Classification)*, 25(10):40–52, October 1992.

[101] B. Meyer. – *Eiffel: The Language.* – Prentice Hall, Englewood Cliffs, NJ, 1992.

[102] B. Meyer. – Systematic concurrent object-oriented programming. – *Communications of the ACM*, 36(9):56–80, September 1993.

[103] B. Meyer. – *Reusable Software: The Base Object-Oriented Component Libraries.* – Prentice Hall, Englewood Cliffs, NJ, 1994.

[104] M. Minsky. – A framework for representing knowledge. – Artificial Intelligence Memo 252, MIT Laboratory for Computer Science, 1974.

[105] D. E. Monarchi and G. I. Puhr. – A research typology for object-oriented analysis and design. – *Communications of the ACM*, 9(35):35–47, September 1992.

[106] J. Musa, A. Iannino, and K. Okumoto. – *Software Reliability: Measurement, Prediction, Application.* – McGraw-Hill, New York, 1987.

[107] G. Myers. – *The Art of Software Testing.* – Prentice Hall, Englewood Cliffs, NJ, 1979.

[108] Peter Naur et al. – Report on the algorithmic language ALGOL 60. – *Communications of the ACM*, 3(5):299–314, May 1960.

[109] Jean-Marc Nerson and Kim Walden. – *Seamless Object-Oriented Software Architectures.* – Prentice Hall, Englewood Cliffs, NJ, 1994.

[110] S. C. Ntafos. – A comparison of some structural testing strategies. – *IEEE Transactions on Software Engineering*, 14(6):868–874, June 1988.

[111] OMG. – The common object request broker: Architecture and specification. – CORBA is available from OMG for a small fee to non-members of the OMG, contact: documents@omg.org.

[112] C. Pancake and D. Bergmark. – Do parallel languages respond to the needs of scientific programmers? – *IEEE Computer*, pp. 13–23, December 1990.

[113] D. L. Parnas. – *Structured Analysis and Design*. – Infotech International Limited, 1978.

[114] D. L. Parnas. – Software aspects of strategic defence systems. – *Communications of the ACM*, 28(12), December 1985.

[115] D. E. Perry and G. E. Kaiser. – Adequate testing and object oriented programming. – *Journal of Object-Oriented Programming*, 3(1):13–19, 1990.

[116] R. M. Poston. – Automated testing from object models. – *Communications of the ACM*, 37(9):48–58, September 1994.

[117] P. Prieto-Diaz. – Domain analysis for reusability. – In *Proc. of COMPSAC*, pp. 23–29, October 1987.

[118] R. G. Fichman and C. F. Kemerer – OO and conventional analysis and design methodologies. – *Computer*, 25(10):22–40, October 1992.

[119] D. T. Ross. – Structured analysis (SA): a language for communicating ideas. – *IEEE Trans. Software Eng.*, SE-6(1):16–33, January 1977.

[120] W. Royce. – Managing the development of large software systems. – In *Proceedings of IEEE WESCON*, August 1970.

[121] James Rumbaugh, Michael Blaha, William Premerlani, Frederick Eddy, and William Lorensen. – *Object-Oriented Modeling and Design*. – Prentice Hall, Englewood Cliffs, NJ, 1991.

[122] Bran Selic, Garth Gullekson, and Paul T. Ward. – *Real-Time Object-Oriented Modeling*. – John Wiley & Sons, New York, 1994.

[123] Ravi Sharma and Mary Lou Soffa. – Parallel generational garbage collection. – In *Proceedings OOPSLA'91*, pp. 16–32, November 1991. Published as *ACM SIGPLAN Notices*, Vol. 26, No. 11.

[124] Robert A. Shaw. – Empirical analysis of a LISP system. – PhD thesis, Stanford University, February 1988. – Available as Technical Report CSL-TR-88-351.

[125] S. Shlaer and S. J. Mellor. – *Object-Oriented Systems Analysis: Modeling the World in Data*. – Yourdon Press/Prentice Hall, Englewood Cliffs, NJ, 1988.

[126] S. Shlaer and S. J. Mellor. – An object-oriented approach to domain analysis. – *Software Engineering Notes*, 14(5):66–77, July 1989.

[127] S. Shlaer and S. J. Mellor. – *Object Lifecycles: Modeling the World in States.* – Prentice Hall, Englewood Cliffs, NJ, 1992.

[128] M. D. Smith and D. J. Robson. – A framework for testing object-oriented programs. – *Journal of Object-Oriented Programming*, 5(3):45–53, 1992.

[129] Philippe Stephan. – Building financial software with object technology. – *Object Magazine*, 5(4):67–68, July 1995.

[130] A. Tantawy. – Réalisation de protocoles à haute performance. – In *Actes du colloque CFIP'93 sur l'ingénièrie des protocoles,* Montreal. Hermès, September 1993.

[131] Leslie G. Valiant. – A bridging model for parallel computation. – *CACM*, 33(8), August 1990.

[132] G. van den Goor, S. Hong, and S. Brinkkemper. – A comparison of six object-oriented analysis and design methods. – Technical Report, Center of Telematics and Information Technology, University of Twente, The Netherlands, 1992.

[133] A. Vermeulen. – Eigenvalues in Lapack.h++. – In *Proceedings of the Object-Oriented Numerics Conference (OON-SKI'93)*, 1993.

[134] D. R. Wallace and R. U. Fujii. – Software verification and validation: an overview. – *IEEE Software*, 6(3):10–17, May 1989.

[135] D. M. Weiss and V. R. Basili. – Evaluating software development by analysis of changes: some data from the software engineering laboratory. – *IEEE Transactions on Software Engineering*, 2(11):157–168, 1985.

[136] E. J. Weyuker. – Axiomatizing software test data adequacy. – *IEEE Transactions on Software Engineering*, 12(12):1128–1138, December 1986.

[137] R. Wiener and R. Sincovec. – *Software Engineering with Modula-2 and Ada.* – John Wiley & Sons, New York, 1984.

[138] George Wilkie. – *Object-Oriented Software Engineering—The Professional Developer's Guide.* – Addison-Wesley, Reading, MA, 1993.

[139] Paul R. Wilson. – Uniprocessor garbage collection techniques. – In *Proc. Int. Workshop on Memory Management*, Number 637 in Lecture Notes in Computer Science, Saint-Malo, France, September 1992. Springer-Verlag, Berlin.

[140] Paul R. Wilson and Thomas G. Moher. – Design of the opportunistic garbage collector. – In *Proceedings OOPSLA'89*, pp. 23–36, October 1989. Published as *ACM SIGPLAN Notices*, Vol. 24, No. 10.

[141] Rebecca Wirfs-Brock and Ralph E. Johnson. – Surveying current research in object-oriented design. – *Communications of the ACM*, 33(9):104–124, September 1990.

[142] Rebecca Wirfs-Brock and Brian Wilkerson. – Object-oriented design: A responsibility-driven approach. – In *Proceedings OOPSLA'89*, pp. 71–76, October 1989.

[143] Rebecca Wirfs-Brock, Brian Wilkerson, and Lauren Wiener. – *Designing Object-Oriented Software*. – Prentice Hall, Englewood Cliffs, NJ, 1990.

[144] Niklaus Wirth. – The programming language Pascal. – *Acta Informat.*, 1:35–63, 1971.

[145] Niklaus Wirth. – *Programming in Modula-2*. – Springer-Verlag, Berlin, 1983.

[146] R. W. Wolverton. – The cost of developing large scale software. – In Ellis Horowitz, editor, *Practical Strategies for Developing Large Software Systems*. Addison-Wesley, Reading, MA, 1975.

[147] Y. Yokote and M. Tokoro. – The design and implementation of ConcurrentSmalltalk. – In *OOPSLA'86 Proceedings*, September 1986.

[148] Y. Yokote and M. Tokoro. – Concurrent programming in ConcurrentSmalltalk. – In A. Yonezawa, editor, *Object-Oriented Concurrent Programming*, pp. 129–158. The MIT Press, Cambridge, MA, 1987.

[149] Akinori Yonezawa, Jean-Pierre Briot, and Etsuya Shibayama. – Object-oriented concurrent programming in ABCL/1. – In *OOPSLA'86 Proceedings*, September 1986.

[150] M. Zitterbart. – High-speed transport components. – *IEEE Network Magazine*, pp. 54–63, January 1991.

[151] Benjamin Zorn. – Comparing mark-and-sweep and stop-and-copy garbage collection. – In *Proceedings of the 1990 ACM Conference on Lisp and Functional Programming*, June 1990.

Index

A

ABCL/1, 137, 140
Abstract ancestors, 246
Abstract classes, 7, 88–89
Abstract data types (ADTs), 6, 19, 67–68, 200
  See also Container classes/CONTAINERS
Abstractions, 168, 222
  in **Tower***Eiffel* Booch components, 238, 242, 246
Acceptance testing, SMDS server, 210–13
access classes, 142
Access criterion, 224
Access hierarchy and COLLECTION, 229–32
Accessors, in Paladin, 262
Active structures/ACTIVE, 230–32
Act 1, 140
Ada83, 17, 18, 71, 151, 234
Ada95, 71
Adapt clause, 106
add, 248, 262–63, 277, 279
add_dblock, 277, 279
Address operator, 117
ADT. *See* Abstract data types
Agents, 237–38, 246
Aggregates, polymorphic, 257–58
ALGOL, 11, 18
alias, 115
Aliasing, 28, 64, 65, 170
all, 81, 106, 109
Ancestors, 246
Anchored declarations
  description of, 79–80
  syntax diagram, 80, 296
and then, 47
ANY, 74–76, 92, 111, 129, 185

append, 66
Application, generating an, 104
ARGUMENTS, 112–14
Arguments, to a routine, 41
ARRAY, 68–70, 111, 232, 294
ARRAY[T], 68–70, 89
ASCII characters, 22, 111
Assembly and configuration
  assembling classes, 103–4
  class name clashes, handling, 106
  description of, 15–16
  excluding and including files, 105–6
  generating an application, 104
  specifying clusters, 105
Assembly of Classes in Eiffel (ACE)
  See also Assembly and configuration
  notation for, 104
  purpose of, 15–16
assertion, 109
Assertion checking
  methods, 107
  with LACE, 107–9
  with run-time control language, 109
Assertions
  defined, 3
  in Eiffel, 12, 19
  and programming by contract, 44
  semantics of, 141
  syntax diagram, 34
Assignment
  description of, 26–28
  operations, 65
  syntax diagram, 27, 296
Assignment attempt (?=), 28, 132
Associative array, 252
ASTOOT, 200–201
Asynchronization, 141

Attribute(s)
 defined, 7
 protection and information hiding, 59–61
Autoregression testing, 205
Awaited object, 140

B

Backus-Naur Form (BNF), 19
BAG, in Tower*Eiffel* Booch components, 240
Bags
 in EiffelBase, 229, 230
 in Tower*Eiffel* Booch components 243–44
Basic types, 22–23
Berard, Edward V., 151, 219–20
BILINEAR, 234
Binary operator, syntax diagram, 48, 297
Bit sequences, 293
Black-box testing, 196–97
BLAS kernel, 283–84
Block synchronous parallel (BSP) model, 143
Boehm, Hans-Juergen, 150, 176
Booch, G., 8, 151
 See also Tower*Eiffel* Booch components
BOOLEAN, 47, 111
Boolean constants, 22, 292
BOUNDED
 in EiffelBase, 233
 in Tower*Eiffel* Booch components, 242–43
BOX, 232
Boyer-Moore algorithm, 254
Branch coverage, 197
Browne, Roger, 311
Bubble sort algorithm, 51
Bug
 implementation, 44
 rates, 193–94
 use of term, 194
Bug-free loops, designing, 35–37
Business object notation (BON), 151, 154, 188

C

C, 11, 16, 17, 116, 275
C++, 137, 154, 200, 234
Call chain syntax diagram, 58, 297
Calling
 external routines, 116–17
 modules and calling other object features, 58–59
 routines, 45
Capability maturity model (CMM), 3, 4
Cardelli, Luca, 134
Caromel, D., 138
CASE tool, 184, 188
CATALOG, 252
Cause-effect graph testing, 196–97
CBox objects, 140
C Eiffel call-in library (CECIL), 117
CHARACTER, 22, 111
Character constants, 22, 292
CharacterInterval, syntax diagram, 31, 297
Check statement
 description of, 37–38
 syntax diagram, 38, 297
Chen, P. P. S., 150
Cholesky algorithm, 270, 282
Class declaration
 lexical components, 21–22
 manifest constants and basic types, 22–23
 notation for describing Eiffel syntax, 19–21
 syntax diagram, 20, 298
Classes
 See also under type of
 abstract/deferred, 7
 assembling, 103–4
 defined, 7
 in Eiffel, 11–12
 naming, 186
 of objects, 6
 required standard, 110–12
 testing of class hierarchies, 201–2
 unit testing of Eiffel classes, 202–5
Class header, 20
Classification, 71
 subtyping, 72–74
Class = module = type

basic principles, 17
class declaration, 19–23
as a module, 17–18
as a type, 18–19
Class name, 21
clashes, handling, 106
Class-responsibility-collaboration (CRC), 151
clone, 57–58
CLU, 6
cluster, 105
Clusters
in SiG library, 253–54
specifying, 105
Coad, Peter, 151
Coleman, Derek, 151
COLLECTION, access hierarchy and, 229–32
Command-query distinction, 174
Comments
layout of, 189
typing of, 186
Common object request broker architecture (CORBA), 137
Communications of the ACM, 199
COMPARABLE, 84, 111
compare_objects, 227
compare_references, 227
Compatibility, 10
Compilers, 12
Completeness, 195
Compound instruction, syntax diagram, 29, 298
Concurrency, model of, 138
ConcurrentSmalltalk, 137, 140
Conditional
description of, 29–30
syntax diagram, 30, 298
Condition coverage, 197
Configuration. *See* Assembly and configuration
Conformance
generic, 73–74
type conformance and expanded types, 83–84
Consistency, 195
Constant entities
description of, 24–26

syntax diagram, 24, 299
Constrained genericity, 91–92
Container classes/CONTAINERs
access hierarchy and, 229–32
bounded, unbounded, fixed, and resizable, 233
description of, 89–91, 224–25
in EiffelBase, 229–34
finite, 233
infinite, 232
primitive, 246
short, 251
in SiG library, 247–49, 251–53
storage hierarchy and, 232–33
in **Tower***Eiffel* Booch components, 246
traversal hierarchy and, 233–34
Contract
assertions and programming by, 44, 107
design by, 9, 44, 107, 167–68, 201, 234
Contravariance, 134–36
convert, 273–75
Correctness, 9
count, 230
COUNTABLE, 232
Coupling, modularity and, 170–71
Covariance policy, 134–36
Covariant signature redefinition, 78
Creating objects, 56–58
Creation
clause, 21
deferred classes and, 85
procedure, 16
Current, 79
Current objects, 58
Cursor structures, 231
Cyclomatic complexity, 173–74, 197–98

D

Data-driven synchronization, 140
Data flow rate measurement, 213
Data parallelism, 257
Data structures, **Tower***Eiffel* Booch components, 235–36
Data type, 18
Data vectorization, 276
DBLOCK-MATRIX, 269, 270, 271, 272
DCOL_MATRIX, 270

Debug/debugging
  designing bug-free loops, 35–37
  difference between verification and validation and, 194
  keys, 38
  statement, 38–39
  syntax diagram, 38, 299
debug, 109
deChampeaux, Dennis, 152
Decoupled code, 61
deep_clone, 58
Default handling of exceptions, 124–26
Default initialization rule for entities, 26
Defensive programming, 167
Deferred classes
  changed in child class, 86, 88
  defined, 7, 20, 84–85
  inheritance and, 86, 88
  as a structuring tool, 88–89
  syntax diagram, 83
  undefining, 88
Deferred feature
  description of, 84
  syntax diagram, 85
Deferred routines, 39
Delegation, 171–72
Deques, in **Tower***Eiffel* Booch components, 244
Description indice, 190
Design by contract, 9, 44, 107, 167–68, 201, 234
DICTIONARY, 240, 246, 252
Dijkstra, E. W., 194
Dispensers, 231
DIST_MATRIX, 267–70
Distributed computing systems (DCSs)
  See also Parallel object-oriented libraries, building of
  other names for, 255
  programming problems with, 256–57
  role of, 255–56
Distributed memory parallel computers, 255
Distribution of matrices in Paladin, 265–67
  implementation of distributed matrices, 267–70

DISTRIBUTION_2D, 265–67, 271
do, 46, 115
Documentation
  analysis and design-level, 188
  code-level, 188–89
Domain analysis, 219–21
Domain error, 107
DOUBLE, 49, 111, 293
DROW_MATRIX, 270
DTE, 209
Dynamically typed language, 18, 19
Dynamic binding, 12, 83, 129, 173
Dynamic modeling, 161, 163–64
Dynamic reconfiguration testing, 211–12
Dynamic redistribution, 271–73, 277
Dynamic structure, in **Tower***Eiffel* Booch components, 243
Dynamic type of an entity, 82

E

Effective feature, 84
Efficiency, 10
  implementation of, 280–83
Eiffel
  background of, 12
  overview of, 11–12
  provisions of, 9–10
  sources of information on, 307–13
Eiffel // approach
  communications, 139
  model of concurrency, 138
  no sharing of objects, 138–39
  parallel, 140–42
  processing requests, 139–40
  synchronization, 140
EiffelBase library
  access hierarchy and COLLECTION, 229–32
  design patterns, 227–29
  overview of, 224–25
  storage hierarchy and CONTAINERS, 232–33
  traversal hierarchy and CONTAINERS, 233–34
Eiffel Outlook, 310
Eiffel parallel execution environment (EPEE), 144–45, 257, 258–59, 275, 276

Eiffel Standard Library Vintage 95, The, 12
  overview of, 109–14
  purposes of, 109–10
  required standard classes, 110–12
  using I/O classes example, 112–14
"Eiffel World," 310
ELLIE, 137
else clause, 31
elseif statement, 29–30
Encapsulation
  distribution, 257–63
  and information hiding, 168–70
  parallelism encapsulation approach, 142–45
end, 185, 189
end --, 189
end -- if, 189
end -- loop, 189
ensure, 42
ensure then, 168
Entities/entity declaration
  constant, 24–26
  default initialization rule for, 26
  defined, 12, 23–26
  dynamic type of, 82
  in Eiffel, 12
  expansion status, 23–24
  polymorphic, 81–82
  syntax diagram, 23, 300
Entity-relationship model, 150–51
Eon Software, 309–10
Equality
  container, 227
  difference between identical and, 222
  testing, 28–29
Error
  domain, 107
  use of the term, 197
European Space Agency, 152
Exceptions
  causes of, 124
  default handling of, 124–26
  trying to repair failures, 126–27
  user-defined, 127
EXCEPTIONS, 112, 123–27
Excluding files, 105–6
Exec mechanism, 259, 267, 276

exhausted, 233
expanded, 66, 74, 265–66
Expanded classes, 20, 23–24
Expanded types
  inheritance and, 74
  type conformance and, 83–84
Export rules, changing, 133
Export status changed, 80–81
extend, 230
Extensibility, 10
external, 115
External routines, 39
  calling, 116–17
  declaring, 114–15
  syntax diagram, 115, 300

F

Failures, 194
Faults, 194
feature, 59, 61
Feature adaptation
  anchored declarations, 79–80
  described, 72, 76–77
  export status changed, 80–81
  redefining, 77–79
  renaming, 77
  select, 81
  syntax diagram, 77, 300
  undefining, 81
Feature clauses, 21
Feature declaration, syntax diagram, 40, 300
Features
  calling object, 58–59
  defined, 7
  in Eiffel, 11
  naming, 186
  universal, 295
FILE, 112–14
fill, 230
Finalization, 120–21
Finite containers, 233
Finite state automaton (FSA), 3
First in, first out (FIFO) channels, 3, 138, 139, 252
FIXED, 233
Flat-short form of a class, 188–89

Formal arguments, syntax diagram, 41, 301
FORTRAN, 11, 265, 275, 283
Frames, units of knowledge, 6
Frameworks, library design and, 221–23
Friendliness, 10
frozen, 41, 83
Functional modeling, 164–66
Functions, pure, 39, 174
Fusion, 151, 154

G

Garbage collection/collector, 28, 211
  controlling, 120
  cost of, 119–20
  defined, 118
  finalization, 120–21
  software correctness and, 118–19
GARME, 209
GENERAL, 74–76, 111, 124
General matrix multiply (GEMM), 283
Generic classes
  arrays, 68–70
  conformance, 73–74
  derivation, 68
  role of, 67–68
  syntax diagram, 68, 298
Generic clause, 231
Genericity
  constrained, 91–92
  defined, 67–68
  inheritance and, 89–92
Grand challenges, 255
Graphs
  in SiG library, 253–54
  in **Tower**_Eiffel_ Booch components, 244

H

has, 66
HASHABLE, 111
Hash table
  in EiffelBase, 232
  in **Tower**_Eiffel_ Booch components, 239–40, 246
head, 66
Header processing speed, 212
"Hello, world!" example, 16
HIERARCHICAL, 234

Hierarchical object-oriented design (HOOD), 151–52
Hoare, C. A. R., 6, 51
Howard, Rock, 311
Hurry, 140

I

Identical, difference between equality and, 222
IEEE, 202, 205
if statement, 29–30, 31
Imperative part of Eiffel, 21
Implementation
  bug, 44
  of distributed matrices, 267–70
  documentation and indexing, 188–90
  indice, 190
  role of, 184
  sequential implementation of a matrix, 263–65
  for SMDS server, 191–92
  style guide, 184–86
  version management, 187–88
include, 105–6
Including files, 105–6
Incremental integration testing, 206–8
Indexing clause
  description of, 20, 189–90
  syntax diagram, 190, 301
Index transformations, optimizing, 276
Infinite containers, 232
Infix function declaration, 47–49
Infix operator, syntax diagram, 47, 302
Information hiding, 61, 168–70
Inheritance
  anomaly, 137
  deferred classes and, 86, 88
  defined, 7–8, 71
  in Eiffel, 12
  expanded types, 74
  genericity and, 89–92
  graphs, 172–73
  module extension, 71–72
  nature of, 71
  repeated, 128–31
  structure, 74–76, 171–73
  subtyping, 72–74
  syntax diagram, 71, 302

Inherit clause, 21
Inspect clause/expression, 30
Inspections, 198–99
Instances, 11
INTEGER, 49, 111
Integer constants, 22, 292
Integer division, 32–33
IntegerInterval, syntax diagram, 31, 302
Integration testing
  assembling SMDS server, 208–10
  incremental, 206–8
  strategies, 205
Intel Paragon, 255, 283
Interaction graphs, 170
Interactive Software Engineering (ISE) Inc., 12, 104, 307–8
Interfaces
  defined, 7
  dependencies, 170–71
  size of, 169–70
Interface specifications, producing, 18, 39
Interfacing with other languages
  address operator, 117
  calling external routines, 116–17
  declaring external routines, 114–15
  linking with external software, 117–18
Interfeature testing, 200–201
Interoperability, 270
Intrafeature testing, 200
Invariants
  loop, 21, 33–34
  routine, 41, 43–44
ISE, 224
is_equal, 79–80
ISO 9000–3 standards, 3
ISO 9001 standards, 3
item, 230, 262, 267
Iteration domains, restricting, 276
Iterative control, 31–33
Iterators
  in Eiffel, 222–23
  in EiffelBase, 227, 229
  in SiG library, 249–51
  in Tower*Eiffel* Booch components, 239, 246

J

Jackson, M. A., 5, 151
Jackson system development (JSD), 5, 151
Jacobson, Ivar, 152
Journal of Object-Oriented Programming, 311

K

Kernel library classes, 23
Keyword-in-context (KWIC) index problem
  DRIVER class, 99–101
  KWIC class, 97
  KWIC_ENTRY class, 95
  object-oriented software, 94
  presentation of, 93–94
  WORDS class, 99
Keywords, typing of, 186
Knuth-Morris-Pratt algorithm, 254
Koster, Kees, 9

L

LACE, 104, 105, 106, 117
  assertion checking with, 107–9
Last in, first out (LIFO) principle, 252
Law of Demeter, 170–71
Lexical components, 21–22
Lexical rules, 186
Library design
  domain analysis, 219–21
  EiffelBase, 224–34
  factors affecting, 218–19
  patterns and frameworks, 221–23
  producing class libraries, 223
  reusability, 218
  SiG, 247–54
  Tower*Eiffel* Booch components, 234–47
Life-cycle testing, 205
LINEAR, 234
Linked list class, building a, 65–67
Liskov, B., 93
LISTE[T], 68, 89
LISTINT, 65–67
Lists, in Tower*Eiffel* Booch components, 244
LME, 209

Local declaration, syntax diagram, 45, 303
local_item, 268–69
LOCAL_MATRIX, 263–65
local_put, 268–69
Loop(s), 31
  designing bug-free, 35–37
  example of, 32–33
  invariants, 33–34
  parts of, 32
  syntax diagram, 32, 35, 303
  variants, 34–35

M

McCabe, T., 173, 197, 200
Mailing lists, 311–12
make, 63
makefile, 16
Manifest constants, 22, 292–94
map_block, 265, 266
MAP/Maps, in **Tower**Eiffel Booch components, 240, 244–45
MATCHER, in SiG library, 254
Matrices/MATRIX, in Paladin, 259–63
  distribution of, 265–67
  dynamic redistribution, 271–73
  implementation of distributed, 267–70
  interoperability, 270
  polymorphic, 275
  sequential implementation of, 263–65
  -type conversion, 273–75
Mellor, S. J., 152
MEMORY, 112, 119, 120, 121
Message sequence specification (MgSS), 201
Method sequence specification (MtSS), 201
Meyer, Bertrand, 12, 74, 137, 140, 167, 170
Miller, H. A., 17
Minimalist school, 169
Minsky, M., 6
Modularity, 17–18
  coupling and, 170–71
Modula-2, 17, 71
Modula-3, 71
Module(s)
  attribute protection and information hiding, 59–61
  building a linked list class, 65–67
  calling other object features, 58–59
  client of, 55
  creating objects, 56–58
  defined, 55–56
  extension and inheritance, 71–72
  restricted export and subjectivity, 61–63
  SMDS support, 209
  strings, 63–65
Monarchi, D. E., 8
Monitor, 6
Multibranch choice
  description of, 30–31
  syntax diagram, 30, 303
Multiple condition coverage, 197
Multiple dispatching, 279–80
Multiple instruction multiple data (MIMD) programming, 142–43
Multiprocessors, 255

N

Naming conventions, 186
Nerson, Jean-Marc, 151, 154
NewExports, syntax diagram, 80, 303
NICE, 12, 104, 110, 310
NME, 209
Nodes, in **Tower**Eiffel Booch components, 246
Nondeferred feature, 84
None, 76, 185
None, 109
Nonprofit International Consortium for Eiffel (NICE), 12, 104, 110, 310
Nonterminal construct, 19
NUMERIC, 91–92, 111

O

Object based language, 71
Object design phase, for SMDS, 175
  algorithms designed, 180
  associations designed, 182
  classes grouped into clusters, 183
  combining the three models, 179–80
  implementation of control, 181–82
  inheritance adjusted, 182

INDEX

optimizations designed, 180–81
representation of object attributes, 183
Object factory for software development (ObjectOry), 152
Object features, calling, 58–59
Object modeling technique (OMT)
  See also Object-oriented design, SMDS and
  background of, 152
  coding statistics, 214–15
  object modeling in, 160–61
  overview of, 153–54
Object-oriented analysis and design (OOAD)
  See also Object-oriented design; SMDS (switched multimegabits data service)
  Eiffel and, 154, 166–75
  overview of, 150–52
  software engineering process, 149–50
Object-oriented approach
  analysis and design (OOAD), 8
  background of, 6
  definitions for, 6–8
Object-oriented design, Eiffel and
  design by contract, 9, 44, 107, 167–68
  design patterns and idioms, 166–67
  encapsulation and information hiding, 168–70
  inheritance structure, 171–73
  modularity and coupling, 170–71
  routines, 173–75
Object-oriented design, SMDS and
  object design phase, 175, 179–83
  object modeling technique phase of, 175
  system design phase, 175–79
Object-oriented methodology, overview of, 150–52
Object-oriented testing, 199–202
Objects
  creating, 56–58
  current, 58
  defined, 6–7
  as machines, 227
  reserving, 141–42
Obsolete clause
  description of, 21, 190
  syntax diagram, 191, 304
Old expression, syntax diagram, 43, 304
once, 46, 115
Once routines, 26, 46–47
OOSD, 152
Operators, 262–63
or else, 47
Owner write rule, 259, 267

P

Paladin, 257, 258
  accessors, 262
  distribution of matrices in, 265–67
  matrices and vectors in, 259–63
  operators, 262–63
  polymorphic matrices, 275
Paragon, Intel, 255, 283
Parallelism
  data, 257
  defined, 3
  Eiffel // approach, 138–40
  encapsulation approach, 142–45
  object-oriented languages and, 137–38
  parallel Eiffel // approach, 140–42
  programming problems with parallel machines, 256–57
Parallel object-oriented libraries, building of
  accessors, 262
  distribution of matrices in Paladin, 265–67
  dynamic redistribution, 271–73
  Eiffel parallel execution environment (EPEE), 257, 258–59, 275, 276
  encapsulating distribution, 257–63
  implementation efficiency, 280–83
  implementation of distributed matrices, 267–70
  implementing distributed aggregates, 258–59
  interoperability, 270
  matrices and vectors in Paladin, 259–63
  matrix-type conversion, 273–75
  operators, 262–63
  optimization techniques, 275–78
  polymorphic aggregates, 257–58
  polymorphic matrices, 275

Parallel object-oriented libraries, building of *(cont.)*
  reuse of external optimized libraries, 283–84
  sequential implementation of a matrix, 263–65
  user friendliness, 278–80
Parallel observable machine (POM), 145, 176, 271
Partial correctness, 34
Partition sort algorithm, 51–54
Partition testing, 196
Path-based testing, 197–98
Patterns and frameworks, library design and, 221–23
PDL/RCL (program description language/run-time control language), 104, 105, 106, 118
Phases, in software development, 3–4
PLATFORM, 112
POINTER, 111, 116
Polymorphic aggregates, 257–58
Polymorphic entities, 81–82
Polymorphic matrices, 275
POOL-T, 137
Portability, 10
Postconditions
  description of, 41, 42–43
  redefined, 79
  syntax diagram, 42, 304
Pragmatic school, 169
Preconditions
  description of, 41, 42
  redefined, 78
  syntax diagram, 42, 304
Prefix function declaration, 47–49
Prefix operator, syntax diagram, 47, 304
PRESTO, 137
Prieto-Diaz, P., 220
Priority queue, 252–53
PROCESS, 138–40
Process entry point, 139
Processing requests, 139–40
Process structure, 138
Programming
  by contract, 9, 44, 107, 167–68, 201, 234
  defensive, 167
  by extension, 71
  in the large, 2, 3–6
  in the small, 2–3
  software crisis, 1–2
  structured, 2, 4–5
Programming languages
  See Eiffel
  importance of, 10–11
  purpose of, 9
prune, 230
prune_all, 230
Puhr, G. I., 8
Pure functions, 39, 174
put, 230, 262, 267

Q

Queues
  in EiffelBase, 231
  in SiG library, 252
  in **Tower***Eiffel* Booch components, 245
Quicksort algorithm, 51–54, 92

R

Rabin-Karp algorithm, 254
raise (name), 127
random, 262–63
Random testing, 196
Rational Software Inc., 234
REAL, 49, 111, 293
Real-time object-oriented modeling (ROOM), 152
Recursion, 49–50
Redefining, 77
  covariant signature, 78
  keeping an original version of a redefined feature, 130–31
  strengthening postconditions, 79
  syntax diagram, 78, 304
  weakening preconditions, 78
Redistribution, dynamic, 271–73, 277
References, matrix-type conversion and, 273–75
Reference semantics
  in Eiffel, 222
  in EiffelBase, 227
  in SiG library, 248
  in **Tower***Eiffel* Booch components, 239–40

Refresh mechanism, 259, 267, 276
Regular, 39
Reliability, 195
remove, 248–49
Renaming
  conflicting classes, 106, 129
  inheritance and, 77
  syntax diagram, 77, 304
Repeated inheritance
  conditions for sharing, 128–29
  defined, 128
  keeping an original version of a redefined feature, 130–31
  replication and selection, 129–30
require, 42
require else, 168
rescue, 124–25
  syntax diagram, 126, 305
Reserved words, list of, 294–95
Reserving objects, 141–42
reset, 56–57
RESIZABLE, 233
Restricted export and subjectivity, 61–63
Result, 45
retry, 126
Reusability, 9–10, 215, 218
  See also Library design
Reuse of external optimized libraries, 283–84
Reversibility, 151
Revision control system (RCS), 187
Revision indice, 190
Rings, in Tower*Eiffel* Booch components, 245
RME, 209–10
Robustness, 10, 195
  testing, 210
Root of the system, 11
Routine(s)
  arguments, 41
  assertions and programming by contract, 44
  calling, 45
  calling external, 116–17
  command-query distinction, 174
  complexity of, 173–74
  declaration, 39–41
  declaring external, 114–15
  defined, 7
  in Eiffel, 11–12
  as a function, 39
  internal body, 45–46
  invariants, 41, 43–44
  once, 26, 46–47
  optional behaviors, 174–75
  postconditions, 41, 42–43
  preconditions, 41, 42
  prefix and infix function declaration, 47–49
  as a procedure, 39
  recursion, 49–50
ROW_WISE_MAPPING, 265–66
Rumbaugh, James, 152, 153
Run-time control language (RCL), assertion checking with, 109

S

Seamless design, 150, 151
Select a feature, 81
  syntax diagram, 129, 305
Selection, 129–30
Semicolons, use of, 185
separate, 141
Sequences, 29, 231–32
SET/sets
  in EiffelBase, 230
  in Tower*Eiffel* Booch components, 240, 245
Settable options, 174
Shlaer, S., 152
Shopping list school, 169–70
short, 18
SHORT, 251
SiG Computer GmbH, 309
SiG library
  abstractions related to containers, 251–54
  design patterns, 248–51
  overview of, 247–48
Simula-67, 6
Single program multiple data (SPMD) mode, 143, 257
Smalltalk, 17, 18, 137

INDEX

SMDS (switched multimegabits data service)
  assembling and testing of server, 208–10
  dynamic modeling, 161, 163–64
  functional modeling, 164–66
  implementation for, 191–92
  ISSIP levels 1 and 2, 159–60
  ISSIP level 3, 158–59
  object modeling, 160–61
  object-oriented analysis, 157–66
  object-oriented design, 175–83
  overview of, 154–55
  problem requirements, 156–57
  protocol service users, 158
  reuse, 215
  server acceptance testing, 210–13
  server problem domain, 157–60
  system design phase, 175–79
Software, linking with external, 117–18
Software components, use of, 15
Software contracting, 151
Software crisis, 1–2
Software development
  See also Programming
  Jackson system development (JSD), 5
  methodology, 4
  object-oriented approach, 6–8, 149–50
  phases in, 3–4
  structured, 2, 4–5
Software Engineering Institute (SEI), 3, 4
s1 := s2, 65
s1 := clone(s2), 65
s1.copy(s2), 65
Sorting data/SORTER
  example of, 50–54
  in SiG library, 254
  in Tower*Eiffel* Booch components, 238
Spiral model, 4, 150, 176
Stability testing, 211
Stacks/STACK
  in EiffelBase, 231
  in SiG library, 252
  in Tower*Eiffel* Booch components, 245
STACK[T], 89
start, 233
State-based test case generation, 198

Statement(s)
  assignment, 26–28
  check, 37–38
  conditional, 29–30
  coverage, 197
  debug, 38–39
  equality testing, 28–29
  loop, 31–37
  multibranch choice, 30–31
  sequence, 29
Statically typed language, 18–19
Static typing, 12
STD_FILES, 112
STORABLE, 112
Storage criterion, 224
Storage hierarchy and CONTAINERs, 232–33
STRING, 111, 127
  in Eiffel, 63–65
  in EiffelBase, 232
  in Tower*Eiffel* Booch components, 245–46
String(s)
  accessing content of, 64
  assignment-like operations, 65
  comparison of, 64
  constants, 22, 293–94
  creating, 63
  using Eiffel, 63–65
Stroustrup, B., 10
Structured programming, 2, 4–5
Style guide
  indentations, 185
  layout, 185
  lexical rules, 186
  naming conventions, 186
  semicolons and **end** keywords, 185
Subclasses/subclassing, 7, 57, 71–72
Subcontracting, 168
Subjectivity
  defined, 18
  modules and, 61–63
SUBSET, 230
Subtyping, 72–74
  true functional, 135
Superclasses, 7
Support, in Tower*Eiffel* Booch components, 246

Symbols
  comparison operators, 64
  double dash (–), 21
  percent (%), 21
Synchronization, 140
Syntax diagrams, notation for describing Eiffel, 19–21
  list of, 295–306
System, 11, 15–16
System design phase, for SMDS
  boundary conditions handled, 177–78
  global resources, access of, 176
  identify inherent concurrency, 176
  implementation of control in software, 177
  organized into components, 175–76
  performance priorities and alternatives, 178–79
  storage, 176
  subsystems allocated to processors and tasks, 176
System-level validity, 136–37

T

TABLE, 230
Tables, 229, 230, 232
tail, 66
Testability, 10
Test case generation for robustness, 210
Testing. *See* Verification and validation (V&V)
tmp_matrix, 272
Total quality management (TQM), 3
Tower*Eiffel* Booch components
  architecture, 240–43
  background of, 234–35
  description of components, 243–47
  design patterns, 237–40
  overview of, 235–37
Tower Technology Corp., 104, 234, 308–9
trace, 109
trace, 262, 263, 277, 279
Traversal criterion, 224
Traversal hierarchy and CONTAINERs, 233–34
Trees, in Tower*Eiffel* Booch components, 246–47
Turing, Alan, 2

Turing machine, 2
Type(s)
  See also Class = module = type; *under type of*
  basic, 22–23
  conformance and expanded, 83–84
Type checking
  changing export rules, 133
  covariance policy, 134–36
  system-level validity, 136–37
Typing errors, 18–19

U

UNBOUNDED
  in EiffelBase, 233
  in Tower*Eiffel* Booch components, 242–43
Undefining
  description of, 81, 88
  syntax diagram, 88, 306
Unique constants, syntax diagram, 25, 306
Unit testing of Eiffel classes
  class-level testing, 202
  development of, 203–4
  embedded tests, 204
  execution and evaluation of, 204–5
  life-cycle and autoregression testing, 205
  testing from client perspective, 203
  testing from subclass perspective, 203–4
Unix, 16
Untyped typed language, 18, 19
Usability, 195
Use clause, 106
USENET, 311
User-defined exceptions, 127
User friendliness, preserving, 278–80

V

Valiant, Leslie G., 143
Validity, system-level, 136–37
Variants, 34–35
Vectors/VECTOR, in Paladin, 259–63
Vendors, list of, 307–13
Verification and validation (V&V)
  black-box testing, 196–97

Verification and validation (V&V) *(cont.)*
  bug rates, 193–94
  cause-effect graph testing, 196–97
  costs of, 194
  defined, 194
  difference between debugging and, 194
  importance of, 194
  inspections and walkthroughs, 198–99
  integration testing, 205–10
  interfeature testing, 200–201
  intrafeature testing, 200
  object-oriented testing, 199–202
  partition testing, 196
  random testing, 196
  SMDS server acceptance testing, 210–13
  state-based test case generation, 198
  testing of class hierarchies, 201–2
  testing process, 194–95
  testing techniques, 195–99
  unit testing of Eiffel classes, 202–5
  white-box testing, 197–98
Version management, 187–88
V model, 4, 149
Void, 76, 124

W

Wait-by-necessity principle, 140, 141, 143
Walden, Kim, 151
Walkthroughs, 198–99
Waterfall model, 4, 149
Weyuker, E. J., 201
when clauses, 31
White-box testing, 197–98
Wiener, R., 93
Wilkie, George, 152
wipe_out, 230
Wirfs-Brock, Rebecca, 151
World Wide Web (WWW), 312–13

Y

Yourdon, Edward, 151